Structures of Protection?

FORCED MIGRATION

General Editors: Tom Scott-Smith and Kirsten McConnachie

This series, published in association with the Refugees Studies Centre, University of Oxford, reflects the multidisciplinary nature of the field and includes within its scope international law, anthropology, sociology, politics, international relations, geopolitics, social psychology and economics.

Recent volumes:

Volume 39
Structures of Protection? Rethinking Refugee Shelter
Edited by Tom Scott-Smith and Mark E. Breeze

Volume 38
Refugee Resettlement: Power, Politics, and Humanitarian Governance
Edited by Adèle Garnier, Liliana Lyra Jubilut, and Kristin Bergtora Sandvik

Volume 37
Gender, Violence, Refugees
Edited by Susanne Buckley-Zistel and Ulrike Krause

Volume 36
The Myth of Self-Reliance: Economic Lives Inside a Liberian Refugee Camp
Naohiko Omata

Volume 35
Migration by Boat: Discourses of Trauma, Exclusion and Survival
Lynda Mannik

Volume 34
Making Ubumwe*: Power, State and Camps in Rwanda's Unity-Building Project*
Andrea Purdeková

Volume 33
The Agendas of Tibetan Refugees: Survival Strategies of a Government-in-Exile in a World of Transnational Organizations
Thomas Kauffmann

Volume 32
The Migration-Displacement Nexus: Patterns, Processes, and Policies
Edited by Khalid Koser and Susan Martin

Volume 31
Zimbabwe's New Diaspora: Displacement and the Cultural Politics of Survival
Edited by JoAnn McGregor and Ranka Primorac

Volume 30
Politics of Innocence: Hutu Identity, Conflict and Camp Life
Simon Turner

For a full volume listing, please see the series page on our website:
https://www.berghahnbooks.com/series/forced-migration

Structures of Protection?

RETHINKING REFUGEE SHELTER

Edited by
Tom Scott-Smith and Mark E. Breeze

berghahn
NEW YORK · OXFORD
www.berghahnbooks.com

First published in 2020 by
Berghahn Books
www.berghahnbooks.com

© 2020, 2023 Tom Scott-Smith and Mark E. Breeze
First paperback edition published in 2023

All rights reserved. Except for the quotation of short passages for the purposes of criticism and review, no part of this book may be reproduced in any form or by any means, electronic or mechanical, including photocopying, recording, or any information storage and retrieval system now known or to be invented, without written permission of the publisher.

Library of Congress Cataloging-in-Publication Data
Names: Scott-Smith, Tom, 1980- editor. | Breeze, Mark E., editor.
Title: Structures of protection? : rethinking refugee shelter / edited by Tom Scott-Smith and Mark E. Breeze.
Description: New York : Berghahn Books, 2020. | Series: Forced migration ; volume 39 | Includes bibliographical references and index.
Identifiers: LCCN 2020006152 (print) | LCCN 2020006153 (ebook) | ISBN 9781789207125 (hardback) | ISBN 9781789207132 (ebook)
Subjects: LCSH: Refugees. | Shelters for the homeless.
Classification: LCC HV640 .S744 2020 (print) | LCC HV640 (ebook) | DDC 362.87/83--dc23
LC record available at https://lccn.loc.gov/2020006152
LC ebook record available at https://lccn.loc.gov/2020006153

British Library Cataloguing in Publication Data
A catalogue record for this book is available from the British Library

ISBN 978-1-78920-712-5 hardback
ISBN 978-1-80073-630-6 paperback
ISBN 978-1-78920-713-2 ebook

https://doi.org/10.3167/9781789207125

Contents

List of Figures   viii

Introduction
Places of Partial Protection: Refugee Shelter since 2015   1
    Tom Scott-Smith

Part I. Shelter, Containment and Mobility

1. Moving, Containing, Displacing: The Shipping Container as Refugee Shelter   15
  Hanna Baumann

2. At the Edge: Containment and the Construction of Europe   31
  Ċetta Mainwaring

3. Shifting Shelters: Migrants, Mobility and the Making of Open Centres in Malta   45
  Marthe Achtnich

4. Moria: Anti-shelter and the Spectacle of Deterrence   57
  Daniel Howden

5. Moria Hotspot: Shelter as a Politically Crafted Materiality of Neglect   71
  Polly Pallister-Wilkins

6. Architectures of Trauma: Forced Shelter and Immigration Detention   83
  Petra Molnar

7. Settling the Unsettled: Forced Shelter in the Negev Desert   97
   Renana Ne'eman

Part II. Shelter, Resistance and Solidarity

8. The Contingent Camp: Struggling for Shelter in Calais, France   111
   Maria Hagan

9. Sounding the Shelter, Voicing the Squat: The Sonic Politics of Refugee Shelter in Athens   123
   Tom Western

10. Redignifying Refugees: A Critical Study of Citizen-Run Shelters in Athens   135
    Ashley Mehra

11. A More Personal Shelter: How Citizens Are Hosting Forced Migrants in and around Brussels   149
    Robin Vandevoordt

12. Life in the Aluminium Whale: A Study of Berlin's ICC Shelter   163
    Holly Young

13. Structures to Shelter the Mind: Refugee Housing and Mental Wellbeing in Berlin   175
    Esther Schroeder Goh

Part III. Architecture, Design and Displacement

14. Protection or Isolation? Humanitarian Evacuees in Australian Quarantine Stations   187
    Benjamin Thomas White

15. *Silos* in Trieste, Italy: A Historical Shelter for Displaced People   199
    Roberta Altin

16. Flexible Shelters, Modular Meanings: The Lives and Afterlives of Danish 'Refugee Villages'   211
    Zachary Whyte and Michael Ulfstjerne

17. Shelter as Cladding: Resourcefulness, Improvisation and Refugee-Led Innovation in Goudoubo Camp   223
    Craig Martin, Jamie Cross and Arno Verhoeven

18. Adhocism, Agency and Emergency Shelters: On Architectural
    Nuclei of Life in Displacement   235
    Irit Katz

19. Social Media, Shelter and Resilience: Design in Za'atari Refugee
    Camp   249
    Diane Fellows

20. Confinement, Power and Permanence in Informal Refugee
    Spaces: Syrian Refugees in Lebanon   263
    Faten Kikano

21. From Emergency Shelter to Community Shelter: Berlin's
    Tempelhof Refugee Camp   275
    Toby Parsloe

Conclusion
Towards Better Shelter: Rethinking Humanitarian Sheltering   287
    Mark E. Breeze

Index   301

Figures

1.1	Tempohomes in Berlin, Germany	14
2.1	Safi Military Barracks in Malta	30
3.1	Hal Far Open Centre in Malta	44
4.1	The camp drawbridge in Moria, Greece	56
5.1	Improvised shelters in Moria, Greece	70
6.1	Central East Correctional Centre in Ontario, Canada	82
7.1	Holot Residence Centre and the Negev Desert, Israel	96
8.1	The Invisible Church, near Calais, France	110
9.1	Sounding the shelter in Athens, Greece	122
10.1	The Melissa Day Centre in Athens, Greece	134
11.1	A more personal shelter in Brussels, Belgium.	148
12.1	The International Congress Centre (ICC) in Berlin, Germany	162
13.1	Rathaus Friedenau in Berlin, Germany	174
14.1	Point Nepean Quarantine Station near Melbourne, Australia	186
15.1	*Silos* in Trieste, Italy	198
16.1	Modular shelter from the 'refugee villages', Denmark	210
17.1	Aluminium-clad improvised shelter in Goudoubo camp, Burkina Faso	222
18.1	MSF IPERJUNGLE shelter in Grande-Synthe near Dunkirk	234
19.1	Za'atari refugee camp	248
20.1	Informal settlement in Kab Elias, Bekaa, Lebanon	262
21.1	Tempelhof Airport in Berlin, Germany	274

Introduction
Places of Partial Protection: Refugee Shelter since 2015

Tom Scott-Smith

Shelter has received surprisingly little attention in Refugee Studies, which is surprising given how important it is to the experience of displacement and the way in which it intersects so closely with so many themes in our subject area. Notions of home and belonging, after all, have long been central to the anthropological literature (Hammond 2004; Korac 2009). Ideas of protection suffuse a range of research from law to politics (Betts 2009; McAdam 2007). There is a vast literature on the subject of camps and their spatiality, which has started to cover urbanism and shelter in more detail (Jansen 2018; McConnachie 2016). However, shelter itself somehow seems too material, too banal, too small-scale and technical to generate a great deal of scholarly interest.

In this edited collection we seek to change that, bringing shelter to the very forefront of analysis. This is, in part, a response to the events of 2015, which marked something of a turning point when it came to discussions of shelter. The arrival of hundreds of thousands of refugees into Europe during the 'summer of migration' sparked a wave of interest amongst designers, architects and journalists, flooding the media with new and often optimistic ideas. The problem with sheltering, protecting and accommodating large numbers of refugees could no longer be seen as an issue 'out there', associated with camps in the developing world; it became an issue 'right here', requiring a level of attention that surprised many staff in aid agencies.

Shelter and sheltering rose up the agenda, and it soon became a common theme in exhibitions, design competitions, architectural magazines and other promotional outlets.

This edited collection brings together twenty-one short chapters, illustrating new work on refugee shelter and broadening our understanding about the conditions faced by forced migrants on the move. The chapters cut across a variety of disciplines, from politics, law and anthropology to medicine, history and architecture, but they are united by an interest in the material forms of refugee shelter and their manifold implications. Each chapter has a focus on shelters themselves, offering a detailed analysis of specific examples and exploring how these shelters have been designed, constructed, negotiated and lived in. The volume presents case studies primarily from Europe, while also branching out to Canada, Australia and the Middle East. This geographical balance largely reflects the origin of debates about shelter since 2015, but should not be taken as a limit to this topic. It is, in fact, just the start of a much bigger conversation in Refugee Studies about shelter, protection, and the role of design.

This volume emerged from a series of discussions held at the University of Oxford in the summer of 2018, generously hosted by St Cross College and funded by the Global Challenges Research Fund. I convened these discussions in order to extend a research project founded at the Refugee Studies Centre at Oxford in 2016, funded by the U.K. Economic and Social Research Council (ESRC) and Arts and Humanities Research Council (AHRC). This project was entitled 'Architectures of Displacement', and it engaged in the detailed study of particularly significant humanitarian schemes for sheltering refugees in Europe and the Middle East from 2015 to 2018. The discussions at St Cross College represented an attempt to create links with other scholars interested in the topic, reaching across the disciplines to collect a much wider range of examples and perspectives. These discussions touched on architecture and the limits of design, health and the wellbeing of refugees, humanitarianism and the turn to technology, and incarceration and the rise of border controls. Our interlocutors at St Cross began to unpack what was at stake in this fertile new area of Refugee Studies, teasing out how refugee shelter spoke to so many different debates. Many went onto write chapters for this book, which all have a similar structure: beginning by describing a particular shelter or outlining a particular site, before exploring the issues that arose from this example and the debates that emerged as a result.

Defining 'Refugee Shelter'

We started our project by establishing a broad definition of 'refugee shelter'. The idea, from the very beginning, was to be inclusive: looking at all the places in which refugees and other migrants found a place to stay, whatever their forms and however long they lasted. One of the central aims of 'Architectures of Displacement' was to move beyond humanitarian responses that so often focused on the tent, camp and caravan, and to expand the idea of refugee shelter accordingly. Forced migrants, it seemed, live in a much wider network of accommodation than the phrase often suggests, stretching from the formal to the improvised, the expansive to the compact. Among other things, refugees often stay with friends, construct their own homes, transform abandoned buildings, live in the natural environment, and draw on forms of sanctuary and local hospitality. The term 'refugee shelter', therefore, should never be restricted to what humanitarians provide, but can be seen as an opportunity to think outside the structures and systems that are notionally designed, planned and temporary.

Our first challenge emerged from the first part of that phrase: the word 'refugee'. This has been used very differently by journalists, academics, lawyers and in public discourse over the past few decades. The legal definition, set out in Article 1A(2) of the 1951 Refugee Convention, is relatively narrow, specifying individuals who are outside their country of nationality and who have a well-founded fear of persecution for reasons of race, religion, nationality, membership of a particular social group or political opinion. The colloquial understanding of refugees is far wider, applying to anyone who has been forced from their homes, while some people restrict the term to individuals who have been granted status officially by a state. Language in the media complicates the issue still further, drawing distinctions between 'forced' and 'voluntary' migration, between 'refugee' and 'economic migrant', and ascribing value in the process. It is therefore hard to find a way through these thickets when looking at how people shelter themselves. The word 'refugee', if seemingly simple, immediately generates a problem.

For the purposes of this collection, we decided, in the end, to adopt a deliberately inclusive approach to the word 'refugee'. The chapters in this book tend not to dwell on the legal status, citizenship or label applied by others. Our interest is not on people's reasons for migrating or the borders they have crossed. In contrast, the focus of these chapters is on places, spaces and buildings. We are interested in the shelters people pass through, regardless of how the individuals are categorized or defined. To mark this inclusivity, we sometimes draw on the phrase 'refugees and other migrants', which has the advantage of subverting the dichotomy between forced and voluntary movement. At other points, we use more the general category of 'displaced people', which often stands in as a useful and inclusive alternative. Specific terms, such as 'asylum seeker', have been sometimes employed to mark a specific moment, but in general the word 'refugee' in 'refugee shelter' should be interpreted expansively unless otherwise indicated.

The second challenge came from the other half of the phrase: the word 'shelter'. This, at least initially, had several advantages. It is a much wider category of structure than a building or a house, and it illustrates how forced migrants find shelter in many different places. Whereas a house has connotations of domesticity, and a building implies something purposeful and solid, a shelter captures how forced migrants live in sites that fit into neither of these categories: within improvised structures, under bridges and sometimes even carved out of forests and fields (see Hagan in this volume). In addition, the word 'shelter' is dynamic as well as general. It draws attention to sheltering as an *activity*. Shelter, it is often said, is a process as much as a place; it is achieved with communities as much as individuals (Davis 2011). Therefore, this word captures how refugees often find shelter through social processes. It embraces how refugees often live with relatives, friends, contacts, or how they join forces with citizen activists to produce more collaborative forms of shelter (see Western and Vandevoordt in this volume).

On the other hand, the word 'shelter' has a disadvantage because it implies an impermanent state. This can be quite misleading. Shelter is meant to be something temporary, but permanence is always relative – both materially and socially. It is materially relative because all permanent buildings decay and deteriorate, while so-called temporary shelters may in fact last for decades. It is socially relative because it is very difficult to declare when something has become permanent, since opinions are bound to differ. How do any of us really know when we have found a permanent place to stay? What does permanency even mean? When do we declare that we have found a place we can call home? These issues are further complicated because some refugees find temporary accommodation in 'permanent' structures that are repurposed: refugee shelters in Berlin constitute perhaps the most well-known example (see Baumann, Parsloe and Young in this volume). Alternatively, refugees may stay for many years in structures that were originally intended to be temporary, building and developing seemingly impermanent structures into something far more long-lasting (see Kikano in this volume).

Theorizing Refugee Shelter

During the workshop, we were aware of these definitional difficulties and often explored and discussed what 'shelter' meant as a concept. The attraction of this word was always its inclusiveness, generating a wide range of analytical possibilities. Indeed, shelter, as a notion, serves to cut across debates in various disciplines, and the chapters in this volume consequently connect the word to a number of theoretical apparatuses. Among other things, our authors discuss the idea of 'forced shelter' (Molnar), 'shifting shelters' (Achtnich), 'anti-shelters' (Howden) and the 'personal shelter' (Vandevoordt). There are chapters in this book on the 'container model of shelter' (Baumann), 'shelter as cladding' (Martin, Cross and Verhoeven), and 'shelter as a politically crafted materiality of neglect' (Pallister-Wilkins). There are reflections on the 'invisible shelter' (Hagan), the 'sonic shelter' (Western) and the idea of 'shelters for the mind' (Schroeder). Underneath these contributions and conceptualizations is a common thread, which sees shelter in terms of protection. This idea unifies the whole collection, appearing in dictionary definitions that frame shelter as protection from the elements. However, the idea of shelter as protection also generates a series of tensions and ambiguities that make these chapters so rich and fruitful.

What are these tensions and ambiguities? In this book we suggest that shelters are structures of protection in that they offer protection from bad weather, violence or insecurity, but this protection is only ever partial. Shelters are basic, which means that they protect in some ways, but not in others. Shelters can have many positive connotations, but they are not necessarily 'good' because they often expose their inhabitants in more significant ways than they protect. The question mark in our title is meant to highlight this ambivalence about the relationship between shelter and protection. If shelters are structures of protection, there always remains a great deal of flexibility in the dynamics of who is protected, how, and what they are being protected from. As the examples in this volume will demonstrate, many shelters are in reality multifaceted and do not offer protection at all, while others only offer limited protection that benefits some people more than others.

The most obvious example of the latter is perhaps government-run reception or detention centres, which can provide cover from the rain, but they might also serve to contain or restrict people's movement (Pallister-Wilkins). Such buildings might be oriented to a spectacle of deterrence (Mainwaring) or they might serve protection for the state rather than for refugees (Molnar). This, as our authors put it, constitutes a form of 'forced shelter'. There are, however, also more mundane examples where shelters offer protection, but are still squalid and leaky (Altin), shelters that lock people into exploitative relationships (Kikano) or shelters that protect the body but are harmful for mental health (Goh). This is a theme that runs throughout the book: shelters protect in some ways, but not in others. They can be defined by their provision of limited protection, and the way in which this protection is patterned reveals a great deal about the realities of life for refugees.

This volume is divided into three main parts, which consider the conceptual facets of refugee shelter under broad headings. Part I looks at the politics involved in shelter, the dynamics of containment and control. Part II looks at the social lives formed in shelters and the opportunities for resistance. Part III then looks at the material forms, history and design of refugee shelters. In each of these sections, the authors conceive of a shelter as a place where people seek greater protection than they would otherwise have available, even if this protection ends up being woefully inadequate.

Summarizing Refugee Shelter

Part I of this book, 'Shelter, Containment and Mobility', looks at how political authorities can use shelter to contain and manage human movement. It opens with Hanna Baumann's study of the shipping container: an object that stands as a metaphor for enclosure and rigidity, while simultaneously being portrayed as flexible. The great irony of the shipping container's popularity as a refugee shelter lies in the contrast between its use for commodities and its use for people. Containers are used to transport objects seamlessly across borders and are then used to prevent people from crossing the same borders. By examining the so-called Tempohomes in Berlin, Baumann teases out some of these ironies and contradictions, drawing attention to the way that shipping containers can become all things to all people. They are standardized yet to a certain extent flexible; they are mobile yet nevertheless stable; they are durable yet easy to remove; they function to isolate refugees while also linking them into urban infrastructures.

These characteristics, which Baumann identifies with a 'container model' of refugee shelter, reappear throughout this volume. In Chapter 2, Ċetta Mainwaring scales up the implications to look at how containment functions for Europe as a whole. Focusing particularly on Malta, whose pivotal position in the central Mediterranean plays a crucial role for European border management, Mainwaring opens with a description of the warehousing of refugees inside a military zone behind the international airport. This chapter shows how refugee shelter can serve distinctly political functions, not just by criminalizing migration but also by constructing an image of a unified Europe with a hard external border. Refugee shelter, she shows, can be symbolically constructive as well as materially destructive. Malta then reappears in Chapter 3, where Marthe Achtnich takes a more anthropological look at the lived experience of the Maltese 'open centres'. She highlights the complicated interplay between containment and the construction of social networks in these centres. In doing so, she draws attention to another recurring theme in the volume: flexibility. Refugee accommodation, she argues, often constitutes a form of 'shifting shelter'; even when it is restrictive, it is never static. Shelters are emergent spaces and, far from being simple protection from the elements, they are also deeply *social* forms that can protect human relations as well.

As both Mainwaring and Achnich point out, models of shelter in Malta have been reproduced around the edges of Europe more broadly, not least in those zones known as 'hotspots'. Chapters 4 and 5 turn to another hotspot, this time in Greece: the infamous camp of Moria on the island of Lesvos. In Chapter 5, Daniel Howden, a journalist who has been based in Greece for many years, builds an account of Moria as a form of 'anti-shelter'. Describing the politics of the camp, its context and history, he argues that Moria is an instructive microcosm of broader European border practices, featuring 'an architecture that is the very antithesis of shelter', designed to produce a spectacle of fear, uncertainty and danger for possible migrants. This theme is then developed further in Polly Pallister-Wilkins' chapter, which takes a closer look at the structures of Moria camp itself. Developing the notion of shelter as a 'politically crafted materiality of neglect', Pallister-Wilkins shows how poor conditions have become a purposeful deterrent within a wider system of border practices. In other words, refugee shelter is part of an exclusionary politics, which becomes written into the materiality of the shelters themselves.

Chapters 6 and 7 focus more specifically on detention centres, which, in the words of Petra Molnar, constitute a form of 'forced shelter'. At first glance, this seems to be an oxymoron, yet detention centres simply change the terrain of protection and safety by focusing on the state rather than the migrant. In Chapter 6, Molnar describes 'forced shelters' as particularly concentrated forms of state power. Drawing on an example from Canada, she explains how immigration detention often resembles a prison, removing migrants away from the general population, limiting their freedoms and choices, giving them uniforms and placing them behind bars in far-flung locations. This all takes place against people's will, yet it is still a form of shelter, which comes with a tantalizing possibility of permanent immigration. In Chapter 7, Renana Ne'eman offers a deep and detailed story of another detention centre, this time in Israel: Holot. This centre, she points out, is more than just a form of 'forced shelter', because it represents the complex and changing relationship between Israel and the Negev Desert. By looking at political culture as much as material conditions in the centre itself, Ne'eman builds a fascinating account of how forced shelters are coercive, traumatic and exclusionary, while also coming with layers of meaning and ideological significance. In particular, Holot illustrates how Israel manages populations through the desert. After many attempts to 'tame' and 'civilize' the desert, she argues, the Negev has become a place of banishment. This 'forced shelter' did not just contain people, but also demarcated territorial zones of exile.

This brings us to Part II of this volume, 'Shelter, Resistance and Solidarity'. The chapters in this part look at the other side of the coin: shelter not as a form of containment and coercion, but as an opportunity for creativity, community and social life. They focus on the lived experience of refugees, taking a more optimistic look at the way in which inhabitants are not simply the passive recipients of political agendas and coercive policies, but end up engaging in political acts themselves. This begins in Chapter 8, where Maria Hagan introduces the concept of a 'contingent camp', a barely perceptible form of shelter that has a very light material imprint. In contrast with coercive shelters examined in Part I of this volume – which were marked by the solidity of steel containers, the barbed wired of detention facilities, and a desire for fixed and firm boundaries – Hagan's contingent shelter is light, mobile and flexible. Her case study is northern France, where the destruction of the Calais 'Jungle' has pushed migrants into subtle and hidden forms of living in the local countryside, giving rise to spaces that are 'lived in but denied material consolidation', shelters that are 'in a constant state of becoming and unbecoming'. Here immateriality generates communal strength and invisibility becomes a concrete strategy. Such places are described in the local vernacular as a 'green hotel': shelter found in the forest and field. The value of shelter, in this example, comes from human relationships rather than bricks and mortar.

Chapter 9 continues the theme of the immaterial, looking instead at the role of sound. In this chapter, Tom Western highlights what he calls the 'sonic politics of refugee shelter', focusing on squats in Athens. The chapters in this collection often examine what protection means beyond the basics, and Western suggests that shelter can be thought of as a place where identities and cultures are protected, sustained and adjusted. Much of this takes place through sound. In his words, 'shelter is also something that is voiced', and the squats of Athens are a good example of spaces that have developed their own voices, identities and cultures. Western, once again, draws our attention to shelters as a site of resistance, ways of 'speaking back' to structures of power.

The next two chapters look at the way that shelters also generate new and lasting bonds between displaced people and citizens in the host country. Chapter 10 continues the focus on Athens, in which Ashley Mehra discusses two citizen-run shelters: the Melissa Day Centre and the City Plaza hotel, which she identifies as examples of 'redignification'. These are shelters that take the participation of refugees seriously: whereas camps and formal facilities fail to promote dignity, these shelters are oriented around equality, recognition and the sharing of power and control. As Mehra points out, dignity can be defined as 'having one's claims recognized by others', 'having some measure of control over one's life' and 'having a say in decisions' – features, she argues, that should be central to the process of sheltering. 'If the purpose of shelter is to protect and nurture people', she concludes, 'then it must involve inclusion and democratic participation.' These dynamics then reappear in Chapter 11, where Robin Vandevoordt takes us to Brussels to look at another attempt to promote participation and solidarity: a citizen initiative to host migrants in ordinary homes. Vandevoordt describes this as a 'more personal shelter', which revolved around strong interpersonal relationships. The hosting programme in Brussels was particularly successful, he argues, because it looked beyond biological needs and responded to the humanity of the displaced. It was founded on social dynamics rather than concrete material forms. Through personal bonds, vibrant virtual spaces and forms of connection into a larger community, shelter was built on human action.

Part II closes with two chapters focused on Berlin, which both show how life in refugee shelters does not always involve democracy, solidarity and resistance; many are also characterized by discomfort, boredom and uncertainty. In Chapter 12, Holly Young turns our attention to the vast International Congress Centre (ICC) in Berlin, an enormous building that was repurposed as a refugee shelter in the summer of 2015 and described by locals as 'the Aluminium Whale'. Young followed the story over several years and her account shows how the inhabitants had such little certainty about their fates, reduced to waiting for many months. This chapter provides a stark contrast with the more expansive political narratives that unfolded in Part I, focusing instead on the everyday concerns of refugee shelter residents: sleep, food, privacy and hygiene. Such issues reappear in Chapter 13, by Esther Schroder Goh, a medical doctor who examines how life in refugee shelters has a negative impact on mental health. Drawing on the study of another collective shelter in Berlin, Rathaus Friedenau, she shows how the organization and adaptation of these former council offices caused a litany of daily problems, once again centred on food, odours, cleanliness and privacy. Refugee accommodation, she argues, needs to consider the impact not just on physical health, but also on mental health, providing a structure to shelter the mind.

The final part of this collection, 'Architecture, Design and Displacement', concentrates on material structures of protection, beginning with three chapters that delve into the history of physical shelters around the world. Chapter 14, by Benjamin Thomas White, provides a biography of two fascinating Australian sites: the old quarantine stations at North Head, Sydney, and Point Nepean near Melbourne. After ceasing to be used as quarantine stations, these structures were used to protect humanitarian evacuees from conflicts as diverse as Kosovo and Vietnam. Drawing attention to the dynamics between protection and isolation in these sites, White argues that site biographies can provide a rich understanding of the human experience of displacement, grounded in the architecture of the buildings themselves. This approach is then taken up again in Chapter 15, by Roberta Altin, who offers a biography of a different site in Trieste: a huge three-storey structure that was built as a warehouse for commodities for the Austro-Hungarian Empire and was subsequently used to accommodate a variety of displaced people, from Jewish concentration camp victims to Italian refugees leaving Istria and Dalmatia, and more recently Afghan migrants moving towards

Western Europe. Altin shows how this structure accrued layers of meaning, serving to both protect and detain people while demonstrating dynamics of mobility and immobility. In Chapter 16, Zachary Whyte and Michael Ulfstjerne then offer a different kind of history, not so much a biography of a site, as a biography of a mobile shelter. Their study concerns the Danish 'refugee villages' of the 1990s, which were conceived to house Bosnian refugees fleeing the Balkan Wars, but whose modular, prefabricated forms could be packed up and moved elsewhere. These shelters became reused in various ways: as a part of a state removal facility, a kindergarten, as well as for repatriated refugees back in Bosnia. Again, this chapter emphasizes how refugee shelters can develop deep social meanings as they are re-placed and reinscribed in a variety of different contexts.

The next three chapters move more concretely to look at the role of architecture and design in forming material shelters. In Chapter 17, Craig Martin, Jamie Cross and Arno Verhoeven look at another instance of repurposing refugee shelter, this time from Goudoubo Camp in Burkina Faso. Like the Danish refugee villages, this is an instance of humanitarian design taking on a new life after change and adaptation; however, the authors of this chapter use their example to theorize how a top-down, imposed design can become encrusted with layers of adaptation and creativity, and how shelter can be thought of in terms of 'cladding', with a basic structure becoming amended with a range of vernacular additions. Chapter 18 then looks at another story of adaptation and 'cladding', focusing on the timber prefabricated shelters erected in Calais and Dunkirk by Médecins Sans Frontières (MSF) in 2015–16. In this chapter, Irit Katz examines emergency shelters not as end products, but as part of an 'ongoing spatial process'. By contrasting the way that MSF imagined a particular user in its handbook with the way that this shelter was adapted in practice, Katz demonstrates the reality of what she calls 'adhocism'. Chapter 19, while sticking with design, builds on this account by providing an example of how adaptation and design works in practice. Diane Fellows explores how social media can contribute to the process of sheltering and how collaborative designs can be furthered through social connectivity, which she describes as an 'emotional protective envelope' constructed through everyday life.

The final two chapters bring us full circle. Written from an architectural angle, they both hark back to themes of containment and immobility. In Chapter 20, Faten Kikano picks up the Middle Eastern focus of the previous chapter and looks further at the dynamics of encampment. Examining the accommodation of Syrian refugees in Lebanon – particularly an informal settlement at Kab Elias, Bekaa – she shows how creativity and self-construction does not necessarily mean freedom from top-down camp controls. The informal settlements of the Bekaa, she argues, were damaging ghettoized spaces, sodden with unequal power relations, poor-quality accommodation and a great deal of suffering. It is a theme that returns again in Chapter 21, when Toby Parsloe looks back at the subject of our first chapter: Berlin and temporary homes. Examining the spatial distinctions between emergency and community shelters at Tempelhof Airport, he argues that the highly symbolic former airport should be seen as an icon for the 'inflexibility, unpreparedness and exclusory housing systems of the contemporary European neo-liberal city'. The new urban structures at locations like Tempelhof, he argues, stand as an indictment of a whole continent: 'incapable, and perhaps even unwilling, to enact the ideals of European liberal democracy'.

Studying Refugee Shelter

The chapters in this collection propose a range of openings into the study of refugee shelter, which we hope will be taken up by others in the coming years. There are a variety of themes running through the collection, with many of the chapters, for example, identifying a central purpose to shelter that could apply more generally: the formation of social ties, the maintenance of border regimes, the creation of solidarity or the isolation of populations in liminal zones, to give just a few examples. Another common theme in the volume is the importance of history, and the way that buildings can put to such different uses over time: from quarantine stations to granary stores and shipping containers, there are a variety of biographical stories in this volume. Furthermore, many of the chapters touch on how sheltering is a process, an activity that changes and evolves, or they return to the idea of social shelter, illustrating how shelter is not just material, but needs to include lived experiences and complex human relationships.

Shelter, in this way, can become an extension of politics, and the different chapters illuminate a range of political positions. Whether it is furthering a liberal framework of rights, a communitarian framework of belonging, or an anarchist politics of radical participation, shelter is a way for identity and ideology to be communicated, a way to construct ideas of unity or fear. Shelter, in summary, can stand for many things, and this volume is just an opening. The examples illustrate how shelter can be fixed as well as fluid, how it can be material as well as symbolic, and how shelter can be public as well as private, a form of coercion as well as liberation. The examples touch on how shelter can encompass everything from substantial forms made from steel and iron to 'contingent' shelters that exist through social relations and are hardly there at all. In short, shelter is a place of ambiguity. Yet, beneath it all, shelter is always form of protection, however partial and contingent that protection turns out to be.

Tom Scott-Smith is Associate Professor of Refugee Studies and Forced Migration at the University of Oxford. His first book, *On an Empty Stomach: Two Hundred Years of Hunger Relief*, was published by Cornell University Press.

References

Betts, A. 2009. *Protection by Persuasion: International Cooperation in the Refugee Regime.* Ithaca: Cornell University Press.
Davis, I. 2011. 'What Have We Learned from 40 Years' Experience of Disaster Shelter?' *Environmental Hazards* 10(3–4): 193–212.
Hammond, L. 2004. *This Place Will Become Home: Refugee Repatriation to Ethiopia.* Ithaca: Cornell University Press.
Korac, M. 2009. *Remaking Home: Reconstructing Life, Place and Identity in Rome and Amsterdam.* Oxford: Berghahn Books.
Jansen, B. 2018. *Kakuma Refugee Camp: Humanitarian Urbanism in Kenya's Accidental City.* London: Zed Books.
McAdam, J. 2007. *Complementary Protection in International Refugee Law.* Oxford: Oxford University Press.
McConnachie, K. 2016. 'Camps of Containment: A Genealogy of the Refugee Camp'. *Humanity* 7(3): 397–412.

Part I

Shelter, Containment and Mobility

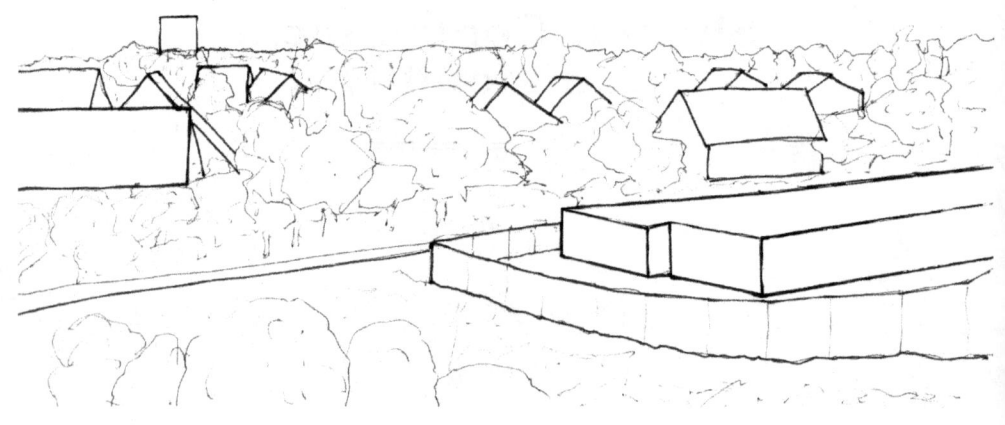

Figure 1.1 Tempohomes in Berlin, Germany. © Mark E. Breeze, based on an image supplied by Hanna Baumann.

1
Moving, Containing, Displacing
The Shipping Container as Refugee Shelter

Hanna Baumann

Modified containers or 'caravans' have been used as temporary refugee housing in countless situations of mass displacement, whether due to forced migration or natural disaster. This is not surprising, given their relatively low cost and durability, as well as their ease of transport, setup, modification and eventual removal. In this chapter, I analyse the container shelter by examining its origins as a core infrastructure of global trade. The shipping container is mainly distinguished from other forms of prefabricated emergency shelter by its adherence to ISO standards. Its standardized size, stackability and corner fixtures allow for numerous possibilities of modular combination and enable seamless transport across air, sea and land. Due to its original use as an infrastructure of commercial exchange – indeed, one that reshaped the international economy – the shipping container used as refugee shelter also provides an occasion to investigate the links between global and urban regimes of (im)mobility.

I argue that shipping containers act as an infrastructure that facilitates the movement and redistribution of people across space using the example of container villages, the so-called 'Tempohomes' created in Berlin to accommodate large numbers of refugees and asylum seekers who have arrived in the city since 2015. I highlight the capacity of containers, on the one hand, to redistribute goods and wealth and, on the other, to contain and displace populations. As a form of shelter, containers are sturdy enough to form a first step in the process of settling people, but also flexible enough to move them elsewhere, or be removed entirely if no longer needed. This dual material quality of permanence and mobility makes container shelters an ideal technology for distributing and redistributing refugees and asylum seekers in response to fluctuating refugee policies.

The Shipping Container as an Infrastructure of Global Trade

The integration of the movement of goods across various surfaces and modes of transport – from freight ship to train to flatbed truck to plane – caused the so-called 'intermodal' container to revolutionize the shipping industry from the 1960s onwards. In integrating trade across the 'transitional zone' of the coast (Martin 2013), the standardized shipping container was able to minimize the time-consuming and costly process of loading and unloading ships, and thereby decrease the cost of maritime shipping substantially (Levinson 2006; Martin 2016). Not only did it increase the speed and rate at which goods moved across the globe, but the price of goods was no longer linked to the distance they had travelled, leading to what Harvey (1989) has called 'time-space compression'. The shipping container thus became a 'key innovation' facilitating economic globalization (Harvey 2010).

The worldwide standardization of shipping containers by the International Organization for Standardization (ISO) increased the scale of change by many magnitudes. Currently over 33 million ISO containers are in operation worldwide (World Shipping Council n.d.). The adoption of the so-called Twenty-Foot Equivalent Unit[1] as industry standard (in recent years replaced by the Forty-Foot Equivalent Unit) might be considered the real building block of the global 'space of flows' (Castells 1999). In mobility studies, 'moorings' are conceived of as the immobile infrastructures that enable flows (Hannam et al. 2006), but in the case of containers, the movement is facilitated by an element that is itself mobile. Furthermore, in addition to the steel cubes themselves, we might see the immaterial standard specifications applied to them as the infrastructure of globalization (cf. Bowker and Starr 1999; Easterling 2014). Containers thus function as both a 'hard' and a 'soft' infrastructure: they 'mediate exchange over distance' and thus form the 'base on which to operate modern economic and social systems' (Larkin 2013: 330) through their physical apparatuses as well as their adherence to a common set of norms and processes.

The shipping container not only spurred a massive increase in international trade, with world seaborne trade trebling between 1975 and 2015 to 1.75 billion metric tons (UNCTAD 2015); it also resulted in the redistribution of centres of commerce through the ascendancy of new economic powers such as Japan, and new port cities such as Busan, Korea (Levinson 2006: 271). *Within* cities too, it shifted the focal points of economic activity. Urban ports were severely affected by the rise of container shipping, and not only because longshoremen were no longer needed in the close-to-automatized processes of loading and unloading cargo. Due to the much higher volumes of goods moving through ports and the possibility of storing containers in situ, more space was needed than inner-city ports could offer. Many urban docksides and waterfronts thus declined as ports moved elsewhere (Martin 2016: 55ff). The container, then, both moves goods and redistributes the profits from those goods and movements, boosting some spaces by linking them to the international network of exchange, and causing the decline of others.

In addition, the shipping container is deeply embroiled with technologies of both war and humanitarianism. As Levinson (2006: 186ff) details, the Vietnam War marked a turning point for the expansion of global container-based trade. The U.S. military fully adopted this system for moving its cargo across the world, indirectly igniting Japan's economic ascendancy, as it became profitable to fill empty containers on U.S. war ships in Japan as they returned from Vietnam on their way to California. Logistics has grown due to the just-in-time manufacturing and shipment flows that developed in the wake of containerization, but it is originally a military discipline that has become a core determinant of corporate success. Not only are corporate logistics based on martial precedents, but current supply chains relying on the orchestration of countless complex flows are highly securitized, and even defended with military might (Cowen 2014). At the same time, humanitarian logistics often use the same sites, paths, expertise and sometimes even personnel as their military counterparts (see Attewell 2018; Khalili 2018; Ziadah 2018) – with aid and reconstruction following in the footsteps of destruction, completing a circle of profit. Ticktin (2016) notes the dehumanization at work when people are forced to live in vessels made for commercial goods. When refugees are sheltered in shipping containers, their position in the context of these wider circulations is brought into sharp relief.

Berlin's Tempohomes

In 2015, following the arrival of close to one million refugees in Germany, thousands of people were housed in emergency shelters that included office buildings, barracks, factories and gymnasiums. While 55,000 were housed in such shelters in Berlin at the peak of the so-called 'crisis', by mid 2018, only 900 individuals remained in these temporary situations (Abel 2018). In lieu of a permanent housing solution, shipping containers had been converted to residential units, called Tempohomes. These were intended to serve as shelters for an intermediate period of a maximum of three years – a short-term solution permitting the circumvention of regular planning laws.[2] The State of Berlin's call for tender specified that shelters should be '20-foot standard containers', corresponding to the ISO norm (State of Berlin 2016).

Berlin's borough of Pankow explained the choice of container shelters as follows: 'The mobile accommodations can be set up quickly, have a good standard, are relatively inexpensive and can be converted and used elsewhere if required' (Stiftung SPI 2015). However, the agency in charge of Berlin's refugee affairs also acknowledged that moving Berlin's refugees into another temporary form of housing, after they had lived in emergency shelters, without privacy and often for years, was 'not ideal' and 'provisional'. In an official communication, it explains that the 'strain' on the city's housing market is to blame for the fact that only 3,500 refugees found accommodation in regular flats in 2017 (Landesamt für Flüchtlingsangelegenheiten 2017) – a number that decreased to just over 2,000 in 2018 (Berlin Senate 2019). Property prices in the city increased by twenty per cent in 2017 – the highest rate worldwide (Knight Frank 2018), leaving Berlin with a lack of affordable housing.

While the city's initial plan was to erect thirty container villages made up of Tempohomes in order to house a total of 15,000 people, these targets were later lowered to seventeen sites with accommodation for 5,300 people, in part because fewer asylum seekers were arriving and in part because of the higher than anticipated cost of the shelters. The left-of-centre coalition that took over Berlin's state government in late 2016 claimed that this downward correction reflected its policy priority of avoiding housing refugees in containers, but the previous right-of-centre coalition had in fact already reduced the scale of the plan because of the high number of asylum seekers in Berlin who were gaining refugee status (*Berliner Zeitung* 2016). The new plan provides for medium-term Modular Accommodation for Refugees (*Modulare Unterkünfte für Flüchtlinge* (MUFs)) to be built in fifty-three sites, suggesting that Tempohomes served mainly as an interim solution for those whose asylum claim had not been processed.

A typical Tempohome site consists of 244 containers arranged in single-storey configurations. Five hundred people are housed in sixty-four flats across eight accommodation buildings, with each flat made up of three containers. In addition, there are two buildings for communal activities and administration (twenty-four containers each) and one four-container unit for a 'porter' or security guard (Senatsverwaltung für Gesundheit und Soziales 2016). Externally, the appearance of the sites is often bare, with amenities such as greenery and playgrounds only added after refugees moved in. Internally, the flats, consisting of three containers, offer 45 m^2 of space for four to eight individuals – meaning 11.25 to 5.6 m^2 per person. This is still above the minimum standard in humanitarian response, specified as 3.5 m² per person (Sphere Project 2011), but well below the Berlin average of 40 m² (*Der Spiegel* 2015). More significantly, the ceiling height of just 2.2 m is quite low.

Each flat includes a small washroom with a shower, and a pantry kitchen including an oven/stove and refrigerator. While basic furniture items including beds, tables and cupboards are provided, sites do occasionally lack essential furniture. For instance, while 30 per cent of residents at the communal Tempohome accommodation at Finckensteinallee in Steglitz-Zehlendorf are infants and toddlers, no baby cots were included in the original setup, and the State Office for Refugee Affairs took some time to approve the additional items (German Red Cross 2018). Therefore, the visual impression related by residents of the surrounding neighbourhoods ranges from 'sparse and functional' (*Berliner Kurier* 2017a) to 'dismal' and 'bleak' (*Berliner Kurier* 2017b). While some Tempohome residents have expressed relief at the increased degree of privacy – as anything was perceived as better than living and sleeping in a gymnasium with hundreds of strangers – many others complained of the lack of privacy due to the density of accommodation and the lack of sound insulation and visual barriers between units (Vey 2018: 38–39). In addition, being fenced in, especially in an area used for leisure activities such as the former airfield of Tempelhof Airport, made one boy fear he would be stared at as if he were in a zoo (Frühauf n.d.).

Containment, (Re)Distribution and Displacement

As Katz (2015, 2017) notes, camps can be used for both 'concentrating' and 'spreading' populations, and this is true for container camps as well. The qualities of the shipping container can impact the spatial position of refugees in the city in both ways. On the one hand, when container villages are placed in low-density environments and sequestered off by physical obstacles and administrative barriers – albeit for security reasons – this serves to isolate and contain their residents. On the other hand, when they are linked to existing urban infrastructures, container shelters can serve as a first step to integrating refugee housing into the wider urban fabric. However, this kind of dispersal can also hinder integration. The provisional nature of the shelter makes the container an ideal technology to distribute (and redistribute) refugees across the city in line with changing administrative and policy requirements, undermining the development of local ties.

The outside of the shipping container, as a standardized form of packaging, rarely reveals the assemblages of items and materials inside (unless they spill out). To contain, then, is to shield something from public view, but also to stop it from permeating into that public. Most of the seventeen Tempohomes sites are outside central Berlin (with only a handful within, or near, the S-Bahn Ring around the urban core). This is in part because large empty plots are required to build the single-storey villages – approximately 12,000 m² for a standard site housing 500 people. A 'double site' accommodating 1,000 refugees, such as Elisabeth-Aue in Pankow, requires 26,000 m². This site takes up a small portion of a large field near an area of single-family homes and is visually separated from the main road and built-up area by a row of trees. Fences surround the perimeter of each site and, while residents may receive visitors, visits must be pre-announced and approved (Dalal et al. 2018). This security arrangement is explained as based on the need to protect refugee accommodation. In 2017, there were close to 2,000 attacks on refugees across Germany, resulting in 300 injuries, as well as over 300 attacks on refugee shelters (*Der Spiegel* 2018), twenty-six of which took place in Berlin (Pro Asyl 2017). Due to the securitization and the threat it reflects, it is perhaps not surprising that Tempohome residents complain of their isolation from their surroundings and, based on this, from German society at large (Vey 2018: 51). Even if the intention is to protect inhabitants from outsiders, the effect is also to contain refugees and minimize their interaction with the city around them.

Yet efforts have also been made to ensure the spatial integration of Tempohome residents in the city. Locations for Tempohomes were selected in a thorough process that was not only concerned with availability of space and technical feasibility; instead, links to social as well as 'hard' infrastructures were evaluated. For instance, the decision to build the Refugium Buch site in the Karow neighbourhood of the borough of Pankow, rather than using existing buildings, considered the proximity to schools, child daycare centres, shops and hospitals, in addition to transport links and the burden on water and electricity networks (Pankow Council 2015). Further, some of the Modular Accommodations for Refugees (MUFs) will be built in locations adjacent to the Tempohomes, suggesting that there is a longer-term plan for settling and spatially integrating residents. As politicians never fail to note, the MUFs, made from prefabricated concrete modules and with a lifespan of eighty years, can be added to the Berlin property market when they have outlived their purpose as refugee housing. In the MUFs, up to 500 people will be living in close quarters in one building (Abel 2018), at times in sparsely populated areas in which they will outnumber local residents (*Berliner Morgenpost* 2018), suggesting that the effect of concentration and containment will remain a challenge in the longer term.

A key factor in the decision for Berlin to invest some seventy-eight million Euros in Tempohomes (Landesamt für Flüchtlingsangelegenheiten n.d.) was the ease with which the containers could be moved to the desired locations. One supplier of containers for refugee shelter, a Dutch company called Tempohousing (2015), notes the versatile possibilities of delivering its shelters based on the twenty-foot shipping container: 'by sea, road and train'. Highlighting the shipping origins of its containers, Tempohousing (2010) explains their advantages as housing for displaced people in various humanitarian situations in a company brochure: 'modules are shipped world wide – by truck to the construction site – with a simple crane building is set up [sic]'. It continues: 'All modules comply with international transport standards and with international building codes, to get the best of both worlds: easy to transport to everywhere and simple to construct a building.' Thus, as in global trade, the container's movability, enhanced by standardization, is key in the context of refugee shelters too. The container reveals its ability to distribute and redistribute – in this case, people rather than goods. Utilized as housing, its modular nature enables easy expansion, recombination and eventual removal. From the point of view of the state, this makes it a suitable means of housing displaced people even over longer periods of time: the shelter situation can be altered in order to adapt to site specificities as required by the urban context and can respond to shifting policy priorities and directions.

In Berlin, such shifts include the potential (re)distribution of refugees across boroughs or states, in line with updated 'burden-sharing' agreements. As there is within the European Union, there is constant debate among Germany's federal states and Berlin's districts regarding the distribution of refugees. In Germany, the *Königsteiner Schlüssel* formula is employed to calculate the distribution of asylum seekers based on each state's population and tax payments. However, the formula does not consider the availability of living space as a factor, meaning that higher quotas are assigned to city-states like Berlin, which was allocated around 5 per cent of all refugees between 2017 and 2019 (Bundesamt für Migration und Flüchtlinge 2019). In the debate over this, alternative models suggest moving refugees and asylum seekers to allow a 'fairer' distribution from the point of view of 'overburdened' federal states like Berlin (Gerl et al. 2016).

Within the city, initial distributions were made according to the availability of space for emergency shelters (Berlin Senate 2016), resulting in unequal distribution and debates on what a 'fair' share would be. Administratively, responsibility was then allocated based on individuals' birthdates, which meant that many asylum seekers had to attend official appointments in a different office from their family members, and sometimes had to travel long distances. Furthermore, local officials in their assigned district were often unfamiliar with the resources in their area of residence. Because asylum seekers often do not have papers or recorded birthdates, many listed January as their birthdate. As a result, the district of Mitte was allocated a disproportionately high number of refugees, a share that then had to be corrected, meaning a renewed reallocation (Fahrun 2018). As such, the temporary nature of the shelters, and the possibility of moving them, appear well-suited to a situation in which governmental responsibility is constantly reshuffled.

In addition to their ability to contain and (re)distribute displaced populations, containers can also act as harbingers of forthcoming displacement. As part of the trend in 'sustainable' small-scale architecture (Roke 2016), shipping containers have increasingly been used for other urban purposes besides emergency shelter. There are an estimated 500,000 idle shipping containers, especially in the United States. In light of reports of a large 'surplus', trade organizations such as the ISBU Association have been advocating for the reuse of containers for various purposes, including as homes (ISBU n.d.). The shipping container as housing or commercial space conveys the impression of 'upcycling' (despite the fact that most containers used for these purposes are new or heavily cleaned and refurbished), appealing to proponents of urban sustainability. At the same time, it encapsulates the aesthetic of a revitalized industrial waterfront as well as that of 'pop-up' urbanism, both associated with gentrification.

The Platoon Kunsthalle Development Center, a commercial art space made up of stacked containers, has been set up in different sites across Berlin since 2002 and has subsequently expanded to Seoul and Mexico City. The company's name and its olive green colour serve as reminders of the container's military history, but the producer of the containers mainly creates temporary sites for the purpose of promoting luxury brands. Similarly, temporary leisure and commercial and leisure spaces made up of containers have been set up in unused lots in cities across the world, with shops, bars and restaurants promising revitalization through a bourgeois version of urban informality. In London, food and retail parks such as Boxpark Shoreditch and PopBrixton draw a predominantly white middle-class clientele, despite the diversity of the surrounding neighbourhoods, and have become symbols of gentrification. Yet shipping containers are also touted as affordable housing for students and people on low incomes. In Brighton, a metal scrap yard was repurposed when the Richardson's Yard homeless shelter, made of shipping containers, was set up on its site. Isolation and the lack of security were seen as problems by residents (Rippingdale 2014), but the shelter was only ever intended for temporary use. The longer-term plan was to utilize the site's new aesthetic to attract creative industries that would become permanent tenants (Brighton & Hove City Council 2009).

The supposedly temporary repurposing of an area through 'meanwhile use' urbanism embodied in container retail parks and housing may result in its longer-term spatial change. In their function of developing and attracting new groups to supposedly underexploited urban sites, containers thus also embody the potential displacement of existing residents. Like Tempohomes, these other urban container spaces function almost like Special Economic Zones on an urban level: their temporariness denotes exceptional regimes where planning processes are bypassed to house people on an ad hoc basis or to 'revitalize' a neighbourhood. In Berlin, Tempohomes are also a response to ongoing gentrification and the rise in housing costs across the city, especially due to foreign investment. On the other hand, MUFs, their longer-term cousins, might be seen as urban development tools where interim use by refugees is merely one step on the way to densifying and reconfiguring an urban area. Again we see how containers are not only used to move objects, and thereby redistribute wealth, but also to redistribute populations across the city, channelling their flow in line with the requirements of capital.

The crowded and bare living conditions of the Tempohomes ensure that this form of interim housing is not too comfortable for residents. Because the container housing is often isolated, the refugee 'problem' appears to be contained. The mobile and temporary architecture of the containers allows for the possibility of the large-scale return of their inhabitants to their home countries. While Tempohomes are justified as quick solutions, they reflect a lesser commitment to permanent settlement that would involve spatial integration and long-term housing solutions. But shipping containers are not by nature isolating, as we have seen in other uses of their typology; they can also be used to settle groups in new locations and may also have displacing effects. They are an infrastructure that can both contain and distribute, exclude or expand. The question then arises as to why Berlin's 'container villages' were planned on such a large scale, and in so segregated a fashion, that isolation was bound to result.

Conclusion: The Shipping Container and Global (Im)Mobilities

We know that globalization does not mean the end of nation states or borders. While enhanced mobilities facilitate the movement of goods and the 'kinetic elite' (Cresswell 2006) across boundaries, the movement of less desirable subjects is curtailed through mobility regimes (Shamir 2005). Yet there is not only a 'mobility gap' (Turner 2006) in the sense that some goods and groups are less mobile than others. Rather, the mobility of some people and goods is *predicated* on the containment of those immobilized and contained others. And, indeed, the forced migration of some can be viewed as a result of the 'free' movement of global markets; poverty and displacement are 'expulsions' due to resource extraction, climate change and the financialization of housing (Sassen 2014). Some nonhuman cargo is deemed so valuable that military violence is employed to protect the supply chain, potentially causing displacement. At the same time, *people* transported on boats in the Mediterranean are not consistently deemed worthy of rescue when their vessels capsize and they are left to drown.

The shipping container participates in both processes: the seemingly boundless movement across the surface of the earth, and the containment and management of those who wish to move, often as a result of the unequal effects of globalization. In acting as a tool for the redistribution of goods and people across space on a grand scale, the shipping container can create temporal, spatial and political transitional zones that are not just useful for optimizing global (and local) trade and value extraction, but also to manage their fallout. While social scientists often focus on the immaterial and deterritorialized nature of flows of capital (Coole and Frost 2010), the shipping container points to the physically tangible nature of much of worldwide trade and mobility. Moreover, through its use as refugee housing, it physically embodies some of the consequences of these global flows – poverty, war and displacement.

While the Dutch producer of inhabitable containers refers to the ISO container as 'our most sturdy and durable solution' (Tempohousing n.d.), shipping containers do not facilitate 'durable solutions' in the sense of the United Nations High Commissioner for Refugees (UNHCR) – local integration, resettlement to a third country or voluntary repatriation. The shipping container's basic physical qualities make it stable enough to protect what it contains in the short term, but flexible and impermanent enough to be moved when required. It is therefore ideal for facilitating transitions in a variety of situations and contexts. Goods and people can be moved and (re)distributed across space swiftly, but they can also be stored or warehoused in an already-protected environment until longer-term solutions are found. Yet, we have seen that the temporary presence of large numbers of containers can also initiate longer-term urban changes, as the surrounding socio-spatial arrangements are affected. As a refugee shelter, the shipping container's dual qualities (mobile/durable, temporary/stable) make it an interstitial form of housing, both spatially and temporally. While it allows for individual or family occupancy (unlike emergency reception centres), it is still a 'collective' form of accommodation – with the lives of large groups of refugees managed by an agency rather than self-determined. Indeed, the size and scope of the MUFs, which will house up to 30,000 refugees across fifty-three sites, suggest that there is no long-term plan to disperse all refugees into individual accommodation. Like other forms of temporary shelter, the shipping container is a space for awaiting longer-term solutions.

In the German context, these qualities of the shipping container allow the state to respond flexibly, fulfilling its basic obligations of shelter provision and setting a potential path to local settlement without committing to long-term housing and integration. The easy disassembly, movability and reuse of the shipping containers, as well as the possibility of repurposing medium-term modular housing, mean that no excessive spatial commitments have been made; large numbers of refugees can easily be moved to a different city district, federal state or European country, or can even be refouled. In light of the shifting policy vis-à-vis refugees on various political scales, such a spatially and temporally flexible approach to refugee shelter should perhaps not be understood as a failure to respond quickly, but rather as a 'rational' response from the point of view of a state keeping its spatial options open.

Despite the specificities of the shipping container as a standardized form, what we might call the 'container model' of refugee housing permeates many of the official responses to sheltering displaced people. These types of mobile infrastructures, which can barely be called housing, enable survival, but not living. They protect those inside from what lies beyond, but also contain them, limiting their ability to develop ties to adjacent areas. Continuously transmitting the embodied message not to get too comfortable in a given location, their very materiality asserts their temporariness, their capacity to uproot inhabitants again at short notice.

Hanna Baumann is a Leverhulme Early Career Fellow at the Bartlett's Institute for Global Prosperity, University College London. She completed her Ph.D. in Architecture at the University of Cambridge in 2017. Her current work in examines the role of infrastructures in the urban exclusion of noncitizens.

Notes

1. The standard shipping container, following ISO 668, is approximately 2.4 m (8 feet) wide and 2.6 m (8.5 feet) high, with a length of either 6 m (20 feet) or 12.2 m (40 feet). So-called 'hi-cube' versions follow the same measurements, except that they have a height of 2.9 m. The corner locking mechanism that enables lifting and stacking follows ISO 1161. ISO 6346 specifies standards for coding and marking shipping containers. See Levinson (2006: 137–49) for details on the process of standardization.
2. As stipulated by law: Baugesetzbuch (BauGB) § 246 Sonderregelungen für einzelne Länder; Sonderregelungen für Flüchtlingsunterkünfte.

References

Abel, A. 2018. 'Senat uneinig über Bedarf an Flüchtlingsunterkünften'. *Berliner Morgenpost*, 28 June. Retrieved 10 October 2019 from https://www.morgenpost.de/berlin/article214704565/Senat-uneinig-ueber-Bedarf-an-Fluechtlingsunterkuenften.html.

Attewell, W. 2018. 'From Factory to Field: USAID and the Logistics of Foreign Aid in Soviet-Occupied Afghanistan'. *Environment and Planning D: Society and Space* 36(4): 719–38.

Berlin Senate. 2016. 'Press Release: Beschluss des Senats zum Umgang mit der Standortauswahl für die Flüchtlingsunterbringung', 23 February. Retrieved 10 October 2019 from www.berlin.de/rbmskzl/aktuelles/pressemitteilungen/2016/pressemitteilung.448168.php.

———. 2019. 'Press Release: Runder Tisch zur Verbesserung der Situation geflüchteter Menschen auf dem Wohnungsmarkt', 20 March. Retrieved 10 October 2019 from https://www.berlin.de/sen/ias/presse/pressemitteilungen/2019/pressemitteilung.794236.php.

Berliner Kurier. 2017a. 'Flughafen Tempelhof: Erste Flüchtlinge ziehen in Container ein'. *Berliner Kurier*, 4 December. Retrieved 10 October 2019 from https://www.berliner-kurier.de/berlin/kiez---stadt/flughafen-tempelhofa-erste-fluechtlinge-ziehen-in-container-ein-28995406.

Berliner Kurier. 2017b. 'Tempohomes: Tag der offenen Tür Hunderte Berliner wollen die tristen Container sehen'. *Berliner Kurier*, 12 February. Retrieved 10 October 2019 from https://www.berliner-kurier.de/berlin/kiez---stadt/-tempohomes---tag-der-offenen-tuer-hunderte-berliner-wollen-die-tristen-container-sehen-25720794.

Berliner Morgenpost. 2018. 'Der große Streit um Berlins neue Flüchtlingsunterkünfte'. *Berliner Morgenpost*, 4 March. Retrieved 10 October 2019 from https://www.morgenpost.de/berlin/article213617491/Der-grosse-Streit-um-Berlins-neue-Fluechtlingsunterkuenfte.html.

Berliner Zeitung. 2016. 'Flüchtlingsheime Statt Containersiedlungen: nun mehr Wohnungen geplant'. *Berliner Zeitung*, 7 June. Retrieved 10 October 2019 from https://www.berliner-zeitung.de/berlin/fluechtlingsheime-statt-containersiedlungen-nun-mehr-wohnungen-geplant-24187676.

Bowker, G., and Star S.L. 1999. *Sorting Things out: Classification and its Consequences.* Cambridge, MA: MIT Press.

Brighton & Hove City Council. 2009. 'SPD10 – London Road Central Masterplan'. Retrieved 10 October 2019 from https://www.brighton-hove.gov.uk/sites/brighton-hove.gov.uk/files/London%20Rd%20SPD%2017%20Dec%2009%20with%20appendices_1.pdf.

Bundesamt für Migration und Flüchtlinge. 2019. 'Erstverteilung der Asylsuchenden'. Retrieved 10 October 2019 from www.bamf.de/DE/Fluechtlingsschutz/AblaufAsylv/Erstverteilung/erstverteilung-node.html.

Castells, M. 1999. 'Grassrooting the Space of Flows'. *Urban Geography* 20(4): 294–302.

Coole, D., and S. Frost. 2010. 'Introduction', in D. Coole and S. Frost (eds), *New Materialisms: Ontology, Agency, and Politics.* Durham, NC: Duke University Press, pp. 1–46.

Cowen, D. 2014. *The Deadly Life of Logistics: Mapping Violence in Global Trade.* Minneapolis: University of Minnesota Press.

Cresswell, T. 2006. *On the Move: Mobility in the Modern Western World.* New York: Routledge.

Dalal, A., A. Darweesh, P. Misselwitz and A. Steigemann. 2018. 'Planning the Ideal Refugee Camp? A Critical Interrogation of Recent Planning Innovations in Jordan and Germany'. *Urban Planning* 3(4): 64–78.
Der Spiegel. 2015. 'Deutsche brauchen immer mehr Platz', 21 August. Retrieved 10 October 2019 from https://www.spiegel.de/wirtschaft/service/wohnungen-in-deutschland-so-viel-platz-brauchen-die-deutschen-a-1048708.html.
Easterling, K. 2014. *Extrastatecraft: The Power of Infrastructure Space.* London: Verso.
Fahrun, J. 2018. 'Berliner Senat gibt 900 Millionen Euro für Flüchtlinge aus'. *Berliner Morgenpost,* 10 January. Retrieved 10 October 2019 from https://www.morgenpost.de/berlin/article213061723/Berliner-Senat-gibt-900-Millionen-Euro-fuer-Fluechtlinge-aus.html.
Frühauf, H. n.d. 'Tempohomes, eine Glaubensfrage?' Neuköllner Blog. Retrieved 10 October 2019 from www.neukoellner.net/alltag/tempohomes-eine-glaubensfrage.
Gerl, M., A. Reimann and F. Kalinowsk. 2016. 'So könnte eine gerechtere Verteilung der Flüchtlinge aussehen'. *Der Spiegel,* 10 March. Retrieved 10 October 2019 from www.spiegel.de/politik/deutschland/fluechtlinge-so-koennte-eine-gerechte-verteilung-aussehen-a-1081169.html.
German Red Cross. 2018. 'GU Finckelsteinallee'. DRK Berlin SüdWest GmbH Liveblog weblog, 13 April. Retrieved 10 October 2019 from https://www.drk-berlin.net/angebote/flucht-und-migration/gu-finckensteinallee/live-blog.html.
Hannam, K., M. Sheller and J. Urry. 2006. 'Editorial: Mobilities, Immobilities and Moorings'. *Mobilities* 1(1): 1–22.
Harvey, D. 1989. *The Condition of Postmodernity: An Enquiry into the Origins of Cultural Change.* London: Wiley-Blackwell.
———. 2010. *The Enigma of Capital and the Crises of Capitalism.* London: Profile Books.
ISBU. n.d. 'Intermodal Steel Building Units and Container Homes, ISBU Shipping Container Benefits'. Retrieved 10 October 2019 from www.isbu-association.org/benefits-container-technology.htm.
Katz, I. 2015. 'Spreading and Concentrating: The Camp as the Space of the Frontier'. *City* 19(5): 727–40.
———. 2017. '"The Common Camp": Temporary Settlements as a Spatio-political Instrument in Israel-Palestine'. *Journal of Architecture* 22(1): 54–103.
Khalili, L. 2018. 'The Infrastructural Power of the Military: The Geoeconomic Role of the US Army Corps of Engineers in the Arabian Peninsula'. *European Journal of International Relations* 24(4): 911–33.
Knight Frank. 2018. 'Global Residential Cities Index 2017 – Q4'. Retrieved 10 October 2019 from www.knightfrank.com/research/global-residential-cities-index-q4-2017-5413.aspx.
Landesamt für Flüchtlingsangelegenheiten. 2017. 'FAQ zu den TempoHomes auf dem Tempelhofer Feld'. Retrieved 10 October 2019 from www.berlin.de/laf/wohnen/dateiablage/faq_tempelhofer_feld.pdf.
———. n.d. 'Tempohomes FAQ'. Retrieved 10 October 2019 from https://www.berlin.de/laf/wohnen/allgemeine-informationen/tempohomes-faq.
Larkin, B. 2013. 'The Politics and Poetics of Infrastructure'. *Annual Review of Anthropology* 42: 327–43.

Levinson, M. 2006. *The Box: How the Shipping Container Made the World Smaller and the World Economy Bigger*. Princeton: Princeton University Press.
Martin, C. 2016. *Shipping Container*. London: Bloomsbury.
——. 2013. 'Shipping Container Mobilities, Seamless Compatibility, and the Global Surface of Logistical Integration'. *Environment and Planning A* 45(5): 1021–36.
Pankow Council. 2015. '2nd Letter of the Borough Council on the Refugee Accommodation' (in German). Retrieved 10 October 2019 from www.berlin.de/ba-pankow/politik-und-verwaltung/beauftragte/integration/dokumente/zweiter_brief_des_bezirksamtes_pankow_zur_fluchtlingsunterkunft_buch.pdf.
Pro Asyl. 2017. 'Gewalt gegen Flüchtlinge 2017: Von Entwarnung kann keine Rede sein', 28 December. Retrieved 10 October 2019 from https://www.proasyl.de/news/gewalt-gegen-fluechtlinge-2017-von-entwarnung-kann-keine-rede-sein.
Rippingdale, J. 2014. 'Sneaking into Brighton's New Homeless Shipping Container Ghetto'. *Vice*, 9 May. Retrieved 10 October 2019 from https://www.vice.com/sv/article/gq8jyq/i-spent-the-night-in-brightons-homeless-shipping-container-housing-project.
Roke, R. 2016. *Nanotecture: Tiny Built Things*. London: Phaidon.
Sassen, S. 2014. *Expulsions: Brutality and Complexity in the Global Economy*. Cambridge, MA: Harvard University Press.
Senatspressekonferenz. 2018. 'Weitere Standorte für Modulare Unterkünfte in allen Berliner Bezirken'. Presentation, 27 March. Retrieved 10 October 2019 from www.berlin.de/sen/finanzen/presse/pressemitteilungen/neue_muf_standorte.pdf.
Senatsverwaltung für Gesundheit und Soziales. 2016. '"Tempohomes": neue Containerdörfer zur Unterbringung von Flüchtlingen in Berlin'. Retrieved 10 October 2019 from www.berlin.de/laf/wohnen/dateiablage/laf_anlage_1_grundrisse_tempohomes.pdf.
Shamir, R. 2005. 'Without Borders? Notes on Globalization as a Mobility Regime'. *Sociological Theory* 23(2): 197–217.
Sphere Project. 2011. *Sphere Handbook: Humanitarian Charter and Minimum Standards in Disaster Response*. London: Sphere.
——. 2018. 'Angriffe auf Flüchtlinge und ihre Unterkünfte', 28 February. Retrieved 10 October 2019 from https://www.spiegel.de/politik/deutschland/fluechtlinge-2219-angriffe-auf-asylbewerber-und-ihre-unterkuenfte-in-2017-a-1195738.html.
State of Berlin. 2016. 'Ausschreibung – Mobile, modulare Containergebäude in Berlin 18 February 2016 (ID:11505226)'. Retrieved 10 October 2019 from https://www.dtad.de/details/Mobile_modulare_Containergebaeude_10243_Berlin-11505226_3.
Stiftung SPI. 2015. 'Die mobile Unterkunft für Flüchtlinge und Asylsuchende am Standort Karower Chaussee in Pankow – Häufig gestellte Fragen', 13 January. Retrieved 10 October 2019 from www.berlin.de/ba-pankow/politik-und-verwaltung/beauftragte/integration/dokumente/faq-s-zur-containerunterkunft-in-buch.pdf.
Tempohousing. 2010. 'Rapid Shelter Solutions'. Retrieved 10 October 2019 from http://tempohousingnigeria.com/content/files/file/THN_Rapid%20Shelter(1).pdf.

——. 2015. 'Quick Tempohousing Shelters for Urgent Situations'. Retrieved 10 October 2019 from http://tempohousing.choosewebdesign.com/wp-content/uploads/2016/11/refugee_shelter_systems.pdf.
——. n.d. Homepage. Retrieved 10 October 2019 from www.tempohousing.com.
Ticktin, M. 2016. 'Calais: Containment Politics in the Jungle'. *The Funambulist* 5: 29–33.
Turner, B.S. 2007. 'The Enclave Society: Towards a Sociology of Immobility'. *European Journal of Social Theory* 10(2): 287–304.
UNCTAD. 2015. *Review of Maritime Transport 2015.* New York: United Nations Conference on Trade and Development. Retrieved 10 October 2019 from https://unctad.org/en/PublicationsLibrary/rmt2015_en.pdf.
Vey, J. 2018. 'Leben im Tempohome: Qualitative Studie zur Unterbringungssituation von Flüchtenden in temporären Gemeinschaftsunterkünften in Berlin'. Discussion Paper 40. Zentrum Technik und Gesellschaft. TU Berlin. Retrieved 10 October 2019 from www.tu-berlin.de/fileadmin/f27/PDFs/Discussion_Papers_neu/discussion_paper_Nr._40_18.pdf.
World Shipping Council. n.d. 'Global Container Fleet'. Retrieved 10 October 2019 from www.worldshipping.org/about-the-industry/containers/global-container-fleet.
Ziadah, R. 2018. 'Constructing a Logistics Space: Perspectives from the Gulf Cooperation Council'. *Environment and Planning D: Society and Space* 36(4): 666–82.

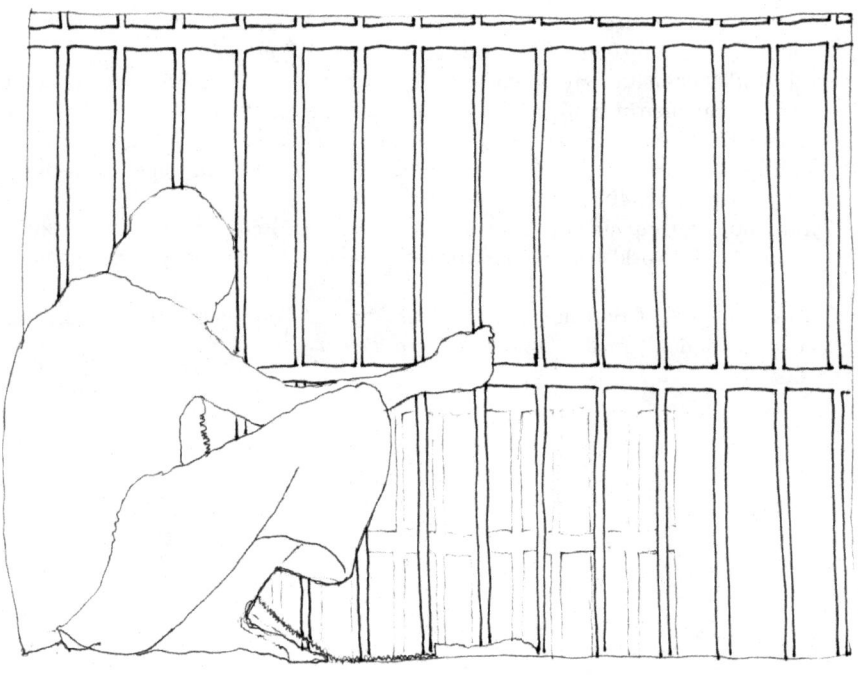

Figure 2.1 Safi Military Barracks in Malta. © Mark E. Breeze, based on an image supplied by Ċetta Mainwaring.

2

At the Edge

Containment and the Construction of Europe

Ċetta Mainwaring

> I don't call it detention, I call it a prison...
> —Tesfay, imprisoned for twelve months, 2009

In 2006, the so-called migration 'crisis' in Malta had reached fever pitch. Arrivals of people by boat had increased from fifty-seven in 2001 to 1,780 in 2006. Yet even at their peak – at 2,775 in 2008 – the numbers were small in absolute terms, a fraction of the overall migration that Malta received.[1] Nevertheless, these travellers were automatically detained for up to eighteen months upon arrival. Indeed, the EU's most southern and smallest Member State, Malta, had already established and expanded a punitive immigration detention system that was designed to punish and deter.

The Maltese islands have acted as a refuge for many seafarers over the centuries due to their geopolitical position in the straits between the eastern and western Mediterranean basins, and their natural deep harbours. The Phoenicians, who first colonized Malta in the seventh century BCE, called the islands 'Maleth', meaning shelter or haven. Although the islands have been known for their hospitality – reputedly giving shelter to a shipwrecked St Paul around 60 CE and providing a safe haven for the Knights of St John to establish their new headquarters in 1530 after the Ottomans took Rhodes – shelter has historically been extended inconsistently, especially under Roman and Crusader rule. Today, similarly, although hospitality is fundamental to the dominant tourist industry, the treatment of people seeking refuge in Europe reveals a process of racialized and classed exclusion. While citizenship is sold to the super-rich, ports and harbours are closed to those compelled to take dinghies across the sea.[2]

In 2006, I had just started my research on migration in the Mediterranean and had the opportunity to visit two of Malta's detention centres, despite the limited access given to researchers, journalists and nongovernmental organizations (NGOs).[3] The detention centres were located within operational military barracks, securitized spaces surrounded by layers of barbed wire and checkpoints that ostensibly justified this limited access. The largest detention centre housed single men and was located inside Safi Military Barracks. When I visited, around 300 people were detained in the centre. Turning off a small road behind Malta's International Airport, we entered the barracks through a security checkpoint. As we drove through the base, fifty ramshackle boats that had carried the men to these European shores filled our view as they languished in the sun, giving the base the air of a junkyard. There were tall fences everywhere, topped with barbed wire. Having arrived at the warehouse that acted as the detention centre, guards granted us entry through a heavy set of doors and into an austere office, which was bare except for a desk and chair. Here, we signed our names and ID numbers into the visitors' log. Only then did the guards open another set of heavy iron gates that led into the centre itself.

The majority of men were kept in a warehouse: one large room filled with rows of bunk beds just a few feet apart, with no more space than strictly necessary to walk between them. Men occupying lower bunks had hung tattered and dirty sheets around their narrow beds to create some sense of privacy. The floors were dirty and flies buzzed everywhere, attracted to food that had not been removed by the detention staff. The office space where the guards generally remained connected this warehouse to another wing with a series of smaller rooms, equally overcrowded with twenty-five to thirty people in each. Here, those with a bed were more fortunate than those who were merely allocated a mattress on the floor. With little to do, most of the men were sleeping despite it being late afternoon; the lack of windows at human height intensified the cramped and oppressive atmosphere. Above one bed, someone had scrawled: 'God, why do you remain silent?'.

Soon, a strong stench indicated that we had arrived at the bathrooms. This was a long, narrow space with toilets at one end. The three or four small sinks provided the only water source, and it was here that the men were forced to bathe, access drinking water, as well as wash clothes and plates. As in the other wing, flies circled everywhere. Charles,[4] a half-Sudanese, half-Nigerian man, explained how the appalling conditions had encouraged the spread of tuberculosis. When he had arrived a year ago, two men had contracted the contagious disease, and after the guards refused their repeated requests to be separated, a further fifteen had fallen ill. The only limited medicine provided, most often paracetamol, was stamped with old expiration dates. When the men informed the guards, they responded that 'all Africans take expired medicine'.

The heat in summer exacerbated deteriorating medical conditions, causing skin rashes to be prevalent. With no fans installed, the detained men had removed the panes from the barred windows in order to let more air in the rooms. Although they had subsequently been accused of vandalism, Charles assured me that the panes were all intact and under their beds. He also explained how they had removed the doors that led out to an empty courtyard surrounded by a tall fence topped with barbed wire. The guards routinely locked the men inside at 5 p.m. and did not open the doors again until 10 a.m., effectively only allowing the men outside during the hottest parts of the day into an area with no shade. Confined inside these overcrowded, hot spaces during months when temperatures regularly reached over 35°C, the men had taken the situation into their own hands.

The overcrowded conditions would only get worse. Two years later, the same centre incarcerated three times the number of people detained when I had visited: 950 in July 2008, according to an interview I conducted with the then Head of Detention Services. Then, and for years after, the government did little in response to continued migrant arrivals, an increasing backlog of asylum claims, and predictably deteriorating conditions in detention. These conditions were regularly criticized and well documented by detainees and activists working in detention centres and with the migrant population (e.g. Médecins Sans Frontières 2009; Jesuit Refugee Service – Malta 2010).

Although particular to the Maltese islands, this form of 'shelter' is reproduced around the edges of Europe. For example, the EU's 'hotspots' have also been criticized for their similarly inhumane conditions (e.g. Human Rights Watch 2016). Such detention facilities are often imagined as a form of temporary shelter, before asylum claims are processed and people are either released or deported, yet they are in fact a permanent feature of the European project in the twenty-first century that works to dehumanize the bodies they contain. Moreover, they are explicitly intended to act as a form of deterrence, though there is little evidence to corroborate this logic (Edwards 2011: 13; Sampson 2015). In Malta and across Europe, detention acts as a spectacle, portraying an image of a cohesive state – and EU – in control of its borders, able to deport those deemed to be unwanted (Mainwaring and Silverman 2017). In reality, in Malta and across the EU, most people who are detained are released rather than deported. According to the European Commission (2017), there is a significant gap between those issued with a return order and those removed from EU territory: for example, in 2016, of the 500,000 people given a return order, only 226,000, or 45 per cent, were deported. These numbers were lower in 2012 (37 per cent), 2011 (34 per cent) and 2010 (37 per cent) (European Commission 2014a).

In this chapter, I analyse how this form of shelter was initially framed as an emergency measure in response to increased migrant arrivals in Malta and how, nevertheless, it continues in much the same form to contain, criminalize and isolate the detainee population. I argue that the containment of migrants at the edge of Europe is illustrative of the contested construction of a unified, discrete Europe. This type of shelter serves to project an image of a cohesive Europe with a hard border, reinscribing differences between 'us' and 'them'.

Malta: A Brief History of Immigration Detention

EU membership, along with Malta's position in the central Mediterranean, has shaped the country's contemporary immigration detention policy. The origins of the policy lie in the 1970 Immigration Act, which first allowed the government to detain immigrants indefinitely. Periods of detention ranged between twenty-two and twenty-four months on average (United Nations 2010: 9), but the number of migrants in detention remained small until 2002, when the number of illegalized migrants arriving on the island increased exponentially, from fifty-seven the previous year to 1,686, an almost 3,000 per cent increase. Over the next decade, the majority of travellers came from Somalia and Eritrea, and had journeyed across the Sahara, through Libya and then across the Mediterranean on small, fibreglass boats. The vast majority would apply for asylum and receive some form of protection in Malta (Mainwaring 2019). Nevertheless, once they arrived on the island, they were automatically detained. Although Malta decriminalized unauthorized entry into its territory in 2002 as part of the pre-accession process to the EU, detention remained in place as an administrative fiat (Council of Europe 2004: 4). An eighteen-month time limit was established in 2005 after substantial pressure from international and local organizations. Yet, until 2015, Malta was still the only EU Member State that automatically detained all migrants and asylum seekers who arrived without authorization.[5] Therefore, for most of the twenty-first century, Malta maintained the longest and arguably harshest detention policy in the EU. In 2013, the average time spent in detention in Malta – 180 days – was more than three times longer than in any other EU Member State (European Commission 2014b: 5).[6]

By early 2002, the Maltese government had also opened Malta's first dedicated detention centre in the Hal Far military barracks. The centre had a capacity to hold eighty people, on the assumption that migrant arrivals would remain relatively low. According to an interview I conducted at the Ministry for Justice and Home Affairs in April 2009, the government responded to the increase in arrivals that year with an 'ad hoc arrangement' that was 'made by the police immigration authorities' (cf. Mainwaring and Cook 2018). The response included forcibly confining those who arrived in detention centres established in the Hal Far and Lyster military barracks (Calleya and Lutterbeck 2008). However, despite being framed as an ad hoc and emergency measure, these detention centres and the broader policy remained and expanded over the next decade.

The policy of automatic detention coupled with lengthy asylum and expulsion processes quickly resulted in overcrowded detention centres (Council of Europe 2004). As the detainee population increased and conditions deteriorated, NGOs campaigned for fundamental reform and abolition of detention. In 2003 and 2004, delegations sent by the Council of Europe (2004, 2005) lambasted the government for its unnecessarily punitive policy and for subjecting detainees to violence and inhumane conditions. Although these challenges prompted Malta to establish an eighteen-month limit to detention, the government deflected responsibility for any legal transgression, locating the source of the problem 'beyond its shores'. Responding directly to the Council of Europe, the government insisted that as 'the smallest EU member state, possessing very limited resources, and, to complicate matters, having one of the highest population densities in the world', Malta 'cannot be expected to adequately address this complex and multi-faceted problem having roots beyond its shores by itself'. The statement went on: 'Malta will continue to insist that the European Union and its member states need to show solidarity with the border states that are bearing the brunt of this problem; at the same time, the countries of origin and the countries of transit must also shoulder their responsibilities' (Council of Europe 2007: 6).

It was only in December 2015 that the Maltese government announced it would end the automatic and mandatory detention of asylum seekers. The announcement came after arrivals by boat decreased substantially from 2,000 in 2013 to 106 in 2015 due to an informal Italian-Maltese agreement that saw disembarkations occur in Italy rather than Malta (National Statistics Office 2018). Today, the government operates an 'Initial Reception Centre', where people are supposed to be held for up to seven days and assessed on a case-by-case basis before being released or transferred to detention. However, organizations like JRS and Aditus Foundation have claimed that people arriving by boat are sometimes taken directly to detention. Indeed, the government still operates a detention centre in 'Block B' of Safi Barracks and, in 2016, detained twenty people there (AIDA 2017).[7] Moreover, with the unravelling of the informal Italian-Maltese agreement in 2018, the question of detention is back on the table as arrivals increased substantially in 2019.

The change in detention policy came after years of campaigning by migrants and NGOs, who condemned the detention policy and the conditions inside the centres as inhumane and degrading, with particularly inadequate protections for vulnerable persons (e.g. Médecins Sans Frontières 2009; Human Rights Watch 2012). Building on these efforts, former detainees won two important cases at the European Court of Human Rights in 2013. In these cases, the Court found violations of the right to liberty, the right to an effective remedy, and the prohibition of inhuman and degrading treatment (European Court of Human Rights 2013a, 2013b). For example, in the case brought by Aslya Aden Ahmed, a Somali national detained for eighteen months, the Court noted the terrible conditions, including the 'exposure of detainees to cold conditions, the lack of female staff in the detention centre, a complete lack of access to open air and exercise for periods of up to three months, an inadequate diet, and the particular vulnerability of Ms Ahmed due to her fragile health and personal emotional circumstances' (European Court of Human Rights 2013c). In short, it found that Malta's immigration detention policy was a 'defective national system hindering human-rights protection' (European Court of Human Rights 2013b).

A public inquiry, published in 2014, echoed many of these findings. The inquiry was launched in 2012 after the death of Mamadou Kamara, a 32-year-old Cameroonian asylum seeker. This was the second death to occur inside detention (Aditus Foundation et al. 2012). The inquiry revealed how detention officers recaptured Kamara after he escaped from detention; they then handcuffed him, placed him inside a steel cage in the back of their detention van and beat him to death. The forensic expert concluded that Karma died from a heart attack due to blunt trauma.[8] The inquiry also documented systemic violence and abuse within detention. For example, a former head of detention services disclosed that one sergeant would prey on women in detention, 'entering their rooms during the night and taking a woman back to his office with him ... Even condoms were found in the room'. The report revealed multiple relationships occurring between members of staff and detained women, noting that consent was questionable under the circumstances. No disciplinary action was taken (Valenzia 2014; cf. Diacono 2015).

The Anatomy of Detention: Violence and (In)Visibility

The expansion and contraction of immigration detention as a form of containment in Malta is intimately linked with Malta's role as a migration gatekeeper and its geopolitical position on the edge of Europe. In the twenty-first century, Maltese politicians have consistently constructed a crisis around the issue of migration in order to attract attention and support from the EU, as well as court the national popular vote (Mainwaring 2014, 2019). Immigration detention plays an important role in this crisis, both contributing to its construction and acting as an ostensible solution (Mainwaring 2012). This dual role is only possible through the interplay between visibility and invisibility. In the state's narrative, particular facets of immigration and detention are made hypervisible. Others, in contrast, are concealed (cf. Mountz 2015).

The government has defended its immigration detention policy on the grounds of security, deterrence and Malta's geopolitical position on the edge of Europe. In these narratives, the risks ostensibly posed by those incarcerated are exaggerated and made hypervisible through their criminalization. Government officials have associated migrants with criminality and even terrorism. Practices such as handcuffing people while transporting them to hospital or to and from detention centres also contribute to their criminalization. The judiciary has often replicated this narrative of suspicion. For instance, in a case brought against the Commissioner of Police in 2009, the Constitutional Court (2014: 13) ruled that detention 'can be considered, in the particular circumstances of our country, as a necessary measure'. Detention, the ruling continued, is 'required for the stability of the country so as to, as much as possible, avoid a deluge of "irregular" people running around Malta, and this without having established the prima facie interest and disposition of the person'. This criminalization overshadows the fact that the vast majority of people in detention in Malta are released, and many remain on the island due to Malta's limited success at forced returns (Eurostat 2017).

In these sovereign narratives, the 'problems' associated with detention are placed outside of the nation state, attached to the number of people arriving on the island and to the EU's role in placing migration and asylum responsibility on Malta and other Member States along the periphery. Political and moral liability for conditions in detention is thus placed on the very people being incarcerated. As a senior official in the Ministry of Foreign Affairs explained it to me in April 2009: 'I hope those conditions [in detention] will be improved, but it all depends on the arrivals. The moment you have a sudden influx, it creates problems'.

Meanwhile, the actual infrastructure of detention, with all the violence it produces, is often concealed. As elsewhere in Europe, detention centres in Malta are located in remote, securitized spaces. Established within Maltese military barracks, they remain largely invisible to the local population, outside of the small activist community, and invisible to the millions of tourists who visit the island every year. Only in particular moments, such as during migrant 'riots', do these centres become hypervisible. Here, the state's role in restoring order through the deployment of armed force takes centre stage, while the state's role in creating the conditions for protest is hidden from view (e.g. Ameen 2009; Peregin 2011). The violence inside detention is only made visible by the work of migrants, activists and organizers through public statements, court cases, reports and other forms of protest (e.g. Civil Court, Malta 2007; Médecins Sans Frontières 2009; Valenzia 2014). Moreover, the violence made visible is often spectacular, such as the death of Mamadou Kamara. Less frequently exposed is the daily violence endured by those incarcerated, such as the denial of adequate healthcare and medicine, limited access to the outdoors, and abuse from guards.

The biases and failures of detention are also concealed. Its failure to act as a deterrent is ignored; as recently as 2015, Prime Minister Joseph Muscat maintained that 'detention plays a role as a deterrent' in an interview I conducted. Even detention's ability to contain is questionable: between 2004 and 2012, 1,614 detainees escaped from the Safi and Lyster Barracks detention centres alone (Parliamentary Question 2014). Moreover, although detention is mandatory for 'prohibited immigrants' who either arrive or are found in Malta without leave to remain, in practice the policy is racialized and classed: the detainee population has comprised primarily African migrants and refugees arriving by sea. In contrast, those asylum seekers arriving by plane have not generally been detained.[9]

The spectacle of detention – the order it purportedly establishes in the face of chaotic migration flows – has been politically useful for Malta as it reinforces the sense of crisis and thus warrants calls for more 'burden sharing' within the EU. Indeed, as the government responds to the migration 'crisis' with immigration detention as a 'solution', detention simultaneously creates and reinforces the crisis: it corroborates the populist impression of out-of-control flows of noncitizens amassing at and within the border while also signalling that the state is in control, working to identify and punish this population (Mainwaring and Silverman 2017).

Conclusion: Project Europe

The processes of containment seen on the edges of Europe, from detention centres to hotspots, from Malta to Italy to Greece, project an image of a united, cohesive and discrete Europe in control of its clearly demarcated borders (de Genova 2016: 89). Thus, the migrant and refugee 'shelter' acts as a way to forge political unity by isolating and containing the 'other'. Such processes of containment obscure the fissures in Europe between and within Member States. Simultaneously, these shelters cement the constructed differences between 'us' and 'them'. The often impermanent nature of structures of detention distract from the permanent, inherent violence of Europe's bordering practices. Europe's colonial past and present shape the migration flows as well as the shelters themselves. As Ida Danewid (2017: 1675) has argued, the 'historicisation and contextualisation of the [migration] crisis – placing the ongoing tragedy in the context of Europe's constitutive history of empire, colonial conquest, and transatlantic slavery . . . unveil the umbilical cord that links Europe to the migrants washed up on its shores'.

For those detained, marginalization and containment continue after release. In Malta, they are released to 'open centres', where they are still contained in warehouses, tents and shipping containers, despite more freedom of movement. Throughout Europe, migrants remain at the edges of society, socioeconomically marginalized sometimes generations after they have arrived (Calavita 2005). For Europe, they are the abject 'other', a straw man to remind us of our enlightened civilization.

Ċetta Mainwaring is a Leverhulme Early Career Research Fellow in the School of Social and Political Sciences at the University of Glasgow. She holds a D.Phil. in International Relations from the University of Oxford. Her research interests lie at the intersection of migration, borders and state controls.

Notes

1. In 2008, over 6,000 'long-term' immigrants arrived in Malta, including EU and non-EU nationals. This number has increased steadily since then and was 17,000 in 2016 (Eurostat 2018). The island also received 1.3 million tourists in 2008 (National Statistic Office 2009).
2. In 2014, Malta launched an Individual Investor Programme. In exchange for citizenship, applicants must pay a €650,000 contribution to a national development fund, invest €150,000 in government stocks or bonds, and own a property worth at least €350,000 in Malta for at least one year (Cooper 2016).
3. The description of the centre draws on my first-hand experience of visiting detention centres during fieldwork in 2006, as well as subsequent conversations with people who had been released from detention and NGO staff who worked in detention. The conditions described here were widely reported at the time (e.g. Médecins Sans Frontières 2009).
4. Pseudonyms are used throughout.
5. In line with the EU's 2003 directive on minimum reception standards, asylum seekers were released once their claim was successful or after twelve months' detention if their claim was still pending. Rejected asylum seekers were held for eighteen months.
6. Estonia had the second-longest detention period of fifty-eight days. The average across all Member States was forty days, with the lowest averages seen in Sweden (five days) and Finland (11.8 days) (European Commission 2014b: 5).
7. Block B has a capacity to hold 200 people; the warehouse facility described above was closed for refurbishment in 2014. Lyster Barracks was closed in mid 2015 because of the decrease in arrivals (AIDA 2017).

8. Three former soldiers are charged with Kamara's murder. At the time of writing, the case was ongoing (Schembri 2017).
9. This trend changed in 2016. Jesuit Refugee Service reported that in the absence of boat arrivals, all asylum seekers arriving by plane in 2016 were immediately detained rather than being taken to the Initial Reception Centre. Moreover, those using false documents to enter the country were brought before the Court of Magistrates and most were sentenced to a prison term. JRS and other NGOs raised concerns about the criminalization of asylum seekers in this manner and reminded the government that the 1951 Refugee Convention prohibits states from penalizing refugees who enter their territory irregularly (AIDA 2017: 14–15).

References

Aditus Foundation. 2016. 'Joint NGO Input on Temporary Humanitarian Protection N'. Retrieved 10 October 2019 from http://aditus.org.mt/Publications/THPN submissions_2016.pdf.

Aditus Foundation et al. 2012. 'NGO Statement on the Death of a Migrant in Detention', Malta: July 1. Retrieved 13 November 2019 from http://www.jrsmalta.org/content.aspx?id=328754#.V7QpG47QuRs.

AIDA (Asylum Information Database). 2017. 'Country Report: Malta. European Council on Refugees and Exiles', 24 May. Retrieved 10 October 2019 from http://www.asylumineurope.org/reports/country/malta.

Ameen, J. 2009. 'Somalis Protest at Safi'. *Times of Malta*, 11 January.

Calavita, K. 2005. *Immigrants at the Margins: Law, Race, and Exclusion in Southern Europe*. Cambridge: Cambridge University Press.

Calleya, S., and D. Lutterbeck. 2008. *Managing the Challenges of Irregular Immigration in Malta*. Valletta: The Today Public Policy Institute.

Civil Court, Malta. 2007. 'Tefarra Besabe Berhe Vs Kummissarju Tal-Pulizija Noe Et. Civil First Hall', 8 May.

Constitutional Court, Malta. 2014. 'Essa Maneh et. v. Commissioner of Police'. Appeal Number 53/2008/1, Civil Court, First Hall, Malta, 29 April. Retrieved 13 November 2019 from http://www.refworld.org/cgi-bin/texis/vtx/rwmain/opendocpdf.pdf?reldoc=y&docid=51a86d424

Cooper, H. 2016. 'Malta Slammed for Cash-for-Passports Programme'. *Politico*, 17 August.

Council of Europe. 2004. 'Report by Mr. Alvaro Gil-Robles, Commissioner for Human Rights, on His Visit to Malta, 20–21 October 2003'. CommDH(2004)4, Office of the Commissioner for Human Rights, Council of Europe, Strasbourg, 12 February.

———. 2005. 'Report to the Maltese Government on the Visit to Malta Carried Out by the European Committee for the Prevention of Torture and Inhuman or Degrading Treatment or Punishment from 18 to 22 January 2004'. CPT/Inf (2005) 15, Strasbourg, 25 August.

———. 2007. 'Report to the Maltese Government on the Visit to Malta Carried Out by the European Committee for the Prevention of Torture and Inhuman or

Degrading Treatment or Punishment from 15 to 21 June 2005'. CPT (2005) 76, Strasbourg, 10 September.
Danewid, I. 2017. 'White Innocence in the Black Mediterranean: Hospitality and the Erasure of History'. *Third World Quarterly* 38(7): 1674–89.
De Genova, N. 2016. 'The European Question: Migration, Race, and Postcoloniality in Europe'. *Social Text* 34(3): 75–102.
Diacono, T. 2015. 'Detention Centre Security Proved No Match for over 1,000 Fleeing Migrants'. *MaltaToday*, 15 January.
Edwards, A. 2011. 'Back to Basics: The Right to Liberty and Security of Person and "Alternatives to Detention" of Refugees, Asylum-Seekers, Stateless Persons and Other Migrants'. PPLA/2011/01.Rev.1. Geneva: United Nations High Commissioner for Refugees.
European Commission. 2014a. 'Communication from the Commission to the Council and the European Parliament on EU Return Policy'. COM(2014) 199, Brussels, 28 March.
———. 2014b. 'The Use of Detention and Alternatives to Detention in the Context of Immigration Policies'. Synthesis Report for the EMN Focused Study.
———. 2017. 'Towards a More Efficient EU Return Policy'. Retrieved 10 October 2019 from https://ec.europa.eu/home-affairs/sites/homeaffairs/files/what-we-do/poli cies/european-agenda-migration/20171114_factsheet_towards_an_efficient_and _credible_eu_return_policy_en.pdf.
European Court of Human Rights. 2013a. *Aden Ahmed v. Malta*, Application No. 55352/12, Strasbourg, 23 July.
———. 2013b. *Suso Musa v. Malta*. Application No. 42337/12, Strasbourg, 23 July.
———. 2013c. 'Conditions in Maltese Immigration Detention Centre Constituted Degrading Treatment'. Press Release, ECHR 231 (2013), 23 July.
Eurostat. 2017. 'Third Country Nationals Returned Following an Order to Leave: Annual Data (Rounded)'. Retrieved 10 October 2019 from http://appsso. eurostat.ec.europa.eu/nui/show.do?dataset=migr_eirtn&lang=en.
———. 2018. 'Immigration'. Retrieved 10 October 2019 from https://ec.europa.eu/ eurostat/tgm/table.do?tab=table&init=1&language=en&pcode=tps00176&plu gin=1.
Human Rights Watch. 2012. 'Boat Ride to Detention: Adult and Child Migrants in Malta'. Report. USA: Human Rights Watch, July. Retrieved 9 December 2019 from https://reliefweb.int/sites/reliefweb.int/files/resources/malta0712webwco ver.pdf.
———. 2016. 'Greece: Refugee "Hotspots" Unsafe, Unsanitary', 19 May.
Jesuit Refugee Service – Malta. 2010. 'Becoming Vulnerable in Detention: National Report Malta'. Retrieved 10 October 2019 from https://drive.google.com/file /d/0B9dE4MlylERgdjBNdFUyTHlfYjQ/view.
Mainwaring, Ċ. 2012. 'Constructing a Crisis: The Role of Immigration Detention in Malta'. *Population, Space and Place* 18(6): 687–700.
———. 2014. 'Small States and Nonmaterial Power: Creating Crises and Shaping Migration Policies in Malta, Cyprus, and the European Union'. *Journal of Immigrant and Refugee Studies* 12(2): 103–22.

——. 2016. 'Transnational Migration and Control: Immigration Detention on the Edge of Europe', in R. Furman, D. Epps and G. Lamphear (eds), *Detaining the Immigrant Other: Global and Transnational Issues*. Oxford: Oxford University Press, pp. 117–28.

——. 2019. *At Europe's Edge: Migration and Crisis in the Mediterranean*. Oxford: Oxford University Press.

Mainwaring, C., and M. Cook. 2019. 'Immigration Detention: An Anglo Model'. *Migration Studies* 7(4): 455–476.

Mainwaring, Ċ., and S.J. Silverman. 2017. 'Detention-as-Spectacle'. *International Political Sociology* 11(1): 21–38.

Médecins Sans Frontières. 2009. '"Not Criminals": Médecins Sans Frontières Exposes Conditions for Undocumented Migrants and Asylum Seekers in Maltese Detention Centres', April. Retrieved 13 November 2019 from https://www.msf.org/malta-report.

Mountz, A. 2015. 'In/Visibility and the Securitization of Migration Shaping Publics through Border Enforcement on Islands'. *Cultural Politics* 11(2): 184–200.

National Statistics Office. 2009. 'Departing Tourists: December 2008'. Information Society and Tourism Unit, 27 January.

——. 2018. 'World Refugee Day: 20 June 2018'. News Release, 20 June.

Parliamentary Question. 2014. 'Ċentri ta' Detenzjoni – ħarbiet irreġistrati'. No. 13155. House of Representatives, Malta, XII Legislature, 22 December.

Peregin, C. 2011. 'Migrants Riot as Police and Army Fight Back'. *Times of Malta*, 17 August.

Sampson, R. 2015. 'Does Detention Deter?' IDC Working Paper No. 1, Australia: International Detention Coalition.

Schembri, G. 2017. 'Former Soldier Recalls Colleague Kicking Malian Escaped Migrant Who Died in 2012'. *Malta Independent*, 14 March.

United Nations. 2010. 'Report of the Working Group on Arbitrary Detention – Addendum: Mission to Malta (19 to 23 January 2009)'. Human Rights Council, 13th Session, A/HRC/13/30/Add.2, 18 January.

Valenzia, G. 2014. 'Inkjesta bis-shha tal-artikolu 4 tal-Att Dwar l'Inkjesti rigwardanti l'harba tal- immigrant Abdalla Mohammed (maghruf ukoll bhala Mamadou Kamara) ta'32 sena mill-Mali li gie certifkat mejjet wara li ttiehed ic-Centru tas-Sahha ta'Rahal Gdid minn ufficjali assenjati mas- Servizz ta'Detenzjoni'. Malta.

Figure 3.1 Hal Far Open Centre in Malta. © Mark E. Breeze, based on an image supplied by Marthe Achtnich.

3

Shifting Shelters
Migrants, Mobility and the Making of Open Centres in Malta

Marthe Achtnich

It was a hot Sunday afternoon in 2013 and I was sitting on the floor in a metal container in one of Malta's open centres, drinking coffee with a group of Eritrean men. After several months in closed detention in Malta and having arrived by boat together from Libya, they had made this container their temporary home. The man sitting next to me told me to look at the island sky through the small and only window. From time to time, the silhouette of a plane interrupted the intense blueness of the sky: Malta's international airport was close by. Pointing towards one of the planes, the man said he used to live close to the airport in Khartoum in Sudan and was looking at planes then as well, imagining that one day it would be him flying away. Instead, nothing had changed; he was still engaged in 'plane watching'.

The open centre was situated in Hal Far, a remote part of the island about a five-minute drive from Malta's airport. Originally established for migrants who had applied for asylum, Hal Far hosted a closed detention centre, a small open centre run by a nongovernmental organization (NGO) and three large open centres operated by the Maltese government. During the course of my long-term fieldwork in 2013, I found that the residents of these open centres were mainly from countries in Sub-Saharan Africa, including Somalia, Ethiopia, Eritrea, Sudan, Niger, Nigeria, Mali, Burkina Faso, Cameroon, Ivory Coast and Senegal. Most had arrived by boat after moving to and through Libya with human smugglers, and were now awaiting the next stage of their journey.

Hal Far was often bustling in the evenings, especially around the Tent Village, which was situated at the bottom of a small hill. With boat arrivals in Malta at its height back then, the cluster of open centres was not simply a space housing people, but a social space. People slept, cooked, ate together and sat in the evening sun around these structures, and residents would often gather outside the main entrance of the Tent Village where a Maltese man sold African food. Not cordoned by a fence, the Tent Village was open. Residents and their visitors could move in and out more or less freely. People who had long left the open centre for private apartments elsewhere on the island would often return in the evenings to meet their friends still in the centre and at times even stay for the night. Intricately linked to migrants' journeys, the metal containers of these open centres therefore did not simply offer physical protection, but also contained migrants' dreams, their social networks and aspirations to mobility.

In this chapter I argue that open centres are not static spaces or bounded sites, but emergent spaces constructed through migrants' mobilities: their very materiality and architecture has a strong bearing on the shelter's scope and purpose. Second, I will argue that what is at stake in such spaces is not simply a shelter in a physical sense, but a social process of 'sheltering', enabled and constituted through networks that migrants establish on journeys. Drawing on this interplay between the sociality and materiality of shelters, traced through an ethnography of Maltese open centres, I argue that mobility and shelters intricately coconstitute one another in ways that exceed a shelter's initial design or conception. Even restrictive shelters can morph and end up playing crucial social roles for coping, sustenance and onward journeys.

Background: Malta's Open Centres

Boat arrivals from Libya have played a major role in the emergence and development of Malta's migrant reception structure. When Malta joined the EU in 2004, the small island had already been a site of increasing boat arrivals from Libya since 2002, peaking roughly at around 2,500 arrivals per year (UNHCR 2018). The United Nations High Commissioner for Refugees (UNHCR) estimated in 2018 that 30 per cent of the approximately 19,000 people who had arrived by boat from Libya since 2002 remained in Malta, with over 2,800 beneficiaries of protection being resettled or relocated to the United States and other EU Member States (UNHCR 2018). During my multisited ethnographic fieldwork in Malta and Libya in 2013 and 2014, many of the migrants had not originally aimed for Malta as their country of arrival (but Italy instead). They often had plans of onward movement. Until 2015, Malta had a system of mandatory closed detention that led to imprisonment directly after arrival by boat for up to eighteen months, or until the end of the asylum application process (UNHCR 2018). Many actors, including the European Court of Human Rights, described the conditions in detention in Malta as detrimental (Brigden and Mainwaring 2016; Mainwaring 2012; MSF 2009).

Malta's open centres served as a form of voluntary transitional assistance, which lasted for a maximum of one year. This was in recognition of the fact that people did not always have a place to live after their release from detention. The first open centres in Malta were founded in 2004 and the Hal Far Tent Village was opened in 2006 (AWAS 2018). The Agency for the Welfare of Asylum Seekers (AWAS), which was responsible for the open centres, was set up in 2009 under the Ministry for Home Affairs and National Security (AWAS 2018). At the time of my fieldwork, Malta had nine official open centres that differed in their architecture – from houses to clusters of containers – and hosted migrants from a variety of different countries, including single men or women, families or mixed groups. Overall, in 2013 Malta housed around 1,499 people in open centres (UNHCR 2018), mainly providing accommodation, language classes, information on employment, housing, resettlement and return, a small transport and food allowance, as well as free access to state health services and education for children. The financial allowance varied according to legal status, with a maximum amount of around €130 per month, and it was only paid if the recipient confirmed their residence through signing in three times a week. There was no systematized programme for integration in Malta (Caruana 2016).

Coming from a vast range of countries and with different needs and aspirations, migrants' movements through the open centres were not uniform. Some only stayed for a few days, some remained for a year or longer, and others returned after unsuccessful asylum applications in other EU Member States (deportations back to Malta in line with the Dublin Regulation were common). Altogether, the open centres accommodated asylum seekers, beneficiaries of protection and rejected asylum seekers. In the following sections, I first show how Malta's open centres in Hal Far emerged as a particular form of shelter, shaped through migrants' mobilities. I also explore the interrelationship between mobility and shelter by focusing on the material form of the open centres and their geographical distancing from Maltese society, as well as the durations and temporalities of people's movements through them. I then show how shelters like these isolate migrants and create tensions between residents, but, in doing so, also enable people from a broad range of backgrounds to form new sources of support and deepen existing social networks. In a brief conclusion, I argue that the sociality and materiality of shelters is important to consider when studying this important new topic, in this case, shaping migrants' future mobilities beyond the open centres.

Emergent Shelters

Migrants' journeys have shaped reception structures in Malta; the island's open centres have structurally morphed in response to migrant arrivals. During the time of my fieldwork, migrant boat arrivals in Malta were often framed as a 'crisis' scenario by policy-makers and the media, justifying the implementation of strict detention on the island (Mainwaring 2012). The Tent Village in Hal Far, for example, began as a cluster of large tents, erected when the first boats started to arrive in the early 2000s. Rudimentary, they were low-cost structures (US$500 each) with a lifespan of only around eight months (*Malta Independent* 2012). The tents had rows of bunk beds and were not suitable for housing a large number of migrants in the long term, and older prefabricated structures, which had served to house earthquake victims and were donated by the Italian Civil Protection Department, were also incorporated into the emerging space (*Malta Independent* 2012). In 2012, the tents were replaced with mobile metal containers, with 80 per cent of the €900,000 project funded by the European Regional Emergency Fund (*Malta Independent* 2012; *Times of Malta* 2012). During my fieldwork in 2013, the tents that gave the Tent Village its name were therefore gone, replaced with rows of white and mobile metal containers erected on concrete structures. Depending on how many people arrived by boat, residents were frequently moved around these mobile containers, and having to share a small space with several unfamiliar people from different countries was difficult for most: sheets hung from the ceiling served as the only partition between beds and many residents were concerned by the lack of privacy.

Metal, as part of the material of the containers, generated considerable heat. Coupled with poor sanitary facilities and the accumulation of rubbish in some of the alleys between containers meant that flies and cockroaches proliferated. Pointing towards a cockroach in the container one day while we were sitting on the floor, a woman from Somalia exclaimed angrily: 'You see, this is life!' For her, the conditions in the open centres were particularly difficult, as she was pregnant. The heat inside the container not only forced her to lie outside on a mattress with little privacy but also affected her skin tone, she was convinced, as it had become much darker in the intense sunshine of Hal Far.

If shelters provided people a place to live on the island, their distant location from Malta's cities worked to spatially exclude migrants from mainstream Maltese society. Hal Far was around one hour away by bus from Malta's capital, Valletta. It had been formed by repurposing an old building and an airfield hangar, as well as erecting the Tent Village. Although the hangar, like the tents, was later replaced by rows of metal containers, the old airfield control tower could still be seen towering over the reception structures, pointing to a multilayered, makeshift architecture. The centres were purportedly 'open', allowing for free movement, but many residents felt imprisoned in geographical terms, and the bus fare to Valletta was often unaffordable. One day when the bus company gave away free tickets because the public transport system had shut down due to a technical fault, the Tent Village seemed deserted, highlighting how eager people were to get away from Hal Far when they were not prevented by the cost of doing so. This geographical isolation was exacerbated by the fact that many migrants believed that Maltese people perceived them as 'dark-skinned' foreigners. The bus stop in front of the Tent Village was often crowded, with Hal Far's residents waiting for a bus to Valletta that did not always arrive or, worse, drove by without stopping. They were convinced that this was on account of their skin colour. The bus to and from Hal Far was mostly populated by residents of the open centres, and many passengers mentioned that more often than not, the air conditioning did not work as well, creating an unpleasant, hot environment – another result of discrimination, they believed.

Sheltering: Physical Isolation to Social Process

Hal Far's residents often felt stuck and isolated not just from the rest of Malta, but from Europe as well. Whilst some perceived the social bonds they had formed during the journey through Libya to be artificial, others capitalized on this closeness to fellow migrants, extending their sources of support. Containers, and their setup, facilitated these social networks. A group of men and women from Eritrea, for example, who shared a container had met in Sudan and travelled to Libya and Malta together. Their container was furnished with only a small gas cooker, bedsheets hanging from the ceiling in an attempt to separate the two beds, and an old mattress on the floor. They were detained when trying to leave Libya the first time, but their second attempt at taking a boat was successful and they spent a few weeks in detention in Malta before being released. Their journey was difficult, the group told me, but they at least had each other for support. It helped, they told me, to be able to talk to other Eritreans in Hal Far about what they experienced, and very often conversations would revolve around the crossing of the Sahara Desert in smugglers' trucks or of the Mediterranean Sea by boat. At times, migrants would play short videos they had taken with mobile phones during the boat crossing or in the desert, where people would pray and sing together. It was almost 'magical' how everybody had united as a group, they said: at sea, in the Sahara Desert and now in Hal Far.

The structure of the Tent Village as an open space, as well as the proximity between the different centres in Hal Far, facilitated networking beyond the journey as well. Arriving together and often living in close physical proximity to one another meant that people's mobilities were intertwined in the long term. Furthermore, shared exposure to suffering and near-death experiences at sea created tight bonds of solidarity among those travelling by boat. Time spent in detention also played a role in knotting together people's journeys and fostering networks. The latter were particularly helpful for migrants who were still detained. Their boat companions would regularly visit once they were released from detention, exchanging information and extending support. A man from Somalia, who was among the only ones from his boat group released early from the centre, went back to detention every week, during visiting hours, to talk to his friends. In addition to delivering items of food through regular channels, he also provided emotional support to those still detained, calling them on a mobile phone someone had managed to keep inside in order to lift their spirits, as he explained to me. Some migrants referred to the people from their boat as their 'family'. In situations where support provided by the government was often not sufficient, networks that stretched along migrants' journeys helped people to cope, shaping their future mobilities. This ranged from welcoming new arrivals in the open centres after their release, accompanying each other to doctor's appointments, helping with childcare, and finding private accommodation and employment. Community support, formed through close proximity, was essential for people's everyday lives and long-term futures.

Through these networks, formed through the intertwining and knotting of people's journeys, it was possible to witness a move from shelters as a physical space to a social process of *sheltering*. To many vulnerable migrants, the open centres were a temporary space to rest and gather strength after the physical and mental exhaustion of the boat crossing and subsequent detention; moreover, some were sick with illnesses that had been left untreated since their journeys. A man from Somalia, for example, had just been released from detention when I first met him in the open centre, and he confided that he was exhausted, in pain and unable to eat properly. His wife was also suffering from an injury sustained when she was attacked in Libya, an injury that became worse after contact with sea water. They spent most days sleeping. One afternoon, sitting on his bed in the container, he shook his head rapidly to demonstrate that everything was still moving and that he could feel the boat and the water underneath his feet. He later showed me an injury his child had sustained, and although they had gone to the local clinic for three days in a row, 'nothing', he exclaimed, had been done. Instead, they were told to wait for a letter with an appointment, which would be sent to the open centre. He did not understand why he had to wait for so long for medical care when his child was sick. What was more, the injury his wife had sustained in Libya was by now severely infected, but still untreated. A few days later, she was examined by a doctor and was sent a letter asking her to wait for another appointment three months later. Struggling to understand the letter written in Maltese and English, they showed it to me. His wife was in pain, so why was she not treated immediately? The man's frustration was compounded by an incident the previous day. Having gone to hospital with another girl from their boat in need of support, he walked up to a doctor and mentioned he was in pain too and was in need of medical care. They told him to wait, but after waiting until midnight, he had to come back to Hal Far – by taxi, at great expense, as they had missed the last bus.

A few days later, while I was sitting in another container, this man came running to tell me that his wife had fallen off the bed. I went to their container and she was lying there, eyes closed. The group of Somali women surrounding her were all convinced she would be fine and gave her some water, but I suggested we get a doctor. They refused, blaming the heat in the container and exhaustion from the journey, while noting that collapses like this had happened before. When I saw them again a day later, the lady seemed much better and was sitting on the bed, laughing and chatting to me while doing her hair. Long-term effects of the journey, compounded by immediate detention experiences in Malta, had generated a negative impact on her health. Yet life in the open centre, and particularly her networks of community support, had also allowed her to receive care, understanding and assistance.

Beyond Shelters

Processes of sheltering through community bonds stretched far beyond Hal Far. Many residents of the open centres perceived the financial independence that came with employment to be crucial to moving out, but uncertainty on many levels complicated this process. Most of the Maltese economy open to migrants was seasonal and dependent on tourism, and employment was therefore rarely stable. Increased rental prices and perceived discrimination on the housing market also made moving out of the open centre difficult. To counter these difficulties, social networks often filled the gap: private accommodation was often found through contacts formed during journeys. Jobs were at times handed over to friends. Meanwhile, people without such networks often struggled to move out of the open centres at all.

A couple I met from Somalia, who were struggling to find an apartment, illustrates this problem very clearly. Despite desperately trying to find options to leave the open centre, they did not have a big network of people they knew in Malta, as they had just been forcibly returned to the island after having spent time in another EU Member State (where they had tried to apply for asylum). To make matters worse, they felt that they were discriminated against by Maltese landlords: they had recently managed to sign a rental contract, but this was cancelled at the last minute when the landlord found out that they were from Somalia. I spoke to them on a very hot day, when they were cooking plain pasta, the only food they could afford, on the gas cooker in their container. They were back in the same open centre they had lived in before they left Malta, but this time they were only allowed to stay for a further three months, which was the rule for anyone who had been forcibly returned after trying to apply for asylum in another country. They seemed frustrated. Referring to how unhappy they were about being back, the lady and her husband said that Malta is 'not Europe'. This was a common sentiment. Another returnee told me that he felt like he was 'going backwards' when he was back in Hal Far. The idea of 'another Europe' was mentioned frequently. Coming back to Malta's open centres after having lived in other reception centres abroad made this couple, like others, feel truly stuck and ever further away from their goal.

Not long afterwards, this couple moved to an apartment they had finally found with contacts made in their boat. The actual move happened very quickly – within one day, in fact. On their last evening in Hal Far, sitting in front of their container with children playing nearby and watching other people chatting around us, I asked them how they felt about leaving the open centre. They would miss some people, they laughed, but the change would be good for them, as they needed to move on. When I visited them at their new apartment a few days later, they seemed happy in the larger and more private space, but also mentioned that they missed Hal Far's community. Like many other people who had left, they would also return from time to time to meet friends and buy the African food sold outside the Tent Village. A few weeks later, they told me excitedly that they had an interview to start the official relocation process from Malta. A move away from Hal Far was the first step to move on from Malta. A few months later, the lady from Somalia and her husband had indeed started a new life in another country. In subsequent years, they would from time to time remember the difficult, very hot, but also very social few months they spent in Hal Far, which illustrates the crucial roles of shelters in building community networks and support.

Conclusion: Mobility and the Social Making of Shelters

This chapter has examined a particular collection of refugee shelters in Malta by bringing them into conversation with dynamic lived experiences of mobility. It has focused on migrants' experiences in a cluster of Malta's open centres, their relations with one another, and their link to journeys to and from the open centre. Looking at the interplay between socialities and materialities of shelters, it has shown, first, that the open centres are not static spaces, but architecturally and materially malleable, with multiple spatiotemporal durations. In other words, these shelters emerge as a place through which the relations between these socialities and materialities, as well as the dynamics of migrants' journeys, can be formed. Second, the chapter has argued that these relations can be generative, leading to the establishment of new bonds, enabling migrants to cope with precarious situations and negative experiences. This thus brings to the fore a process of social 'sheltering': arrangements and relations between people, often culturally and geographically distant, emerging as a result of their journeys both within and outside formal practices of assistance and care. Together, it is an example that enables us to reflect further on a number of ideas about shelters and sheltering more widely.

First, understanding shelters as emergent rather than static spaces points to their dynamic nature. This chapter has argued that the temporalities of shelters and their materiality are closely related, with bearings upon social relations. Existing structures can be repurposed. Shelters may be constructed with materials that allow for rearrangement, contingent upon the intensity of migrant flows. But the very materials, and the atmospheres they conjure up, also regulate people's everyday lives and experiences in these shelters. Mobile metal containers generate heat in summer months, forcing people outside and therefore forging social interactions. Whilst these containers allow for minimum privacy, which can be a problem, they also foster important social bonds. Not all relations, of course, have to do with conviviality. As this chapter has shown, there are a number of spatial exclusions at work in the placement and arrangement of shelters and their geographical distance from mainstream Maltese society segregates migrants. Discrimination can be written into the very networks that migrants seek; transport in place for migrants to access Maltese towns is limited, expensive and often unreliable. Whilst these shelters purportedly remain 'open', mobility within Malta, in both a physical and a social sense, is very limited.

Recent developments in migration policy also play an important role in shaping shelters. In 2014, Italy and Malta entered into an agreement, which resulted in all migrants discovered at sea being disembarked in Italy, unless they were medical evacuations. As a result, the number of boat arrivals in Malta drastically reduced to 568 (2014) and twenty-three (2017) from the 2,008 in 2013 (UNHCR 2018). Therefore, instead of travelling by boat from Libya, many migrants now arrive by plane or through relocation programmes from other EU Member States such as Greece (IOM 2017; UNHCR 2018). Despite such changes, the number of asylum applications in Malta is still at a similar level to previous years, with 1,600 in 2017 (UNHCR

2018). Malta's strong economy now makes the island a desired country of destination, which stands in contrast to the situation at the beginning of my research around a decade ago. In 2015, Malta's reception system underwent changes, including an end to mandatory detention and the establishment of an Initial Reception Centre. This temporarily housed migrants applying for asylum in order to conduct health screenings before transferring them to an open centre. Structures in the open centres changed in relation to these developments, and the latest figures show that the number of residents in Malta's open centres has increased again to 907 (Bonnici 2018; UNHCR 2018). If this trend continues, it could increase pressure on the open centres, but could also mean more permanent structures, fences to restrict access to only residents, and making open centres into established accommodation centres rather than social spaces. Certainly, this seems to be the recent trend (Barry 2015).

A second contribution of this chapter is to develop an understanding of sheltering as a process, emerging in spaces like the open centres. Here, people's journeys overlap, intertwine and knot together, and in times of precarity sheltering is not solely about having a place to stay, but also about enabling coping strategies in a range of different registers. These include the sharing of memories and information, support with healthcare, food and childcare, as well as finding employment or accommodation and onward movement. Compared to the government-run reception networks, alternative networks enabled through social 'sheltering' have the potential to create alternate forms of support shaping migrants' future mobilities, offering information on leaving Malta, and help when returning. None of these are written into the 'design' of shelters, which are often about housing people. Through its ethnographic exploration of open centres in Malta, this chapter has drawn attention to these relations between mobility and shelters, the former including not just movement but immobility as well. Malta's open centres have bearings upon migrants' mobilities in different ways: slowing them down, forcing them to stay still and creating feelings of being stuck, but also accelerating or propelling their journeys onwards. Migrants' mobilities mean that shelters are emergent and ephemeral, shifting according to the contingencies and ebbs of journeys. Sheltering as a process of the formation of community networks emerges as more important than the shelter as a physical space. Shelters, even when restrictive and confining, can shift and change, playing crucial social roles on migrants' journeys. It is these social networks emerging through mobility rather than only the policies that render centres 'open': meaningful and accessible to fraught and precarious lives.

Marthe Achtnich is an anthropologist working on mobility and migration with a focus on unauthorized migrants' journeys through Libya and by boat to Europe. Her interests include ethnographies of mobility, borderwork, migration and the (bio)economy. She is currently a postdoctoral Fellow by Examination in Anthropology at Magdalen College, University of Oxford.

References

AWAS. 2018. 'History'. Retrieved 10 October 2019 from https://homeaffairs.gov.mt/en/MHAS-Departments/awas/Pages/History.aspx.

Barry, D. 2015. 'Outsiders Barred from Entering Hal Far Open Centre, "Centre Not Living up to its Name"'. *Malta Independent*, 10 August. Retrieved 10 October 2019 from http://www.independent.com.mt/articles/2015-08-10/local-news/Outsiders-barred-from-entering-Hal-Far-open-centre-centre-not-living-up-to-its-name-6736140252.

Bonnici, J. 2018. 'Population at Open Centres in Malta Grows by a Third in Light of Rising Rental Prices'. *Malta Independent*, 10 May. Retrieved 10 October 2019 from http://www.independent.com.mt/articles/2018-05-10/local-news/Population-at-open-centres-in-Malta-grows-by-a-third-in-light-of-rising-rental-prices-6736189586.

Brigden, N., and C. Mainwaring. 2016. 'Matryoshka Journeys: Im/mobility during Migration'. *Geopolitics*. DOI: 10.1080/14650045.2015.1122592.

Caruana, J. 2016. *Struggling to Survive: An Investigation into the Risk of Poverty among Asylum Seekers in Malta*. Birkikara and Hamrun: Jesuit Refugee Service and Aditus Foundation Malta.

IOM 2017. 'Relocation from Italy and Greece to Malta'. Retrieved 10 October 2019 from https://malta.iom.int/relocation-italy-and-greece-malta.

Mainwaring, C. 2012. 'Constructing a Crisis: The Role of Immigration Detention in Malta'. *Population, Space and Place* 18: 687–700.

Malta Independent. 2012. 'Hal Far Open Centre: New Structures Replace Tents'. *Malta Independent*, 20 April. Retrieved 10 October 2019 from http://www.independent.com.mt/articles/2012-04-20/news/hal-far-open-centre-new-structures-replace-tents-308922.

MSF. 2009. *'Not Criminals': Médecins Sans Frontières Exposes Conditions for Undocumented Migrants and Asylum Seekers in Maltese Detention Centres*. Paris: Médecins Sans Frontières.

Times of Malta. 2012. 'Hal Far "Tent Village" Being Dismantled', 19 April. Retrieved 10 October 2019 from https://timesofmalta.com/articles/view/migrants-tent-village-is-no-more.416232.

UNHCR. 2018. 'Malta Asylum Trends'. Retrieved 2 July 2018 from http://www.unhcr.org/mt/charts.

Figure 4.1 The camp drawbridge in Moria, Greece. © Mark E. Breeze, based on an image supplied by Daniel Howden.

4

Moria

Anti-shelter and the Spectacle of Deterrence

Daniel Howden

On the western flank of Moria, jutting out over a stream of effluent, is the camp's drawbridge. It is a metal cage on stilts that cuts through the riotous, sewage-powered vegetation, but does not quite reach the far bank of the stream. The final distance can only be spanned by a wooden drawbridge that is lowered using a heavy chain. There is no sign to announce its purpose. The apparatus is not an entrance – it is an emergency exit. It was not built to serve the more than 8,000 people who currently shelter inside Moria, but for the staff of the European Asylum Support Office (EASO), whose office is just inside the perimeter on the eastern bank. Fires, fights and protests have become so commonplace here that asylum agency personnel had refused to enter the camp unless a rapid escape route was established. Their offices are located less than 100 metres from the official entrance-exit of the reception centre, but the threat level is deemed to be such that this distance is too great. The representatives of the same EU and national government agencies who will ultimately decide which of the camp's residents will be legally able to move on from its confines to a future in Europe therefore demand their own escape route from Moria as a condition for even entering the site – hence the drawbridge.

Moria is a 46,480 square-metre site carved from a hillside three kilometres inland from the sea on Lesvos. Its entire aspect is in direct opposition to the natural environment. Amid the olive groves with their twisted trunks in silver, green and grey, the hotspot is composed almost entirely of right angles. Its palette is white, concrete grey and stainless steel. Ranks of nested wire fences are sunk into rough concrete foundations, with single or stacked containers for buildings. Lookout boxes mark its southernmost corners. The camp's only circles come in the form of the spirals of razor wire that top the perimeter and divide internal sections.

The inconvenient fact of Moria's slopes, which prior to its construction authorities were warned would make the site unsuitable, have been combated with concrete terracing. Tons of gravel have been poured to banish the mud of winters past. The handful of permanent structures include concrete shower and toilet blocks, plus two single-storey buildings on the eastern corner used by the Greek army. The remainder are prefabricated structures ranging from canvas hangar tents to individual containers on breeze block foundations. Suvendrini Perera and Joseph Pugliese (2016) put it clearly: 'It is an architecture that is the very antithesis of shelter: they are spaces designed to engender fear, compound uncertainty and maximize a sense of exposure to danger.' They were referring not to Moria, but to Australia's offshore refugee and migrant holding camps, but their words chime with this and many other sites. 'They are producing mentally disordered people here', said Samuel Chidi Nduka, a 32-year-old Nigerian, who spent ten months in Moria. 'If you want to go mad, just come to this camp for one week' (Howden 2017). This is Moria as a spectacle of detention, designed for an audience of possible migrants beyond Europe's borders.

A Mirror for Outside Tensions

The delineation of space inside Moria reflects the tensions that called it into existence: between human rights and perceived political imperatives; protection and deterrence; and between national and supranational sovereignty. At its conception in 2013, Moria was a national facility: the land was handed over by the Greek army to the Greek police. It was intended as a temporary shelter (no more than twenty-five days) for a relatively small number of irregular arrivals from Turkey. It was later renamed the First Reception and Identification Centre (Greek First Reception Service 2016), reflecting increased pressure on Greece to conform with EU requirements to fingerprint and register all new arrivals prior to their departure for the mainland.

In its earliest form, the camp had three main projected areas: an identification centre with a capacity for 100 people, a first reception area with accommodation for 220 and a larger closed 'pre-departure centre' where deportees would be held before their expulsion from Greece. It was constructed by Athens-based AKON Techniki, whose previous works included migrant detention centres elsewhere in the country. Security at the camp would be managed by local and national police forces, while the Greek military retained a presence. However, by the beginning of 2015, an increasing number of EU Member States were dissatisfied with Greece and Italy's implementation of the Dublin Regulation, and they stipulated that irregular arrivals must be identified, registered and have their asylum claims heard in the country of first entry (Howden and Fotiadis 2017). The Agenda on Migration in April that year accelerated and refined the 'hotspot approach' (Europa 2015) as an answer to this dissatisfaction. Trumpeted by the European Commission as a way of coordinating EU support for frontline states, it meant the concentration of all relevant agencies in one location. The European Asylum Support Office (EASO), Frontex (the European Border and Coast Guard Agency), Europol (the EU police office) and Eurojust (the agency for judicial cooperation) would all work together on the ground.

By mid November 2015, it was clear that policy papers and statements from the European Commission had not changed the situation in Greece's putative hotspots. A European Council team that conducted spot checks in Evros, and on Chios and Samos reported that 'nothing seems to be prepared or planned ... The whole system seems to be organized to register migrants and let them leave' (Howden and Fotiadis 2017). A Greek policeman serving at Moria at the time put it more succinctly when he said that his job was to get a copy of an ID and a fingerprint and then speed them on their way to Germany. 'Copy, finger, Merkel', he explained (Howden and Fotiadis 2017).

In the Greek context, the norms of migration management under the previous conservative government of pushbacks, arbitrary detention, police brutality and impunity were superseded by the emerging norms of a new leftist government, including administrative paralysis, humanitarian rhetoric and state withdrawal (Fotiadis 2017). At the EU level, a similar unresolved conflict emerged between a hotspot approach meant to facilitate burden-sharing among Member States via the relocation of asylum seekers and one that envisaged a fast-track approach to asylum as a mechanism for the mass return of border-crossers (Asylum Information Database 2017). In Moria all of these norms coexisted. Police brutality, existing since the days of the Pagani detention centre (the precursor to Moria), was present. In one notorious incident on 24 July 2016, children in the unaccompanied minors' section were tear-gassed, while some were taken to a Greek police station where they were forced to spend hours in the 'chair position' and beaten when they were no longer able to do this (Médecins Sans Frontières 2017). Administrative paralysis was manifested by the absence of a general director for the camp: the ranking official from the time, Spyros Kourtis, complained of 'the absence of the state' (Kalir and Rozakou 2016) and turned to nongovernmental organizations (NGOs) to cover emergency needs. The new alternate minister for migration policy, Yiannis Mouzalas, repeatedly spoke of bringing 'order from chaos' (Howden 2017). However, it seemed that he was doing no such thing.

Meanwhile, the EU language of solidarity was expressed by Dimitris Avramopoulos, the European Commissioner for Migration, Home Affairs and Citizenship, who promised that the hotspot would ensure human rights (Kathimerini 2015). 'If this had taken place 10 months ago, we could have avoided what we went through this summer', he said. 'More importantly, we would have been able to treat all those people who are seeking for a better life in Europe in a more humane manner.' While the Commissioner spoke, heads of Member States were in negotiations with Turkey to find an expedient way to reduce the flow of people across the Aegean regardless of their protection needs. The resulting EU-Turkey statement in March 2016 (Consilium 2016) imposed geographical restrictions on new arrivals crossing the Aegean, as well as a returns mechanism to Turkey for asylum seekers, particularly Syrians. It was deliberately framed as a joint statement rather than a 'deal' so as to avoid scrutiny by the European Parliament (Greens/European Free Alliance 2018).

In Moria itself, this competition of rhetoric and purpose manifested itself in a switch from an overwhelmingly chaotic and violent place of transit to an overcrowded, expensive and still violent place of indefinite confinement. In terms of its spatial layout, this meant that the camp of 2014, with its three areas of identification, accommodation and detention, needed to be overhauled (UNHCR 2014). The largest expansion was in accommodation, which was achieved in a denser formation of containers and the ad hoc addition of tents. The arrival of EU agencies saw a similar expansion in the services area where extra layers of identification were conducted. By now, the predeparture detention centre had shrunk to a capacity of roughly 150 and had come to be known as 'Section B' (Tazzioli 2016).

An Institutional Grey Zone

The confusion over sovereignty at Moria became clearest during the winter of 2016–17, when freezing conditions contributed to at least three deaths in the camp. The flawed investigations and the lack of accountability that followed these deaths offer a stark illustration of the way in which Moria occupies an institutional grey zone (Pro Asyl and Refugee Support Aegean 2017). In the space of one week in January 2017, a 22-year-old Egyptian and a 45-year-old Syrian died in the same tent in Moria, while a Pakistani man, aged twenty, lost his life and an Afghan man was found in a critical condition and transferred to an intensive care unit on Lesvos, where a lengthy battle ensued to save his life. Camp residents, aid workers and members of the local community agreed that the deaths were the result of the inhalation of toxic fumes from stoves in which people had been burning rubbish to keep warm.

Despite these testimonies, an investigation by Refugee Support Aegean found no official cause of death. Blood tests, which experts said could effectively establish whether poisonous fumes caused the deaths, were not carried out. Without such evidence, no action has been taken by Greek prosecutors (Pro Asyl and Refugee Support Aegean 2017). Previous deaths at Moria had followed a similar pattern. In November 2016, a 66-year-old woman and a six-year-old child were killed when a portable cooking gas stove exploded inside their tent. An investigation opened by the Greek fire service has remained pending. Delays in the probe were blamed on an incomplete forensic report. Surviving family members were transferred to another EU state. An Refugee Support Aegean (RSA) report concluded that 'it appears that the very structure of hotspots – spaces not clearly integrated into the Greek administrative structure and legal system – is creating confusion regarding competence over the premises, thus leading to a legal void regarding their management and monitoring' (Pro Asyl and Refugee Support Aegean 2017).

Until February 2017, Moria, along with other hotspots, did not have a general director. Responsibility for the site was therefore handed from the Greek Ministry of Migration to the ranking official of the First Reception Service. Even this was done on short rotations of less than one month. Then there is the issue of EU responsibility. A report from the European Court of Auditors in March 2017 makes it clear that the European Commission and EU agencies were present on the ground and were therefore aware of events and conditions. The Commission had created a body called the Structural Reform Support Service, the head of which chaired biweekly interagency meetings in Athens where they were updated with all events on Lesvos and at Moria. The report concluded that urgent steps should be taken to appoint 'a single person to be in charge of the overall management and functioning of each individual hotspot area on a more permanent basis' (European Court of Auditors 2017), as well as the adoption of hotspot standard operating procedures, which would establish a chain of responsibility in case of serious harm coming to camp residents. Without this, everyone could evade responsibility and Moria would remain an institutional grey zone.

Despite its fierce appearance, Moria is not a prison. It contains one in the form of Section B, but the vast majority of camp residents can come and go via its two exit points. This distinction has regularly led to confused media reports on the facility. Headlines such as '"Welcome to Prison": Winter Hits in One of Greece's Worst Refugee Camps' (Smith 2017) and 'Conditions are Horrific at Greece's "Island Prisons" for Refugees: Is That the Point?' (Witte 2018) are representative examples. Another popular trope speaks to the hazards of accessing the camp, such as 'Rare look at life inside Lesvos' Moria refugee camp' (McElvaney 2018). Both tropes are problematic.

In fact, Moria is full of back doors: between four and six improvised entry and exit points have been almost constantly present from 2015 on the northern and western perimeters. For large sections of the perimeter, there is a single chain-link fence. On the north side next to a section most often occupied by West African and Bangladeshi or Pakistani asylum seekers, one of the back doors, a hole in the fence, has its step fashioned from an olive tree trunk. The area is scattered with discarded condom packets and drinks cans. On the eastern perimeter atop the bank of the polluted stream, the fence has been replaced in a 30-metre stretch by a shanty-like open structure. The shelter, which abuts the more formal camp, is home to a group of Syrians from Deir ez-Zor in eastern Syria. The men and boys sleep twenty to a single tent-like structure. On their phones, the Syrians have videos of gang violence from inside the camp. The pictures show stabbings and unidentified males being beaten with metal bars and improvised clubs. Violence between some Syrians from Deir ez-Zor and Syrian Kurds has intensified inside Moria since May 2018, and medical charities have highlighted the presence of large numbers of asylum seekers from former Islamic State-held areas in Iraq and Syria and have warned of a mental health epidemic. 'It is harrowing and incredibly disempowering to see the mental health status of the asylum seekers in Lesvos progressively getting worse', said a Médecins Sans Frontières (MSF) psychologist. 'We do our best to help those that we can, but the situation they are in is so horrendous', stating that the organization received news of an average of fifteen suicide attempts every month (Médecins Sans Frontières 2017).

Prior to 2013, the site now called Moria was a Greek army compound called Paradellis, in an area known as Marmaro, or 'the marble' in Greek. The proximity of the island to the mainland of Greece's geopolitical rival, Turkey, means that it is dotted by army properties, many of them in some state of disrepair. The military site covered two-thirds of the current reception centre, and was made up of an administration block and several rudimentary concrete dormitories for young men fulfilling their national service. All but two of these structures were subsequently demolished.

When the site was originally chosen for Greece's First Reception Service, the main local objection was the use of the name (Frydenlund and Diaz, 2018). The nearby village of Moria did not want to be associated with an asylum seeker detention centre, as had happened previously to the area of Pagani. Pagani was a straight-up detention centre, opened in 2009, with inmates kept in a crudely converted warehouse. Originally designed to accommodate 250 people, Pagani's population swelled to more than 1,200 and detainees had no regular access to an outdoor space. Media coverage of the 2015 sea crossings from Turkey to the Greek islands has tended to create the impression that this was an unprecedented event; in fact, flows of migrants and asylum seekers have been present since 2000, with arrivals ebbing and flowing depending on conditions at Greece's land border with Turkey at Evros (Howden 2017). Pagani was opened during a previous peak in 2009, in the hills outside Mytilene, the port of Lesvos, and accommodation was arranged in large dorms with barred windows and bunk beds stacked up to four high. The population was managed by regular deportations, many of them without due process or access to asylum procedures. When 160 young refugees, including unaccompanied minors, were crammed into a single room, activists succeeded in drawing wider attention to the facility (Welcome to Europe 2009). In 2010, with Greece under a new centre-left government, unrest at Pagani, which was violently suppressed by the police, saw the centre closed.

The controversy over the Pagani detention centre stalked the early days of Moria, with activists dubbing it the 'Pagani of the Troika', a reference to the EU's representatives in debt negotiations with Greece: the European Commission, the European Central Bank and the International Monetary Fund. Stavros Miroyiannis, then an officer with the Greek civil protection force and now the director of another camp on Lesvos, Kara Tepe, was among the crews that set up the first emergency tents at Moria in early 2015. He was surprised to find that there was no development plan for the site, no demarcation of common spaces or recreation areas (Miroyiannis 2018). 'They didn't seem to understand that you need to plan this in the way you would a village.' Miroyiannis says he told the relevant authorities that the hilly site was the wrong location, advising that flatter areas further north on the island would work better. 'They had no plan of any kind except an evacuation plan [for staff]. I warned them, you are going to make a favela.'

Local Perspectives

The first thing that strikes any new visitor to Moria is the extraordinary number of cars parked along the road outside the camp. It is common to see as many as 200 vehicles. Every one of these represents jobs and income, often for members of nearby communities. A form of codependency has emerged between the islanders and the local community, despite mainly local complaints about the camp. Discontent with the facility chiefly focuses on petty theft from warehouses and livestock to olive orchards, chopped down by camp residents for firewood. Sitting at a table in the shade of a grapevine, Dimitris Tsintiris is the only one of the twenty-nine local businesses in Marmaro that have endured since 2014 (Tsintiris 2018). His auto shop is on the other side of the footpath from the stream that demarcates the western perimeter of Moria. Tsintiris gives the example of his uncle who lost thirty sheep, suspected to have been slaughtered for food by asylum seekers in Moria. The other focus of the community's ire is the sewage system. Despite clear wording on the development of waste water disposal being included in public works documents related to the site since its creation in 2013, Moria has not been connected to the mains sewage system. The first legal complaint alleging pollution of local waterways was made by local landowner Stratos Kerimis in August 2014 (Empros 2014).

In response to the claim, environmental inspectors from the North Aegean regional authority visited the site, confirmed waste water leakage and requested access to the sewage system plans from the Greek police. According to local media reports, they found that the new facility had been connected insecurely to pre-existing septic tanks. Four years on, and after the official expenditure of €5.5 million in EU funds (Trevizo 2017), the same problems exist and local protests that have shut the access road outside the camp focus on raw sewage leaks from Moria. Unconfirmed local estimates suggest that the site's septic tanks need to be emptied every second day at a weekly cost in excess of €30,000.

The presence of the camp and its continued operation into the future has created winners and losers in the local community, and this is aptly expressed by the fact that Kerimis, the same landowner who sued camp authorities over pollution, now owns one of the two profitable roadside canteens that service the camp, its residents and workers. Hundreds of other jobs have been created inside the camp and lucrative contracts have been awarded to Lesvos businesses, typically subcontracted by larger Athens-based construction groups like AKON. Tsintiris speculates that for the money spent servicing Moria's aged septic tanks, a proper sewage pipe system connecting to the mains in Panagiouda 3.5 kilometres away could have been built many times over. Repeated fines of up to €100,000 (To Vima 2018) have been levied by regional authorities against the Greek police for illegal pollution of local waterways. The garage owner blames local and national greed and short-termism more than the migrants and asylum seekers in the camp for the violence he has witnessed, which includes rapes and stabbings. 'All of this architecture results in violence. If these people were in something like a village it would be different but this is a warehouse of people. There's nothing done properly, everything has been done wrong.' (Tsintiris 2018).

However, Moria is not the only local response to the arrival of refugees and other migrants. Indeed, on Lesvos there are two clear alternatives that do not the share the same features of violence, short-termism and containment. One is Pikpa on Lesvos, an abandoned holiday campsite that has been transformed into a refugee shelter just outside the island's capital. Something wholly unexpected happens when you open the door to the laundry in this place. Multicoloured lights dance across the chrome and white fronts of the donated washing machines, as nearby speakers belt out ABBA music, and a disco ball spins and sparkles. This disco laundrette is the brainchild of Simos Simoleon, the volunteer caretaker whose Mohican hairstyle and slightly crooked smile have become everyday staples of life at Pikpa. Simos has fond memories of bygone summers when he was a DJ at a bar on the island, and he thought others might enjoy a revival. Outside there are picnic tables, simple wooden chalets and inflatable shelters that appear to have rolled into place under the trees like giant footballs. Colourful murals that owe more to enthusiasm and peace slogans than artistry decorate the administrative building. The vibe here, as in many of the charitable refugee shelters in Greece, is more kibbutz than camp. The only chain-link fence to be found belongs to an adjoining tennis club. It could scarcely be more different from Moria. The same basic elements of shelter are performed, as they are on Moria, but no attempt is made in the architecture to reinforce the sense of illegality and insecurity.

Kara Tepe, the other comparatively large refugee shelter on Lesvos, has been constructed on the site of a former children's road safety park. Its recreational area sits on the still visible, child-sized roundabouts and junctions. Adjacent to it is a communal garden planted with vegetables and sunflowers. The camp was opened in June 2015 as an alternative to Moria for Syrians and other vulnerable asylum seekers. Kara Tepe's smaller population, which has never climbed above 2,000, contrasts with the wild expansions and contractions that have occurred at Moria. While Kara Tepe has a current population of 1,600 against a capacity of 2,000, Moria has a population that has regularly exceeded 10,000 against a stated capacity of 2,500. While Kara Tepe accommodates residents in containers similar to those in Moria, they are spaced out completely differently. Each container has been stencilled with geometric patterns in blue and orange to break up the monotony. A camp maintenance worker explains that each container has also been given its own step, clothesline and awning, both for functional reasons and to give occupants some sense of autonomy. The contrast with Moria drives home the sense that there are deserving (vulnerable) asylum seekers and undeserving, criminal asylum seekers, with the latter forced to shelter in Moria.

Conclusion

Moria is an instructive microcosm of broader European border practices and their local impact. It offers a physical manifestation of the effects of

European asylum and migration policy: a permanent-impermanent shelter (Sayigh 2005) composed of prefabricated structures; expensive, insufficient infrastructure that remains unconnected with host community systems; an architecture dominated by security imperatives and yet violent and chaotic; a nexus for formal and informal jobs and money that co-opts sections of the local community while creating unrest; and a divisive relationship with nongovernmental agencies that offers contracts and access to those willing to limit criticism and mute advocacy. Moria and the other Greek hotspots are anti-shelters that have turned the islands into a buffer zone, separate from mainland Europe but able to create a spectacle of detention for an audience of possible migrants beyond Europe's borders.

Moria's architecture is shaped by containment and punishment, inspiring fear and violence. But responsibility for these anti-shelter choices is evaded by everyone involved. The impact of these choices is excused by the responsible national and supranational authorities in a number of ways, which transfers the blame or obscures the nature of the shelter (Howden and Fotiadis 2017). Even in planning documents, Moria is asserted as temporary in a way that can then be used to excuse its ad hoc nature. When the extreme consequences of this short-termism become too obvious, they are blamed on a lack of resources devoted by an absent national government or the EU. Alternatively, they are, as the European Commission has asserted, the fault of Greek maladministration. The fact that these conditions create a forceful deterrence to future migratory flows is never officially acknowledged. EU laws on asylum and fundamental rights mean that Moria must be a shelter rather than an outright detention centre as its predecessor Pagani, but it consists of shelter inspired by the model of incarceration and punishment where the suffering of those sheltered is performed as a deterrent to those who might otherwise choose to follow them.

Daniel Howden is an award-winning journalist focused on migration. He was the editor of *Refugees Deeply* and has previously been a foreign correspondent with *The Economist, The Guardian* and *The Independent*, spending much of his career in Africa and Southern Europe. He is now Director of the media non-profit Lighthouse Reports.

References

Asylum Information Database. 2017. *Accelerated, Prioritised and Fast-Track Asylum Procedures Legal Frameworks and Practice in Europe.* AIDA. Retrieved 11 October 2019 from https://www.ecre.org/wp-content/uploads/2017/05/AIDA-Brief_AcceleratedProcedures.pdf.

Consilium. 2016. 'EU-Turkey Statement'. Retrieved 11 October 2019 from http://www.consilium.europa.eu/en/press/press-releases/2016/03/18/eu-turkey-statement.

Danish Refugee Council. 2017. *Fundamental Rights and the EU Hotspot Approach*. Retrieved 11 October 2019 from http://www.statewatch.org/news/2017/nov/danish-refugee-council-fundamental-rights.pdf.

Empros. 2014. 'Pollution in Stream!' Retrieved 11 October 2019 from https://www.emprosnet.gr/article/61849-lymata-se-rema.

Europa. 2015. 'The Hotspot Approach to Managing Exceptional Migration Flows'. European Commission. Retrieved 11 October 2019 from https://ec.europa.eu/home-affairs/sites/homeaffairs/files/what-we-do/policies/european-agenda-migration/background-information/docs/2_hotspots_en.pdf.

European Court of Auditors. 2017. *EU Response to the Refugee Crisis: The 'Hotspot' Approach*. Retrieved 11 October 2019 from https://www.eca.europa.eu/Lists/ECADocuments/SR17_6/SR_MIGRATION_HOTSPOTS_EN.pdf.

Farahat, A., and N. Markard. 2016. 'Forced Migration Governance: In Search of Sovereignty'. *German Law Journal* 17(6): 923–48.

Fotiadis, A. 2017. *Exousies Ektos Elegxou*. Athens: Kastaniotis Press.

Frydenlund, E., and L. Diaz. 2018. 'This is Moria . . .' *The Migrationist*. Retrieved 11 October 2019 from https://themigrationist.net/2018/06/08/this-is-moria.

Greek First Reception Service. 2015. 'Emergency Assistance in Support of the Organisation, Provision of Legal Information and Interpretation for the Effective Management of Immigration Flows in the Eastern External Borders'. Retrieved 11 October 2019 from http://firstreception.gov.gr/news-detail.php?lang=en&type=press&id=36.

———. 2016. 'Emergency Support Enhancing the Operational Capacity of FRS to Manage the Extreme Rise in Migration Flows into Greek National and European Territory'. Retrieved 11 October 2019 from http://firstreception.gov.gr/news-detail.php?lang=en&id=40.

Greens/European Free Alliance. 2018. 'The EU-Turkey Statement and the Greek Hotspots'. Retrieved 11 October 2019 from https://www.greens-efa.eu/en/article/document/the-eu-turkey-statement-and-the-greek-hotspots.

Howden, D. 2017. 'Greece: Between Deterrence and Integration'. *Refugees Deeply: Quarterly Reports*. Retrieved 11 October 2019 from http://issues.newsdeeply.com/greece-between-deterrence-and-integration.

Howden, D., and A. Fotiadis. 2017. 'The Refugee Archipelago: The Inside Story of What Went Wrong in Greece'. *Refugees Deeply*. Retrieved 11 October 2019 from https://www.newsdeeply.com/refugees/articles/2017/03/06/the-refugee-archipelago-the-inside-story-of-what-went-wrong-in-greece.

Kakissis, J. 2018. '"Europe Does Not See Us as Human": Stranded Refugees Struggle in Greece'. NPR. Retrieved 11 October 2019 from https://www.npr.org/sections/parallels/2018/03/09/589973165/europe-does-not-see-us-as-human-stranded-refugees-struggle-in-greece.

Kathimerini. 2015. 'First Hotspot Inaugurated on Lesvos'. Retrieved 11 October 2019 from http://www.ekathimerini.com/202586/article/ekathimerini/news/first-hotspot-inaugurated-on-lesvos.

Kalir, B., and K. Rozakou. 2016. '"Giving Form to Chaos": The Futility of EU Border Management at Moria Hotspot in Lesvos'. *Society & Space*. Retrieved 11 October 2019 from http://societyandspace.org/2016/11/16/giving-form-to-chaos-the-futility-of-eu-border-management-at-moria-hotspot-in-lesvos.

McElvaney, K. 2018. 'Rare Look at Life Inside Lesvos' Moria Refugee Camp'. *Al Jazeera*. Retrieved 11 October 2019 from https://www.aljazeera.com/indepth/inpictures/rare-life-Lesvos-moria-refugee-camp-180119123918846.html.

Médecins Sans Frontières. 2017. *Confronting the Mental Health Emergency on Samos and Lesvos*. Retrieved 11 October 2019 from https://www.msf.org/sites/msf.org/files/2018-06/confronting-the-mental-health-emergency-on-samos-and-lesvos.pdf.

Miroyiannis, S. 2018. Interviewed by the author. 24 May.

No Borders. 2009. 'Pagani Detention Centre'. Retrieved 11 October 2019 from http://w2eu.net/files/2009/08/noborder.lesvos.09-pagani.detention.centre-20-08-2009-01.jpg.

Perera, S., and J. Pugliese. 2016. 'Insecurities: Anti-shelter'. *Medium*. Retrieved 11 October 2019 from https://medium.com/insecurities/anti-shelter-55842842d4e3.

PROASYL and Refugee Support Aegean (RSA). 2017. 'Greek Hotspots: Deaths Not to Be Forgotten'. Retrieved 11 October 2019 from https://www.proasyl.de/wp-content/uploads/2015/12/2017-06-14-RSA-Policy-Paper_Greek-Hotspots_Deaths-not-to-be-forgotten.pdf.

Sayigh, R. 2005. 'A House Is Not a Home: Permanent Impermanence of Habitat for Palestinian Expellees in Lebanon'. *Holy Land Studies* 4(1): 17–39.

Smith, H. 2017. '"Welcome to Prison": Winter Hits in One of Greece's Worst Refugee Camps'. *The Guardian*, 22 December. Retrieved 11 October 2019 from https://www.theguardian.com/world/2017/dec/22/this-isnt-europe-life-greece-worst-refugee-camps.

Tazzioli, M. 2016. 'Concentric Cages: The Hotspots of Lesvos after the EU-Turkey Agreement'. *OpenDemocracy*. Retrieved 11 October 2019 from https://www.opendemocracy.net/mediterranean-journeys-in-hope/martina-tazzioli/concentric-cages-hotspots-of-lesvos-after-eu-turkey-.

Trevizo, P. 2017. 'A Crisis within a Crisis: Refugees in Lesvos'. *Al Jazeera*. Retrieved 11 October 2019 from https://www.aljazeera.com/indepth/features/2017/05/crisis-crisis-refugees-Lesvos-170502080931359.html.

To Vima. 2018. 'Fine of 100,000 Euros for Moria and VIAL from the Regional Prefecture of the North Aegean'. Retrieved 11 October 2019 from https://www.tovima.gr/2018/09/22/politics/prostimo-100-000-gia-moria-kai-vial-apo-tin-perifereia-voreiou-aigaiou.

Tsintiris, D. 2018. Interviewed by the author. 28 May.

UNHCR. 2014. 'Moria Site, Lesvos'. Retrieved 11 October 2019 from https://data2.unhcr.org/en/documents/download/46995.

Welcome to Europe. 2009. 'Police Repression in Pagani Increasing'. Retrieved 11 October 2019 from http://w2eu.net/2009/10/26/police-repression-in-pagani-increasing.

Witte, G. 2018. 'Conditions are Horrific at Greece's "Island Prisons" for Refugees: Is That the Point?' *Washington Post*, 15 January. Retrieved 11 October 2019 from https://www.washingtonpost.com/world/europe/conditions-are-horrific-at-greeces-island-prisons-for-refugees-is-that-the-point/2018/01/15/b93765ac-f546-11e7-9af7-a50bc3300042_story.html?utm_term=.733bbf3df41e.

Figure 5.1 Improvised shelters in Moria, Greece. © Mark E. Breeze, based on an image supplied by Polly Pallister-Wilkins.

5

Moria Hotspot

Shelter as a Politically Crafted Materiality of Neglect

Polly Pallister-Wilkins

The bright yellow Lipton Ice Tea display fridge, with its large glass door and refreshing looking bottle illustrated with a splash of water and a sprinkling of tea leaves, stands unevenly on a wet concrete slope, surrounded by the skeletal frames of an old torn lawn gazebo and a flimsy dome tent. A man sits huddled in the fridge, the door slightly ajar, with a plastic bag on his hands. The hood of his rain jacket is pulled up and wet hair is stuck to his forehead. He is sleeping. This display fridge is his temporary shelter against the incessant rain, a dry if not a comfortable or private place to sleep for the night at the Moria reception centre, now hotspot, in Lesvos, Greece on 22 October 2015. The following evening, the Lipton Ice Tea display fridge lies on its back like a coffin, the white plastic insides are now lined with gold and silver thermal space blankets. The glass door is propped slightly open with a piece of wood and another man sleeps inside. Across the sodden concrete slope, down which water streams in torrents, stands an a-frame tent made from green and black plastic, wearing a ripped United Nations High Commissioner for Refugees (UNHCR)-logoed tarp like a toga.

At the bottom of the slope – lined with old, gnarled olive trees and dotted with flimsy nylon tents of the type usually found at music festivals – stands a large white marquee. When it rains, water runs through the front door; inside, sodden wooden boards attempt to level the floor. Colourful matting has been placed on the boards. On some mats, a human figure stands under a shelter made of two hands surrounded by an olive wreath. On others, the letters 'UNHCR' can be read, while others simply say 'The UN Refugee Agency'. On top of this mosaic of woven plastic, rows of two-tier bunk beds sit covered in sodden grey woollen blankets, with the turquoise letters that spell 'UNHCR' just visible. Some of these blankets can be found outside amongst the olive trees, draped over sticks to form simple bivouacs.

To one side of this large marquee stands a crumbling building from which flies a small Médecins Sans Frontières flag, while to the other stands a small white plastic portacabin with a Médecins du Monde logo on the door. Behind the portacabin is a fenced compound, within which sit neat rows of prefabricated buildings with solar panels on their roofs and AC units under their windows. These buildings house the computers that make up the frontline of the European Union (EU) system for registering irregular entries, sorting the refugees from the migrants, and are the principal reason for Moria's present existence.

Moria contains many different examples of refugee shelter, all of it in some way accidental and improvised. The space itself is not designed for the purpose of shelter, lying as it does on a steep slope surrounded by thick olive groves. Meanwhile, it contains a range of different shelters: from display fridges, to nylon festival tents that offer little to no protection against the elements, to structures cobbled together from discarded materials and the more 'mainstream' IKEA/Better Shelter housing that offers a front door, four walls, and a roof (Scott-Smith 2018). The variety of accidental and improvised shelter on offer in Moria speaks to more than just the diversity of refugee shelter itself, or how various materials, objects and technologies become repurposed to address needs in a humanitarian crisis. It also speaks to the wider response of the Greek government, the EU and the international humanitarian community to the 'refugee-crisis' when it arrived in Europe in 2015 and up to the present day. As Lisa Smirl (2015) made clear in her work on the role of spaces and materials of aid, solutions to perceived problems are shaped by how the problem is framed and understood as well as how those formulating any response think about the 'space' of crisis. With this in mind, the response in Moria was shaped by the framing of the 'crisis' as a *border* crisis first and foremost. The accidental and improvised shelters therefore came to represent the privileging of state security concerns over human security, a failure to address the needs of refugees effectively, a callous disregard for the wellbeing of those seeking shelter in its broadest definition and a purposeful policy of neglect intended to act as a deterrent within a wider system of exclusionary border practices. In short, it reflects shelter as a politically crafted materiality of neglect.

A Brief Genealogy of Moria

Exploring the materialities of refugee shelter in the 'hotspot' of Moria makes visible the processes of what Estella Schindel (2018) has called 'politically crafted suffering' and the EU's either ad hoc or purposefully neglectful approach to 'managing its undesirables' (see Agier 2011). Meanwhile, an uncovering of how Moria came into being highlights a clear symbiosis between the failures of Moria as a space and place of shelter and its material geographies. Additionally, Moria is home to the full range of diversity in refugee shelter, both in material and temporal terms, as it is concurrently a site of high-tech solutions and the informal, and where shelter and the spatial planning of that shelter changes over time.

The site of Moria was an old, abandoned, run-down army base located close to the village of the same name and approximately 10 km from Mytilene, the capital of Lesvos. It emerged in Europe's consciousness as a place of 'shelter' and refugee management in the summer of 2015, having been working as a place of registration for irregular arrivals since 2013. In 2015, however, the temporalities of shelter were very different, as Moria became a registration and screening site for newly arrived refugees on the island, who were expected to leave the island for mainland Greece and beyond. During this period, Lesvos was predominantly a space of transit, where refugees, once registered and 'made visible' statistically and biometrically to the Greek state and the EU more broadly, would use their expulsion orders as a way of exercising their onward mobility to the rest of Europe (Franck 2017).

The original inception of Moria as a registration and transit space is important because of the geographical suitability of the site itself and the dynamics involved in the initial provision of shelter. I have written elsewhere about the mobility of refugees and the role such mobility plays in creating temporally limited spaces of refugee management (Pallister-Wilkins 2018a). This mobility of refugees, combined with Moria's original iteration as a registration point and space of transit serving the border security regime, meant that the use of the former military base, with its clearly defined and walled boundaries and built on the steep slope, was not necessarily unsuitable for the sheltering of registration architectures. After all, the EU border security regime needs to know who has entered EU territory, including their biometric markers, and how they are to be classified (e.g. refugee, migrant, citizen, other). Such a regime requires suitable 'shelter' for the devices that make such a regime possible – computers, mobile databases, satellite uplinks – and suitable places for the security personnel to work. The military base therefore provided a quick solution to the needs of the EU border security regime. It served to register the arrivals on Lesvos of increasing numbers of refugees in the summer of 2015.

Moreover, Moria was not intended as a space of refugee shelter; it was conceived of as a place of registration and transit. Its suitability as a site of shelter and residence was always limited by its geography, which was not at all characterized by flat (or at least flatter) ground, or room to expand, or adequate water and sanitation facilities, which would suit such projects. However, over time and with the introduction of the hotspot approach in combination with the EU-Turkey Statement (which prevented onward mobility from the Aegean islands, hereinafter referred to as the EU-Turkey deal), Moria became a space of residence. The hotspot approach, while predominantly intended as an emergency, border security response, required basic humanitarian assistance, including shelter, and refugees effectively ended up warehoused on Lesvos. However, the changing European political landscape changed Moria from a transit space into a space of residence, altering its shelter needs in turn. The 'chaos' of an informal approach that saw refugees seeking shelter in abandoned display fridges was replaced with a sense of more (material) order. Meanwhile, the temporality of transit that excused the poor quality of shelter in Moria, which was more akin to the short-term liminal tented shelter of the music festival, gave way to something more concrete. However, as the rest of this chapter will show, the extent to which such needs have been actualized have been severely limited by the politics Moria represents and the very geography of the site itself.

Order from Chaos

As hinted at in the introduction, refugee shelter in Moria is and has been diverse. It has ranged from the highly temporary, experimental and ad hoc use of whatever materials can be found around the site, such as fridges, woollen blankets, space blankets, tree branches, items of clothing including ponchos and rain jackets, to prefabricated units housing the architecture of border security that has taken up an apparent permanent presence. In between these two extremes, Moria has seen a range of other types of shelter, including tents of various sizes, designs and suitability. The majority of these shelters have changed over time in reaction to the changing nature of the site and the changing dynamics of emergency. From the initial months of apparent chaos to an attempt at order in line with longstanding practices of refugee camp management, a look at shelter in Moria tells a wider story of many actors involved in governing the space, as well as refugees and other migrants' relationship to the site.

In October 2015, the number of actors present in Moria was visible from the logoization of the space alone (see Franck 2018). Various services were adorned with the logos of well-known humanitarian organizations such as Médecins Sans Frontières (MSF), Médecins du Monde, Action Aid and the

Danish Refugee Council. The presence of the UNHCR was also visible from the use of its branded tarps to make temporary shelters, its plastic mats being used on the floors of the large marquees and its logo appearing on the – at the time – limited number of prefabricated IKEA kit 'houses', with four walls, a door and small windows. Intended for families and single women, these IKEA kit 'houses' still lacked suitable flooring, allowing water to collect on the floor as they were placed on uneven surfaces and rain could seep in at the base of the walls, and there were not enough of them to provide shelter for the numbers of families and single women transiting the space. As well as refugee shelter, Moria also contained a number of run-down derelict buildings, the remains of the army camp. During this time, the overall impression of Moria, in terms of the provision of refugee shelter, was one of chaos. What order there was came in the form of those architectures created to house and facilitate the EU border security regime.

From its inception as a space of refugee management, the flattest part of Moria, and its most substantive architecture, has been used to house the computer systems, generators, AC units and secure communication links required for registration. Further-fenced within the external fences and walls of the hotspot, the security of these border security architectures has been foregrounded from the creation of the space. Therefore, shelter in Moria should not only be conceived as the shelter of refugees, but also as the shelter of logistical systems necessary for their creation as a population to be governed (see Bulley 2014; Newhouse 2015). Moria has therefore always been a place of attempted order in terms of the border security regime, even if there has been 'chaos' in the provision of basic needs, from shelter, to Water, Sanitation, and Hygiene (WASH) facilities, food and medical care.

The border security logic preceded that of human security in Moria from the very beginning. As mentioned above, the crisis was primarily understood as a border crisis rather than a humanitarian crisis, or one in which the needs of displaced people were placed front and centre. It was suggested to me by European politicians, policy-makers and pundits that the provision of basic needs to refugees and migrants constituted a pull factor for those making the journey from Turkey. Within the wider context in which the EU understood and characterized the arrivals of significant numbers of people on the Greek islands, the response was unsurprisingly securitized around upholding the integrity of the border. The needs of refugees and migrants using the spaces created by the border security regime appeared, from the failures in the provision of shelter and other basic humanitarian needs, to have been a secondary concern. However, the presence of international humanitarian organizations in Moria, with long histories of providing order in sites of displacement (see Agier 2011; Pallister-Wilkins 2018b; Redfield 2013; Reid-Henry 2014), carefully carved out a level of architectural and thus governmental order in Moria in the autumn of 2015. Materially, this involved triage tents replaced with prefabricated portacabins and the slow erection of greater numbers of IKEA kit houses.

As the role of the hotspot evolved from one of pure transit to one of residence following the introduction of the EU-Turkey deal, many humanitarian organizations pulled out of the hotspot, and the EU was pushed into the provision not only of border security in the hotspot but also of basic human security focused on longer-term residence. As a result, refugee shelter in Moria slowly developed a more long-term and rationalized aesthetic, accounting for and making better use of its location on a steep slope.

Within the walls of the hotspot itself, the improvised shelters and insecure, large marquees filled with bunk beds have been gradually replaced with multitiered and stacked prefabricated container like shelters that cascade down the steep slope of the site. These stacked, two-storey prefabs run in long terraces along the contours of the site and the second storey is accessible via outside staircases. Solar panels are used for the generation of electricity and some prefabs have AC units. The units are basic, containing beds and sleeping approximately four persons to a unit. In other parts of the hotspot, the IKEA housing remains, but attempts have been made to level the ground on which they sit. Meanwhile, grey Nissen hut-style housing units have also popped up, which results in the hotspot of 2018 offering a range of different forms of rationalized forms of shelter designed to provide longer-term residence and to bring order to the space.

However, all these different units, while suggesting permanence through their use of solid walls, roofs, doors and windows, are still temporary in design and intention. The use of quick-assembly systems made from lightweight materials, while rational and efficient, sit lightly on the landscape and can be as quickly removed as erected. Such units can be either assembled from flatpacks, like the IKEA houses, or transported into the hotspot on the backs of trucks and dropped into position using lifting equipment. In other words, they do not require the digging of foundations, which would alter the physical geography of the site, or the laborious erection of masonry, the remains of which would linger, like the old derelict buildings of the army camp, if and when the hotspot ceased being an emergency response space in a site of 'migratory pressure'.

In addition, the hotspot's internal site has been carved into a range of fenced enclaves, separating different communities of refugees from each other and channelling them around the space in specific, deliberate ways (see Pallister-Wilkins 2016). The highly securitized space of 'Section-B' houses single women and unaccompanied minors, who are in fact eligible for onward travel to mainland Greece under the EU-Turkey deal as recognized 'vulnerable' groups. Meanwhile, the compound of the border security regime remains heavily fortified and the overall impression of the hotspot site today is of a prison as opposed to a refugee camp, due to the abundance of wire, fences, gates and other assorted security architecture such as watchtowers and loudspeakers. This suggests that the securing of migration remains the primary function of the hotspot rather than the provision of a meaningful or comfortable life for the residents. With the foregrounding of state security in the face of migration over that of refugees and migrants, what order there may appear to be in terms of refugee shelter should not overshadow Moria's unsuitability as a site of residence. Indeed, it was never conceived to be a place of residence in the first instance, but a place of registration and transit.

Materialities and Spatialities of Neglect

If an exploration of refugee shelter in Moria shows an attempt at the imposition of order, the governing of space and the provision of humanitarian protection, such an exploration also highlights processes of neglect that have become a common feature of EU approaches to refugee management (see Davies et al. 2017). On 25 November 2016, a woman and a young child died in Moria after a gas canister used to heat a hot plate exploded inside their small nylon tent. Later that same November, three men died of asphyxiation after burning cardboard and small scraps of wood inside the tent they shared. Both incidents were the result of refugees trying to keep warm inside shelters, which were not suitable for the approaching winter weather (MSF 2017).

Both within the walled space of the hotspot itself and outside its perimeter, there have long been improvised shelters made from UNHCR tarps, ropes, tree branches and lightweight camping tents. These improvised shelters pop up in the gaps and small spaces that exist between the slowly developing, permanent-appearing, yet light-touch, portable housing units. Meanwhile, such shelter fills the olive grove to the northeast of the hotspot perimeter and can be seen on satellite images of the site. This space has become known as 'Afghan Hill' and has itself taken on an apparent semi-permanence, even while the shelters that appear there disintegrate in the rain and sun and blow away with the wind.

It is estimated that approximately 2,000 people live in tents and improvised and unheated shelters in and around Moria (Malafeka 2018). The continued use of improvised and dangerous refugee shelter in Moria is the result of the inability of the site to expand in size, flanked as it is on one side by a road and on the other three sides by privately owned olive groves. It is also due to the continued arrival of people to Lesvos even after the EU-Turkey deal and the use of Moria as a semi-carceral space of residence for refugees stuck on the island as a result of this deal. Together, these issues have led to massive overcrowding, where a space originally conceived of as a transit space with a capacity for 3,000 people passing through at any one time has become 'home' for at least 18,000 people in early 2020, with unofficial reports putting the number much higher. The continued use of improvised and unsuitable shelter results in continued protection issues relating to inadequate heating, poor sanitation and risks to public health. Such poor conditions raise particular protection concerns for women and girls, especially in relation to safe access to toilets and showers due to the lack of running water and overall poor sanitation facilities (HRW 2017).

The provision of WASH facilities remains a huge problem. One of the few brick-and-mortar buildings in Moria is the old toilet and shower block of the army barracks. Run down and unsuitable for use when Moria was first opened, the high levels of overcrowding six years on mean that the sanitation and sewage system is unable to cope with the needs of the residents, resulting in raw sewage running through the camp space aided by gravity and the site's location on a steep slope. Amid such abject conditions, questions arise concerning how three years later such conditions can persist, or have been allowed to come into existence, in contradiction of the humanitarian logics of protection that are meant to govern refugee camp management.

Conclusion

In recent years there has been an increased focus on designing, innovating and building the optimum refugee shelter: a range of designs have been exhibited, funded and in some cases erected in various sites of displacement, and most of these shelters share the common features of attempting to mimic or elicit the feeling of 'home' while articulating a temporariness of presence in order to assuage fears of the temporary camps becoming permanent settlements. However, what happens when ideas of impermanence come to structure approaches to shelter in the main? This chapter has attempted to answer these questions through an exploration of the Moria 'Hotspot'. It has examined how the accidental and improvised approach to shelter reflects a politically crafted materiality of neglect and suffering. This neglect and suffering is facilitated through the unsuitability of the initial site and its shift in use from a space of transit to a space of waiting, de facto detention and deportation.

The materialities of suffering in Moria, I have argued, can only be understood as the result of a European approach to migration and border security that privileges the security of the border over the human security and protection needs of migrants. This enactment of neglect is intended as a deterrent within a wider system of exclusionary border practices, which rejects European responsibility under international law and the EU's own fundamental rights framework to shelter refugees within its borders, fostering continued processes of externalization of both responses to migration *and* protection. The thinking behind such policies of neglect rests on the idea that the provision of protection, including safe forms of shelter and basic needs, act as a 'pull-factor' for refugees and migrants who are excluded from accessing similar in their countries or regions of origin. Europe, so the argument goes, must avoid seeming like a soft touch. Such an argument comes to be materially written into and spatially articulated by shelter in the hotspot of Moria.

In terms of rethinking refugee shelter and its role in humanitarian action more broadly, a study of shelter in Moria shows us that technical solutions can never stand in for political solutions or 'fix' what are primarily, first and foremost, political problems (Scott-Smith 2016). It may be possible to design a 'better shelter' like the IKEA better shelter with the right designers and the economic resources to do so, or to build a migration hotspot that meets the basic needs of those seeking shelter and then some. But unless there is political will to shelter refugees, migrants and others that extends beyond designing a better shelter, then such better shelters cannot meet the needs of those displaced, as the tent, container or kit house will lack the necessary sociopolitical infrastructure to ensure that the wide-ranging shelter needs of the displaced are met.

Polly Pallister-Wilkins is a senior lecturer in politics at the University of Amsterdam and Scientific Collaborator at L'Université Libre de Bruxelles. She has been researching humanitarianism in Greece's borderlands since 2012 and is a principal investigator in the Horizon2020 ADMIGOV project examining humanitarian protection in response to border violence.

References

Agier, M. 2011. *Managing the Undesirables: Refugee Camps and Humanitarian Government.* London: Polity Press.
Bulley, D. 2014. 'Inside the Tent: Community and Government in Refugee Camps'. *Security Dialogue* 45(1): 63–80.
Davies, T, A. Isakjee and S. Dhesi. 2017. 'Violent Inaction: The Necropolitical Experience of Refugees in Europe'. *Antipode* 49(5): 1263–84.
Franck, A.K. 2017. 'Im/Mobility and Deportability in Transit: Lesvos Island, Greece'. *Tijdschrift voor Economische en Sociale Geografie* 108(6): 879–84.
———. 2018. 'The Lesvos Refugee Crisis as Disaster Capitalism'. *Peace Review* 30(2): 199–205.
HRW. 2017. 'Greece: Dire Risks for Women Asylum Seekers'. Retrieved 13 October 2019 from https://www.hrw.org/news/2017/12/15/greece-dire-risks-women-asylum-seekers.

Malafeka, M. 2018. 'Moria Refugee Camp: Restriction of Movement and Living Conditions'. *Border Criminologies*. Retrieved 13 October 2019 from https://www.law.ox.ac.uk/research-subject-groups/centre-criminology/centreborder-criminologies/blog/2018/04/moria-refugee.

MSF. 2017. *One Year on from the EU-Turkey Deal: Challenging the EU's Alternative Facts*. Retrieved 21 January 2019 from http://www.msf.org/sites/msf.org/files/one_year_on_from_the_eu-turkey_deal.pdf.

Newhouse, L. 2015. 'More than Mere Survival: Violence, Humanitarian Governance, and Practical Material Politics in a Kenyan Refugee Camp', *Environment and Planning A: Economy and Space* 47(11): 2292–307.

Pallister-Wilkins, P. 2016. 'How Walls Do Work: Security Barriers as Devices of Interruption and Data Capture'. *Security Dialogue* 47(2): 151–64.

———. 2018a. 'Médecins Avec Frontières and the Making of a Humanitarian Borderscape'. *Environment and Planning D: Society & Space* 36(1): 114–38.

———. 2018b. 'Hotspots and the Geographies of Humanitarianism'. *Environment and PlanningD:Society&Space. OnlineFirst*:https://doi.org/10.1177/0263775818754884.

Redfield, P. 2013. *Life in Crisis: The Ethical Journey of Doctors without Borders*. Berkeley: University of California Press.

Reid-Henry, S.M. 2014. 'Humanitarianism as Liberal Diagnostic: Humanitarian Reason and the Political Rationalities of the Liberal Will-to-Care', *Transactions of the Institute of British Geographers* 39(3): 418–31.

Schindel, E. 2018. 'Border Deaths Conference'. Vrije Universiteit Amsterdam, Amsterdam, 14 June.

Scott-Smith, T. 2016. 'Humanitarian Neophilia: The "Innovation Turn" and Its Implications'. *Third World Quarterly* 37(12): 2229–51.

———. 2018. 'A Slightly Better Shelter?' *Limn* 9: 67–73.

Smirl, L. 2015. *Spaces of Aid: How Cars, Compounds and Hotels Shape Humanitarianism*. London: Zed Books.

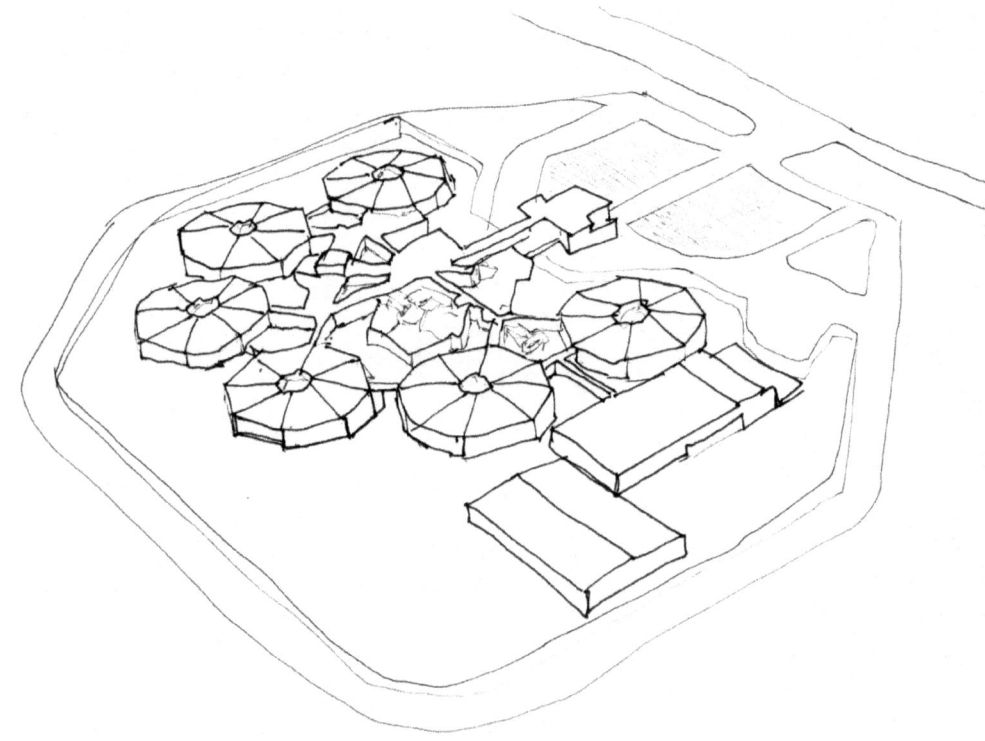

Figure 6.1 Central East Correctional Centre in Ontario, Canada.
© Mark E. Breeze, based on an image supplied by Petra Molnar.

6

Architectures of Trauma
Forced Shelter and Immigration Detention

Petra Molnar

Elizabeth sits perched on the edge of an uncomfortable plastic chair, jumping up at every robotic announcement barking over the tinny announcement system: 'Santiago, Room 9', 'Okafor, report at the reception window'. Her three children, all under the age of five, sit quietly at her feet, crying occasionally as the wait stretches longer and longer.

Elizabeth is at a Canadian Border Services Agency (CBSA) check-in facility. She is seeking protection in Canada, after escaping her violent ex-husband who repeatedly sexually assaulted her and then kidnapped her eldest son to try and force her to come back to him. Elizabeth is waiting on the decision for her application for permanent residence on humanitarian and compassionate grounds, yet she is still reliving the trauma of having been detained upon arrival at the Canadian border, separated from her children for weeks, before she was connected with a lawyer and a support community and was told to apply for asylum.

'Every visit is like a new knife to the heart: Will we be detained again? What will happen to my children? Why am I being punished for wanting to keep my family safe and give my children a new life in Canada? I haven't done anything wrong . . .'[1]

As this vignette demonstrates, the Canadian immigration detention regime is rife with violence. Detainees are frequently separated from their families, denied access to counsel, faced with the prospect of having their children taken away and segregated in far-flung locations with little access to medical care and psychosocial supports (Silverman and Molnar 2016). At least sixteen people have died in Canadian detention since 2000, and immigration detention in Canada is highly racialized and gendered (Molnar and Silverman 2018a, 2018b).

While the separation of thousands of children from their parents at the US–Mexico border has rightly dominated public discourse (American Civil Liberties Union 2018), Canada also has its own immigration detention that perpetuates trauma. People like Elizabeth and her children experience the ramification of this carceral system daily. The spectre of detention looms large over every decision and interaction they have with the Canadian immigration bureaucracy, from the first interaction at a port of entry or immigration office to the end of the road when trying to prevent deportation. Detention in Canada functions in the shadows, relegated to windowless rooms at the airport or to Immigration Holding Centres (IHCs), which eerily try to blend in as forgettable downtown buildings that you pass by without a second look. Immigration detention is a form of forced shelter, in which detainees are also housed in wings of maximum-security provincial jails, comingling with convicts and forced to wear orange jumpsuits that further link them with presumed criminality (American Civil Liberties Union 2018).

Detention can be indefinite in Canada.[2] Unlike other countries, Canada does not have statutory time limits controlling how long a person can languish in immigration detention. When a migrant lives in detention for years at a time without the prospect of freedom, detention becomes both impermanent and permanent at the same time: always threatening deportation while bureaucratically languishing behind bars for years. The psychosocial impacts of this process reach deeply into communities. Detention impacts thousands, if not tens of thousands, of family and community members (Global Detention Project 2018). When men are detained, they are often separated from their family and children for prolonged periods, resulting in loss of income, support, and housing for the family. Family members waiting for the release of their loved ones are further harmed by having to endure harsh visiting conditions. Children are also harmed across axes of dependency, abuse, insecurity, poverty, racialization, discrimination, stigma, and physical and emotional violence (Gros and Song 2017). Detention can occur in cycles, with migrants detained and redetained during the course of years, which disrupts migrants' ability to find permanent shelter or housing and leaves them vulnerable to further trauma with every new prospect of being detained.

In this chapter, I expand the concept of shelter to include sites of incarceration in Canada's immigration detention system, arguing that detention functions as a form of 'forced shelter', moving migrants away from the general population, limiting their freedoms and choices, and exacerbating their trauma. I argue that incarcerating migrants behind bars in far-flung locations amounts to geographical segregation, and the architecture of detention highlights both the symbolic and real conflation between administrative detention and criminality (Mountz et al. 2013). Drawing on theoretical insights concerning access to justice in immigration detention, carceral and legal architecture, and its impacts on psychosocial wellbeing, as well as examples from practice when representing immigration detainees and visiting detention centres in Canada, this chapter will highlight the lived experiences of detainees and how they cope in a system where shelter and trauma coexist on a daily basis.

Hidden from View: Detention in Canada

Immigration detention is a form of administrative incarceration. The people who are being held have not committed a crime under Canada's Criminal Code. Instead, they are being detained for immigration infractions under the Immigration and Refugee Protection Act (IRPA),[3] the statute that governs Canada's immigration and refugee system, and the accompanying Immigrations and Refugee Protections Regulations (IRPR). As with most facets of immigration law, detention is highly discretionary and opaque, with many procedures hidden away from the public eye.[4] Exact numbers and statistics are often difficult to come by; however, in 2017, Canada detained 7,215 individuals (Molnar and Silverman 2018a).

Detainees are mostly housed in IHCs, with multiple facilities in Toronto, Montreal and Vancouver, Canada's major urban hubs. IHCs are akin to medium security prisons, fenced with razor wire, surrounded by cameras and uniformed guards who regulate limited daily leisure activities. Detainees do not have access to the internet and have to relinquish their mobile phones upon arrival (Silverman and Molnar 2016). IHCs separate fathers from their children, who remain with their mother in detention. Families are able to occasionally visit, but the practice of detaining children at all has been widely criticized (Gros and Song 2017).

Over 3,000 detainees have also been housed in provincial facilities (Silverman 2013), including maximum-security prisons, with nearly 1,500 nonviolent immigration detainees locked up in the most restrictive conditions possible in 2018 (Kennedy 2019). Their existence here is even more securitized. Detainees relinquish their street clothes for bright orange jumpsuits and while they are relegated to one specific wing for 'immigration cases', they comingle with the rest of the prison population in the mess hall, hallways and courtyards. Cleveland and Sousseau (2013) show that such overt criminalization has profound mental health issues on detainees, not to mention access to justice issues (Silverman and Molnar 2016). Preparing for refugee hearings or other types of applications for protection and status is incredibly difficult due to the geographical segregation of provincial facilities, many hours away from urban centres, and hence far away from the majority of lawyers (Silverman and Molnar 2016). Gathering evidence, taking testimony and bringing in mental health professionals for Post-Traumatic Stress Disorder (PTSD) assessments is incredibly difficult, and detainees are cut off from their communities of support. There are no counselling supports inside the prisons for immigration detainees (Nakache 2012) and many people report that their mental health significantly worsens during their time in detention, with reverberations felt for years after release (Gros and van Groll 2015).

Immigration in Canada can also be indefinite. While the law does mandate that detention be reviewed at predetermined intervals,[5] there is no upper time limit. Some detainees have languished in maximum-security prison for more than nine years (Black 2015), often without access to counsel or other psychosocial support (Silverman and Molnar 2016). Detainees can be trapped in a cycle of cursory detention reviews, which in effect become a rubber-stamp process when they cannot provide new evidence to assist in their release. However, detention does not have to be indefinite to be harmful. Psychiatrists have documented that even a brief period in immigration detention results in lasting symptoms of posttraumatic stress, anxiety and depression (Cleveland and Rousseau 2013). It is the very architecture of Canada's immigration detention regime that is violent and that exacerbates suffering and trauma of this vulnerable group.

Unlike the deprivation of liberty in the criminal justice context, with delineated rights and responsibilities of the state to provide defence counsel and bail, the legal architecture of immigration detention is governed by opaque and discretionary policies and norms in the realm of administrative law. It is presided over by tribunals and decision-makers who make decisions without oversight and with limited appeal procedures. Immigration detention departs from the central norms and ethics animating liberal political communities. It is extrajudicial in almost every way, with few oversights and rights protections. No warrants are needed to arrest an immigration detainee, and often no bail hearings or readings of rights are provided (Silverman and Nethery 2015). Detention operates with virtual impunity in every state around the world.

International human rights law clearly stipulates that lawful immigration detention should be nonpunitive, nonarbitrary and not applicable to vulnerable persons.[6] Like other modes of incarceration, detention should be a measure of last resort. Noncustodial measures – such as bail, sureties, community supervision or reporting mechanisms – should be considered, weighed up and ruled against before making the decision to incarcerate a noncitizen for migration-related reasons. At least in theory, there should be a presumption against immigration detention unless absolutely necessary. However, in reality, detention is cemented into worldwide immigration, asylum and border control apparatuses to a dangerous degree.

'The Slow Death': Intersecting Vulnerabilities on the Frontlines

> On a sunny Tuesday at the office, Elizabeth drifts in an out of her thoughts. She is preparing for another visit to CBSA. Every month, a new one-page paper arrives in the mail, summoning Elizabeth and her three children to check in with an officer to determine if they are allowed to stay in Canada until she receives a final decision for permanent residence on humanitarian and compassionate grounds. She can be redetained at any one of these visits. Elizabeth dreads the skinny envelope because she now knows very well what is involved: piling all her children onto the bus at 7 a.m. and taking the 1.5 hour journey to the suburbs of west Toronto, so she can sit for hours in the sterile waiting room which acts as a strange type of meeting place for people from all over the globe, exchanging knowing glances, or looking down and avoiding eye contact when someone does not return to the main lobby after their interview.

> 'This happened to me', Elizabeth whispers. 'When I was taken into one of these rooms, I didn't come out. They put me in shackles, and for what? I don't know. This whole system is a mystery to me. They hold so much power over us and every new appointment is an opportunity to break me further. I can't sleep, I can't eat. Is this all worth it? I don't know anymore . . .'

Despite maintaining a relatively low public profile[7] until recently, people with precarious or otherwise irregular immigration status are highly aware of detention and its impacts. Indeed, it is an ever-present shadow in their lives, one that causes anxiety, PTSD and other mental health issues. Each interaction with Canada's detention apparatus causes these symptoms to resurface. It is this opaque yet ever-present dimension of immigration detention that is extremely damaging (de Zayas 2005; see also Silverman 2014). The majority of asylum seekers must routinely visit a CBSA office as they await word on their protection claims. The threat of arrest and incarceration underwrites each visit. For people like Elizabeth, this means that each visit is laden with trauma, anxiety, and fear of being stigmatized and punished. It also means harm to their children, who watch their caretaker suffer by prolonged exposure to stress and traumatization, often being unable to engage in their parenting and caretaking duties. After each visit, Elizabeth needs about a week to recover, often misses work and is late to pick up her children from school as she relives the trauma of interacting with Canada's immigration detention apparatus.

Incarceration in the criminal justice system also presents significant harms and traumas. However, the inherent time limit of criminal incarceration separates it from the amorphous open-ended nature of immigration detention. The literature on trauma shows that events without resolutions, which create a situation of limbo, are the most damaging to mental health (Alvarez and Alegria 2016; Collier 2015; Suárez-Orozco et al. 2010). A person stuck in an endless cycle of detention is not able to heal and move on with their life in a meaningful way (Rinaldi and Shah 2017). They are constantly reminded of the possibility of being placed in detention, separated from their family and eventually removed from Canada. Moreover, the threat of deportation to a place of persecution and torture has extreme effects – numerous immigration detainees in Canada have committed suicide while in detention. In recent years, these deaths have included women like Lucia Vega Jimenez, who hanged herself in an airport holding cell on the eve of her deportation to Mexico (Woo 2018) and Teresa Gratton (Kennedy 2017), who was held in a maximum-security prison without charge and the details around whose death remain opaque.

While the violence of the lived experiences in immigration detention has damaging and life threatening repercussions, detention reverberates far outside the walls of the holding cells and prisons. Newcomer communities are affected when family members are incarcerated, when families are separated and when livelihoods are disrupted (Molnar and Silverman 2018b). Immigration detention and its ever-present threats haunt communities, damaging family dynamics and shredding the social fabric of marginalized groups. Similar effects on have been documented in the impact of ongoing police violence on Black communities in the United States and Brazil, showing that in addition to the direct deaths caused, family members are also killed slowly through prolonged exposure to state-induced trauma, pain and loss (see e.g. Smith 2016). As such, immigration detention should be thought of as a social determinant of health, which has negative repercussions on a person's wellbeing that extend long after release and even formal status to remain in Canada.

Punishment as Daily Existence: Symbolic Power of the Criminalization of Migration

> Elizabeth often cries. Sometimes she does so discreetly, wiping her tears on her sleeve as she turns away, at other times weeping openly. Any mention of her time in detention has the effect of reducing her to tears. For Elizabeth, it is the hot shame of being seen as a criminal that stays with her, the injustice of being treated as a convict when all she wanted to do was escape a violent situation to a place of safety.

Regardless of how many conversations about the legality of the system she has had, Elizabeth staunchly believes that she was treated unfairly: 'I am not a criminal. So why was I behind bars, watched over by guards, unable to leave? Let me leave. Why would I hide or do something bad if I came here to seek protection and rebuild my life?'

The criminalization of migration is on the rise globally. As nation states all over the world seek to control, manage, detain and deport migrants, equating them with criminals is a powerful way to justify increasingly hardline policies of exclusion (see e.g. Atak and Simeon 2018). By creating increasingly harsher ways of detaining migrants or, as in the case of the United States, by taking away their children, the state is signalling to others who may be coming that they had better think twice, lest they wish to end up in prison. However, using immigration detention as a deterrent to claiming asylum is contrary to international law (Sampson 2015). Detention as deterrent is also ineffective (Silverman and Lewis 2017), as people will continue to arrive due to ongoing conflicts and unstable situations.

The criminalization of migration also weakens the procedural safeguards that are already less robust than in the criminal justice system. For example, immigration detainees do not have an automatic right to counsel, bail or even internet access as they prepare for their detention reviews and refugee claims (Silverman and Molnar 2016). Immigration and refugee decisions often have incredibly high stakes for people's lives, risking death or torture, prolonged family separation or lifelong traumatization. Sometimes migrants are also presented with a false choice: either continue living without status on the edges of society, unable to access social services, attend schooling or work legally, or make yourself known to CBSA and risk detention as you file your refugee claim or deportation as you file your discretionary application for immigration status.[8]

The tendrils of criminalization extend far beyond the walls of prisons. Sometimes the messaging of the state is in plain view: immigration detainees housed in provincial prisons wear the same jumpsuits as convicts and often arrive in shackles at their refugee hearings.[9] This overt link to symbols of criminality negatively prejudices the adjudicator and further entrenches the idea that a person in immigration detention should be presupposed to be criminal until proven otherwise (see also Evans Cameron 2018). The expansion of presumed criminality further permeates people's lived reality even as they navigate their interactions with the detention apparatus after release. People like Elizabeth often report feelings of shame and embarrassment for having to continually return for check-ins with CBSA or even for being detained in the first place. Proposed alternatives such as introducing electronic monitoring bracelets only work to further stigmatize migrants, so much that when a group of five men who were held in detention under

Canada's security certificate regime were given the option to wear the bracelets instead of being detained, they found the process so onerous and traumatic for them and their families that they all chose to return to detention (Silverman and Molnar 2016).

Ultimately, the Canadian state relies on the symbolic capital of its detention apparatus to instil fear, acting as a spectacle (Mainwaring and Silverman 2017). This is how forced shelter works in practice: not just negatively affecting the lives subjected to immigration detention, but also signalling policies on deterrence, border enforcement and immigration as a whole. Some migrants (such as economic investors) are welcome with open arms into the polity, while others are only expedient when they are able to win public sympathy and votes (Molnar 2016).[10] Detention is allowed to operate largely out of the public eye with little oversight, while risking violations to people's lives, liberties and freedoms under the guise of national security and migration management. This system is incredibly costly in financial terms, averaging nearly CAD$300 a day (Minsky 2015), but also in social terms: traumatizing a large swath of the newcomer population has lasting repercussions on social cohesion, prosperity and future outcomes for children. Immigration detention is an unjustly punitive system against a population that has not committed a crime.

Conclusions: Carceral Violence of Canada's Immigration Detention

> Elizabeth and her children continue to wait for the outcome of their refugee claim. It is unclear how long this decision will take, so for now, they are living in limbo. The children have made friends, and are beginning to adjust to life in Canada. Elizabeth is having a harder time, isolated from friends and family back home, alone with three small children. She has filled her home with bright light and colour, in stark contrast to the grey-on-grey concrete in immigration detention: 'This way, I keep the dark thoughts at bay'.

> Elizabeth's time in immigration detention continues to haunt her. Every time she sees a police car or there is a forceful knock at her door, her heart jumps into her throat and her knees go weak. Ever her children have taken note, cowering when they spy a police cruiser. Unlike other children who wave at uniformed officers, for Elizabeth's children, they are a visceral reminder of their mother being ripped away from them, left alone in a strange land. A land which presents itself as welcoming to migrants, yet not welcoming everyone equally.

The impact of forced shelter extends far beyond the period of incarceration in immigration detention. In Canada, thousands of people are affected every year, detained in holding centres or provincial prisons, facing prolonged family separation, retraumatization and limbo, sometimes for years after their incarceration. Detention is also not reserved for new arrivals like Elizabeth. People who have been in the country for decades can be detained and threatened with deportation even if they have no other place to go or their country of origin will not take them. This can lead to immigration detention over months and years. In some cases, immigration detention is a shelter by no other choice – a shelter for people who have fled their homes to Canada, but are not allowed to leave, yet not allowed to stay.

The lasting traumatic experiences of people like Elizabeth highlight the far-reaching repercussions of immigration detention. While the sheer scale of the problem may differ from jurisdiction to jurisdiction, incarcerating migrants exacerbates the trauma of an already highly vulnerable population. Detention separates families, weakens procedural safeguards, makes preparing for status determinations very difficult, and segregates a subset of the newcomers population away from psychosocial and community supports. It is a violent system without oversight mechanisms, time limits and safeguards for vulnerable populations such as children, pregnant women and people with mental health issues. International law and norms dictate that immigration detention should be used as the absolute last resort. Yet globally, this is clearly not the case. The legal and physical architectures of immigration detention highlight the moral and legal failures of an international migration management system that detains migrants as if they are criminals. Criminalizing migrants and imposing sanctions such as the deprivation of liberty works against the presumption that people should be fully able to exercise their right to claim asylum.[11] Forcibly sheltering detainees only exacerbates their inability to exercise their rights, without access to counsel and community support to assist them in fully participating in presenting their case and having a fair chance for asylum and status.

'Forced' shelter may seem like an oxymoron, as shelter usually evokes ideas of protection and safety. Yet with the tantalizing promise of eventually attaining permanent immigration status, the incarceration of migrants shows that often there is no other choice than succumbing to the state's mechanism of control with the hope of surviving the period of sheltering. It also creates a coercive false choice: with few safeguards, opaque policies and violent rights-infringing mechanisms, detention forces people to choose between freedom from incarceration and their right to seek protection under international and domestic refugee law. Nowhere is this dichotomy clearer than the incarceration of migrants and the systematic separation of children in the U.S./Mexico detention regime, used as a deterrent to prevent people from exercising their right to seek asylum. An even more extreme example is the forced sheltering of migrants in offshore detention camps on Nauru and Christmas Island off the coast of Australia far from public oversight, or the sites of extreme violence, human trafficking and slavery endemic in Libyan detention facilities.

With global migration numbers on the rise, immigration detention presents a clear example of how traumatic architecture can create instances of forced shelter. Instead of upholding systems of forced shelter that are violent, punitive and extremely costly, states should critically examine their commitments to basic human rights principles in light of their own actions as perpetrators of violence and trauma on newly arrived people seeking safety and protection. Only then will it be possible to return to the concept of shelter-as-safety instead of shelter-as-trauma.

Petra Molnar is a lawyer and researcher specializing in immigration and human rights. Since 2013, she has been writing on immigration detention in Canada and internationally. She holds a Juris Doctorate from the University of Toronto and an LL.M. specializing in international law from the University of Cambridge.

Notes

1. Vignette based on a real case seen in practice by the author. Names and identifying features have been changed to protect the identity of the client and her family, but the story remains true and is shared with 'Elizabeth's' permission.
2. The lack of upper time limits on detention in Canada compares poorly with thresholds in other countries of destination across Europe, including Ireland (thirty days), France (thirty-two days), Spain (forty days) and Italy (sixty days). When contextualized with other states that receive a high number of immigrants and asylum seekers annually and that lack upper limits on time spent in immigration detention, the shortcoming of contestation in Canada is notable.
3. Immigration detention is governed by sections 54–61 of the IRPA and in sections 244–250 of the IRPR.
4. Such as the practice of placing detainees in solitary confinement or why a detainee may be transferred from one detention facility to the next.
5. Section 57(1) and (2) of the IRPA.
6. See Amnesty International UK 2017: for example, International Covenant on Civil and Political Rights (ICCPR), Art. 9(1); Universal Declaration of Human Rights (UDHR), Arts. 3, 7, 9; HRC General Comment 35; General Assembly Body of Principles, Principle 2; European Convention on Human Rights (ECHR), Art. 5(1); Refugee Convention, Art. 31; Migrant Worker Convention, Art. 16(1); Declaration on the Human Rights of Individuals Who Are Not Nationals of the Country in Which They Live, A/RES/40/144, Art. 5(1)(a); African (Banjul) Charter on Human and Peoples' Rights OAU Doc. CAB/LEG/67/3 rev. 5, 21 I.L.M. 58, Art. 6; American Convention on Human Rights, Art. 7(1); American Declaration on the Rights and Duties of Man, Art. 1; Arab Charter on Human Rights, Art. 14; United Nations High Commissioner for Refugees (UNHCR) Detention Guidelines, Introduction.

7. See, for example, the exposé first published by the *Toronto Star* in a series of articles: https://www.thestar.com/projects/short/2017/03/17/caged-by-canada.html (retrieved 14 October 2019).
8. For example, for humanitarian and compassionate applications, there is no statutory stay of removal, or the ability to remain in the country while the application is decided; these are governed by section 25 of the IRPA and are the discretionary applications of last resort for many refused refugee claimants or people with precarious status in Canada.
9. While there are no publicly available guidelines regarding the shackling of claimants at their refugee hearings, it is a phenomenon often seen in practice, one to which many refugee counsel take very strong opposition and seek to have their client released so they can have the opportunity to change into more comfortable clothing before being seen by the adjudicator of their claim. This works against the stigmatization of the refugee claimant, while also making them more comfortable during difficult testimony.
10. Such as in the case of the resettlement of 35,000 Syrian refugees, an election issue that may have contributed to the victory of the current Trudeau Administration.
11. As enshrined in UN General Assembly, *Convention Relating to the Status of Refugees*, imported into Canadian domestic legislation through sections 96 and 97 of the IRPA.

References

Alvarez, K., and M. Alegría. 2016. 'Understanding and Addressing the Needs of Unaccompanied Immigrant Minors'. *American Psychological Association*, June. Retrieved 14 October 2019 from http://www.apa.org/pi/families/resources/newsletter/2016/06/immigrant-minors.aspx.

American Civil Liberties Union (ACLU). 2018. 'Immigrants' Rights and Detention'. Retrieved 14 October 2019 from https://www.aclu.org/issues/immigrants-rights/immigrants-rights-and-detention.

Amnesty International UK. 2017. 'A Matter of Routine: The Use of Immigration Detention in the UK', 14 December. Retrieved 14 October 2019 from https://www.amnesty.org.uk/node/53550.

Atak, A., and J. Simeon. 2018. *The Criminalization of Migration: Context and Consequences*. Montreal: McGill-Queens University Press.

Black, D. 2015. 'Canada Border Services Agency Confirms Identity for "Man with No Name"'. *Toronto Star*, 22 August. Retrieved 14 October 2019 from https://www.thestar.com/news/immigration/2015/08/22/canada-border-services-agency-confirms-identity-for-man-with-no-name.html.

Cleveland, J., and C. Rousseau. 2013. 'Psychiatric Symptoms Associated with Brief Detention of Adult Asylum Seekers in Canada'. *Canadian Journal of Psychiatry* 58(7): 409–16.

Collier, L. 2015. 'Helping Immigrant Children Heal'. *Monitor on Psychology* 46: 58. Retrieved 14 October 2019 from http://www.apa.org/monitor/2015/03/immigrant-children.aspx.

De Zayas, A. 2005. 'Human Rights and Indefinite Detention'. *International Review of the Red Cross* 87(857): 15–38.

Evans Cameron, H. 2018. *Refugee Law's Fact Finding Crisis: Truth, Risk, and the Wrong Mistake*. Cambridge: Cambridge University Press.

Global Detention Project. 2018. 'Canada Immigration Detention'. Retrieved 14 October 2019 from https://www.globaldetentionproject.org/countries/americas/canada.

Gros, H., and Y. Song. 2017. 'Invisible Citizens: Canadian Children in Immigration Detention'. International Human Rights Program, University of Toronto Faculty of Law Reports. Retrieved 14 October 2019 from https://ihrp.law.utoronto.ca/page/working-group-and-clinic-reports/invisible-citizens.

Gros, H., and P. van Groll. 2015. '"We Have No Rights": Arbitrary Imprisonment and Cruel Treatment of Migrants with Mental Health Issues in Canada'. International Human Rights Program, University of Toronto Faculty of Law Reports. Retrieved 14 October 2019 from http://ihrp.law.utoronto.ca/We_Have_No_Rights.

Immigration and Refugee Protection Act, SC 2001, c 27. Retrieved 14 October 2019 from http://canlii.ca/t/529s2.

Immigration and Refugee Protection Regulations, SOR/2002-227. Retrieved 14 October 2019 from http://canlii.ca/t/529xj.

Kennedy, B. 2017. 'Held in Maximum Security without Charge, She Begged Her Husband to Get Her out. A Week Later, Teresa Gratton Was Dead'. *Toronto Star*, 16 December. Retrieved 14 October 2019 from https://www.thestar.com/news/investigations/2017/12/16/held-in-maximum-security-without-charge-she-begged-her-husband-to-get-her-out-a-week-later-teresa-gratton-was-dead.html.

———. 2019. 'Hundreds of Nonviolent Immigration Detainees Sent to Max-security Jails as Part of "Abhorrent" Government Program'. *Toronto Star*, 24 January. Retrieved 14 October 2019 from https://www.thestar.com/news/investigations/2019/01/24/hundreds-of-nonviolent-immigration-detainees-sent-to-max-security-jails-as-part-of-abhorrent-government-program.html.

Kronick, R., C. Rousseau and J. Cleveland. 2011. 'Mandatory Detention of Refugee Children: A Public Health Issue?' *Paediatric Child Health* 16(8): 65–67.

Mainwaring, C., and S. Silverman. 2017. 'Detention-as-Spectacle'. *International Political Sociology* 11(1): 21–38.

Minsky, A. 2015. 'Feds Spend $265M over 5 Years on Controversial Detainee Program: Documents'. *Toronto Star*, 24 June. Retrieved 14 October 2019 from https://globalnews.ca/news/2070097/feds-spend-265m-over-5-years-on-controversial-detainee-program-documents.

Molnar, P. 2016. '"The Boy on the Beach": The Fragility of Canada's Discourses on the Syrian Refugee "Crisis"'. *Contention Journal: Civil Society and Uncivil Times* 4(1–2): 67–75.

Molnar, P., and S. Silverman. 2018a. 'Canada Needs to Get out of the Immigration Detention Business'. *CBC News*, 5 July. Retrieved 14 October 2019 from https://www.cbc.ca/news/opinion/immigration-detention-1.4733897.

———. 2018b. 'How Canada's Immigration Detention System Spurs Violence against Women'. *The Conversation*, 15 April. Retrieved 14 October 2019 from https://

theconversation.com/how-canadas-immigration-detention-system-spurs-violen
ce-against-women-95009.
Mountz, A., K. Coddington, T. Catania and J. Loyd. 2013. 'Conceptualizing Detention: Mobility, Containment, Bordering, and Exclusion'. *Progress in Human Geography* 37(4): 522–41.
Nakache, D. 2012. *The Human and Financial Cost of Detention of Asylum-Seekers in Canada*. Geneva: United Nations High Commissioner for Refugees.
Rinaldi, T., and A. Shah. 2017. 'Immigration Limbo is a "Tug of Emotions": It's Also a Mental Health Issue'. *Public Radio International's The World*, 22 August. Retrieved 14 October 2019 from https://www.pri.org/stories/2017-08-21/imm igration-limbo-tug-emotions-it-s-also-mental-health-issue.
Sampson, R. 2015. 'Does Detention Deter?' *IDC Working Papers*. Sydney: International Detention Coalition. Retrieved 9 December 2019 from https://idcoalition.org/wp-content/uploads/2015/04/Briefing-Paper_Does-Detention-Deter_April-2015-A4_web.pdf.
Sanchez, R., S, Jones, D. Alsup and K. Allen. 2018. 'The Chill of Detention: Migrants Describe Their Experiences in US Custody'. *CNN*, 7 July. Retrieved 14 October 2019 from https://www.cnn.com/2018/07/07/us/separated-families-de tention-conditions/index.html.
Silverman, S. 2013. 'Detention and Asylum in Canada and Abroad', in J. Hyndman and D. Nakache (eds), *Detention and Asylum Research Cluster Working Papers*, 2013.
———. 2014. 'In the Wake of Irregular Arrivals: Changes to the Canadian Immigration Detention System'. *Refuge* 30(2): 27–34.
Silverman, S., and B. Lewis. 2017. 'Families in US Immigration Detention: What Does It Mean to Do "the Right Thing"?' *Contemporary Readings in Law and Social Justice* 9(2): 95–115.
Silverman, S., and P. Molnar. 2016. 'Everyday Injustices: Barriers to Access to Justice for Immigration Detainees in Canada'. *Refugee Survey Quarterly* 35(1): 109–27.
Silverman, S., and A. Nethery. 2015. 'Understanding Immigration Detention and Its Human Impact', in A. Nethery and S.J. Silverman (eds), *Immigration Detention: The Journey of a Policy and its Human Impact*. London: Routledge, pp. 1–12.
Smith, C. 2016. 'Facing the Dragon: Black Mothers, Gendered Necropolitics, Anti-Black Violence and Radical Refusal in the Americas'. *Transforming Anthropology* 24(1): 31–48.
Suárez-Orozco, C., H.J. Bang and H.Y. Kim. 2010. 'I Felt Like My Heart Was Staying Behind: Psychological Implications of Family Separations & Reunifications for Immigrant Youth'. *Journal of Adolescent Research* 26(2): 222–57.
UN General Assembly. 1951. Convention Relating to the Status of Refugees, 28 July 1951, United Nations, Treaty Series, vol. 189, p. 137.
Woo, A. 2018. 'Woman Who Died in CBSA Custody Feared Returning to Domestic Trouble in Mexico'. *Globe and Mail*, 11 May. Retrieved 14 October 2019 from https://www.theglobeandmail.com/news/british-columbia/woman-who-died-in-cbsa-custody-feared-returning-to-domestic-trouble-in-mexico/article16644691.

Figure 7.1 Holot Residence Centre and the Negev Desert, Israel.
© Mark E. Breeze, based on an image supplied by Renana Ne'eman.

7

Settling the Unsettled
Forced Shelter in the Negev Desert

Renana Ne'eman

Since December 2013, Israel has sent thousands of African asylum seekers for a one-year detention in Holot Residence Centre (hereinafter Holot), an open detention facility located in the midst of a closed military zone on the outskirts of the Negev Desert. It operated for over four years, until a failed attempt to deport the detainees led to its closure in March 2018 (Zur 2018). The facility was defined as 'open', since the detainees were permitted to leave in the morning and return by night, yet its isolated location in a remote part of the Negev Desert severely restricted the detainees' freedom of movement. In fact, Holot's location in the Negev dramatically transformed it from an open residence facility into a de facto prison. Considering Israel's explanation that the main purpose of Holot is to prevent the settling of asylum seekers in cities, the decision to locate it in the Negev Desert is of great significance. Holot's location also signifies a change in the Zionist mythos of the Negev as a place of redemption to the Jewish people, a vision that was manifested over the years in many state projects.

Holot (חולות), which in Hebrew means 'sand dunes', represents a transformation in Israel's relationship to the desert and provides an insight into Israel's history and ideology of settlement and displacement of populations in the Negev. Following the state's longstanding failure to materialize the Zionist vision to 'tame' and 'civilize' the Negev through Jewish settlements, Holot has recast the Negev as a place of banishment. The Negev, I argue, is no longer a locus for civilization, but has been transformed into a place of exile. This contextualization of place and purpose, I conclude, has lasting significance in the way that we examine refugee shelter and detention more generally.

Holot Residence Centre

Between 2006 and 2013, Israel was a major destination country for asylum seekers, primarily from Eritrea, Sudan and Darfur (Paz 2011). Thousands of asylum seekers crossed the Sinai Desert and entered Israel through its southern border with Egypt, hoping for protection. The journey to Israel was a perilous one; many were held in torture camps, where they were beaten, enslaved and sexually assaulted by Bedouin traffickers who were seeking to extort ransoms from their families (Paz 2011). Those who took these risks hoped to receive assistance, support and protection from Israel, a country they perceived as a democracy that protects and respects human rights.

The legal status of asylum seekers in Israel is regulated under the amendment to the Anti-Infiltration Law (1954), which was originally written to secure Israel's borders from infiltration by Palestinian fedayeen.[1] The law defines an infiltrator as an individual who entered Israel 'illegally', i.e. not through a formal border station. African asylum seekers who enter the country irregularly through Israel's southern border with Egypt are therefore classified as 'infiltrators' and according to numbers provided by Israel's Population and Immigration Authority, there are currently 32,604 'infiltrators' in Israel. A total of 71 per cent of these are Eritreans and 20 per cent are from Sudan (Population, Immigration and Border Authority 2019). The detention of asylum seekers has been regulated through a long process of court hearings and back-and-forth negotiations between the court and the government. The High Court of Justice (as the supposed protector of democratic values) and the government (as the protector of ethnic virtues) ended up mainly disputing the duration of detention rather than its existence. The initial plan of the state was to detain in Holot all asylum seekers residing in Israel for an indefinite period. However, the Supreme Court ruled against it and agreed to a twelve-month 'open detention' in Holot of single male asylum seekers. This excluded parents in charge of minors, women, children, elders and men with extreme illness or disabilities (*Desta v. The Knesset* 2015).

Yet, the purpose of Holot remained unclear: unlike other detention facilities in the world, Holot did not serve as a transition point before deportation or asylum, since Israel cannot deport asylum seekers back to Sudan and Eritrea due to its international obligations of *non-refoulement*. At the same time, the recognition rate of asylum requests in Israel is almost nonexistent.

The state declared that Holot serves to deter future 'infiltrators' (Shani et al. 2014; Population, Immigration and Border Authority 2018), while refugee rights organizations have claimed that Israel's real incentive is to make the life of asylum seekers so miserable that they will voluntarily leave (Drori-Avraham 2015).

According to Nicholas de Genova, detention and deportation are defining features of the state's management of noncitizens more generally: detention is perceived as an 'inevitable reality', a 'mundane' act of the state, merely 'holding back' the noncitizen, without having to 'recourse to the formalities of any due process of law' (de Genova 2016: 3). Detainees, he argues, are 'outside of the purview of the law altogether' (2016: 6), and since the logic of the nation state requires the securing of its borders, noncitizens who cross the border irregularly are considered to be a danger to the nation state. In that sense, de Genova argues that noncitizens' lives 'are plainly judged to be unworthy of justice' (2016: 6), a description that seems accurate in the case of African asylum seekers in Israel.

While not legally defined as a prison, Holot is surrounded by two tall fences and is operated by Israel's prison service (IPS). It is inhabited by asylum seekers in three major wings, each containing four cell-blocks divided into twenty-eight rooms, with five bunk beds, allowing the accommodation of ten people. When the facility operated, most of the rooms were constantly in full capacity. The size of a room in Holot is 46.15 square metres, meaning that each detainee had a living space of 4.5 square metres (Guthmann 2017: 25). Overcrowding was not the only problem in the facility: the food was of extremely poor quality, served in small portions, and detainees were not allowed to bring in food from outside or cook for themselves (*Ismail v. The IPS* 2016).

Detainees were free to leave the facility from 6 am until 10 pm, after which the gates would close, locking the detainees inside. At the entrance there was a biometric gate, and several others were located between the different cell-blocks. This allowed the IPS to keep track of the location of each detainee, restricting their movements inside the facility (Rozen 2016). However, the detainees' freedom of movement was also restricted when the gates were open. Holot is located in a closed military training zone ('fire zone') in the Negev Desert, next to the southwestern border of Israel with Egypt, where the weather is either extremely hot in the summer or very cold in the winter (Berman and Zeigler 2015). The closest city, Be'er Sheva, was too far and too expensive to get to, especially since detainees are not allowed to work and are consequently short of cash (Rozen 2016). Holot, in other words, was essentially isolated from civilization.

The location of Holot in the Negev Desert, I argue, has fundamentally transformed what Holot is and how it has affected detainees' lives. As one asylum seeker from Sudan put it during his detainment in Holot: 'They call it an "open facility", but we can't get out . . . There are guards everywhere, and a lot of desert. There's really nothing to do here, it's a prison' (Voices from Holot 2015). An asylum seeker from Eritrea, who was also detained in Holot, echoed this point: 'We, the asylum seekers: no one sees us. Although we are black, we are invisible. Now they've put us as far as possible, in the middle of the desert, and no one remembers that we exist'. As these quotes reveal, refugees in Holot did not experience it as an open camp, but rather as a prison. Its isolated location in the desert, combined with prison-like characteristics (guards, counts, gates, etc.), made it impossible for refugees to fulfil their freedom of movement, transforming it from an open facility into a de facto prison.

In this sense, Holot is an example of the twofold virtue of Israel as democratic and Jewish, the dynamics of containment and exclusion: the high court approved of Holot as an open facility and thus less harmful to the liberal-democratic virtue of freedom of movement, while knowingly ignoring the fact that the 'openness' of Holot lacked substance. Indeed, Holot enabled the state to maintain simultaneously its democratic façade, while executing a policy of exclusion. More significantly, Israel's decision to locate Holot in the Negev was far from coincidental, since it illustrated the transformation of settlement in the Negev. As will become clear, Holot is more than just a detention centre, a form of 'forced shelter'; it signifies a failure to materialize the mythos of civilizing the desert through settlement by Jewish immigrants.

Will the Desert Bloom?

A Sabra (צבר) is a prickly pear cactus – the fruit of the desert. It is also a nickname in Hebrew referring to Jews born in Israel, *Tzabar*, and a metaphor of the Israeli character: a rough appearance covering a delicate soul. The term was coined in the 1930s to describe the 'New Jew', the first generation of Zionist Israelis to be socialized in the *Yeshuv* (the Jewish settlement in Palestine). The 'New Jew' was finally born in his homeland, free of the distortion of the diaspora: he was bronzed and courageous, a labourer and a fighter, at once local and superior. The Sabra's duty was to settle the land and defend the *Yeshuv*. His labour was not mere work, but represented an historic mission of collective redemption.

Palestine's vast area of desert – the Negev or el-Naqab in Arabic – was the paradigmatic project of the Sabra, a long-forgotten wilderness yearning for salvation and for the building of civilization through labour and settlement (Almog 2000). In early Zionist ideology, the Negev was prominently conceptualized and romanticized as a place where Jews would achieve redemption. The settling of the Negev, it was believed, would prove the superiority of men over nature and of the Jews over the native Arab population of Palestine. David Ben-Gurion, Israel's first Prime Minister, believed that 'making the desert bloom' was an existential matter, which will determine the survival of the Jewish State (Ben-Gurion 1970). As he put it (1986: 82), 'the sages of Israel, sages of land, rain and plant, will tell the sage men of the world the new truth of Eretz-Israel: the truth of a land with a soul who awaits a redemption – the redemption of labor and building'. This idea had its roots in the Bible, particularly in its passages pertaining to the Hebrews' forty-year-long exodus in the desert. The redemption therefore had two elements: the Negev would be redeemed from its savage wilderness and the Jewish people would be redeemed from their exilic nature.

Thus, the desert was often presented as even more appropriate than Jerusalem to fulfil the Zionist vision. Theodor Herzl, who is considered to be the founding father of Zionism, thought that the desert areas were better suited for Jewish settlement, since the Arabic population there was less dense than in Jerusalem. He even proposed building a Jewish state in El-Arish, located in the Sinai Desert (Elon 2004). Ben-Gurion expressed similar notions: 'to me, it seemed more important to re-establish our authority over the Negev than even to attempt the rescue of Jerusalem's Old City' (Ben-Gurion 1970: 137). In 1956, Ben-Gurion left Tel Aviv and moved to Sde-Boker, a newly built Kibbutz in the Negev. In an introduction to his memoir from 1970, the editor wrote: 'His abrupt retirement from politics to the Negev Kibbutz has been represented by some as an act of self-exile, an immurement in the wilderness. This interpretation is far from the truth. For Ben-Gurion developing the Negev is Israel's greatest task and his move there underlines his determination to participate in this vital undertaking' (Dorman 1986: 135). In other words, moving to the desert was not a form of exile, but a return to his determination to participate in the most central task. As he proclaimed: 'On what is accomplished in the Negev ... Israel will stand or fall' (Dorman 1986: 135).

The settlement of new Jewish immigrants in the Negev was a prominent characteristic of the state in its early stages, when hundreds of villages were built for Jewish immigrants (Hacohen 2003). Spatial planning became a crucial and prominent tool in the hands of the Israeli apparatus, when new settlements were created as frontiers, with a view to expanding Israel's territory and sovereignty (Tzfadia 2009). Oren Yiftachel describes pre-1948 Jewish settlements in Palestine as 'colonialism of collective survival' (Yiftachel 2003: 169). All land that was cultivated and settled by Jews was considered vital for the continuation of the Jewish sovereignty, and as a Jewish-settler state, Israel had a continuous demographic battle with the native Arab population. Accordingly, it 'pursue[d] a deliberate strategy of ethnic migration and settlement that aims to alter the country's ethnic structure' (Yiftachel 2006: 2): The first form of Zionist settlement were the agricultural cooperative villages, built in the beginning of the twentieth century by 'pioneers' – young Jewish European immigrants driven by Zionist ideals. Yet it was hard to convince the masses to join the new villages, since they were extremely isolated and not connected to water or electricity. However, by the end of the independence war, construction and settlement in the Negev gained new impetus and, in a famous speech entitled 'Mission or Career' in 1954, Ben-Gurion praised the special characteristics of the desert and said that the state needed a desert more than the desert needed a state. Thus, under Ben-Gurion's administration, developing the Negev was prioritized, many villages and factories were built, and agriculture flourished (Hacohen 2003).

In the 1950s, upon the arrival of new Jewish *Mizrahim* (eastern) immigrants, a policy of 'aggressive population movement dispersal' began (Katz 2016: 151). This was utilized for the enhancement of Israel's control over land and for territorial expansion. A new kind of settlement – 'the Development Town' – was designed for the new immigrants. These new towns were the home of workers in the new factories and providers of services for agricultural villages in the area; the planning was carried out by state architects trained in Europe and who were therefore unfamiliar with the special circumstances of the desert. The population in the Development Towns soon suffered from decades of neglect and discrimination by the state, leading to severe inequalities in Israeli society (Efrat 1984). This discrimination, which began with the *Ma'abara*, the refugee camps for Mizrahi Jews, and continued with the Development Towns, was not coincidental. It originated in the deeply rooted racism of the state against non-European Jews: those who had arrived primarily from Arab states (Katz 2016).

Prior to the arrival of Jewish settlers, the Negev had previously been inhabited by Bedouin tribes and villages. Before 1948, around 130,000 indigenous Arabs, the Bedouins, resided in the northern Negev, mostly within the Be'er-Sheva metropolis region. However, during and immediately following the 1948 war, around 80–85 per cent of the Bedouin population of the Negev fled or were expelled by the Israeli Army to neighbouring Arab countries, or to Gaza and the West Bank. Those who remained were transferred from their original lands to the *Siyag*, an area to the northeast of Be'er-Sheva known for its low agricultural fertility. The Siyag was under military rule until 1966 and no concrete building was allowed. There are now around 200,000 Bedouin citizens of Israel, constituting 32 per cent of the Negev's population, and although the Bedouins have full Israeli citizenship, the shrinking of their land along with state discrimination led to their persistent economic marginalization in modern Israel (Abu-Sa'ad 2004; Yiftachel 2003). In attempt to coerce the urbanization of the Bedouin community, most of the Bedouin villages are officially unrecognized. These villages are not connected to water or electricity, lack access to adequate healthcare and welfare, and have no planning outlines. In addition, hundreds of Bedouin houses were destroyed over the last decade or are under demolition orders (Rotem 2015).

A turning point in Israel's policy towards the Negev came in 1977, when, for the first time in Israel's history, Ben-Gurion's party Mapai was defeated by the revisionist party Herut. Under the revisionist party, funding and resources were now directed towards developing and building new settlements in the Occupied Territories in the West Bank, Gaza and the Golan Heights (Tzachor 2001). Such a shift of focus was never subsequently reversed, so the focus on the Negev declined and investment in settlement in the Occupied Territories intensified (Gazela and Natanzon 2016). Three different yet parallel approaches of settling the desert can thus be traced: the first settlers were motivated pioneer ideologists – embodying the Zionist utopia of redeeming the land by labour. The second group of settlers, the Mizrahi Jews, were used by the state to settle the Negev since nobody else was willing to do so by then. The Mizrahi Jews were included by their nationality, yet were ethnically, geographically and economically excluded (Bar-On 2007). This has led to their discrimination and channelling into the working class via unskilled labour in factories. The third approach can be discerned in the treatment reserved for the Bedouins. Since they are Muslims, their presence in the Negev does not have the effect of redemption. While Zionism was desperately looking for new Jewish settlers, it was displacing Bedouins from their lands. The lack of new pioneers to 'redeem' the land, the economic failure of the development towns and the dispute with the Bedouins over their land have pushed the state towards ever more aggressive strategies in its quest to 'tame the Negev'. As attention shifted to civilian settlement on the West Bank instead, the Negev was subsequently dominated by the military.

The Noncivilian Settlement

In 1949, as the war of independence ended and new training areas for the military were needed, the state declared large areas in the Negev as 'fire zones' or closed military areas. This was done under Article 125 of the Defence (Emergency) Regulations, enacted in 1945 by the British Mandate government and incorporated in Israeli law by 1948 (Mortski 2011). Although the regulations were intended to operate only during war or times of emergency (Tzur 1999), they remained in place after the end of the 1948 war and were used as legal basis for the military rule imposed on Israel's Arab citizens until 1966, as well as to control the Occupied Territories during the 1967 war (Association for Civil Rights Israel 2012). Since 1992, the regulations are anchored in the Basic Law: the government, which authorize the Knesset to institute the regulations once a State of Emergency is declared. A national state of emergency has existed since the country's inception in 1948, and is extended every year. Today, closed military zones cover over 30 per cent of Israel's territory, mainly in the Negev Desert (Mortski 2011).

In the 1970s, another major event in Israel's history changed the situation in the Negev for years to come: the peace agreement with Egypt in 1978 led to the retreat of all military forces from the Sinai Peninsula into the Negev. The local authorities in the Negev had hoped that this would lead to a positive change, since more military officers would settle there and new construction plans would enhance its development and revive settlement in the desert, which was now being neglected after attention had shifted to the Occupied Territories. However, the officers moved to the centre of Israel, and new plans for the Negev were devised for military needs in a way that did not benefit the civil society. It was at this point that the desert became a space dominated by the military, punctuated by some civil enclaves, a process that has continued in more recent decades (Ezra 2011). Indeed, in recent years the process of militarization has intensified. In 2016, 'The Training Bases City', a complex of military bases, was finally opened in the Negev. As bluntly written in a website aimed to prepare young teenagers before their draft, 'this project was born as part of the plan to move Israel's military bases to the Negev, in order to strengthen it and settle it, or in short "to make the wilderness bloom"' (Meitav 2016). The official website of the 'new city' also has a section called 'Ben-Gurion's vision', describing in detail his vision to settle the wilderness, and its roots in the bible (Mabat La-Negev 2016).

However, the process of militarization of the desert has led to a new configuration of the Zionist myth of redemption. The 'newest city of the Negev', the Training Bases City, now stands as the antithesis to a civilian settlement. Although the Zionist rhetoric has remained similar, a vision of civil settlement has been transformed into the reality of military dominance. Large areas of the desert are now either closed military zones or inhabited by noncivilians: soldiers and detainees. Besides military bases, there are seven detention centres and prisons mainly for Palestinian prisoners, and two for African 'infiltrators': Saharonim and Holot.

The Negev from Redemption to Exile

The question of Israel's sovereignty is tightly connected to the ability to control the settlement of its population in accordance with an ethnic logic, as part of the ongoing battle with the Arab population over demographic dominance in Israel/Palestine (Yiftachel 2006). As such, Israel's sovereignty is most vulnerable when the state loses control over the entrance to its territory. Consequently, the contestation of Israel's southern border with Egypt, represented by the irregular entry of African asylum seekers, has led

Israel to commence two major and costly projects: the first is a 245 km-long border fence along Israel's southern border with Egypt, built at a cost of 1.6 billion NIS (Lior 2018); and the second is Holot, which is the continuation of the fence in the sense that it aims to 'create a normative barrier to potential infiltrators' (*Desta v. The Knesset* 2015: 39). Like the fence, Holot deters future asylum seekers by the intimidation of detention.

Interestingly enough, these initiatives were not prompted by the long-lasting threat to the border posed by terrorists and drug smugglers, who have been infiltrating Israel through its border with Egypt. The border fence and Holot were only constructed when African refugees began crossing the border to seek asylum in Israel. This is worth an explanation, considering that terrorist attacks and drugs smuggling are evidently more dangerous to Israel's security than asylum seekers. According to Wendy Brown (2014), the recent revival of walls built by states serve as mere *performances of sovereignty*, covering up the waning sovereignty of the nation state in a globalized world. Similarly, the border crossing of asylum seekers is a threat to Israel's *performance of sovereignty*, since it alludes to a gap in the control over the ethnic structure of its population through the management of migration and settlement.

In the court hearing that eventually legalized Holot, the state explained that 'Holot is intended to serve clear and distinct social interests relating to Israel's sovereignty and its ability to deal with the consequences of the settlement of thousands of infiltrators in its cities' (*Desta v. The Knesset* 2015: 40). Since Israel's existence relies on a Jewish majority, the presence of African asylum seekers, being non-Jews, is a threat to Israel's sovereignty. Accordingly, in order to preserve Jewish demographic dominance in Israel's urban core and to protect its sovereignty, refugees were detained in the desert. By doing so, Holot, like the militarization of the desert, underscores the Negev's peripheral status and the fact that the civilization project in the Negev had been abandoned. In other words, the detainment of refugees in Holot produces the Negev as a space of segregation and banishment; not from this city or another, but from the institution of the polis, of civilization itself. The Negev, no longer a candidate for redemption, transforms with the construction of Holot into a place of exile.

When it comes to the study of shelter, this example demonstrates the need to move beyond contemporary conditions to also consider the location, history and environment. In the case of Holot, these elements took on a much wider significance: it was not just the design and management of the facility that mattered, but also its placement in the desert, which revealed much deeper themes about Israel's history and ideology. Many other spaces of detention and confinement have similar resonances. The use of former barracks, airports and bunkers in historically laden sites are not just of academic interest; they shape the whole way that the treatment of noncitizens is connected to political culture and the establishment of nation states. In the case of Holot, its isolated and remote location, combined with the low availability of transportation, prevented residents from fulfilling their freedom of movement and acted as a deterrent. But simultaneously, this same location indicated the transformation of a mythos: Ben-Gurion's vision of redemption for the Jewish people through the labour and settlement of the Negev seems to have failed and a new reality is now apparent, one of ever-growing disparity, violence and despair.

Renana Ne'eman received her B.A. from Tel Aviv University in History and her M.Sc. from the University of Oxford in Refugee and Forced Migration Studies. Since 2009, she has worked in various human rights non-governmental organizations in Israel and participates in musical projects as a harpist and singer. She currently studies law in Tel Aviv University and is working on her second solo album.

Note

1. Fedayeen in Arabic is one who gives his life for another or for a cause. From 1951 to 1956, Palestinians crossed the border of Jordan into Israel in order to carry out attacks on Israeli civilians (Morris 1993).

References

Abu-Sa'ad, Ismail. 2004. 'Education as a Deportation Tool in the Unrecognized Villages' (Hebrew) (online), *Adalah electronic issue* 8. Retrieved 10 June 2017 from https://www.adalah.org/he/content/index/1422?Content_sort=.

Activstilles. 2014. 'Holot Photo Diary, Day 1: "This Is a Real Prison"'. *+972*, February. Retrieved 15 October 2019 from https://972mag.com/holot-photo-diary-day-1-this-is-a-real-prison/88627.

Almog, Oz. 2000. *The Sabra: The Creation of the New Jew.* Berkeley: University of California Press.

Association for Civil Rights Israel. 2012. 'Supreme Court Rejects Petition to End Continual State of Emergency' (Hebrew). Retrieved 15 October 2019 from https://www.acri.org.il/en/2012/05/08/state-of-emergency-petition-rejected.

Bar-On, Shani. 2007. 'A Contract Breached: Workers and State in Ofakim, 1955–1981'. *Iyunim Betkumat Israel (Studies in Israel's Resurrection)* 17: 287–317.

Ben-Gurion, David. 1986. *On the Settlement.* Tel-Aviv: Hakibbutz hameuchad.

Ben-Gurion, David. 1970. *Memories.* Geneva: Covenant Communications Corporation.

Berman, Yonatan, and Ruvi Zeigler. 2015. 'The Union of Securitisation and Demography: Immigration Detention in Israel', in A. Nethery and S. Silverman (eds), *Immigration Detention: The Migration of a Policy and its Human Impact*. New York: Routledge, pp. 154–62.
Brown, Wendy. 2014. *Walled States, Waning Sovereignty*. New York: Zone Books.
De Genova, Nicholas. 2016. 'Detention, Deportation and Waiting: Towards a Theory of Migrant Detainability'. *Global Detention Project Working Paper* 8: 1–13.
Desta v. The Knesset [2015] HCJ 8665/14.
Dorman, M. (ed.). 1986. *On Settlement: An Anthology, 1915–1956*. Tel Aviv: Hakibbutz Hameuchad.
Drori-Avraham, Adi. 2015. 'Report: Where There Is No Free Will: Israel's "Voluntary Return" Procedure for Asylum Seekers'. Tel Aviv: ASSAF. Retrieved 23 December 2019 from https://hotline.org.il/wp-content/uploads/2015/04/free-will-web-.pdf.
Dvora, Hacohen. 2003. *Immigrants in Turmoil: Mass Immigration to Israel and Its Repercussions in the 1950s and after*, trans. Gila Brand. Syracuse: Syracuse University Press.
Efrat, Elisha. 1984. *Urbanization in Israel*. London: Croom Helm.
Elon, Amos. 2004. *Herzl*. Tel Aviv: Am Oved.
Ezra, Eyal. 'The Spatial Implications of IDF Deployment in the Negev through the Prism of the Implementation of Israel-Egypt Peace Treaty'. *Planning* 8(1): 219–37 (Hebrew).
Gazela, Itamar, and Ruvi Natanzon. 2016. *Settlements Monitoring – A Special Report: The Settlements of Judea and Samaria's 2017–2018 Budget*. MACRO: Center for Political Economics (Hebrew).
Guthmann, Anat. 2017. *Immigration Detention in Israel: Annual Monitoring Report* Tel Aviv: ASSAF.
Ismail v. The IPS [2016] HCJ 4581/15.
Katz, Irit. 2016. 'Camp Evolution and Israel's Creation: Between "State of Emergency" and "Emergence of State"'. *Political Geography* 55: 144–51.
Landau, Yaron. 'Netanyahu Vows to Reopen Detention Facilities for Asylum Seekers after Israel Tells Court Deportation No Longer an Option'. *Haaretz*, April. Retrieved 15 October 2019 from https://www.haaretz.com/israel-news/israel-admits-no-way-we-can-forcefully-deport-african-asylum-seekers-1.6028656.
Lior, Gad. 2018. 'Cost of Border Fences, Underground Barrier, Reaches NIS 6bn'. *Ynet Online*. Retrieved 15 October 2019 from https://www.ynetnews.com/articles/0,7340,L-5078348,00.html.
Mabat La-Negev. n.d. 'David Ben-Gurion's Vision'. Retrieved 28 May 2017 from http://www.mabat-lanegev.co.il.
Meitav. 2016. 'The Training Bases City' (Hebrew). Retrieved 10 May 2017 from https://www.mitgaisim.idf.il.
Morris, Benny. 1993. *Israel's Border Wars, 1949–1956*. Oxford: Clarendon Press.
Mortski, Elad. 2011. 'The Legal Foundations for Determining Training Areas Facing Basic Constitutional Rights'. *Planning* 8(1): 238–58 (Hebrew).
Paz, Yonatan. 2011. 'Ordered Disorder: African Asylum Seekers in Israel and Discursive Challenges to an Emerging Refugee Regime'. *New Issues in Refugee*

Research, 25. Geneva: UNHCR Policy Development and Evaluation Service. Retrieved 9 December 2019 from https://www.unhcr.org/research/working/4d7a26ba9/ordered-disorder-african-asylum-seekers-israel-discursive-challenges-emerging.html.

Population, Immigration and Border Authority. 2018. 'Data of Foreigners in Israel' (Hebrew), January.

———. 2019. 'Data of Foreigners in Israel' (Hebrew), June.

Rotem, Mical. 2015. 'A Community under Attack: The Human Rights of the Bedouin Population in the Negev 2015'. *Negev Coexistence Forum for Civil Equality* (Hebrew). Retrieved 15 October 2019 from http://www.dukium.org/wp-content/uploads/2015/12/HRDR_HEB_WEB1.pdf.

Rozen, Sigal. 2016. *Detention Monitoring Report*, trans. Merav Zonenshtein and Sigal Rozen. Tel Aviv: Hotline for Refugees and Migrants.

Sade, Shuki. 2015. 'This Place Is the Death of the Young'. *The Marker*, August (Hebrew). Retrieved 15 October 2019 from http://www.themarker.com/markerweek/1.2717989.

Shani, Eli, Ayal Shira, Yonatan Berman and Sigal Rozen. 2014. *No Safe Haven: Israeli Asylum Policy as Applied to Eritrean and Sudanese Citizens*. Tel Aviv: Hotline for Refugees and Migrants.

Tzachor, Ze'ev. 2001. 'The Negev in the Zionist Ideology and Actions' (Hebrew). *Ariel: A Periodical for the Research of Eretz-Israel* 150: 11–20.

Tsfadia, Erez. 2009. 'Settlements in Israel: A Perspective on Militarism', in Oren Amiram (ed.), *Space of Security: New Approaches to the Use of Land (Resources) of Security and Military Needs*. Jerusalem: The Van Leer Jerusalem Institute, pp. 46–58. (Hebrew).

Tzur, Mical. 1999. *The Defence (Emergency) Regulations 1945*. Position Paper No. 16. Jerusalem: Israeli Institute for Democracy (Hebrew).

Weizman, Eyal, and Fazal Sheikh. 2015. *The Conflict Shoreline: Colonialism as Climate Change in the Negev Desert*. Brooklin: Steidi and Cabinet Books.

Voices from Holot. 2015. 'Weblog'. Retrieved 15 October 2019 from http://www.holotvoices.co.il (Hebrew). Yiftachel, Oren. 2003. 'Ethnocratic Policies and Indigenous Resistance: Bedouin Arabs and the Israeli Settler State'. *Holy Land Studies* 1(2): 161–69.

———. 2006. *Ethnocracy: Land and Identity Politics in Israel/Palestine*. Philadelphia: University of Pennsylvania Press.

Zur, Yarden. 2018. 'Last Asylum Seekers Released from Holot Detention Center as Mass Deportation Campaign Moves Ahead'. *Haaretz*, March. Retrieved 15 October 2019 from https://www.haaretz.com/israel-news/last-asylum-seekers-leave-holot-as-mass-expulsion-campaign-moves-ahead-1.5908461.

Part II
Shelter, Resistance and Solidarity

Figure 8.1 The Invisible Church, near Calais, France. © Mark E. Breeze, based on an image supplied by Maria Hagan.

8

The Contingent Camp
Struggling for Shelter in Calais, France

Maria Hagan

There is an invisible church in Calais. Standing inside it, you can see right through: to the right, a row of houses beyond a road; to the left, a motorway noisy with lorries heading to and from the port. It's Sunday, and for two hours faith blots out the vehicles and the vicious promise of a better life across the Channel. Within the confines of a simple pétanque pitch in a little forest, a community of Eritreans gather for prayer. We enter, remove our hats and stand shoulder to shoulder in tight rows facing east, to pray and sing. Afterwards, we walk a few hundred metres through the forest, to a shaded area where several men are already gathered. Habtom laughs: 'Welcome to the Green Hotel sister!' I look around at the wood we are standing in; it is anything but a hotel. Men and boys sit grouped around campfires on makeshift wooden benches and crouched on the muddy earth. Some chat and share food; others stare into the fire silently or scroll through their mobile phones. A teenager with a broken voice plays a homemade kraar and sings to the background noise of traffic. The 'green hotel' is a living room, immaterial as it may be. Kifle pulls a football from its hiding place in a low shrub. A heated match kicks off and before long trees are used as coat hangers for excess jumpers and coats. I wonder if the community sleep here, but there's not a tent in sight. Habtom tells me of homes without doors, shelters of tarp and sticks with invisible thresholds tucked away in the woods. He describes the tireless game of hide-and-seek they play with the French police: everyone knows their shelter may be uncovered at any moment, torn down, leaving them shut out of what is already outside, and forced to build again. He shrugs, 'there's nothing more we can do'. Later that evening, I pass by the green hotel and the social place has vanished. There's not a soul in sight, and little to suggest there ever was.

–Field diary, 10 December 2017

Calais is a border city, serving as a policy testing ground and performance site for French migration politics. For decades, informal camps of displaced populations at the border have had an overlapping existence. However, since 2015, the visibility of asylum seekers and other migrants has increased, with conflicting interpretations circulating among the general public. Alongside rising visibility has come an increasing demand that these groups be actively acted upon rather than neglected in their informality. The demolition of the infamous Calais Jungle in October 2016 reflected this shift from inaction to action on the ground, and the act of destroying the massive makeshift camp marked a desire for greater control; informality would no longer be tolerated. To justify this 'zero-tolerance' policy, the French state developed an institutional system of official processing centres. These centres became non-negotiable 'humanitarian' spaces, and, as such, legitimized violent and active policing of asylum seekers and other migrants beyond the official system. This was most visible in Calais, where hundreds of displaced people continued to settle in the border zone in scattered encampments known as 'jungles', which the police systematically sought to destroy. While the Jungle was a destitute place unfitting to human life, it was a publicly visible place where makeshift infrastructure was tolerated, allowing even those in France illegally to claim ownership of a place and nurture social life within it (Katz 2017). However, in the more recent 'jungles', the routine destruction of shelter enforces invisibility and nomadism on the displaced, undermining their human rights even further.

In this chapter, I explore the implications of authorities maintaining the absence of camps, proposing that displaced people in Calais have ended up inhabiting 'contingent camps': spaces lived in yet denied material consolidation. These camps are not fixed places, but involve a coming together of activities and processes, which are in a constant state of becoming and unbecoming. The invisible church described in the opening to this chapter is a good example. Building on five months of ethnographic research in 2017 and early 2018, I describe and analyse the dynamics of these 'contingent camps', before reflecting on how these politics signal a transition from a humanitarian response to one driven by a logic of securitization. In this process, structures of protection end up turned on their head.

During my fieldwork, the numbers of displaced people in Calais fluctuated between 400 and 800 people, primarily of Afghan, Eritrean and Ethiopian origin, as well as smaller Sudanese and Kurdish groups. A minute proportion were women. Spatially, their lives revolved around five food and material distribution points, various car parks, roundabouts, stretches of motorway, the port, and scattered informal encampments in forests and on industrial waste sites, hidden as well as possible from marauding police. Most of these people were trying daily to cross to the UK, usually by sneaking onto vehicles headed for the ferry port or the Channel Tunnel when they were stationary at petrol stations, car parks or stuck in traffic. Many used smugglers to facilitate this process, as strategic points of attempted crossing were heavily policed. The presence of international aid agencies like the United Nations High Commissioner for Refugees (UNHCR) was very limited in this period, and French and British charities relied heavily on volunteers who were acting on their own initiative and often criminalized by the state.

Protective Containment: The Paradox of 'Unconditional' Shelter

Following the hasty destruction of the so-called Calais 'Jungle' in October 2016, President François Hollande (2012–17) set up a 'disperse-contain-process' policy, according to which asylum seekers and other migrants were sent to centres across the country for processing. On the back of this policy, centres for hosting (or arguably sorting) the displaced opened, and continued to develop through late 2017 under President Emmanuel Macron. This ever more complex system of processing centres marked a shift towards greater control and the sorting of people according to administrative status. The functions of these places of containment are often as abstract as their acronyms (CAO, CHU(M), PRAHDA, DPAR, CAES, DEMIE,[1] etc.) and their role seems to match that suggested by Minca (2015: 76), who has argued that the institutionalized camp is a violent political technology that emerges when a state does not know how to qualify people spatially, but seeks to govern their mobility. Similarly, Pallister-Wilkins (2016) understands these processes as ones of ambiguous humanitarian triage, describing them as 'sovereign processes of control designed around exclusive practices of exclusion', which involve 'exile through deportation rather than the inclusive ideal of universal humanity'. In other words, this is a framework that seeks an institution in which to fit each migrant 'type', guaranteeing that there should be no such thing as being outside of the state system.

In France, a discourse of care and control rationalizes the state's desire to contain people in institutionalized camps, while simultaneously attacking the existence of informal camps. In January 2018, President Macron stated: 'If migrants don't accept the propositions for shelter that are systematically made to them by state services, if they refuse that their fingerprints are taken according to the Dublin regulation, if they commit offences, notably by damaging lorries or private property, then they do so actively and are held responsible'. Contrasting their prospects in formal and informal camps, he went on: 'We owe them this truth: to stay in Calais, building makeshift homes in the undergrowth and marshlands, sometimes squats, is a dead end. The alternative is clear and open: to be hosted in accommodation centres where each person's situation will be examined with great attention' (Macron 2018).

In this way, the existence of an efficient processing system, which the state claims can welcome and host (contain) everyone unconditionally, seems to legitimize its 'zero tolerance' of people living outside of that system. In his speech, Macron explained this further, stating that 'the objective is, yes, to host everyone unconditionally, to verify their status straight away, determine it rapidly, so as to protect some and send others back'. However, he also emphasized that while the unconditional provision of shelter to vulnerable people is morally essential, 'unconditional shelter does not mean undifferentiated welcome'. The slipperiness of this discourse concerning different 'types of welcome' – some of which are in fact closer to detention – is revealed here. It is perhaps not so much welcome as domination. However, for the state, human rights commitments go hand in hand with control, legitimizing the destruction of any attempted encampment. 'In no case will we allow a jungle or an illegal occupation of the territory to come together again', Macron declared.

There is a stark contrast between the infrastructure for control being put together by the state in Calais and the imposed precarity of the informal camps constantly being taken apart alongside it. Permanence is built up while impermanence is imposed. It becomes clear that the promise of 'unconditional shelter' only applies to people willing to receive humanitarian care on the terms set out by the state. Instead, practices are put in place for the dehumanization of the displaced who circumvent the institutional system. While in Calais, I spoke to a number of volunteers who had long worked with the migrant community, and one, an active French volunteer in his sixties, told me about recent restrictive developments. 'It is no longer relevant to speak of the camp', he told me, 'because people cannot settle':

> If they could settle and the police would leave them be for a few weeks or a few months, we could speak of a camp. [But] today they are just homeless people from whom the police confiscate everything that might make it possible to settle, to take shelter. Tarps, but also duvets, sleeping bags, and even their personal belongings, shoes, documents etc. The situation now is worse than at the time of the camp because before, people could set up squats or shacks and it would take the police weeks or even months to expel them. But now there are far more police patrols, more police officers and CRS.[2] 'No point of fixation' politics mean that we are in a constant state of expulsion.

The numbers of police to deal with this situation in Calais was remarkable: in January 2018, there were 1,130 police and gendarmes stationed in the area

(Macron 2018), and only 700 asylum seekers and other migrants. By seeking to continue their journey beyond France and refusing the offer of formal shelter, they positioned themselves in defiance of the state. Refusing to be contained by the institutionalized system, they 'stripped themselves' of the identity of asylum seeker – the one potential legitimizer of their presence. Politically dispossessed, the displaced became what Agamben (1998) calls *homines sacri*: bare life whose body and thus spaces of life – home, sites of memories and survival – are vulnerable to material dispossession. Displaced people in Calais underwent frequent and cyclical destructive acts by the police, designed to take apart their structures of shelter, dehumanizing them as well as enforcing a state of nomadism. These people often came 'home' at the end of the day to devastation: crushed planks and slashed tarps, sleeping bags and blankets tear gas-soaked. Sometimes, everything would be gone. An Afghan man I spoke to described how these cycles unfold:

> You see those trees on the other side of the field? Inside those trees we made a hole and small shelter with blankets and plastic. It is for five people but it is too small and not really waterproof. The rain comes in and our sleeping bags get wet. We can't dry them outside or maybe someone will take them. This is a problem. Before, we had a very hidden place. But the police: they found it and destroyed it. We've had eight tents total together and we've only been here for forty days. Always they find us in the end. It is so cold at night but if we make a fire the police will find us easily. We sleep together to be warm and safe, but we are always afraid. Him – we call him Mama [laughs] because he is big and old – he sleeps beside the door to protect us. When they come we try to take our things, but they threaten us with spray and say 'don't come near – otherwise pssscht'. So we stay away. Some days we are so so angry. But we can do nothing, so just we make the tent every time again, every time make it again.

Police infringe on the scattered spaces of the contingent camp far more readily than they did in the more contained, established and materially visible former Jungle. Although the police manned the peripheries of the former camp, they would only rarely venture in. In 2018, local voluntary organizations reported an average of three destructions per week regardless of weather conditions, enforcing a perpetually nomadic existence even within the confines of one forest or wood. An Eritrean exile conveyed the state of imposed nomadism when he said to me: 'If the police know a place, they will come and destroy it. So we move all of the time'. This enforced mobility within an already restricted area is draining for a community deprived of any certainty, from their administrative future down to where they might sleep for the night. It is a situation of enforced precarity and temporariness, of being 'fixed in mobility' (Jackson 2012).

The effects of the routine harassment described above are particularly devastating. Restlessness and deprivation of material comfort and protection weigh on the communities, who complain of tiredness and stress. As one Eritrean explained it to me: 'We sleep three, maximum four hours every night. We are thinking all the time, when are they coming to wake us up?' The police strategy seems designed to wear people down and it is effective. Indeed, the constant attack on shelter, the threat of material dispossession at any time of the night or day leads to sleep deprivation that is experienced not only as unpleasant but also as unjust. As one person explained:

> If I am in a lorry and they hit me – OK. But if I am sleeping and they come ... That is the cruellest thing. When we're here minding our own business or sleeping, and they come and get us with tear gas. Is that really their job? If we are committing a crime, then I get it. But our crimes are not here. When we are sleeping and they spray us, what exactly is our crime?

Attacks on shelter and human dignity resonate with Derrida's descriptions of 'zoo-power' or 'zoo politics'. In his words, 'the most inhuman violence has been unleashed against living beings, beasts or humans, and humans in particular who precisely were not accorded the dignity of being fellows' (2009: 108). While police attacks on material (such as tents, tarpaulins and sleeping bags) generally cause less outrage than attacks on bodies, attacking material allows for a subtle encroachment of violence as routine, with devastating effects on the body and psyche. This politics of dehumanization is counterproductive, generating resentment of the state by displaced people as opposed to a desire to peacefully coexist or integrate.

Reclaiming the Camp: Resistance in Persistence

In Calais, shelter is not so much a place as an active and contested process. In May 2017, the police carried out sixteen 'anti-squat' operations in Calais: thirty-three sites were 'dismantled' and 20,900 kg of objects were destroyed. By August, these figures had risen to twenty-six 'anti-squat' operations: 103 sites were dismantled and 31,000 kg of objects were destroyed (IGPN, IGA and IGGN 2017: 32). These spectacular figures reveal the extent of the police crackdown on material expressions of presence, but the considerable weight of objects removed also reveals the ability of that materiality to regenerate; the process of shelter-making is ongoing and dynamic. One volunteer argued that it is inevitable that migrants will persist in being present in Calais, drawing attention to their resourcefulness and drive to persist. As he put it, 'the goal of the state and local government in Calais is that there be no migrants here at all. But the migrants are still here. The police, the mayor, the authorities generally, try to dislodge and discourage them from staying. But humans have arms, eyes, they think ... It's a perpetual game of hide-and-seek'.

This analysis of the situation in Calais is simple yet insightful, acknowledging the agency of asylum seekers and other migrants in a hostile environment. As long as the cliffs of Dover lie across the water from Calais and the European asylum system continues to fail, they will be drawn to this border zone. The human drive to act, nurture and pull together shelter even in the face of resistance challenges the idea that the death of the camp may be declared. So long as there are people, there will be attempts at temporary home-making and the establishment of spaces of life. This is a game of visibilities and strategizing as to how, when and where to reconstruct unnoticed.

The rebuilding of shelter and the camp is collaborative in Calais. In response to absurd cycles of destruction, the displaced and volunteer humanitarians strategize to re-establish camp spaces. This is mainly achieved through the provision of material supplies for rebuilding by humanitarians, from which people then strategize to build concealed shelters. Material donations are acquired by grassroots organizations and charities from across the European Union (mainly France and the United Kingdom), and many of the same organizations that were present in the Jungle remained after its inhabitants were dispersed, working with many of the same people. This continuity is crucial, as it has allowed organizations to simply adapt their aid strategy in response to the 'zero-tolerance' situation. As displaced people have dispersed and become less visible, humanitarians have rendered their service provision mobile: food, water, hygiene products and clothing distributions, WiFi provision and legal advice follow recipients rather than staying fixed. Several central elements of the former camp are thus still to be found in Calais, but in a rather different form. Service provision, even if for just a few hours each day, creates a semblance of the camp-that-was. These instances humanize a group whose humanity is attacked through the denial of a material living space. It is a provision of aid that emphasizes the argument for a right to be and live at the border; as well as making the displaced visible by performing a camp space, aid provision rejects the image of presence at the border as criminal and strives to humanize and reclaim the dignity of asylum seekers and other migrants. The defiant solidarity of the European citizen offers a moment of respite. It reaffirms the right to a camp for the displaced and offers a visual counternarrative to migrants as outlaws by presenting them as deserving aid recipients. As a result, the problematic situation in Calais stays tangible, materially symbolic and visible as a humanitarian crisis.

Invisible Places: 'We Live at the Green Hotel'

The invisibility of encampments in Calais is striking, considering the estimated 400–800 displaced people present at the time of my fieldwork. While encampments themselves are visible when assembled, they are impermanent and hidden from the public and marauding police, often embedded into bushes. 'Zero-camp tolerance' strategies therefore drive people into invisibility. This makes it difficult for the outsider to witness and document disproportionate attacks on her or his home and body. Resistance to this destruction does not so much emerge through explicit protest as through a refusal to cease living, by strategizing to persist even when the threat of attack on shelter is imminent. Car parks and roads, roundabouts and motorways in Calais are heavily policed; the streets of the city are patrolled at length by police vans, giving an impression of constant surveillance and limiting the routes that asylum seekers and other migrants may take to navigate the city. However, this attack on presence prompts a creative and immaterial reappropriation of space by the displaced, who have traced and treaded an invisible, parallel mapping of the city: secret routes and shortcuts through the greenery, away from asphalt and the city's immediate threats.

Communities of asylum seekers and other migrants also appropriate secondary spaces of life, which are somewhat visible to the public and thus materially invisible. The 'green hotel' described in the opening passage is a social place of life for the Eritrean community; it is where they gather to rest, sit, talk or eat, on makeshift benches or crouched around fires. The immateriality of such places is jarring, as well as the fact that they become invisible when nobody is around to perform their social function. In these places there is nothing left to destroy. Quite simply, they are places in which to be, and be together. This appropriation of a place of togetherness is a powerful form of resistance because it cannot be materially attacked. When the place is empty, it is unremarkable, but when it is inhabited, it is vested with sociality and ownership. It is the place to which guests might be invited to spend time, and although the threshold to the 'green hotel' is invisible, the transition from an abstract public space to a nurtured social place is clear when walking into it from the nearest road. This appropriation of space allows for a role reversal between the humanitarian/citizen and the refugee/migrant in the form of a threshold beyond which the roles of giver and receiver can be transformed. Receivers become hosts in a way that the constant destruction of the camp otherwise makes impossible.

Despite the contingency of the camps they inhabit, displaced people around Calais tend to perform everyday activities. Many Muslims, for example, perform several daily prayers despite the immaterial conditions. Some have managed to hold on to prayer mats, which they lay down on elevated concrete slabs or wooden pallets to avoid the muddy ground. Similarly, many Orthodox Catholic Eritreans attend prayer in the invisible church described in the opening vignette on Sundays. When in progress, the space of the church functions as a peaceful place of 'ceasefire' and humanization, resisting strategies of animalization and exclusion put in place by the state. Remarkably, almost every Sunday, a CRS police van drives by during prayer, stops and announces its presence with a quick whoop of the siren and lights. While a few worshippers glance sideways at the van nervously, long-termers do not flinch; although the CRS might sit and watch the mass from a distance for a while, they would not get out of the van or intervene during prayer. The church may be invisible, yet the space is seemingly sacred, and therefore material in some sense. Prayer becomes a fleeting moment during which shared humanity is recognized through dedication to a culturally familiar ritual.

Such social places play a significant role in reclaiming the right to shelter and the camp. When shelter is attacked, simple and persistent social acts to remake it become a form of resistance (Hammami 2016). Those who inhabit contingent camp spaces in Calais perpetuate practices that provide a *social* form of shelter, despite an absence of materiality; these practices lay claim to a right to shelter. While asylum seekers and other migrants in Calais may not engage in constant and active protest very often, they are by no means depoliticized; through persistent struggles for everyday life and immaterial spaces of appearance like the 'green hotel' that render the body visible, the act of resistance grows concerned not just with the possibility of appearing in public, but with struggling for the basic means to live, be recognized and sheltered.

Conclusion: Living the Everyday

Preserving a routine as similar to 'normal' everyday life as possible is an important aspect of resistance. It is the pursuit of 'liveable life' through the pursuit of everyday acts (Hammami 2016: 172), daily activities that give shape and materialization to a persistent presence. Although the routines are somewhat unremarkable, they are humanizing and bear witness to appropriation of a space as one in which life may be pursued. As one Afghan man explained it to me in Calais, 'when we wake up in the morning we go for tea and breakfast at the other distribution place, where the Africans eat. Then we come back to this distribution place to charge our phones and eat lunch. When it is open we go to the day centre, otherwise we go here and there, eat in the evening and then, well, you know what we do, we all have our problems so we "try"'.

This 'trying' to cross the Channel illegally is the most important part of the daily routine and is described in a way that gives it a privileged place: like a job. Residents of the encampments tend to stick to a strict timetable and strategize their 'trying' with commitment. To an extent, the day is spent preparing the body for this activity, through eating and trying to rest as well as gathering appropriate clothes. One might wonder what drives people to try and cross the Channel considering the risks involved, and conversations on the ground reveal that the United Kingdom is not a gilded dream for all. While some indeed picture an easy life within a tight-knit community in London or Manchester, there are many for whom the United Kingdom is little more than a last resort, the next place to try. After surviving an often perilous dinghy-crossing over the Mediterranean, many are left to drift through the European asylum system, running from fingerprints snatched from them on the shores of Italy or Greece. Most have already been disappointed by an application process elsewhere that cost them months if not years of waiting time. The 'UK dream' is often not for lack of trying elsewhere; it is a last opportunity to seize self-determination in a system so eager to strip you of it. To 'try' is to find some meaning in otherwise absurd living conditions and in a European asylum system in which no individual state wants to take responsibility for you. Being in Calais, perpetually rebuilding shelter and trying to cross becomes a positive act. The border zone is appropriated as a place of productive waiting, in which one can hold a sliver of agency over what happens next in one's life.

The cycles of shelter destruction and reconstruction in Calais described in this chapter reflect a broader logic in France. Namely, it reflects the transition from a humanitarian response to one driven by securitization, in which structures of protection are turned on their head. The flaws in this shift are reflected in the space of the contingent camp, which undergoes cycles of destruction and reconstruction. This chapter has shown how a system that seeks to police and control inadvertently multiplies the number of people seeking informal alternatives, whatever the living conditions. Relationships of trust with the state are jeopardized; asylum seekers and other migrants are weary of approaching a system into which authorities seek to force them and that they are convinced has been designed to trick them. Despite camp destruction, these displaced people alongside grassroots humanitarians strive to perform the humanitarian camp space in Calais, to claim the right to the camp and the recognition of the displaced person through the constant rebuilding of shelter. The contingent camp is both a source of vulnerability and a source of resistance. Its very immateriality makes it unconformable, but also easy to render invisible. An unexpected strength emerges in this invisibility of spaces in which human presence may nonetheless persist – a fundamental act of resistance to material violence. The true value of these places lies in their existence as social spaces, as forms of shelter that draw their power from the interwoven human networks that constitute them.

Maria Hagan received her M.A. (Res) from the University of Amsterdam and is currently a Ph.D. candidate in the Department of Geography at the University of Cambridge. Her research explores the spatial regulation of displaced people in France and Morocco through ethnography.

Notes

1. Centre d'Accueil et d'Orientation (CAO); Centre d'Hébergement d'Urgence pour Migrants (CHU(M)); Programme d'Acceuil et d'Hébergement des Demandeurs d'Asile (PRAHDA); Dispositif de 'Préparation au Retour' (DPAR); Centres d'Accueil et d'Examination des Situations (CAES); Dispositif d'Évaluation des Mineurs Isolés Étrangers (DEMIE).
2. Reference to the Compagnie Républicaine de Sécurité (CRS), the general reserve of the French National Police charged with general security missions, crowd and riot control.

References

Agamben, G. 1998. *Homo Sacer: Sovereign Power and Bare Life*. Stanford: Stanford University Press.
Derrida, J. 2009. *The Beast and the Sovereign*, vol. 1, trans. G. Bennington. Chicago: University of Chicago Press.
Giorgio, A. 2005. *State of Exception*, trans. K. Attell. Chicago: University of Chicago Press.
Hammami, R. 2016. 'Precarious Politics: The Activism of 'Bodies that Count' (Aligning with Those that Don't) in Palestine's Colonial Frontier', in J. Butler, Z. Gambetti and L. Sabsay (eds), *Vulnerability in Resistance*. Durham, NC: Duke University Press, pp. 167–90.
Human Rights Watch. 2017. '"Like Living in Hell": Police Abuses against Child and Adult Migrants in Calais'. Retrieved 15 October 2019 from https://www.hrw.org/report/2017/07/26/living-hell/police-abuses-against-child-and-adult-migrants-calais.
IGPN, IGA and IGGN. 2017. 'Evaluation de l'Action des Forces de l'Ordre à Calais et dans le Dunkerquois'. Retrieved 15 October 2019 from https://www.interieur.gouv.fr/Publications/Rapports-de-l-IGA/Rapports-recents/Evaluation-de-l-action-des-forces-de-l-ordre-a-Calais-et-dans-le-Dunkerquois.
Jackson, E. 2012. 'Fixed in Mobility: Young Homeless People and the City'. *International Journal of Urban and Regional Research* 36(4): 725–41.
Katz, I. 2017. 'Between Bare Life and Everyday Life: Spatializing Europe's Migrant Camps'. *Architecture_MPS* 12(1): 1–20.
Macron, E. 2018. 'Transcription du Discours du Président de la République Auprès des Forces Mobilisées'. Retrieved 15 October 2019 from https://www.elysee.fr/emmanuel-macron/2018/01/16/discours-devant-les-forces-de-securite-a-calais.
Minca, C. 2015. 'Geographies of the Camp'. *Political Geography* 49: 74–83.
Pallister-Wilkins, P. 2016. 'Hotspots and the Politics of Humanitarian Control and Care'. *Society and Space*. Retrieved 15 October 2019 from http://societyandspace.org/2016/12/06/hotspots-and-the-politics-of-humanitarian-control-and-care.

Figure 9.1 Sounding the shelter in Athens, Greece. © Mark E. Breeze, based on an image supplied by Tom Western.

9

Sounding the Shelter, Voicing the Squat

The Sonic Politics of Refugee Shelter in Athens

Tom Western

Τούτ οι μπάτσοι που 'ρθαν τώρα, βρε,	The cops that came just now,
Τι γυρεύουν τέτοιαν ώρα;	What are they looking for at this hour?
Ήρθανε να μας ρεστάρουν, βρε,	They've come to take our cash,
Και τα ζάρια να μας πάρουν.	And they've come to take our dice.
Και μας ψάξανε για ζάρια ρε,	And they've searched us for the dice,
Και μας βρίσκουν οκτό ζευγάρια.	And they found eight pairs.

–'Τουτ οι Μπάτσοι Που 'ρθαν Τώρα', song recorded by Giannis Ioannidis, 1928

A pile of cables, a mixing desk, an ashtray. Athens. A refugee squat located somewhere between Exarcheia Square and Omonoia Square. Around a table, three men work to set up a sound system for a gig later that evening. A banner hangs from a wall bearing the slogan 'Squat the World – Rap Against State and Law'. An adjacent wall features an artwork inscribed with the words 'No Borders'. Earlier the squat received a visit from the police – a regular occurrence – and a bunch of us stand in the kitchen trying to figure out what kind of police they were and whether they have the authority to shut down the event.

The squat has become known as a place for music. Throughout much of 2017, one resident – from Brazzaville, Republic of the Congo – organized and hosted an open mic night every Thursday, at which people gathered to perform and listen, dance and socialize.[1] French-language songs from

West Africa played on guitars; rap in Arabic performed over beats played on mobile phones. These weekly events, and the bigger shows that have developed out of them, are part of the social life of a community formed in transit and in waiting, in the 'politicolegal precariousness' (Cabot 2014: 10) of the asylum system in Greece. The squat has become a gathering place for refugees, for Greek solidarians and for volunteers from Western Europe who work at nearby community centres and humanitarian collectives.

This chapter is about this squat and the music nights that happen there. It focuses on the sounds that resound from this shelter and the forms of sociability that are fostered in the process. In doing so, I argue for the importance of studying the everyday, street-level experiences of displacement. This has a specific purpose: refugees are too often discussed only in ideological terms, as if they dwell entirely within a political realm, while shelter is too often considered only as the provision of something essential to survival rather than as a space where life unfolds in all its usual complexity. The result of both is that, in Diana Allan's (2014: 5) words, refugee lives are usually considered 'as if their aspirations and inner lives lacked the fractured complexities of Western consciousness and identity', which in turn results in a number of 'blind spots' regarding social life and agency (2014: 25).

My main contention here is that these complexities play out through politics and practices of vocality. Shelter is something that is voiced. Shelter is protection, but not only from the elements and from danger; shelter is where identities and cultures are protected, sustained, developed, reformulated and recombined. In turn, shelters develop their own identities and cultures – their own voices. Vocal practices generate publics, giving rise to new forms of collective identity and intimacy (Weidman 2014: 44). And they become sites of resistance, 'speaking back' to larger structures of power.

In other words, refugee shelters have sonic politics. Music and sound are ways in which people make claims on belonging and are ways in which solidarity is performed, but they are elsewhere heard as noise and become a means of creating borders in urban space. Certain sounds and people are heard as fitting or not fitting within 'appropriate soundscapes' (Trnka et al. 2013: 2) – of a city, a nation, even a continent. A squat party thus connects with, and speaks out against, current logics of border securitization, and we need to consider how voices at the street and policy levels engage with and distort one another. Focusing on everyday experiences of displacement does not mean tuning out from the bigger political and ideological forces that have created the necessity of squatting in the first place.

This is, then, an attempt to simultaneously study the social life of a refugee shelter and the forces that structure this social life. And this means embracing the messiness of life in protracted displacement, which in turn means dealing with a series of contradictions – sound/silence, permanence/transience, accommodation/eviction, solidarity/tension, invisibility/

audibility – which are threaded through this chapter. To do this, I turn first to the broader landscapes and soundscapes of refugee shelter in Athens, before listening to the squat's music nights as part of a mobile commons of migration. I close by considering how the squat is voiced by those who live there, and how shelter is redesigned sonically as part of broader migrant activisms in the city.

Sounding the Shelter

The squat was established in 2016 through the collaborative efforts of refugees from Central and West Africa, French activists and Greek solidarians – the latter defined by Katerina Rozakou (2018) as those who identify themselves through their activities of solidarity with immigrants, in social as well as legal terms. It houses fifteen people, who are self-organized and manage and maintain the space through weekly meetings. It fits into a broader landscape of shelters, squats and social centres that has expanded in Athens – and elsewhere in Greece – since the 'refugee crisis' hit hard in 2015. (I put the terms 'refugee crisis' in quotes here, not to suggest that there is not a crisis, but to suggest that it is not a crisis of or caused by refugees; rather, it is a crisis of humanitarianism and political will, with refugees at the sharp end.)

Many of these new shelters were founded in response to the inhumane conditions of government and United Nations High Commissioner for Refugees (UNHCR) camps and reception centres. Yet they also extend out of several longer intertwined histories. An asylum crisis in Greece predates the 'refugee crisis', while solidarianism is an outgrowth of earlier forms of anti-state mobilization. Further back, the Greek word for 'refugees' – πρόσφυγες (*prosfighes*) – has strong associations with experiences of displacement following the population exchange between Greece and Turkey in 1922 and 1923 (see Hirschon 1989). All of these histories map onto a particular Greek set of sociopolitics, centring on the concept of hospitality – φιλοξενία (*filoksenia*) – which permeates refugee–host relations and underpins understandings of the modern Greek nation state, but also creates power imbalances and is used to control the possible danger represented by the 'stranger' (Herzfeld 1987; Rozakou 2012).

In other words, Athens has long been an arrival city, a site of hospitality and hostility, of solidarity and anxiety. As an arrival city, it is a site of transition and of waiting, a space of negotiating Europe's borders, a place of transnational migrant communities and networks (Trimikliniotis et al. 2015: 63–64). It becomes a borderland. We can no longer think of borders only as lines on maps or physical barriers that separate nation states; instead, borders – and their enforcement – become part of everyday life, and border struggles become urban struggles (Brambilla et al. 2015; De Genova 2015). This is particularly stark in Greece, where the violent border logics of 'Fortress Europe' proliferate, multiply and permeate city streets as much as island hotspots.

We find this violence in the deployment of border control police (συνοριοφύλακες – *synoriofilakes*) in the centre of Athens. We find it in the rise in xenophobia and racist attacks that have accompanied financial crisis, in the broader criminalization of immigration, and the institutionalization of racial profiling and detention brought in with 'Operation Xenios Zeus' in 2012 (Rozakou 2018). For Giorgos Tsimouris and Roland Moore (2018: 73), 'in Greece, death in the terrestrial and maritime borders for security reasons as well as fatal attacks in the centre of Athens by the Neo-Nazis should be considered in common'. Border logics play out in urban space, and my argument here is that migration and securitization, inclusion and exclusion, squatting and sheltering have a soundtrack.

Again, this has a history. The refugee communities that developed out of the 1920s population exchange were subject to police visits, breaking up musical gatherings in refugee dwellings in Athens and Piraeus. Borders are drawn along sonic lines. David Novak (2014: 28) highlights how ideas of noise have frequently been indexed to foreignness, as something to be eliminated so as to protect or recover 'original' soundscapes. Borders pop up at moments of linguistic, ethnic or cultural division (Nail 2016: 145). Borders materialize on migrant bodies and migrant voices – everyday markers of racialized discrimination (De Genova 2015: 6). Yet, refugee shelters are also sites of agency and strategies of dealing with persecution and exclusion. Participatory architecture involves designing ways to collectively create, while keeping much of that creativity hidden from outside eyes and ears. Refugee communities have long used structures of protection to shelter sounds and other forms of cultural expression. This remains true today.

A Musical Mobile Commons

Four men join hands. They move into a space in front of the band, which becomes an impromptu dancefloor. The musicians are from Syria, Iran, Greece, Nigeria and the United Kingdom. They have formed a group since moving to Athens, and tonight's show at the squat is one of a string of live performances as they forge a reputation for themselves in the city. They are preparing to make professional recordings and perform at festivals across Greece.

The four men form a line and begin the swooping and stomping of *dabke*, an Arabic dance that has been claimed as having various national origins and was manipulated by modern nationalist politics through the twentieth century, but has also been part of efforts to foster a pan-Arabism, reaching its peak in the 1950s and 1960s, and is now part of a movement to cultivate a message of 'borderless humanity' through popular culture (Karkabi 2018; Silverstein 2012). The band are playing 'Wayn A Ramallah'. The song speaks of travelling to the Palestinian city in the title, and of a couple separated in the process. It is part of a setlist that includes songs from all around the Eastern Mediterranean and singing in four different languages.

Mobilities generate socialities. Groups of people come together in displacement in ways that would often be impossible before displacement. The squat is a place where these connections can be forged and sheltered, and is a node in a much larger network of life in the arrival city. These encounters and relations speak to and sit within what has been called a mobile commons of migration. Extending out of theories of urban commons and practices of commoning – whereby spaces, resources and various kinds of knowledge are shared and made public (Stavrides 2016) – the idea of the mobile commons centres on the mundane organizational practices of mobile people. Papadopoulos and Tsianos (2013: 191–92) posit five features of the mobile commons: (1) the invisible knowledge of mobility that circulates between people on the move; (2) infrastructures of connectivity that distribute and circulate this knowledge; (3) a multiplicity of informal economies; (4) transnational communities of justice; and (5) a mutual politics of care. These combine to form an organizational force for supporting freedom of movement.

All this requires effort and organization, and provides us with clear examples of the agency of those building social worlds in migration and displacement. Our host at the squat, during a conversation at a café elsewhere in the city, spoke in explicit terms about starting the music nights as a means of building community and finding people in a situation of separation from family. Dwight Conquergood, relatedly, writes of the tendency for refugee camps to be alive with performance culture, wherein their occupants use expressive culture to secure 'continuity and some semblance of stability', while at the same time playing with 'new identities, new strategies for adaptation and survival' (1988: 180). Musical events constitute part of the 'ad hoc coping strategies' of life in forced displacement (Allan 2014: 21).

These events also form part of refugee economies. The organizers buy crates of beer and sell the cans for profit from the squat's kitchen, which becomes a bar for the night. This tells us two things. First, and in accordance with recent research on refugee economies (Betts 2014), it debunks a string of myths about refugees being economically isolated, a burden on host states and dependent on humanitarian assistance. Second, it subverts ideas about guest–host relations, flipping normative assumptions that local communities 'host' refugee communities (Rozakou 2012: 572). When a building is repurposed as a squat, and a refugee organizes an event attended by people from across Europe, Africa and the Middle East, questions of hosting and host communities get pretty complicated pretty quickly.

This also takes us way beyond conceiving of life in refuge and exile only in terms of what is essential for survival – that which Giorgio Agamben (1995) famously characterized as 'bare life' – and to consider the playfulness and pleasures that people bring and seek in such situations. The music events are at once spectacular and completely mundane. They show displacement in Greece to be about uneasy but peaceful coexistence as much as it is about hot spots and flashpoints of violence. In many ways, they follow the model of invisible knowledge and improvised infrastructures outlined above, yet they also add a creative outlet to these mechanisms of care, exchange and solidarity. In other words, the squat is a space where people can define 'new socialities, new spatialities and reshape new citizenship modes' (Trimikliniotis et al. 2015: 15). It fits into a network of places of musical performance across the city, from public squares to social centres to underground radio stations – a musical mobile commons.

This is not to suggest that Athens is some kind of urban playground for refugees (or indeed that refugee life is somehow fun). Seeking cultural expression involves negotiations with various authorities. Police visiting the squat in relation to the sound produced at the music nights are told that the gathering is a birthday party for one of the residents – part of a set of practices, struggles and strategies for evading control – which is usually met with acceptance. Maybe these police visits are a form of what Didier Fassin (2013: xii) calls 'proactive intervention' on the rise in urban policing, in connection with immigration and security jumping to the top of the political agenda across Europe in the last decade or so: 'random patrolling in search of subjects'. (The organizer of the music nights has been subject to being stopped and searched by the police in Athens.) Maybe they are part of a recursive history of migration, whereby relations between new arrivals and those responsible for enforcing order loop back on themselves – thinking back to the song at the start of the chapter. Or maybe they represent more of a tacit agreement with the police: a 'reciprocal concession', in order to maintain a 'quasi-contract of non-violence' (Trimikliniotis et al. 2015: 70–71).

In any case, these encounters speak to the multiple meanings of the word 'accommodation' – accommodation as shelter, but also as welcome, toleration, reconciliation, mutual adaptation. The material conditions and lived experiences of refugee shelter are tied to state policy on squatting and housing more generally, which in turn is indexed to broader European stances on migration and securitization. This is another way of saying that the squat sits at the intersections of a multitude of border logics, and accommodation is thus always in flux, subject to political vicissitudes, caught up in dynamics of tolerance and eviction. So, while on the one hand, closed borders imbue life with a sense of permanence and stasis, on the other hand, the refugee condition is still thought of as temporary and shelter is conceived of as something provisional or transient: 'spaces people occupy rather than worlds they inhabit' (Allan 2014: 25). Protracted displacement fosters both temporalities at the same time.

Voicing the Squat

The live musicians have finished performing and have packed their equipment away. The squat transforms itself again. Now, it becomes a hip-hop club: the floor is given to emcees who exchange verses in French and Arabic, English and Farsi, over beats supplied by DJs from Greece and France. Rappers jump in and out, passing the two microphones and the multiple languages between themselves. Many refer to the squat itself in their raps, signifying it as a space of creative responses to displacement. The shutters on one side of the building are open as people spill out onto the street to continue conversations or get some air. The beats spill out with them, mocking the idea of a binary between public and private space. Breaks in the music come only to reward someone with acclaim after a particularly compelling performance or to defuse the occasional scuffle that breaks out.

The shifts that the squat has undergone since its founding, that it undergoes over the course of a single night and that I have traced so far in this chapter highlight a theme of rethinking refugee shelter generally: sheltering is an activity – a process, not simply a place. In this final section, I want to argue that shelter is also something that is voiced. And that voicing is also a process rather than something somebody has or does not have. This matters precisely because it is the concept of the 'refugee voice' that is so often used in humanitarian campaigns, but that equally often strap these voices to narratives of victimhood or posit the act of 'giving voice' as necessary for refugees to be heard at all (Cabot 2016). To think about voicing is to think about how shelter is reappropriated and redesigned: creatively, collaboratively, from the bottom up.

'Squat the World: Rap against State and Law'. As is clear from the banner hanging defiantly from the wall, the musical and sonic politics of hip-hop are considered compatible with the anti-authoritarianism of squatting. The music nights can be heard as an example of what Tyler and Marciniak (2013: 143) call 'migrant activism', with 'coalitions of citizens and noncitizens engaging in various forms of advocacy and resistance around the enforced destitution, dispersal, detention, and deportation of refugee populations'. These are uninstitutionalized forms of activism. Mobility and mobilization are tied together. Migrant political practices do not conform to historical models or fit institutional expectations. Instead, they develop their own codes and logics, through which, in the words of Papadopoulos and Tsianos

(2013: 184), 'movement *itself* becomes a political movement and a social movement'.

One way of understanding this is to focus on migrant music and the sonic politics of the squat as acts of citizenship (Isin 2008: 18), whereby subjects make claims on belonging and transform themselves into citizens through particular practices and performances. Another way – again following Tyler and Marciniak (2013: 149–50) – is to consider them as acts *against* citizenship, rejecting exclusionary regimes of national security and control. Probably, and problematically, both are true. Migrant politics involve demanding the rights of citizenship while simultaneously drawing attention to how precarious and violent it is. It might not be possible to resolve these contradictions, but the shelter, the squat, is where they can be thought through, set aside and voiced.

At the same time, voicing the contradictions of asylum and refuge through music and sound brings its own dangers. As well as having to deal with the police, the squat has drawn the attention of the far-right in Athens, who on one occasion visited with a gun with the explicit message that they would *silence* the music nights and their organizer in particular. Noise complaints can have severe consequences in a city of crisis. Alongside familiar questions of the right to the city (Lefebvre 1968) and what Hannah Arendt (1951) wrote of as the right to have rights, we can add *the right to make sound* as a contested social terrain of citizenship.

And yet, musical identities – as with any kinds of identities – do not remain fixed in transit and displacement. Sound cultures – as with any kinds of cultures – are fluid, hybrid and transnational. At the open mic nights in 2017, the host would open the show by performing a song called 'Parakalo' – Greek for both 'please' and 'you're welcome'. 'Parakalo' is a song under constant construction and revision, expanding as the host's Greek language skills expand. Again, the aim is explicitly to connect with people (and has apparently been met with enthusiasm from elderly Greek women when performed in public squares).

All of this is to say that the squat is continually being voiced and that these voices carry within them experiences of and responses to displacement. This connects with theories of voice more generally. As Amanda Weidman points out, because they are at once embodied and performed, voices serve as 'deeply felt markers of class, race, geographic origin, etc'. (2014: 40). But it is a mistake to assume that voices are singular and link coherently with a fixed identity. Instead, speakers can have multiple relationships to their own voices, and a single voice can be collectively produced. Voices are fragmented. This phenomenon is likely heightened through forced displacement, with voicing being less about fixed ethnonational identities and more about encounters and interactions. But voices are also participatory. They *design* sound and they *sound* design. And these sounds structure spaces of shelter as much as the materials and surfaces through which they resonate.

The idea of voicing breaks down the dichotomy of refugees either having (or being given) a voice, or being silent or silenced. Sound and silence are things strategically chosen and performed at particular given moments, based on knowledge accrued in displacement. Such thinking recognizes and reintroduces refugee agency. And it draws attention to the squat as a multivocal site: something voiced and performed, collaboratively and collectively. Athens is a border, but it is also a theatre, where the control of mobility and escape through mobility are performed in countless messy everyday forms (Trimikliniotis et al. 2015: 64).

Outro

Sound and voice help us understand sheltering as dwelling, what spaces of displacement mean to those who live in and occupy them, and how the affective and political dimensions of shelter are intertwined. Material practices and subjectivities are brought together through voicing. Shelter is voiced; shelters develop voices. A final example: at another refugee squat in Athens, I played a New Year's Eve concert with the band featured earlier in this chapter. As the clock struck midnight, the children who lived in the shelter ran to the balcony and yelled the name of the squat down into the street below. Sheltering became belonging; structures of protection became infrastructures of defiance. Broadening out from this, studying shelter requires engagement with the senses, asking what these spaces sound like. It matters what people hear, in the same way that it matters what people see, touch, taste and smell.

At the same time, studying refugee shelter is a study of precariousness. The next time I met with the organizer of the music nights, a couple of weeks after his most recent gig, he told me he had since left the squat and was living elsewhere, having spent a few nights sleeping on the streets. There would no longer be music nights at the squat, but he was already scoping out places for forthcoming events. This chapter is thus recast as an exercise in representing the uncertainty and adversity of refugee shelter. As Allan puts it, ethnographic knowledge is contingent, 'always built on the shifting sands of the historical moment' (2014: 25). I thus close this chapter without closure. And maybe this is the point: refugee shelter is fragile and always in flux, and only those who live in such spaces can really tell their stories. The best that the rest of us can do is to listen.

Tom Western is a Marie Curie Fellow in the Faculty of Humanities at the University of Oslo. He works primarily in Athens, Greece, where his research connects music, sound, borders and citizenships. His first book is forthcoming with Bloomsbury Academic Press and he has recently published in the journals *Migration and Society*, *Sound Studies* and *Ethnomusicology Forum*.

Note

1. The people mentioned in this chapter have been anonymized to protect their identities, but I am immensely grateful to them for welcoming me into their homes and inviting me to participate in their musical activities.

References

Agamben, G. 1995. *Homo Sacer: Sovereign Power and Bare Life*. Stanford: Stanford University Press.
Allan, D. 2014. *Refugees of the Revolution: Experiences of Palestinian Exile*. Stanford: Stanford University Press.
Arendt, H. 1951. *The Origins of Totalitarianism*. New York: Schocken.
Betts, A. 2014. *Refugee Economies: Rethinking Popular Assumptions*. Oxford: Humanitarian Innovation Project.
Brambilla, C. et al. 2015. 'Introduction: Thinking, Mapping, Acting and Living Borders under Contemporary Globalisation', in C. Brambilla et al. (eds), *Borderscaping: Imaginations and Practices of Border Making*. London: Routledge, pp. 1–9.
Cabot, H. 2014. *On the Doorstep of Europe: Asylum and Citizenship in Greece*. Philadelphia: University of Pennsylvania Press.
———. 2016. '"Refugee Voices": Tragedy, Ghosts, and the Anthropology of Not Knowing'. *Journal of Contemporary Ethnography* 45(6): 645–72.
Conquergood, D. 1988. 'Health Theatre in a Hmong Refugee Camp: Performance, Communication, and Culture'. *Drama Review* 32(3): 174–208.
De Genova, N. 2015. 'Border Struggles in the Migrant Metropolis'. *Nordic Journal of Migration Research* 5(1): 3–10.
Fassin, D. 2013. *Enforcing Order: An Ethnography of Urban Policing*. Cambridge: Polity Press.
Herzfeld, M. 1987. '"As in Your Own House": Hospitality, Ethnography, and the Stereotype of Mediterranean Society', in D. Gilmore (ed.), *Honor and Shame and the Unity of the Mediterranean*. Washington DC: American Anthropological Association, pp. 75–89.
Hirschon, R. 1989. *Heirs of the Greek Catastrophe: The Social Life of Asia Minor Refugees in Piraeus*. Oxford: Clarendon Press.
Isin, E. 2008. 'Theorising Acts of Citizenship', in E. Isin and G, Nielsen (eds), *Acts of Citizenship*. London: Zed Books, pp. 15–43.

Karkabi, N. 2018. 'Electro-Dabke: Performing Cosmopolitan Nationalism and Borderless Humanity', *Symposium of the ICTM Study Group, Essaouira - Mediterranean Music Studies: Music and Sound at the Mediterranean Crossroads*, 18–23 June. Essaouira: ICTM.
Lefebvre, H. 1968. *Le Droit à la Ville*. Paris: Anthropos.
Nail, T. 2016. *Theory of the Border*. Oxford: Oxford University Press.
Novak, D. 2014. 'A Beautiful Noise Emerging from the Apparatus of an Obstacle: Trains and the Sounds of the Japanese City', in M. Gandy and B.J. Nilsen (eds), *The Acoustic City*. Berlin: Jovis Verlag, pp. 27–32.
Papadopoulos, D., and V. Tsianos. 2013. 'After Citizenship: Autonomy of Migration, Organisational Ontology and Mobile Commons'. *Citizenship Studies* 17(2): 178–96.
Rozakou, K. 2012. 'The Biopolitics of Hospitality in Greece: Humanitarianism and the Management of Refugees'. *American Ethnologist* 39(3): 562–77.
——. 2018. 'Solidarians in the Land of Xenios Zeus: Migrant Deportability and the Radicalisation of Solidarity', in D. Dalakoglou and G. Agelopoulos (eds), *Critical Times in Greece: Anthropological Engagements with the Crisis*. London: Routledge, pp. 188–201.
Silverstein, S. 2012. 'Syria's Radical Dabke'. *Middle East Report* 263: 33–37.
Stavrides, S. 2016. *Common Space: The City as Commons*. London: Zed Books.
Trimikliniotis, N., D. Parsanoglou and V. Tsianos. 2015. *Mobile Commons, Migrant Digitalities and the Right to the City*. Basingstoke: Palgrave Macmillan.
Trnka, S., C. Dureau and J. Park. 2013. 'Introduction: Senses and Citizenships', in S. Trnka, C. Dureau and J. Park (eds), *Senses and Citizenships: Embodying Political Life*. London: Routledge, pp. 1–32.
Tsimouris, G., and R. Moore. 2018. 'Death in the Greek Territorial and Symbolic Borders: Anti-immigrant Action for Policing the Crisis', in D. Dalakoglou and G. Agelopoulos (eds), *Critical Times in Greece: Anthropological Engagements with the Crisis*. London: Routledge, pp. 73–85.
Tyler, I., and K. Marciniak. 2013. 'Immigrant Protest: An Introduction'. *Citizenship Studies* 17(2): 143–56.
Weidman, A. 2014. 'Anthropology and Voice'. *Annual Review of Anthropology* 43: 37–51.

Figure 10.1 The Melissa Day Centre in Athens, Greece. © Mark E. Breeze, based on an image supplied by Ashley Mehra.

10
Redignifying Refugees
A Critical Study of Citizen-Run Shelters in Athens

Ashley Mehra

Surrounding the neighbourhood of Kypseli in the centre of Athens lies Agios Panteleimonas Square, an area that has become identified with the Greek far right (Human Rights Watch 2012). Since the late 1990s, members of the Golden Dawn party and their right-wing populist allies have been visibly organizing in the area around the square. The influx of migrants after the clearing operations ahead of the 2004 Olympics prompted the party members to take control of the area with the aim of entrenching an anti-immigrant politics of exclusion (Vradis and Dalakoglou 2011). Yet just steps from the square, a very different kind of political experiment is underway. Since 2015, two spaces of refuge have opened, both founded by members of Greek civil society together with refugees and migrants: the Melissa Day Centre and City Plaza.

Kypseli has long been in transition. For most of the twentieth century, middle- and upper-middle-class families flocked to the upmarket district, attracted by its neoclassical architecture, shops and spacious parks. The large, modern apartment buildings were the first in Athens. By the 1980s, however, many residents of Kypseli had decamped to the more affluent northern suburbs, and the well-heeled were replaced by immigrants and refugees from Eastern Europe who found affordable apartments in the once-grand buildings along Patission Street (Balampanidis and Polyzos 2016). The migrants were followed by the forces of reaction: members of the Golden

Dawn party soon established a stronghold in Agios Panteleimonas Square with the aim of spreading ultranationalism and xenophobia throughout the Greek political system (Bampilis 2017). The opposition has continued through the onset of refugee flows to Greece starting in 2015, when the square transformed into a makeshift camp for arriving Afghan refugees (Zikakou 2015).

Activists established the Melissa Day Centre and City Plaza in this area: two multiethnic and diverse citizen-run spaces of shelter, with members from more than forty countries speaking more than a dozen languages. Nadina Christopolou, a cofounder of the Melissa Day Centre, remarked that 'the choice of place is relevant, because this location was a stronghold of the Golden Dawn, we wanted to *reclaim* the space . . . we decided to remake what was strange' (Christopolou 2017a). Nasim Lomani, a cofounder of City Plaza, similarly stated that 'it was important for [us that] the refugees join with the struggle of the locals. People would then stand much more with us than against us. The locals [needed to] at least realize that their problems are not those of the refugees' (Lomani 2017). Although the surrounding neighbourhood originally opposed both Melissa and City Plaza, the spaces successfully opened in July 2015 and April 2016, respectively. I will refer to both as citizen-run shelters, which I define as open spaces regulated[1] by members of civil society who collaborate with refugees to organize and operate the shelter. Beyond providing physical protection, the shelter acts as a form of solidarity and inclusion in the social sphere.

While the Melissa Day Centre and City Plaza share similar purposes, origins, locations and membership, these shelters also differ in important ways. Melissa has repurposed a former two-floor, neoclassical apartment into a centre hosting approximately 150 refugee and migrant women. City Plaza, by contrast, has transformed an abandoned seven-floor hotel into a communal living space for around 500 people, most of whom are refugee families. In this chapter, I argue that citizen-run shelters like the Melissa Day Centre and City Plaza instantiate experiments in integration and democracy that seek to redignify refugees. As I argue, redignification is an evolutionary process that entails the elevation of the relational status of refugees by giving them political and social agency that would otherwise be denied to them in their statelessness. Based on interviews and participation observation in both centres, I observe the limitations of redignification in practice and suggest how it can apply to the study of refugee shelter more broadly.

From Camps to Dignified Alternatives

Spaces of refuge are often characterized by their indignity, and many scholars over the past two decades have invoked a variety of theoretical frames to make sense of this process. Giorgio Agamben's (1998) concept of bare life (*zoē*) has been a particularly fertile concept, describing the physically harsh conditions that refugees face in camps and the way that social and political life ends up neglected. Other scholars have followed Foucault (1979) in coming to understand such settlements as 'heterotopias', where residents exist geographically within the state, but legally and politically have 'no place'. The political condition of the refugee has been characterized with reference to Arendt's (1958) concept of statelessness and total marginalization as well as through Goffman's idea of total institutions (Malkki 1995). More recently, Merril Smith (2004) introduced the concept of 'warehousing' to describe the situation in refugee camps: rather than integrate refugees into the host country while waiting for asylum, Smith argued, camp life disempowers residents and 'warehoused refugees become spectators to their own lives rather than active participants in decision-making' (Smith 2004: 38; see also Agier 2011, Harrell-Bond 1985, 2002; and Verdirame and Harrell-Bond 2005).

If camps and hierarchical state institutions are the de facto practices of refugee shelter, there would seem little hope for resistance, creativity and refugee agency. However, scholars of refugee shelter can also track contemporary shifts away from camps and towards more participatory and collaborative institutional arrangements, such as the Melissa Day Centre and City Plaza. The United Nations High Commissioner on Refugees (UNHCR) and the Greek government have both publicly committed to an 'out-of-camp' policy with the objective to close all camps as soon as possible, and in 2014, the UNHCR published a 'Policy on Alternatives to Camps' with the objective of making camps 'the exception, and, to the extent possible, a temporary measure' (2014: 6).[2] By July 2018, about half of the camps on mainland Greece had closed, with thirty-three remaining, and in Athens, citizen-led actions gained momentum as an alternative method of organizing spaces of refuge that see agentive potential in the refugees and their surrounding communities.

This movement contrasts with the warehousing effects of refugee camps, where residents are subject to paternalism or hierarchy imposed from above and are removed from decision-making or shared governance. Indeed, the levels of engagement by refugees in building and organizing shelter covers a wide spectrum: from neglected and incarcerated spaces to partially self-appropriated spaces to entirely self-built, yet provisional shelters. However, across the spectrum, temporality is baked into the basic architecture of such spaces, and humanitarian materials are generally provided for the sake of constructing *and* deconstructing the shelter. Meanwhile, the citizen-run shelters of Athens are different. They recognize that materials are temporary and ephemeral, and instead emphasize enduring interpersonal relationships rather than enduring physical forms. This collaborative impulse of citizen-activists and refugees to build shelter has initiated an experiment in redignification: the transformation of traditionally sterile and oppositional spaces of containment into vibrant social and political centres that treat migrants and refugees as free and equal persons.

In making sense of this wave of citizen-run shelters, I follow Josiah Ober, who defines dignity as 'having one's claims recognized by others, having their respect, having some measure of control over one's life, having a say in decisions, and having responsibility for one's choices' (2009: 2). Further, Ober (2012) writes that dignity stands against humiliation (disrespect as a moral equal) and infantilization (lack of one's recognition as a choice-making adult). As a relational concept, dignity in citizen-run shelters concerns not only how the individual is treated, but also how a related constellation of people is treated. Members of the citizen-run shelters not only aim to empower each individual, but also to collectively create webs of meaningful relations that help form a community of empowerment. In the following sections, I show how the Melissa Day Centre and City Plaza redignify refugee participants through the organization and operation of *space*, cultivation of *interpersonal relations* and dynamics of *collective action*.

The Melissa Day Centre: An Experiment in Social Integration

In Greek, Melissa (μέλισσα) means 'bee'. The name gives meaning to Melissa's 'vision of society not as a set of isolated cells but as an open beehive of communication, creativity, and exchange' (IIP Interactive 2016). The physically porous design of Melissa resembles a beehive and its organization is transparent: a large, wide, green double-door marks the open entrance; the space is bright and clean, with open windows and French doors leading to an outdoor garden. There is no waiting room; instead, the entrance allows immediate access to a living room with a homely atmosphere, including couches, a dining table and decorative wall art. Melissa's built environment reflects its aspiration to help refugees adapt to their host society, while cultivating the host society's capacity to welcome refugees and accept 'a diverse and cohesive society framework' (CAMOC 2017). Indeed, Melissa has actively transformed the building's spatial dynamics to establish friendly relations with surrounding locals: it opens its doors to visitors, invites and hosts events with local Greek neighbours, and uses social media to broadcast daily activities.

Local businesses, shops and restaurants are a vital part of Melissa's interactive classroom. Refugee women practise their Greek by interacting with neighbouring shopkeepers and locals, and, according to one of the cofounders, 'Melissa was able to reclaim the space by patronizing local shops ... and thereby introducing ourselves and giving them [shopkeepers] a chance to get to know the migrant and refugee women' (CAMOC 2017).[3] In the face of potential hostility from the Golden Dawn party, the organizers of Melissa made it even more open and accessible to the public by creating an open-door policy. Melissa generated high levels of transparency, making it easier to earn the support of its Greek neighbours and thus more effectively protect itself from hostile actors.[4] This lack of boundaries in the physical space mirrors the demographics of its members. Although the leaders of Melissa stressed their intention to limit the 'numbers-based' rhetoric about refugees, many are eager to share the global reach of their organization, telling me that over 700 women and children from over 45 countries participate in their programmes and that, so far, no one has dropped out.

The Melissa Day Centre does not see the varied linguistic profiles of the participants as a source of conflict. Instead, it organizes 'mixed classes' in which migrants and refugees with different linguistic backgrounds have the opportunity to collaborate and learn together. These mixed classes have an integrative function: 'the common denominator here is the *new* language they are learning. The model of the classes is structured thematically ... to "practice" coexistence instead of just preaching it' (Christopolou 2017a). This porousness of Melissa allows it to extend its reach to the neighbourhood in which it is embedded; the process of redignification thus involves expanding open circles of relation, rather than a confining, closed circuit between the refugees and Centre organizers.

While the Melissa Day Centre visibly opens its space to the local neighbourhood, it also provides a space within for international interaction with the local community: ethnic Greeks and longtime immigrant residents regularly circulate throughout the Centre. According to Demir (2017), 'the biggest difference between Melissa and the camps is the human contact, seeing people's faces: by organizing formally, putting people in boxes as accommodation without an address, you lose links with people'.[5] Participants learn a sense of responsibility and they are not treated as passive recipients of services but are empowered as active agents of change 'for their own lives, their families, their societies, as well as for the society that hosts them' (Christopolou 2017b).

With the object of 'learning based on community building', the Melissa Day Centre developed a model called *Alef*, which gives structure to the mutual interactions between refugee and migrant women within the space.[6] *Alef* is built on seven pillars: (1) literacy; (2) psychosocial support; (3) information and referral; (4) advocacy support; (5) art and creativity; (6) skills development; and (7) communal care (Christopolou 2017a, 2017b). Each member of Melissa commits to some of these activities for four to five hours per day.

Between 2015 and 2017, over 700 women have participated in programming at the Centre, and with each pillar, Melissa offers refugee women the space to work by either participating and volunteering or creating and teaching classes. Women who speak more than one language might become translators within the space; an asylum seeker who helped teach and translate at Melissa, for instance, was subsequently employed as a teacher and cultural mediator in Athens (Demir 2017). Moreover, by offering space for women to share their expertise, Melissa helps build and advance their skills and increase their employability. Some refugee women have created films and organized screenings, designed art classes and even launched community engagement activities at the Athens Municipality's home for the elderly.[7] Melissa prioritizes engaging refugee and migrant women to start programmes in the space so that they are validated for their skills as community leaders (Christopolou 2017b).

Such a high degree of mutuality is integral to the functioning of these integration activities and has effectively transformed even the language of relationality within the space. Christopolou (2017a) described her relationship to the other women in the space this way: 'They call us different names ... when they start feeling familiarity, they will call me "mother" ... but they call everybody "teacher".' By calling each other 'teacher', the women – refugees, migrants, Greek citizens and international volunteers alike – elevate one another. All take a position of authority and share their skills and knowledge with one another. The language of respect becomes a vital tool in repositioning members as agents with equal power to build and cultivate their community. By cooperating with and elevating one another as 'teachers', the women at Melissa participate in their own redignification.

Instead of viewing its purpose as charitable, Melissa aims to create a culture of mutual respect, encouraging refugees to harness and share their skills with one another 'to be able to rebuild their lives whether in Greece or in other countries' (CAMOC 2017). Refugees can seek additional support from members of the space but can also provide support to others within the community. The Melissa Day Centre creates porous and open boundaries that prefigure a broader sense of community. It cultivates collaboration and affiliation both between its members, and externally, with the surrounding neighbourhood. It also creates a collective, action-oriented culture by including refugee clients in planning and facilitating their own integration. Through these three processes, Melissa introduces dignity into the space of refuge by opening up its communal space to the outside, facilitating internal and external relations between the refugees and their Greek neighbours, and instituting a pathway towards integration that requires the refugees to be actively involved. It is a form of shelter that offers a stark contrast to camps.

City Plaza: An Experiment in Democratization

In addition to integration, citizen-run shelters employ democratic practices with the aim of redignifying the space of refuge and the refugee community within.[8] This is best illustrated by the operations of City Plaza. City Plaza is a former hotel, which was left abandoned and taken over to create apartment spaces for around 500 people, along with two types of physical space that sustain democratic processes: an 'assembly hall' for centralized decision-making and 'working spaces' for decentralized decision-making. All decisions at City Plaza are made through a consensus-based model, and the creation of these various 'gathering spaces' recognizes that all members of the space assume collective responsibility for the community.

Every fifteen days, all members congregate in the assembly hall to deliberate on issues and make decisions that are relevant to the community. During these meetings, announcements are made, proposals are raised, updates from each of the working group committees are voiced and impromptu discussions take place. Listening to the working group updates is important to all of the residents because working group memberships are always in rotation. The general assembly meetings may principally play an administrative role in the functioning of City Plaza, but the execution of the meetings reflects the process of redignification: refugees are given a voice in the meetings and make choices that affect themselves. They participate in decisions that have consequences for others in the community, and the general assembly meetings provide a space for refugees to have an equal voice in voting on issues relevant to the space of refuge in which they live. City Plaza also offers a space to collaborate with members of the Greek host society and to take on leadership roles. Leadership in the meetings rotates among the residents, so that every participant is given a say on voting items and individuals have equal access to information relevant to vote responsibly.

In principle, the consensus-based model promotes all participants being seen and heard, regardless of their political status, ethnic or national background. Lomani (2017), for example, has commented on the structure of decision-making:

> Some people come a few hours a day, or once a month or once a week, or all twenty-four hours, but what we are struggling against is to not connect the hours with privilege; if someone is doing more things that does not mean that he has a stronger voice here. [It is] much more a process of justice, not only of equality ... [We are] a place that tries to push everyone to participate in decision-making on the field and [to be] active.

If this quotation demonstrates optimism about the future prospects for their experiment in democracy, the organizers of City Plaza also recognize some of the challenges they face. One longtime organizer, for example, observed that: '[City Plaza] creates encounters that are deep, and I don't mean this simplistically. They are not always peaceful encounters. There are conflicts. I fight with my neighbour on the third floor because their children are crying all the time and I want to sleep' (Kalodoukas 2016). These conflicts are resolved through dialogue, facilitated by ground rules posted throughout the building.

These rules aim to manage potential conflict and encourage a culture of taking responsibility for one another. They include the instruction to *always* listen to, respect and empower others; to *always* let everyone, children especially, participate in planning and delivering activities that are related to them; to *never* hit or otherwise physically assault or abuse others; and to *never* act in ways meant to shame, humiliate or degrade others. When conflict arises, the first mode of resolution is to talk to the person one-on-one. If the situation cannot be resolved this way, then the community comes together to render a judgment. So far, these rules have effectively managed conflict in the space. As one organizer explained, 'we have had no problems of violence; problems are only solved through dialogue ... We emphasize respect towards other people and towards the place where we all live' (Scampoli and Cardinali 2017). The community of City Plaza acts as a collective arbiter of conflict, executing a set of agreed-upon rules, and the population (~500) is small enough that collective decisions can be made by direct vote and those who implement these decisions can be held directly accountable by the community.

Members of City Plaza also participate in political activism outside the space. This publicizes the project's initiative while also making it possible 'for the refugees to speak out about their own issues as a way of demand' (Lomani 2017). Greek activists and refugee members of City Plaza hold mass demonstrations in Athens in solidarity with all refugees and migrants, and their investment in promoting refugee voices demonstrates the relational nature of their understanding of dignity: the dignity of the refugees, as political subjects, exists not merely as an individual possession, but inheres in the relationships that they foster between their own community and that of the host community. Being seen and heard does not merely express solitary action, but also the refugees' assertion of their rightful presence in a network of political relationships in Greek civil society. Moreover, demonstrations and protests organized by City Plaza residents often call for the closure of the remaining camps and advocate for full integration of asylum seekers into host societies. An International Day of Action in June of 2017, for example, was meant to gather 'the refugee squats of Athens and groups in more than ten cities around the world [to] participate in a series of protests in order to show solidarity with the refugees and squats of Athens' (Lomani 2017). Here, City Plaza exhibited its connection to the global movements with which it identifies.

Many former City Plaza residents too have shown their continued commitment to hold demonstrations of their own throughout Europe, advocating for more dignified living spaces and for full social integration of refugees and migrants. A group of former residents have started a global, online campaign – Swarming Solidarity (2017) – to help solicit donations for the building. This global campaign demonstrates the strength of community fostered through City Plaza's project: the bonds cultivated within the City Plaza are visibly robust enough that they live on beyond the physical space of the building itself. Even when refugees gain asylum outside Greece, they remain committed to fighting for the dignity of their former fellow residents and continue to harness their political agency in their communities. This shows how City Plaza's political engagement with its wider community highlights refugee concerns and promotes self-organization. These members do not merely engage in political discourse, but also take part in on-the-ground politics. They seek to fundamentally change the decision-making structure of refugee spaces by prefiguring these changes in City Plaza itself. The City Plaza occupation makes a democratic claim: that anyone who uses the space of refuge, regardless of difference, earns an equal stake in its operation. Dignity for the refugees within City Plaza thus emerges from their status as members of a self-governing polity entrusted with making consequential decisions about its daily life.

Conclusion: Shelter as Redignification

Citizen-run shelters do not offer a prescriptive formula but rather represent a vital impulse: they illustrate how refugee shelter can be fluid, flexible and experimental. Instead of designing shelters as exceptional spaces of emergency that focus on narrow physical needs, these citizen-run shelters are bridges to humanity – and dignity – without a time stamp. They demonstrate that redignification is central to shelter. If the purpose of shelter is to protect and nurture people, then it must involve inclusion and democratic participation. More broadly, citizen-run shelters show the value of thinking about 'shelter' as a dynamic, social process rather than a static place. We can observe how the makeup of a shelter is continuously adapted as participants move in and out of it, especially as those who populate the shelter prioritize the space's elements, applying personal skills to change how the shelter functions. In other words, the protean nature of shelter ultimately enables it to survive amid changes in the community and local context. These examples may not be appropriate to solve every kind of refugee crisis, but they do offer a model to redignify and democratize refugee life.

In practice, of course, citizen-run shelters can fall short of their normative aspirations. Although such spaces aim to manifest a de jure horizontal leadership structure, members do take on de facto leadership roles. In City Plaza, for example, the Greek organizers often counsel other members who seek guidance in making decisions about the space. Their steady involvement in the project's initiatives since its inception, dwelling in the space with other residents and willingness to vocalize their opinions have given them licence to assume leadership roles. But the presence of 'natural' leaders is not necessarily in conflict with City Plaza's model of self-organization; after all, these de facto leaders do not usurp power, but rather exercise an important centripetal influence. Indeed, given the nature of continuous change in the populace and activities of citizen-run shelters, leaders introduce some stability to maintain the general functioning and cohesiveness in the space. Successful democratic leadership requires the joint commitment to a goal between the leaders and members of the collective; the primary function then of a leader in a self-organized space, like City Plaza, is to help coordinate action towards achieving a common goal. Instead of being antithetical to participatory self-government, leaders can in fact become integral to making collective agency possible (Beerbohm 2015).

To reduce the threat of leaders seizing authority and becoming a governing elite, members of the space must defend features that promote horizontal leadership: open access to information to all members necessary to form reasoned opinions; a joint commitment to participation in making choices for the community; a general assembly apparatus; and decentralized committees. To a certain extent, the advantages of inclusiveness and equal participation are a product of the space's intimate size. Larger-scale democratic participation might require the delegation of authority to representatives. Like leaders in a direct democratic system, representatives in a successful democracy would be tasked with coordinating political action and voicing the opinions of the collective whole in a debatable arena. The collective would retain *negative* power to contest, criticize and judge the decisions made by its elected representatives and act as a check against its authority. Given continuous communication between the represented and their representatives, a processual model of representation can also be an effective and dynamic political institution for decision-making in a larger, pluralistic democratic space (Urbinati 2006).

As the climate of refugee reception continues to shift away from the camps, a serious consideration of alternative structures calls for reorienting traditional service relationships. The Melissa Day Centre and City Plaza demonstrate the democratic, participatory potential of refugee shelters: experiments in redignification that show the ways in which including refugees in the organization of space can inform how they find a place for themselves in their host community.

Additional research on citizen-led shelters in Athens could provide insight into if and how the alternative approach may persist or change over time, and a survey of the various spatial, social and political features of existing citizen-run shelters in urban centres beyond Athens and outside of Greece would further expand upon the case studies I have presented here. With a more expansive collection of data, we can begin to question why a citizen-led movement thrives in a particular environment or culture, as well as examine the ways in which ethnic, religious, national or gender differences affect the social structure of citizen-run shelters. Do differences in identity create friction between members of a principally 'free and equal' community or even engender hierarchies within the experimental centres? The myriad pathways to continued research indicate the potential to expand upon and advance our understanding of citizen-led movements as a viable alternative to refugee shelter.

Ashley Mehra engages with scholarship in human rights and historical and literary research on democratic institutions in the sociopolitical context of antiquity. A Phi Beta Kappa graduate, she was awarded the best undergraduate thesis for her political science work. She received her M.Phil. in Classics as a Buckley Scholar at the University of Cambridge, King's College in 2019.

Notes

1. I use the word 'regulated' here loosely because the citizen-activists do not hold official titles and do not consider themselves to be official authorities.
2. In the same report, the UNHCR describes its rationale for the shift in policy: 'The defining characteristic of a camp, however, is typically some degree of limitation on the rights and freedoms of refugees and their ability to make meaningful choices about their lives. Pursuing alternatives to camps means working to remove such restrictions so that refugees have the possibility to live with greater dignity, independence and normality as members of the community, either from the beginning of displacement or as soon as possible thereafter'. (2014: 4).
3. Demir (2017), another longtime member of Melissa, adds: 'It is important that they [the refugee women] can walk into a shop and have the ability to say what they need in Greek so that they can independently make those choices'.
4. A cofounder of Melissa (CAMOC 2017) further commented on the organization's strategy: 'We [Melissa] established ourselves in the middle of it. We opened our doors and our windows. We went door to door and became acquainted; we informed everyone about our work, supported the local shop owners and economy, cleaned up our corner, brought out the drug dealers and brought in our plans'.
5. Demir (2017) continues her comment about the value of homegrown initiatives concerning refugee reception: 'I think part of [our approach] stems from the fact that we are housed in the Greek community. We, Greeks, can't do anything

without personal ties . . . Always at Melissa, I am with my conscience as my job, I feel this immediacy and intimacy'.
6. Like the organization's name 'Melissa', *Alef* also has its own significant meaning: *Alef* is the root of 'alpha', the first letter in the Greek alphabet, and thus 'stands for the first steps in a new life' (Christopolou 2017b).
7. Similarly, City Plaza has given its residents the platform to innovate self-directed initiatives, such as the group of young girls who created and circulated their own magazine, *Plaza Girls* (Petrides 2018).
8. The practices at City Plaza also give way to republican claims about the value of civic participation in achieving an ideal of freedom as nondomination. Cf. Pettit 1999.

References

Agamben, G. 1998. *Homo Sacer: Sovereign Power and Bare Life*. Stanford: Stanford University Press.
Agier, M. 2011. *Managing the Undeseriables: Refugee Camps and Humanitarian Government*, trans. David Fernbach. Malden, MA: Polity Press.
Arendt, H. 1958. *The Origins of Totalitarianism*, 2nd edn. New York: Meridian Boooks.
Balampanidis, D., and I. Polyzos. 2016. '"Migrants" Settlement in Two Central Neighborhoods of Athens'. *City* 20(1): 75–90.
Bampilis, T. 2017. 'Far-Right Extremism in the City of Athens during the Greek Crisis', in D. Dalakoglou and G. Agelopoulos (eds), *Critical Times in Greece: Anthropological Engagements with the Crisis*. London, Routledge, pp. 59–72.
Beerbohm, E. 2015. 'Is Democratic Leadership Possible?' *American Political Science Review* 109(4): 639–52.
CAMOC (International Committee for the Collections and Activities of Museums of Cities). 2017. *Migration: Cities Workshop, Athens 2017 – Debbie Carlos Valencia 'Women Building Bridges'*. Retrieved 16 October 2019 from https://www.youtube.com/watch?v=iK658HPNGYg.
Christopolou, N. 2017a. Interviewed by A, Mehra, July.
———. 2017b. 'The Depth of Our Divisions, the Breadth of Our Communities'. Josh Rosenthal Education Fund Lecture. Gerald R. Ford School of Public Policy, 19 September.
Demir, D. 2017. Interviewed by A. Mehra, July.
Foucault, M. 1979. *Discipline and Punish: The Birth of the Prison*. Harmondsworth: Penguin.
Harcourt, B. 2012. 'Political Disobedience'. *Critical Inquiry* 39(1): 33–55.
Harrell-Bond, B. 1985. *Imposing Aid: Emergency Assistance to Refugees*. Oxford: Oxford University Press.
———. 2002. 'Can Humanitarian Work with Refugees be Humane?' *Human Rights Quarterly* 24(1): 51–85.
Human Rights Watch. 2012. 'Hate on the Streets: Xenophobic Violence in Greece'. Retrieved 16 October 2019 from https://www.hrw.org/report/2012/07/10/hate-streets/xenophobic-violence-greece.

IIP Interactive. 2016. 'Welcoming Today's Refugees'. Retrieved 16 October 2019 from https://www.youtube.com/watch?v=cmB2gZF3tR4.

Kalodoukas, A. 2016. 'Η Τζούντιθ Μπάτλερ στο Χώρο Στέγασης Προσφύγων City Plaza'. Retrieved 16 October 2019 from https://www.youtube.com/watch?v=Zi5EFUOfWcY.

Lomani, N. 2017. Interviewed by A. Mehra, July.

Malkki, L. 1995 *Purity and Exile: Violence, Memory, and National Cosmology among Hutu Refugees in Tanzania*. Chicago: University of Chicago Press.

Maloutas, M., D. Emmanuel and M. Pantelidou. 2006. *Athens: Social Structures, Practices, and Perceptions: New Parameters and Changing Trends 1980–2000*. Athens: National Centre for Social Research.

Ober, J. 2009. 'Three Kinds of Dignity'. Yale Law Workshop, 10 December. Retrieved 16 June 2018 from https://law.yale.edu/system/files/documents/pdf/Intellectual_Life/LTW-Ober.pdf.

———. 2012. 'Democracy's Dignity'. *American Political Science Review* 106(4): 827–46.

Petrides, K. 2018. 'City Plaza Teenage Girls Have Published a Magazine and Won the Heart of Our Heart'. *Luben*. Retrieved 16 October 2019 from https://luben.tv/politix/146212.

Pettit, P. 1999. *Republicanism: A Theory of Freedom and Government*. Oxford: Oxford University Press.

Scampoli, M., and M.A. Cardinali. 2017. '"Welcome to Greece": An Interview with Olga Lafazani, Coordinator of City Plaza'. Retrieved 16 October 2019 from http://www.meltingpot.org/Welcome-to-Greece-An-interview-with-Olga-Lafazani.html#.Ws202dPwaqB.

Smith, M. 2004. 'Warehousing Refugees: A Denial of Rights, a Waste of Humanity', in *World Refugee Survey of the U.S. Committee on Refugees and Immigrants*, 38–56. Retrieved 16 October 2019 from http://refugees.org/wp-content/uploads/2015/12/Warehousing-Refugees-Campaign-Materials.pdf.

Swarming Solidarity. 2017. 'The Best Hotel in Europe'. Retrieved 16 June 2018 from https://best-hotel-in-europe.eu/swarming-solidarity.

United Nations High Commissioner for Refugees (UNHCR). 2014. 'Policy on Alternatives to Camps'. Retrieved 16 October 2019 from http://www.unhcr.org/en-us/protection/statelessness/5422b8f09/unhcr-policy-alternatives-camps.html.

Urbinati, N. 2006. *Representative Democracy: Principles and Genealogy*. Chicago: University of Chicago Press.

Verdirame, G., and B. Harrell-Bond. 2005. *Rights in Exile: Janus-Faced Humanitarianism*. Oxford: Berghahn Books.

Vradis, A., and D. Dalakoglou. 2011. 'Spatial Legacies of December and the Right to the City', in A. Vradis and D. Dalakoglou (eds), *Revolt and Crisis in Greece: Between a Present Yet to Pass and a Future Still to Come*. Oakland, CA: AK Press, pp. 77–90.

Zikakou, I. 2015. 'Refugee Crisis in Athens is out of Control'. *Greek Reporter*. Retrieved 16 October 2019 from http://greece.greekreporter.com/2015/12/30/refugee-crisis-in-athens-getting-out-of-control-refugees-sleeping-outside-in-the-cold.

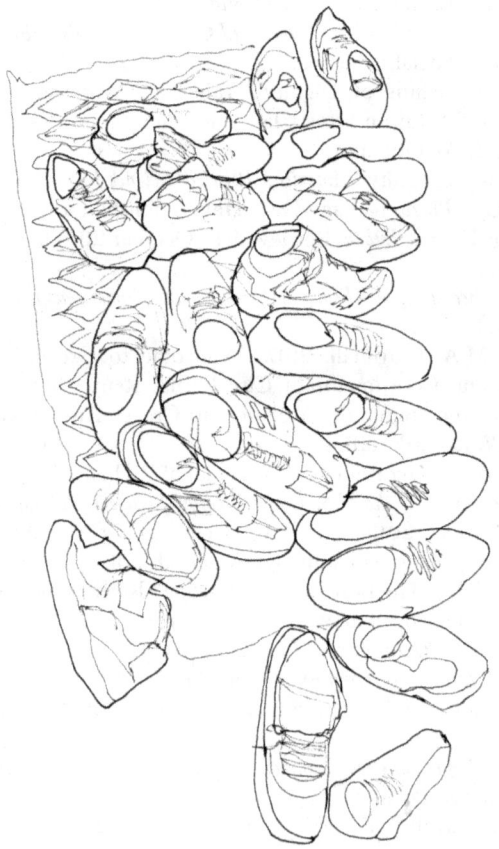

Figure 11.1 A more personal shelter in Brussels, Belgium. © Mark E. Breeze, based on an image supplied by Robin Vandevoordt.

11
A More Personal Shelter
How Citizens Are Hosting Forced Migrants in and around Brussels

Robin Vandevoordt

Surrounded by Brussels' skyscrapers, over a hundred men and women have gathered in a corner of the Maximilian Park. Most hope to cross the Channel into England one day, but now they are simply looking for a place to sleep. Shortly after 7 pm, they are approached by four young men and women wearing white vests with the blue logo of the Plateforme Citoyenne de Soutien aux réfugiés:

> 'Hi there', a young woman says cheerfully to two men who look as if they have yet to turn eighteen. 'Is this the first time you are staying with us?'
> 'Erm, yes', one of them answers hesitantly.
> 'Okay then. Do you have any family or friends with you?'
> 'Yes, just my friend here.'
> 'And you want to stay together tonight?'
> 'Hm', he nods, slightly surprised. 'We stay together.'
> 'Okay. Okay' she murmurs, her gaze fixed to her phone as she swipes through the Facebook posts.

During the day, the Citizen Platform launched several polls on its closed Facebook groups, asking its members to welcome migrants into their homes, just for a night. If all goes well, everyone in the park should be sheltered by the end of the day. It is an exhausting task, but ever since they began providing accommodation in the summer of 2017, the Platform has offered a bed to between thirty and six hundred migrants nearly every single night.

Drawing on in-depth interviews and ongoing participant observation as one of the Platform's volunteers, this chapter describes how this group of citizens in Brussels has established a strikingly personal form of shelter. After briefly sketching the Platform's general background and the practical coordination of the hosting-at-home system, I explore how this unlikely, demanding form of shelter has survived over time. This is largely due, I argue, to three distinctively *social* dynamics: the affective encounters and personal bonds it establishes between hosts and guests; the vibrant virtual spaces through which volunteers are connected into a larger community; and the ambiguous relation it maintains with politics. Combined, these characteristics render the Platform a rather radical example of how civil humanitarians have responded to the arrival of forced migrants in Europe, either in lieu of or as a complement to the efforts of state actors and professional humanitarian actors. By focusing on such a personal type of shelter, I hope to reframe shelter away from its purely material form and towards the complex social dynamics that can make it so successful in circumstances like this.

A Short History of the Citizen Platform

The Citizen Platform is one of the many initiatives emerging from Europe's 'long summer of migration' in 2015. As Belgian authorities struggled to keep up with asylum applications, many migrants were stranded in the Maximilian Park right in front of the Immigration Office. In lieu of a coordinated response by the state or professional nongovernmental organizations (NGOs), citizens set up an informal refugee camp where they offered food, clothes, medicine and companionship (Depraetere and Oosterlynck 2017; Lafaut and Coene 2019). After a few weeks, some of the most active citizens founded the Citizen Platform to coordinate their actions, which has since grown into a large, volunteer-based organization providing a variety of services to different groups of forced migrants. In Brussels' northern suburbs, they established a social centre mainly for asylum seekers and recognized refugees, where they offered language classes for adults and children, a safe space for women, socioadministrative counselling and psychological support. Together with professional humanitarian organizations, they also established a 'humanitarian hub' close to Maximilian Park, providing more urgent humanitarian support to undocumented migrants.

However, this chapter focuses on yet another part of the Platform's activities. In the summer of 2017, the Platform's volunteers were confronted with a rising number of migrants roaming around Maximilian Park. Most had ended up in Brussels due to the continuous destruction of refugee shelters in Calais, Dunkirk and Paris. Others were either unable to apply for asylum in Belgium because their fingerprints were taken in countries like Greece, Italy and Hungary or because they lacked adequate information on their right to protection. As the Platform's members noticed, there were many minors, women and people persons with urgent health problems among the migrants in the park, and so they launched an emergency call to its core volunteers to host the most vulnerable among them into their homes. To their surprise, the number of hosts signing up enabled them to accommodate not only minors and women, but all the migrants staying in the park. It soon became clear that neither municipal nor Federal government agencies would provide shelter, and as new volunteers kept reporting themselves to the Platform, the emergency appeal transformed into a dynamic system of hosting-at-home, dubbed *hébergement* ('lodging' or 'accommodation').

The *hébergement* was coordinated largely through the Platform's closed Facebook groups: every day, a handful of coordinators launched a series of polls asking their volunteers if they were willing to host that night, if they needed a driver to bring migrants to their home or if they could serve as drivers themselves. Spread across the regional groups, the Platform counted close to 50,000 members, of which an estimated 6,000 hosted migrants at home. Every evening, a team of coordinators ventured into the park, matching the migrants in need of shelter to the day's hosts and drivers. Overall, this dynamic, Facebook-based system allowed the Platform to align the availability of their hosts to the changing needs on the ground – something its coordinators liked to contrast with the organizational inertia hampering professional NGOs to take quick and effective action. Whenever the number of (vulnerable) migrants rose or police actions were organized, the Platform reached out to a larger pool of hosts by launching emergency calls or by contacting recently available hosts.

From the very beginning, the Platform's coordinators were well aware that the system of *hébergement* was not a viable solution in the long run. On numerous occasions, they advocated for the establishment of an orientation centre that would not only offer shelter to those in need, but would also provide them with correct information on their rights, under which circumstances they were eligible for asylum in which countries, for instance, or the additional rights of minors irrespective of their refugee status. As winter approached and it became increasingly clear that no one was going to establish such a centre, the Platform changed its strategy. It engaged in lengthy negotiations with more sympathetic municipal and provincial government agencies and professional humanitarian NGOs to acquire material and financial support. In mid December 2017, and with their help, it was able to open a temporary shelter it baptised *Porte d'Ulysse,* in an abandoned wing of an office building on the outskirts of Brussels.

Together with other volunteering groups, the Porte d'Ulysse offered a bed for the night, shower facilities, an evening meal and breakfast for up to eighty people. In the next few months, it gradually increased its capacity to 200 beds. According to the Platform, the Porte d'Ulysse offered more than 23,000 nights and evening dinners over a period of 4.5 months. It was loosely organized by one employed coordinator, around ten coordinating volunteers and a larger pool of around 800 volunteers fulfilling 150 shifts per week.

On 30 April, the renting contract and financial support the Platform received from the municipal government was due to stop, and the Porte d'Ulysse was temporarily closed. This created an opportunity for its key coordinators to reflect on the Platform's overall role as a service provider and a social movement. Negotiations with municipal and provincial government agencies and professional NGOs resulted in more extensive financial support, enabling the Platform to employ twelve of its long-term volunteers to coordinate the centre and professionalize its organization. When it opened its doors again on 12 June, the shelter was rebaptised Porte d'Ulysse 2.0 and its capacity was increased to 300 beds.[1] However, the number of migrants in need of shelter remained stable at around an estimated 700 men, women and minors throughout this period. The system of *hébergement* therefore remained in place. In the rest of this chapter, I reflect upon why it has survived, against the odds, combined with an examination of the Platform's own expectations. I do so by exploring three of its most distinctively *social* characteristics: the affective, personal bonds between hosts and guests; the virtual community among volunteers; and the Platform's ambiguous relation with political action.

Affective Encounters, Personal Bonds

One day in the humanitarian hub, I was talking to Mohamed,[2] a young East African man, when he suddenly saw Elisa walking through the door behind me to start her shift distributing clothes as a volunteer. 'This is my family!' he cried enthusiastically. 'She is taking care of me!' After greeting each other with an affectionate hug, Elisa asked him whether he had a place for tonight:

> 'Yes, I do. Don't worry. I have a place.'
> 'Are you sure? Okay. But don't forget to go to the doctor as we told you.'
>
> After Mohamed said goodbye, Elisa gazed at the door. She mused: 'My family, he said. He's a wonderful kid. So young and all by himself. I hope he'll be okay.'

Later on, as Elisa and I got into conversation, she showed me pictures of the three young men she regularly hosted, sometimes for several days in a row. 'Here are the lads that are now staying with us', she smiled. 'They're great guys. Whenever they need a place to sleep in Brussels, or if they need something to be found out about their rights, they call me.'

The familial, affective way in which Mohamed and Elise treated each other was not an exception. Many guests referred to their hosts as aunties, uncles, cousins, big brothers or sisters – and vice versa. The Platform's coordinators nonetheless repeatedly emphasized that hosts were expected to do little more than offer a bed for a single night. The idea was that they would offer 'bed, bath and bread' with no strings attached, either for the hosts or the guests. Yet hosting strangers in one's home seemed bound to become personal. David, one of the hosts, explained some of the complexities:

> They say it's very simple, just bed, bath, bread, but it also plays into your conscience. You can't do it otherwise. Nobody asks you to put so much energy, time and emotion into it, but there's no one who can do that – just stick to bed, bath and bread and stay silent. You might as well put that man in prison then: bed bath bread, that's what you get there, that's just the same ... Once you welcome someone into your home, feed him, give them towels and try to look for clothes, it's always intense, otherwise you wouldn't do something like that. It's just being human.

Like most hosts, David kept in touch with a large number of his guests. If they did not manage to cross the Channel or were unable to apply for asylum in Europe, many migrants returned to the Belgian hosts they had stayed with before or with their friends. 'I think it makes a massive difference', David said, 'if you already know each other and trust each other. It's a lot easier than going to a different family every time again'. In between receiving their guests, hosts continued to worry about them, and as they committed their available moments to guests from the past, they had less space, both physically and emotionally, to receive new ones. 'I just have my two kids now. So I don't have other guests now, no. It takes a lot of time ... If a person enters your house, he enters your life.'

The affective intensity of these host–guest relations not only motivated hosts, but also wore them out. Sara, a longstanding volunteer at the Platform, told me that she decided to stop hosting largely because it was too much in combination with her regular work as a volunteer elsewhere in the Platform:

> I have hosted people for two or three months, but when I stopped doing it I noticed that I felt a weight falling off my shoulders, without me knowing that it was there. So then I decided not to do that anymore. You see a lot of people that start to feel guilty because they can't host, or because they can't host every day. But they really shouldn't. You need to have some space for yourself, you know. And most people don't really have experience with this kind of thing.

In response to these sometimes puzzling experiences, some of the Platform's members set up conversation groups where hosts could share their experiences and worries under the guidance of professional psychologists who volunteered to do so. Hosting and participating in the conversation groups incited a process of reflection on what drove them to do this, why they responded in a particular way and why they kept doing it. Two regional coordinators of the *hébergement* told me that a large share of their host pool consists of parents whose children have moved out, either temporarily or permanently. From a practical perspective, this makes sense, as these parents are likely to have a spare room and presumably have the financial means and the time to host someone in their home.

In a number of cases, one of the coordinators of the conversation groups suggested that hosting also helped to fill a social and emotional gap. While volunteers were initially motivated primarily by a humanitarian imperative to provide support to those in need, hosting strangers in their homes confronted them with needs they did not know were there. In an interview, the coordinator explained why a particular region, quite distant from Brussels, provided so many hosting families:

> You've got a lot of families there, where the men work in Brussels or in Luxembourg, and they become, erm, do you know *Desperate Housewives?* ... And then you bring those people to their home, and they want to do something. All of a sudden there's something new in their lives ... there's a rupture, a rupture in their lives, and they get this energy ...

While needs such as these may be specific to some individuals, more general dynamics are at work with the majority of hosts. In *The Need to Help*, Liisa Malkki (2015) contrasts the intensity of humanitarian workers' social encounters abroad with their daily lives at home. Whereas the latter are characterized by individualization, distance and alienation, the former result in social experiences that are 'full of life', intense and spontaneous.[3] As Malkki (2015: 8) observes, many professional humanitarians 'sought in their work a partial escape from national belonging – even an escape from their mundane, workaday selves. The safe, well-ordered and in principle predictable home, the welfare society that should have met their social and material needs, had become, for some, burdensome and constraining, and emotionally cold'. This observation may well apply to the Platform's hosts: all of a sudden, they were absorbed by intense, genuine encounters with people they had never encountered before. Whereas the dominant suburban lifestyle has most Belgians use their house like a fortified castle behind which they retreat into a private sphere of family and friends, these citizens turned theirs into a shelter for strangers. As one of the coordinators of the conversation groups recounted, such encounters 'break down all the barriers that we, in Belgium, have erected around us'.

Virtual Social Spaces

The closed Facebook groups through which *hébergement* was coordinated served more than merely a practical purpose; they provided the setting for a vibrant social life. First, through these closed groups, all members were exposed to a plethora of posts by coordinators and volunteers, which turned these closed groups into a set of vibrant social spaces. Some coordinators, for instance, commented extensively on recent developments in asylum and migration policies on local, domestic and European governance levels, and on politicians' statements. By doing so, they provided volunteers with insights in the structural causes of migrants' unfulfilled needs for support – much of which was regularly discussed even among volunteers with little prior interest in politics – and with digital links to more elaborate analyses by human rights organizations, journalists or other opinion leaders. Second, members shared their own hosting experiences by recounting how their initial worries and fears were soon dismantled by the sympathetic behaviour of their guests, by expressing their admiration for migrants' incredible resilience in the wake of the horrors they had gone through and, increasingly, by providing detailed accounts of police intimidation and even violence towards them. These stories kept circulating across the closed Facebook groups and one of the volunteers eventually reached out to a wider audience by gathering them on a website called *perles d'accueil* ('pearls of welcoming'). Third, both volunteers and coordinators continuously affirmed the Platform's moral identity. Amidst emojis of fist bumps and flexing biceps, they pointed out how many migrants they have sheltered, whilst the government failed to act appropriately. It was the Platform, they claimed, and not elected representatives, that were living up to the ideals of human rights and human dignity.

The continuous reaffirmation of this group identity is most succinctly represented by the 'vnous' that widely circulates across posts, cartoons and banners – a contraction of 'vous' and 'nous' ('you' and 'we') – often in expressions of gratitude, such as 'merci à Vnous' ('thanks to you/us) or 'Vnous êtes formidables ('you/we are marvellous'). While this continuous affirmation of the Platform's group identity may seem trivial and slightly self-congratulatory, it is pivotal in keeping up the elevated spirits that are needed to maintain such a demanding form of civil humanitarian action. Indeed, social movement scholars have theorized that, especially when institutionalization and formalization is low, a strongly experienced collective identity is crucial to maintain the movement's dynamic (Jasper 1997; Melucci 1989). As the Platform's coordinators are well aware of the importance of this sense of a shared moral identity, they have regularly organized festivities where volunteers are invited to go out and meet. Complete with concerts, food trucks and speeches, these social events continue to feed what

Durkheim (2001) has described as collective effervescence or what Randal Collins (2001) has dubbed the 'emotional energy' that is required to continue their support in strenuous, exhausting conditions.

In other words, the needs being fulfilled were not only of an affective and personal nature, but of a social and moral one as well. Taking part in the Platform's activities provided volunteers with a strong sense of community that required relatively little imagination as it seemed rooted in shared experiences and frequent interactions.[4] Their intense encounters with migrants, and the vibrant, virtual social life they share with other hosts, created a strong sense of moral identity that distinguished them as collective 'heroes' from the 'villains' embodied by ruling politicians (cf. Jasper 1997).

Political Ambiguities

To scholars of social movements and protests, it came as a surprise that the Citizen Platform and its coordinators did not identify themselves as a protest driven by activists, but as a platform for citizens who wanted to support refugees (cf. Alcalde and Portos 2018). Its core business quintessentially consisted of providing humanitarian aid in the form of shelter, food and clothes. Yet many similar initiatives do engage with politics, albeit in less evident ways (Fleischmann and Steinhilper 2017). In this section I focus on two political ambiguities that I think are crucial for understanding the relative success of the Platform in attracting new and motivating established volunteers: their actions were experienced as a purely moral response to political developments, and this moral motivation often increased citizens' political awareness over time.

First, the Platform's adversarial relationship with its surrounding political climate was pivotal to its relative success in attracting new volunteers. The initial one-off appeal to host migrants in volunteers' homes, for instance, fed into a dynamic system partly as a result of a series of controversies surrounding Theo Francken, State Secretary of Asylum and Migration. In early September, the State Secretary boasted on Twitter about the results of a new series of police actions: 'This morning 14 people arrested in the Parc Maximilien and 9 in the North station, 3 declared minors', he wrote, ending with the hashtag #CleaningUp. This suggestion that migrants should be 'cleaned up' like lingering rubbish or symbolic dirt sparked a debate in the national press and initiated a steep rise in the Platform's pool of hosts. 'That week', one of the coordinators told me, 'we got a few thousand volunteers more. Just like that'. A few months later, a similar process took place in the aftermath of a new controversy. Francken had invited bureaucrats of the Sudanese government to examine the identity of close to eighty arrested migrants. A few weeks later, human rights organizations filed a complaint claiming that several Sudanese men had been tortured upon their return.[5] Both controversies provided a 'moral shock' (Jasper and Poulsen 1995), which brought more citizens into the Platform.

Volunteers' engagement therefore represented a moral response to concrete political actions. As one coordinator explained to me, 'the role of the Platform is not to plan or to organise. Citizens just want to do something, they want to help. And we simply coordinate those citizens and what they do'. At least initially, the Platform did not resort to traditional protest repertoires such as petitions, rallies or letter-writing. Nor did they seem particularly interested in political discussions or the complexities of migration policy and humanitarian work. 'We're not here to *talk* about solidarity, we're here to *act* in solidarity' was something one of the long-term volunteers kept repeating to his friends. In other words, instead of losing themselves in political debates over who should provide which forms of support to migrants, they preferred to take direct social action themselves (cf. Zampioni 2018).

This brings us to a second political ambiguity: the Platform's coordinators soon realized that a seemingly apolitical form of social support was partly what made the Platform appealing to the broader public, but it was precisely this social support that opened up an opportunity to create a greater sense of political awareness among its volunteers. In an interview, one of the coordinators drew a distinction between idle debates in the media and the mobilizing power of direct social action:

> I think people are not informed. They don't look at [the news], they don't give a shit about it. The only thing they hear is one is saying black and one is saying white and pfrt! Keep on fighting guys. [But] if you just call out for more solidarity, for more support, for more humanity, then people join. And the moment you join, the moment they're in, it's done, you cannot close your eyes and go back to sleep, go back to your life.

It was through such forms of direct social action, he claimed, that people became more intensively involved with the cause of forced migrants. As we saw before, the closed Facebook groups through which the support was organized exposed them to an incessant flow of political information, commentaries and witnessing stories, as well as a stronger sense of community. Whether deliberately or not, several initiatives across Europe seemed to facilitate the same process: volunteers initially joined out of an essentially humanitarian imperative to help others in need, yet gradually became more aware of the causes and consequences of migrants' needs, and through their awareness became mobilized into protest (Feischmidt and Zakaria 2019; Fleischmann and Steinhilper 2017; Sandri 2018). Similarly, the Citizen Platform every now and then mobilized its volunteers for more traditional forms of protest such as rallies, letter-writing initiatives to local politicians and social media campaigns. It is through being involved as seemingly apolitical, civil humanitarians that these citizens ultimately became involved in political action.

Putting the Platform into Context

Initiatives such as the Citizen Platform should, of course, be situated in a neoliberal context of increasingly restrictive migration regimes. Over the last few decades, several European states have reduced social support for refugees and other migrants, with the double aim of discouraging (potential) immigrants from entering their territory and of forcing established immigrants to earn their social and political rights (Schinkel and van Houdt 2010; Ticktin 2011). As a result, humanitarian organizations such as Doctors Without Borders and Doctors of the World have expanded their activities in Europe (Ticktin 2011). With the recent advent of a perceived 'refugee crisis' on the continent, these NGOs have struggled to keep up with the needs on the ground (Scott-Smith 2016), and as these needs became ever more visible, partly due to increased media attention in the summer of 2015, citizens stepped in to provide shelter and other forms of humanitarian aid.

From a different perspective, such initiatives can be read as fulfilling the possibly unconscious needs of their volunteers (cf. Malkki 2015; Melucci 1989). In some cases, these needs are personal, depending on their family situation or biographical trajectories. Yet, more generally, they seem to fill in a desire for establishing a community based on intense, communal experiences, regular interactions and a sense of collective moral pride. All of the Platform's activities are socially subversive, in that they break down the formal barriers of everyday life and put people, migrants and citizens alike, into direct, immediate contact with each other (Vandevoordt forthcoming; Vandevoordt and Verschraegen 2019). In this sense, the *hébergement* system seems to fill an experiential, affective and social gap that was created by the formalization of solidarity in European societies. In initiatives such as the Platform, citizens reinvent themselves as active members of a moral community. There, they become part of a higher purpose that transcends their individual selves: restoring their humanity in the face of a humanitarian crisis.

Their actions remind us that displacement is much more than the purely spatial process of being forced to leave one's physical home. Displacement is a social, even a personal matter, of losing one's connection to the world. This simple fact, I think, may help us rethink the notion of shelter not as something that is constructed by tents, bricks and other materials, but as a deeply social process that shields those without a home from the violence of indifference. Maybe that is what a personal shelter does best: offering a sense of humanity.

Robin Vandevoordt is a postdoctoral researcher based at the Universities of Ghent and Antwerp. As an ethnographer, his research interests are in forced migration, civil solidarity and humanitarianism. He holds a Ph.D. from the University of Antwerp and has been an Early Career Fellow at Oxford University's Refugee Studies Centre.

Notes

1. Furthermore, since April 2018, they used a software program developed by one of the volunteers to monitor who is accommodated through *hébergement* and who is sheltered in the Porte d'Ulysse.
2. All names are pseudonyms, except when they appear in full to designate, for instance, official statements by the Platform's spokespersons.
3. Alberto Melucci (1989) made a similar argument with respect to European social movements.
4. In contrast to Benedict Anderson's (2006) description of nations as 'imagined communities', as they depend not so much on direct social contact between its members as on mediation through mass media.
5. This complaint was later found to be unsubstantiated by a separate, independent government agency. However, the results of that report were immediately disputed by the human rights organizations.

References

Alcalde, J., and M. Portos. 2018. 'Scale Shift and Transnationalisation within Refugees' Solidarity Activism: From Calais to the European Level', in D. Della Porta (ed.), *Solidarity Mobilizations in the 'Refugee Crisis': Contentious Moves.* London: Springer, pp. 243–70.
Anderson, B. (2006). *Imagined Communities: Reflections on the Origin and Spread of Nationalism.* London: Verso books.
Collins, R. 2001. 'Social Movements and the Focus of Emotional Attention', in J. Goodwin, J. Jasper and F. Polletta (eds), *Passionate Politics: Emotions and Social Movements.* Chicago: University of Chicago Press, pp. 27–44.
Depraetere, A., and S. Oosterlynck. 2017. '"I Finally Found My Place": A Political Ethnography of the Maximiliaan Refugee Camp in Brussels'. *Citizenship Studies* 21(6): 693–709.
Durkheim, E. 2001. *The Elementary Forms of Religious Life*, trans. C. Crossman. Oxford: Oxford University Press.

Feischmidt, M., and A. Zakaria. 2019. 'Politics of Care and Compassion: Civic Help for Refugees and its Political Implications in Hungary: A Mixed-Methods Approach', in M. Feischmidt, L. Pries and C. Cantat (eds), *Refugee Protection and Civil Society in Europe*. London: Palgrave Macmillan, pp. 59–99.

Fleischmann, L., and E. Steinhilper. 2017. 'The Myth of Apolitical Volunteering for Refugees: German Welcome Culture and a New Dispositif of Helping'. *Social Inclusion* 5(3): 17–27.

Jasper, J.M. 1997. *The Art of Moral Protest: Culture, Biography, and Creativity in Social Movements*. Chicago: University of Chicago Press.

———. 2014. *Protest: A Cultural Introduction to Social Movements*. Chichester: John Wiley & Sons.

Jasper, J.M., and J.D. Poulsen. 1995. 'Recruiting Strangers and Friends: Moral Shocks and Social Networks in Animal Rights and Anti-nuclear Protests'. *Social Problems* 42(4): 493–512.

Lafaut, D., and G. Coene. 2019. '"Let Them in!" Humanitarian Work as Political Activism? The Case of the Maximiliaan Refugee Camp in Brussels'. *Journal of Immigrant and Refugee Studies* 17(2): 185–203.

Malkki, L.H. 2015. *The Need to Help: The Domestic Arts of International Humanitarianism*. Durham, NC: Duke University Press.

Melucci, A. 1989. *Nomads of the Present: Social Movements and Individual Needs in Contemporary Society*. London: Vintage Press.

Sandri, E. 2018. '"Volunteer Humanitarianism": Volunteers and Humanitarian Aid in the Jungle Refugee Camp of Calais'. *Journal of Ethnic and Migration Studies* 44(1): 65–80.

Schinkel, W., and F. van Houdt. 2010. 'The Double Helix of Cultural Assimilationism and Neo-liberalism: Citizenship in Contemporary Governmentality'. *British Journal of Sociology* 61(4): 696–715.

Scott-Smith, T. 2016. 'Humanitarian Dilemmas in a Mobile World'. *Refugee Survey Quarterly* 35(2): 1–21.

Ticktin, M. 2011. *Casualties of Care: Immigration and the Politics of Humanitarianism in France*. Berkeley: University of California Press.

Vandevoordt, R. 2019. 'Subversive Humanitarianism: Rethinking Refugee Solidarity through Grassroots Initiatives'. *Refugee Survey Quarterly* 38(3): 245–65.

Vandevoordt, R., and G. Verschraegen. 2019. 'Subversive Humanitarianism and its Challenges. Notes on the Political Ambiguities of Civil Refugee Support', in M. Feischmidt, L. Priese and C. Cantat (eds), *Civil Society and Refugee Protection in Europe*. London: Palgrave Macmillan, pp. 101–28.

Zampioni, L. 2018. 'From Border to Border: Refugee Solidarity Activism in Italy across Space, Time and Practices', in D. Della Porta (ed), *Solidarity Mobilizations in the 'Refugee Crisis': Contentious Moves*. London: Springer, pp. 99–124.

Figure 12.1 The International Congress Centre (ICC) in Berlin, Germany.
© Mark E. Breeze, based on an image supplied by Holly Young.

12

Life in the Aluminium Whale
A Study of Berlin's ICC Shelter

Holly Young

Broken shelves. Textbooks. Grills. Games. A shard of glass. And, for some inexplicable reason, lots of odd shoes. These are some of the objects Jenny Rumohr, manager of the International Congress Centre (ICC) shelter, found in its empty rooms. Three months after the ICC received the letter for closure, the last residents have now gone. The clatter of the plasterboard cubicles being dismantled echoes around the huge empty hall; their sides still covered in paintings, flags and messages in multiple languages. What's left in the rooms goes to a decontamination room set up on the fifth floor to finally get rid of the bed bugs. After they have been decontaminated, the objects will be given away for free at a market in front of the building: the books, the bunk beds, the washing lines, everything.

Rumohr and I agree: it is strange to see the shelter like this. For almost two years, this place was dense with life, home to 600 people from over twenty different countries carving out slivers of privacy. The smell of cleaning products and canteen food had mingled in the stuffy air. Men sat around power points cradling their mobiles. Little groups of kids speaking snippets of dozens of languages had streamed down the halls and disappeared around corners. Now, the shelter has the sobriety of a party after the lights have gone up.

Between December 2015 and September 2017, I made a series of visits to the ICC to speak with residents, as well as staff of the international humanitarian organization Malteser managing the shelter. I used a set of questions to guide these interviews, although they almost always opened out into wider, freewheeling conversations, sometimes with groups of people speaking at once. Documenting what life is like in a place like the ICC is fraught with challenges: the intractable issue of representation; the loss of nuance through translation; how to observe openly instead of seeking props to advance political argument; how, in essence, to describe things as they were. With this in mind, I have relied heavily on oral testimonies, using the moments where they chimed together to provide guiding principles.

These testimonies confirmed that the ICC was a place that housed multiple, often contradictory, experiences. However, common threads emerged: sleep, food, privacy and hygiene. The conditions of an 'emergency' in which the shelter, like others across the city, was established can threatened to blur the analytical gaze and dominate the conclusions we draw from this period of the city's history. Unintended and unavoidable or not, the domestic conditions within the shelter had a complex and profound psychological impact on those involved: over time, the regulation of mundane acts of eating and sleeping assumed a symbolic and political significance. The shelter was, perhaps more so than the asylum interview room, the most visceral place to observe how the power dynamics between the individual and the authorities were established, reinforced and challenged. The domestic life of a shelter is as political as their existence in the first place.

It will be curious to see how far numbers of asylum applications, denials and approvals will be used to give shape to historical accounts for what happened in Berlin during this period. The texture of domestic life in shelters like the ICC is also vital. And not ephemeral in importance, as one lady, who over a year after the closure told me she found it hard to breathe when she thought of the ICC, might attest to. What does the fragment of glass hidden under a bunk bed tell us about what people worried about as they tried to fall asleep? What do the grills snuck into bedrooms tell us about the frustrations of daily meals? Do the murals tell us that creativity and dignity flourished despite it all?

'Our Little Island'

> I remember one Syrian family standing in front of the building asking me if this was the right address. They thought it just couldn't be true.
> –Jenny Rumohr

Among locals, the ICC is sometimes called 'The Aluminium Whale'. It is an apt description: the building seems born of something both animal and industrial. Built in the 1970s in West Berlin, it is a hulking, grey construction of multiple floors. You get the best sense of its scale from an aerial view on Google Maps, its extensive length resting parallel to a major road and the tracks of the S-Bahn. Its exterior is a dense mesh of silver panels, stairwells, chunky cladding, tubes and ventilation panels; like a building that has been turned inside out. The ICC was built to showcase postwar German architecture, a place for international diplomats and elites in West Germany to rub shoulders. The conference hall is big enough to host 5,000 people. Now its silver panels have dulled: it is an endearingly dated vision of modernity.

Architects can design a building fit for purpose, but cannot predict the way in which history will redefine that purpose in unexpected ways. The wall fell, wealth grew and new people continued to arrive and reshape the city. In 2015, the ICC had a cameo role in a story playing out across Berlin, Germany, Europe and beyond: what became narrativized at the time, rather problematically some would argue, as the European refugee crisis. It was one of many buildings across the city, including gym halls, barracks, former airports and school classrooms repurposed as an emergency refugee shelter. While a complex and improvised world was constructed in these two years, outside the building, Germany, or at least the political zeitgeist, changed. The ICC's doors opened a few months after Angela Merkel's open door policy, where images of welcome signs and teddy bears at German train stations circulated in the media. It closed in the month of the federal election in September 2017, where the far-right Alternative für Deutschland (AfD) rode on an anti-refugee platform straight into the Bundestag. The party's placards of 'Burqas? We'd rather bikinis' could be seen pinned around the city. Among some, anxiety replaced hope; something in the alchemy of society changed, or at least rose to the surface.

On one of the visits I made to the shelter, a few kilometres away, a Nazi rally was taking place. 'A good thing about this isolated place of ICC', Rumohr told me, 'is that there is no way that anyone will put it on fire.' Berlin, a city known for its tolerance, had like the rest of Germany seen a spate of violence and arson attacks on shelters. The ICC is beside a busy junction, but set back from the road, making it feel simultaneously at the centre of its surroundings and isolated. People rolling suitcases along the pavement are a familiar sight here, but most are on their way to somewhere else. 'Our little island, that's what we call it', said Rumohr.

The building, she added, is also really hard to enter. To get in, you use a discreet side entrance, where a security guard signs you in, before taking the lift up several floors. It seems that the more defined the distinction between outside and inside the shelter is, the less easy it is to parse the distinction between control and care, if there is one, in its intentions. In the seclusion, a level of protection could be achieved. But for Rumohr, this also seemed to expose contradictions between the theory and practice of refugee policy. 'Sometimes I wonder whether these camps are really meant to integrate people', she said. 'Or just to store them away until a decision has been reached on their legal status.'

Clocks and Calendars

There is no natural light in the main hall of the ICC. Instead, day and night is scheduled in: the fluorescent lights on at 6 am and off at 11 pm. It's not easy to tune into this collective body clock: if you want to sleep in, or move about after dark, you have to be creative. One lady told me she always made sure her phone was charged, so she had a light to go to the bathroom in the middle of the night. The shelter has its own rhythm. Breakfast is served 7–9 am, lunch 12–2 pm and dinner 6–8 pm. Food is kept for anyone who misses dinner while they are out at lessons or activities. Most days, there is something happening, from knitting to kickboxing. On certain days, you can visit a therapist. The security personnel are there around the clock. The rails in the donation room change with the seasons: jumpers and boots replace shorts and sandals.

Rumohr observed residents going through distinct phases during their stay in the shelter. 'There is a lot of raw emotion we are dealing with', she said:

> And the longer people stay the more intense it gets. The first six months are about arriving: figuring out where you get your money, where the bank or the school is, how the doctors treat you; it is very operational. After six months you have basically figured out everything you need to live your daily life, and that is when you start processing everything that happened to you, how you got here.

The experience of time in the shelter was at once both too rigid and too ill-defined, characterized by both imposed routine and endless waiting. The length of stay in the camp, longer than both residents and the authorities had originally expected, was itself political, a symbol of failed promises. 'We've been here for almost the last two years', one exasperated resident told me; 'How long will we remain in the camp? ... We want to move as soon as possible to get somewhere with our own privacy.' Another told me of his disappointment in the authorities: 'I was expecting very good things from German government', he said. 'We were expecting to only be here in ICC for three to six months.' Waiting for answers on their asylum applications and for the ability to move out of temporary accommodation, they were in a state of suspended arrival. Residents were not yet fully the masters of their own time. They knew precisely when the lights would turn on and food would be served, but not when their new life would begin.

Care and Control

In my interviews with residents at the ICC, just like those in other shelters across the city, food came up with more frequency and passion than any other issue, often before any mention of asylum status. 'Food and cooking was voiced at all protests I participated in Berlin', confirmed a local campaigner. 'I think the general problem was that [refugees] could not choose their own food.'

The food issue at the ICC was both bureaucratic and architectural. 'Catering is a big problem', confirmed Rumohr. 'The caterers we have at the moment are really trying, but we don't get much money per head from the state. And you have 600 people so not every meal can be to everyone's taste. We meet once a month with the heads of other camps and they all basically say the same thing.' The ability to cook for oneself was a key defining distinction between emergency shelters (*Notunterkünfte*) and shelters intended for medium-term stay (*Gemeinschaftsunterkünfte*). In the ICC, despite there being large kitchen areas (previously used to cater for large events) residents were not able to gain access to them due to fire regulations. Regulations also meant that residents were not allowed to cook in their rooms or cubicles.

Some residents were disappointed in the quality of the food, but most said it was a lot better than other shelters, where people had seen mouldy bread and uncooked meat being served. It appeared that the real issue was more about power than taste. 'Food plays an important role in daily life, but here it is not good quality', one resident explained:

> And some people are sick here, so if we don't eat the food we have hunger, so we have to eat something. And when we eat we are sick. I am sick and the doctor advised me I can't eat things with salt and high in fat – so what should I do? If I don't eat I will be hungry, and if I eat I will be sick. This is a very common problem with all of us. It is not that the food isn't fresh, but because we are sick. We have no choice, we have to eat the same food every day.

Eating may be part of what we think of as basic needs, but the desire to control what you eat and when is neither trivial nor mundane. The cultural and social significance of mealtimes differs between families and family members. Often prefixed with an acknowledgement of gratefulness of the provision of food, for many the lack of agency to provide this basic need for themselves took on more meaning as the days went by. It can feel humiliating, putting your empty plate out three times a day for someone else to fill up, one translator told me, speaking of his own experiences of living in another shelter. The serving of food became not an act of nourishment, but a ritual reinstatement of disempowerment. Indeed, for some, food became a political messenger of sorts, symbolic of the relationship between individual and the authorities. 'The food is really the problem we have here', said one resident, 'and this is intentionally happening to us. Everyone knows it.'

The Watchful Shelter

When Rumohr told me of the shard of glass she found under a bed, I thought of something Mariana Karkoutly, a social worker in another emergency shelter in Berlin, told me: 'We found someone who had a knife, and when we asked why, they said it was so scary to sleep there.' As the resident put it, staying in these shelters could be 'like sleeping in the forest'. Rumohr understood the purpose of the shard of glass she found under the bed in that empty room, as she had also confiscated knives, pepper spray and tasers: 'I can understand why people feel they need protection in these places: imagine being here with your family, among so many strangers.'

There were a number of ways in which the architectural limitations of the building were not conducive to good physical or mental health. While the families with young children on the upper levels were able to sleep in rooms, the vast majority of residents slept in the main hall in a series of plasterboard cubicles. Each cubicle had wooden bunk beds to sleep a maximum of eight people. Doors and roofs to the cubicles were prohibited as fire hazards. With so many sleeping in an open room, tightly packed together, both the bed bugs and the noise were difficult to contain. Some women told me they had scarcely ever had a night of unbroken sleep in the almost two years they had spent there.

Privacy and a sense of physical vulnerability were big concerns. Many residents complained that they couldn't sleep and were experiencing mental health issues. 'We are all sick and depressed', said one. 'We have psychiatric problems, like depression and anxiety. We can't sleep. If you lived here you would also be like us.' Rumohr, the manager, concurred:

> Over time people get really depressed. I remember we had a Syrian interior decorator who was really creative. He told me just couldn't take it. He lost lots of weight and couldn't sleep anymore: he got just really very depressed. He said 'I can't live in a place like this, it kills me slowly from the inside'. It was the noise, lack of privacy, the bathrooms located three floors away and you have to share your room with complete strangers.

The search of a place to not be seen could be observed in the pieces of material used to make improvised doors on the cubicles and even to separate bunk beds. In the ICC, the standard lines of public and private space do not correspond to being inside or outside the shelter. Strangers, indeed hundreds of them, were of course in the shelter itself: they were not outside, they were in the next cubicle, the next bed. The impact of this on family dynamics was complex. 'There are social problems', one resident said. 'It is a camp and different people are sent here. Some have bad characters. Some are socially not good. Some are drinking and using drugs and most of them are single and we have families and small children.' Fractures within the camp could run not just between family units and those that were single, but also along cultural and linguistic lines. 'It becomes very difficult for them to live in', said one social worker. 'It is such a close space with so many different cultures. It is always a clash of cultures.' The shelter was simultaneously a place of exposure and isolation, of protection and fear.

One day, Rumohr got a call from the local school. The teacher of a child living in the ICC had some concerns: their uniform was often dirty and they were occasionally aggressive towards their classmates. Rumohr and a colleague called the parents in for a meeting and learned that the child was the middle of three siblings. Rumohr asked about the older child, who was seven and had been wetting the bed. The parents said it was probably a phase, but admitted that there were some other difficulties. Originally there were four children in the family, but the twin of the middle child drowned in the sea on the journey. A doctor in Turkey told them that the best thing would be to pretend to the other siblings that there had never been a fourth child.

The way in which the shelter exposed the private lives of residents to external observation was complex. Despite the cramped conditions, trauma could hide in plain sight in the ICC. One of the advantages of a shelter that was so exposed might be that it was easier to identify vulnerable individuals and those that might need support, but sometimes this took time. Again, care and control, paternalism and much-needed support sat side by side.

Power Play

When you lay in bed, one woman told me, the bed bugs liked to gather around the warmth of your neck. Bed bugs, despite the best efforts of staff, volunteers and residents, were impossible to get rid of. I saw translators and social workers scratching at their arms as they went about their work. I saw a video one father took of bed bugs crawling across his two-year-old daughter's arms and chest. One man told me he collected the bed bugs in a plastic container one day and took it to LaGeSo, the department that dealt with refugee issues. He stood in line and, when it was finally his turn, placed the container on the desk of the German official. I'm sorry, they said, but there is nothing we can do.

There were many ways in which the visceral elements of life in the shelter seemed to lay bare the attitudes of the authorities towards ICC residents. The very act of sheltering people in the institution of an emergency camp reinforces or clarifies them as a separate group. We refer to them as refugee camps, although few in the ICC had legal refugee status. For some residents, being in the ICC seemed to expose how the asylum system was at best inconsistent and at worst directly favoured certain groups in the shelter. As one Afghan resident explained, the authorities told most people that they would only remain in the ICC for a few months before being transferred to somewhere better, 'but that was a kind of lie, because these promises have not been met'. He went on to explain how 'the Syrians, Kurds, and Iraqis have received asylum and gone on to get their own apartments', whereas he had been left in the shelter. Therefore, this was a place where many expectations of life in Germany met with a stark reality. 'We know there are these problems in the bureaucracy', explained another resident, 'but these are intentional in order to suppress us, so that we should return back to our country.'

The shelter was seen for some as a place outside of Germany, a pre-arrival place, that illuminated the contradiction between the daily life of refugees and expectations the state had for them. 'We cannot go outside because we don't have the language, and we feel ashamed', said one. 'It is very shameful thing. We stay at home and play with phones and internet, and other times we stay in our rooms.' In this way, the residents described the shelter playing an active role in hindering 'integration'. They also suggested a type of feedback loop, where the shelter hindered learning, which then led to more social isolation. 'I am going to school for last one year but I came back and I live in this place and I forget everything', one young resident told me. 'In this environment nobody can learn anything. That is [a] problem, when we go back to school teacher says why did you not learn, but it is very noisy so we cannot learn.'

One day, my interviews came to an abrupt end when a female resident began shouting at us, throwing water bottles and then trying to smash up the wooden bench beside where we were sitting. After the security guards intervened, the translator discovered that the outburst was directed at me: the resident had seen a stranger from outside the shelter and assumed I was from a government department. Officials had been around the week before and she believed they had not delivered on their promises.

Complaints and outbursts are to be expected in the intense environment of a mass shelter, and perhaps these frictions are not only real, but also a way of making more abstract frustrations concrete. 'Residents sometimes get angry or loud but they don't have anything else they can negotiate with', said Rumohr. 'Every fight you win in here is because you are in a position of power and the refugee you are arguing with is not.' The shelter was a tangible foothold in the confusing layers of power and agency operating between the individual and the state. Different external elements shaping residents' lives could be collapsed into one.

One translator described the ICC to me as 'jail-like'. 'Jail is a closed unit', he explained, 'and this one is open, but the structure is like jail. You cannot open your window, the eating time is fixed, and everything is fixed so you see only regulations.' The shelter places restrictions on movement, sleep and what can be consumed and when. What began as shelter in the most basic sense of providing safety evolved into something perceived to be ideological. The camp is therefore an intrinsically political space, reproducing through everyday domestic actions the power dynamic between state and refugee, citizen and noncitizen. In its presence and vividness, one could argue that this was as much a political space as the asylum interview room. Partly, the strength of its impact was drawn from the repetition of domestic conditions. Imagine not having natural light or being able to sleep through the night for almost two years, one woman remarked to me: 'it makes you crazy'. It is possible that the experience in the shelter could have long-term consequences too in terms of damaging mental health, hindering language learning and integration. This, in the end, might also strain the nascent relationship between the new arrival and the German state.

From comparison to a '1 star hotel' to being like an 'open jail', the residents and staff I spoke to sought comparisons with other types of institutions when trying to make sense of the ICC, suggesting that 'shelter' was too vague a term to articulate the reality. However, Rumohr's description of the ICC as a 'village' seems particularly useful in the way it recognizes the complexity of its social dynamics. This, after all, was a place where the full spectrum of human experiences and interactions could be observed, and at times they were intensified by the architecture itself. 'We are like a petri dish for human emotion', Rumohr told me:

> Everything else that happens in a city happens here in a very small space . . . We have seen it all. We've had miscarriages, babies been born, people being sick, highly traumatized, people falling in love, but one being Afghan and the other Arab causing family feuds, people trying to commit suicide . . . We've had extreme violence, and extreme joy . . . There is a lot of raw emotion we are dealing with. And the longer they stay the more intense it gets.

What Remained

The ICC had a lasting impact on people after it closed: there are the children who still struggle to sleep through the night, the woman who finds it hard to breathe when she thinks of the place. But not all that remained was negative. In the months following the closure of the ICC, I met with staff and volunteers still in contact with former residents. Many told me of the difficulties of living in the shelter, while in the same breath sharing the lasting friendships they established and gratitude they felt towards the staff and volunteers who tried their best, despite all the limitations they faced. Rumohr estimated that over 1,000 volunteers were engaged with projects over the duration of the camp. Activities that took place included handicrafts, knitting, swimming classes, visits from the state ballet, yoga, kickboxing, soccer, basketball, chess and violin lessons. There was also a classroom and a kindergarten, and a special programme for female integration where they would drink tea and eat cookies while discussing life in Germany. 'We've seen examples of people either falling apart in here or coming back together', said Rumohr. 'We've seen people who were super shy and insecure when they arrived and have left the building smiling with a few friends and a life in Berlin. We had many awful stories and also many beautiful stories. I think that is what happens when you put 600 random people together.'

The modifications that were made to the interior of the building tell a story of creativity, resourcefulness and collaboration: families were placed on the second floor as there were the only rooms with doors and access to a little natural light; a wall was constructed on the second floor to prevent residents from seeing over the top of cubicles into people sleeping or getting changed; rooms were sorted as far as possible based on common spoken languages, and staff tried their best to ensure that groups of friends stayed together. New furniture was built from broken bunk beds and everywhere there was decoration: on walls, inside the cubicles, on the outside plaster board of the cubicles and in communal spaces. Residents and staff worked together to make the aluminium whale colourful. The shard of glass, the grill and the leftover board games in the rooms on the day of closure attest to the ways in which people asserted their agency against all the limitations.

When Rumohr left the ICC, she took a door with her. It was painted in intricate patterns of blue, turquoise and white. An artist living in the camp had drawn a Mihrab on the door and surrounding walls and, because they did not know where this locked door went, the artist named the work 'The Door to Paradise'. As the artist recalled: 'I drew a Mihrab, and spoke in my solitude with its lines. Mihrab – place of the victory of beauty over ugliness and place of divine becoming . . . A place where I pray . . . I drew the memories of my birthplace, hoping that this door would reopen one day and put an end to my problems.' As it turned out, there was a lift behind the door, which went straight down to the LAF office below. LAF, the department responsible for refugee housing, requested it be blocked so that it could not be accessed from the camp.

After the camp closed, Rumohr took the door and sent it to the House of History in Bonn, where it is now displayed: a memento of a place where restriction and creativity coexisted. The artist had feared that it might not survive. 'Maybe the Mihrab, in which I invested all my beautiful feelings, would be destroyed or covered up with new paint', she wrote. 'These thoughts tormented me so much that I would have liked to take the door with me, but where could I keep it? For this reason, I was forced to say goodbye until I learned that a new home was found in the museum for my Mihrab. I thanked God that the door has come to a place of safety and tranquility.'

Holly Young is an award-winning freelance journalist based in Berlin and was previously deputy editor of *The Guardian*'s global development network. In 2016, she completed a journalism fellowship at the Freie Universität, Berlin, where she documented refugee experiences in Berlin's emergency shelters, and has continued to report on refugees, inequality and mental health.

Figure 13.1 Rathaus Friedenau in Berlin, Germany. © Mark E. Breeze, based on an image supplied by Esther Schroeder Goh.

13

Structures to Shelter the Mind
Refugee Housing and Mental Wellbeing in Berlin

Esther Schroeder Goh

Sleep, eat, wash. When Rathaus Friedenau in Berlin, Germany was converted from council offices to temporary housing for refugees and asylum seekers, the outcome was a structure that allowed for basic human physical functioning, but one that was not supportive of their mental wellbeing. Phrases such as 'it's too much', 'I'm not feeling that safe' and a need to 'refresh the mind' were common themes from the residents in Rathaus Friedenau. In this chapter, I explore some of the ways in which the conversion of this structure into a refugee shelter, along with many other repurposed buildings in Berlin, had an impact on mental wellbeing. Based on semi-structured interviews with female residents of the Rathaus, this chapter presents insights as to how the actual physical structures of the building as well as the implications of day-to-day life in the Rathaus affected resident wellbeing. There is no universally accepted definition of mental wellbeing; rather, it is seen as having different connotations for the individuals themselves or within certain groups. Therefore, the subjective views of the residents themselves are invaluable in terms of better understanding the impact of their environment on them, along with the nuances of what it means to be sheltered.

The repurposed Rathaus – an administrative council building in an inner suburb of Berlin – was home to approximately 200 refugees and asylum seekers, including 100 children, when I visited it in 2018. Previously a functioning office building, the building was converted into emergency housing at the start of Germany's great influx of asylum seekers in 2015. It was initially planned for any asylum seekers, but was later converted into housing for particularly vulnerable people. This included single women with children, women who have experienced violence and members of the LGBTQI community. Residents of the Rathaus of varying ages, countries of origin and experiences were involved in the interviews for this chapter, but despite the diversity of backgrounds, there were many common themes about which elements of the Rathaus impacted on their daily lives and what they found to be important stressors. The Rathaus is located within an upper middle-class inner suburb of Berlin with around forty retired locals from the neighbourhood who provide daily German classes, as well as collecting donated clothing and other items. There is a park nearby and there are supermarkets and shops within the surrounding few blocks around the Rathaus, with easy access to public transport.

The policy for using the Rathaus was originally that asylum seekers would only stay there for a few weeks until more permanent housing could be found. However, given the particular needs of some of the residents and the challenges of the current private rental housing market in Berlin, many residents stayed there for up to two years (Hynie 2017). Despite this, new residents continued to be informed that their situation in the Rathaus was a form of temporary housing, coming to view the accommodation as short-term. The residents were all single women and women with children originating from different countries, cultures and religious backgrounds, many of whom did not share a common language.

Housing or Home? Effects of Housing on Mental Wellbeing

Poor mental health can impact an individual's physical health, their ability to perform daily tasks, overcome challenges, interact with others and make decisions for their future. These are important for all people, but particularly those seeking asylum and settling themselves in a new country as refugees. The events that cause people to seek asylum and gain refugee status are diverse and varied, and do not necessarily cause mental health issues. However, many of these experiences can and do have an impact on mental health, presenting a new diagnosis such as Post-Traumatic Stress Disorder, exacerbating existing mental health conditions or impacting on general mental wellbeing (Turrini et al. 2017). Groups working in refugee health, such as Médecins Sans Frontières, have been increasing their focus on refugee mental health in recent years, demonstrating how refugees are at particular risk as a consequence of fleeing their homes, finding themselves in an unfamiliar environment, experiencing specific traumas relating to the reasons for leaving their homes, worrying about family and friends whose outcomes are unknown, and suffering anxiety related to the uncertainty of their futures (Hanquet 2018).

Mental wellbeing can be seen as an important outcome of successful shelter. As Ziersch and Due (2018) have written, to have housing is 'to have a home, a place which protects privacy, contributes to physical and psychological wellbeing and supports the development and social integration of its inhabitants'. In humanitarian settings, interventions that have been shown to improve mental health include water and sanitation improvements, energy infrastructure upgrades, building new transport infrastructures, mitigating environmental hazards, better waste management systems and improved housing (Habib et al. 2006; WHO 2018). Moreover, there are certain elements of the built environment in cities that have long been established as improving mental health (Allen et al. 2014). Examples include green spaces and access to nature, spaces for physical activity, spaces allowing for social interaction, and spaces that are secure and safe. Despite these developments, the design of particular housing units, insofar as health is concerned, remains focused on the impact on physical rather than mental health.

The Rathaus, of course, was not designed and built for its current use. Therefore, it is an interesting example of the interplay between the built environment and mental wellbeing. If the physical elements of being protected, fed, kept warm and given access to proper sanitation are all that is required of a shelter, then the Rathaus fulfils such needs. However, it is clear that shelter involves more than meeting such biological, minimum standards. There is more to effective shelter than this. The women interviewed in this chapter provide important testimony to the need for a shelter that has a positive impact on mental wellbeing. Mothers, in particular, are known for having an increased responsibility at the time of resettlement for maintaining values and culture (Shishehgar et al. 2016). Therefore, for many women in the Rathaus, their shelter is not just a physical building, but a space in which they attempt to shelter the wellbeing of their family, more broadly conceived.

What elements of housing are crucial to improvements in mental wellbeing? The interviews at Rathaus Friedenau provide some interesting insights into this question. In what follows, I examine three main areas that had a particular impact on my informants: first, the physical spaces that directly affect wellbeing; second, the impact of daily tasks and routines; and, third, the consequence of social relationships in a shared shelter such as this. The subsequent sections will consider each in turn.

Physical Spaces Directly Affecting Mental Wellbeing

First, the physical elements of the Rathaus had an impact on the stress of residents, generating a decline in the ability to cope. In the shared spaces of the building, particularly the bathroom and the corridors, the main concerns related to cleanliness and odours. The corridors leading down to the residents' rooms, for example, were often a locus of stress. After spending some time in the building, I noticed that residents were often seen coming in and out of their rooms, mostly alone, not acknowledging each other as they passed. These rooms were of varying sizes, ranging from 2 x 3 metres to 5 x 3 metres; some had up to three single female residents. On each floor, the corridor ran along the inside of the building, with windows looking into the courtyard; the rooms coming off the corridors had their windows looking to the outside of the building. During the day, the corridors themselves were filled with natural light from the windows or were lit by long fluorescent bulbs. Much of the paint was chipped on the walls as well as the window frames, and it was easy to get the impression that this was still an office building – indeed, as it was originally designed.

At the beginning of each corridor were the bathrooms and toilets. The room for the toilets had four toilet stalls, as well as one children's toilet stall. The shower room had individual shower cubicles, which were installed as part of the conversion. Walking past one of the bathrooms, I often saw residents standing at the sink, washing knives and other kitchen utensils, with food scraps in the rubbish bin. Often described in a divisive 'them and us' manner, the bathrooms, despite being cleaned by Rathaus staff twice daily, were a source of stress and discomfort throughout the day. As two residents at the Rathaus told me: 'I'm not complaining about Germany, or the people. It's about the people with whom I'm living. Because they're not trying to keep this place clean. The bathroom is not clean. It's too much.' Another echoed these sentiments: 'I don't like this sharing bathroom. It's too difficult to share. We each have a room, we have each have a dustbin, but they don't throw their food in their own bin . . . They come, throw it in the bathroom. And they don't care about when they use the bathroom, they don't care what they do. They don't care to clean.'

The limitations in opening windows, combined with ventilation problems, created additional problems with the cooking odours. On the floor of some rooms were electric rice cookers, used by residents to make one-pot meals. The variety of cooking created a mix of smells, which combined with the warm spring afternoon sun to make a stuffy environment in many parts of the building. The rooms were sparsely furnished, with plain metal spring-wire single bed frames and mattresses, some without any bedsheets; a few metal lockers were provided for personal items. On the far side of each room were tall, sectioned windows to the outside; only the narrow top section could be opened. The view out of the windows varied, depending on which floor the room was on and which side of the building the room was in. The rooms on the front of the building looked out on to the trees in the square. Other rooms looked out on to the offices or other residential buildings opposite.

Many residents told me that they were particularly concerned about privacy in their rooms. These small rooms, often shared with other women, offered limited opportunities for time alone and for privacy in completing daily tasks. In addition, most of the women interviewed at the Rathaus reported that they had no covering of any type over the window. An even greater impact for residents was the further lack of privacy through a general sense and uncertainty of being watched from neighbouring buildings. Moreover, renovations had also led to a further sense of violation when the scaffolding on the outside of the building led to workers walking directly outside the windows. As one North African resident put it, 'it's also a problem, because we want to sleep more. And the workers are outside watching. We don't feel like [sleeping then] . . . it's a woman's thing'. Another concurred: 'Yes some men are working and making something. I removed my headscarf, and a man was here! He can see me! Before 5 am I now put a blanket on the wall.'

These elements – the cleanliness of the bathrooms, the ill-equipped ventilation for cooking and the lack of window coverings – were direct physical problems with the building itself. They could be solved by better design and were caused by the rapid and insensitive repurposing of an office building, which ended up negatively affecting the wellbeing of its residents. Feelings of frustration that the space was not as clean or as fresh at it should be increased the tension between residents. Moreover, the lack personal privacy in a space that should allow for relaxation and emotional safety had a negative impact over extended periods of time.

Daily Tasks and Identity

For the residents of the Rathaus, the ability to carry out daily tasks was important for their sense of purpose, as well as a sense of control over the separation of private from the public spaces. The design of the building, with shared spaces, introduced additional concerns of security. Not only did the rooms not have locks on the doors, but the bathrooms and foyers were shared with other residents and their insecurity was compounded by the unfamiliar neighbourhood that they are in. The combination of outdoor public neighbourhood, indoor public shared spaces and easily accessible shared bedrooms came together to create a widespread sense of insecurity.

Given that they were once offices, these rooms did not have any locks. Therefore, the residents were unable to lock their rooms. Not having locks on the doors of the rooms led to stress, and this was a crucial factor in increasing past anxieties about safety for many women, as well as leading to a feeling of a lack of control. Many women reported how the addition of some kind of physical separation from other residents through a locked door could lead to greater emotional security. As one mother from Syria with four children put it: 'I'm not allowed to lock up my room [so] I'm not feeling like I'm really enjoying my privacy ... I like to, you know, feel safe in my room, but I'm not feeling that safe.' Another woman, a Palestinian from Lebanon, echoed this point. 'When I first came here, because I didn't feel so safe because of the door, I kept having nightmares', she told me. To add to this, the absence of any kitchen facilities for the residents to cook in had an impact on the ability for mothers to provide a sense of 'home', cooking culturally appropriate food for their children. Having been an office building, which had no kitchens at all, a cafeteria had been set up to cater for the residents, but the cultural diversity of residents made for difficult catering challenges.

Having found the cafeteria food to be not to their liking, some mothers decided to cook simple food in their own rooms with electric cookers. For them, sheltering their families became not so much a physical action as a sheltering of family, of culture and of the identity of being a mother. One mother was discussing how her children only like 'the food of me, their Mama', and another mother agreed, admitting tension between her child and herself: 'My son ... usually he don't want eat', she told me; 'When I cook for him, I cook what he likes. But here I don't have this opportunity. That's why I sometimes fight with him.'

A positive element of Rathaus Friedenau was the external security of the building. The building had a grand wide entrance with many stone steps leading up to the double doors. Once through those doors, there were further steps leading up to what once served as an information desk for the council building and is now a security station for residents. Two security staff sat behind the desk, with a further four security standing around on the steps in front of it. On each level of the building, security staff sat in the foyer, and despite the intimidating nature of some security guards in their blue uniforms, the staff smiled and chatted to residents as they passed in and out of the entrance. Most residents agreed that having security at the door was reassuring, letting them know that everyone within the building was there because they had the right to be. Particularly for mothers, the building security provided the peace of mind that their children were safe to play within the building confines without the danger of getting lost outside. As one mother from Eritrea told me that the building 'is one hundred per cent safe ... There is a playing room. I rest my mind ... My mind rest. This is good, I like it'.

Social Interactions and Relationships

It was not only the physical elements of the building that affected mental wellbeing or the way in which it had an impact on daily routines; they also affected the way in which the building shaped social interactions and relationships between residents. All of the residents were either attempting to start a life in Germany or were still waiting on news regarding their status to remain in the country. With these underlying stressors and challenges, living in a house with other women with cultural and religious differences and almost no common language between them resulted in loneliness amongst the residents, many of whom did not feel they could trust each other fully.

In the small paved square in front of the Rathaus, with roads on two sides and cafés on another, boys in their early teens speaking Arabic could often be found playing football. At the tables in front of the cafés, retired women chatted in German over coffee. On the benches lined up against the façade of the Rathaus, women residents of the Rathaus sat, and, on one bench, I found two women speaking Arabic sitting together, talking. On another bench, a woman of African background sat alone, with no acknowledgement from her fellow residents as they walked past her to join those on the next bench. Residents have reacted to living with so many unusual people and nationalities by keeping to themselves. Many have ever fewer interactions with fellow residents, either by sitting in their room or, for some of the younger single women who are sharing rooms with others, by staying outside away from the Rathaus for as long as possible each day. As one Syrian mother told me, 'there's nobody that gives me the community feeling, because everyone sits on their own and does not share anything with the others'. Another described how she spent her day: 'I go to school in the morning, and then I just go to a park and come back late in the evening. That's how I do not stay too much in the building.'

Despite tactics to avoid conflict and interactions between residents, tensions and outbursts still existed within the Rathaus. This was perhaps unsurprising, given the lack of activities with purpose, which is further compounded by the language barriers. These tensions manifested through petty measures, such as not letting someone sit on a bench in the foyer, or standing in front of the only empty washing machine and preventing others from using it. These provocative actions, which were all reported to me in interviews, often had no easy form of resolution, due to barriers in communication. One resident told me how simple acts of walking along the corridors of the Rathaus could cause tensions. 'Everybody here is stressed, but we will not come outside and tell each other what is paining us. You need to bear the pain by yourself. If our country was better, we would not be here. So you cannot bring your own problems and put it on another person. They will definitely slap you.'

Some residents felt that these tensions were not only between individuals, but were also racially motivated, and that certain residents acted in a racist manner. As one Ghanain resident told me with frustration: 'We are all refugees. They should treat us the same, whether we are black. Whether we are monkeys or what!' The way in which many of these residents dealt with the tensions emotionally continued a mantra of the temporary nature of the housing. Despite the Rathaus being intended to be short-term emergency housing, the reality was that many residents had lived there for up to two years due to not having found other suitable housing options. The newer arrivals to the Rathaus were largely unaware of this, and believed that the situation was bearable because it was short-term. As one Palestinian resident put it, 'there are too many people in this place, but it's good for the moment because it is temporary . . . I am going to go'.

Passing further through the glass doors, with the creamy yellow paint of the wooden door frames chipping off slightly, the building opened up into a large foyer. The foyer had high ceilings and concrete flooring, with walls painted a brighter yellow, appearing relatively newer. This was the main common area, and the only area in the building that had access to wireless internet. One could usually find residents on the wooden benches lining the walls of the foyer, using their phones and watching videos together.

The staff at the Rathaus, when asked about what issues they were aware of, mentioned the lack of internet access in the residents' rooms as a problem because they are unable to complete their German lessons and school homework easily. Whether this was the case, the residents explained the need for internet as a respite from their current situation. Younger women voiced a desire to have internet access, while the older women preferred television access somewhere in the building. One resident from Eritrea told me how important this was for her wellbeing: 'Someone need for example television. You watch movie or something, you relax maybe. You thinking about something, when you see movie, you refresh your mind.' In such comments, the residents described the need for this shelter to not only to be a physical space merely fulfilling the requirement of basic needs, but also to provide areas of relaxation and stress relief through mediums such as music or having quiet and private places to spend time. Another resident from Nigeria agreed: 'if you cannot solve a problem you need to walk, you do exercise. Maybe you can play music'.

Without opportunities to unwind and recharge and without effective ways of communicating and engaging with their roommates and neighbours, these women and children suffered from accumulated stress and anxiety and decreased coping mechanisms.

Conclusions: Sheltering the Mind

For residents of the Rathaus, living in a safe shelter was more than having security staff at the front entrance. A place to live required elements of privacy where they could be emotionally secure, as well as spaces that provided social and mental respite. The physical elements of the building, the ability to carry out daily tasks, and the social and relational impacts of the setup of the Rathaus all appeared to have a significant impact on the mental wellbeing of the residents. These findings should make us rethink what it means to have shelter. Too often shelter is conceived as a purely physical form of protection from the elements, but this narrow approach gives insufficient attention to the ways in which mental health should also be supported.

Rathaus Friedenau, adapted from an office as a space of physical accommodation for residents, had significant gaps in terms of how it sheltered the mental wellbeing of those living there. The concept of shelter, according to the residents of Rathaus Friedenau, should have provided a safe space, a space where privacy was available, where there was infrastructure to relax and unwind, where they could mentally escape and emotionally recharge. The unlocked doors and the lack of kitchens in Rathaus Friedenau changed the residents' abilities to carry out the daily tasks and routines that they were used to. A true shelter should provide a space where such daily routines could be carried out in a way that affirms identity, sheltering the family unit and culture. A true shelter should be a space where social interactions can take place in an atmosphere of trust. The residents of Rathaus Friedenau demonstrated that shelter should go beyond providing a place to eat, sleep and wash; rather, the physical building must be adapted to support mental wellbeing in a culturally and contextually appropriate manner. Finding a way for shelters to accommodate residents' current and future mental wellbeing and moving beyond a place for people to just physically function is not just a design challenge; it requires a change of focus.

Esther Schroeder Goh is a medical doctor with a particular interest in interdisciplinary approaches to mental health. Previously a Worcester College Provost's Scholar at the University of Oxford, she is currently a Westpac Future Leaders Scholar in Australia, pursuing further research into mental health in emergency settings.

References

Allen, J., R. Balfour, R. Bell and M. Marmot. 2014. 'Social Determinants of Mental Health.' *International Review of Psychiatry* 26(4): 392–407.

Chen, W., B. Hall, L. Ling and A. Renzaho. 2017. 'Pre-migration and Post-migration Factors Associated with Mental Health in Humanitarian Migrants in Australia and the Moderation Effect of Post-migration Stressors'. *The Lancet Psychiatry* 4(3): 218–29.

Habib, R., S. Basma and J. Yeretzian. 2006. 'Harboring Illnesses: On the Association between Disease and Living Conditions in a Palestinian Refugee Camp in Lebanon'. *International Journal of Environmental Health Research* 16(2): 99–111.

Hanquet, G. 2018. *Refugee Health: An Approach to Emergency Situations*. Paris: MSF.

Hynie, M. 2017. 'The Social Determinants of Refugee Mental Health in the Post-migration Context: A Critical Review'. *Canadian Journal of Psychiatry* 63(5): 297–303.

Rasmussen, A., and J. Annan. 2009. 'Predicting Stress Related to Basic Needs and Safety in Darfur Refugee Camps: A Structural and Social Ecological Analysis'. *Journal of Refugee Studies* 23(1): 23–40.

Shishehgar, S., L. Gholizadeh, M. DiGiacomo, A. Green and P. Davidson. 2016. 'Health and Socio-cultural Experiences of Refugee Women: An Integrative Review'. *Journal of Immigrant and Minority Health* 19(4): 959–73.

South-East Asia Regional Office. 2018. 'Promotion of Mental Well-Being'. Retrieved 17 October 2019 from http://www.searo.who.int/entity/mental_health/promotion-of-mental-well-being/en.

Turrini, G., M. Purgato, F. Ballette, M. Nosè, G. Ostuzzi and C. Barbui. 2017. 'Common Mental Disorders in Asylum Seekers and Refugees: Umbrella Review of Prevalence and Intervention Studies'. *International Journal of Mental Health Systems* 11(51): 1–14.

WHO. 2018. *Social Determinants of Mental Health*. Geneva: World Health Organization.

Ziersch, A., and C. Due. 2018. 'A Mixed Methods Systematic Review of Studies Examining the Relationship between Housing and Health for People from Refugee and Asylum Seeking Backgrounds'. *Social Science & Medicine* 213: 199–219.

Part III

Architecture, Design and Displacement

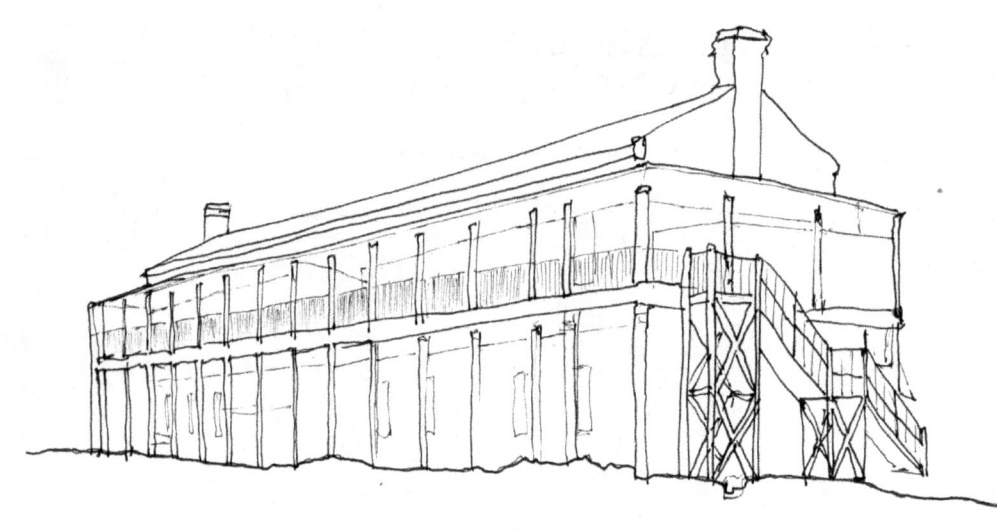

Figure 14.1 Point Nepean Quarantine Station near Melbourne, Australia. © Mark E. Breeze, based on an image supplied by Benjamin Thomas White.

14

Protection or Isolation?
Humanitarian Evacuees in Australian Quarantine Stations

Benjamin Thomas White

The refugee camp, Liisa Malkki once wrote, is a technology of both care and control (Malkki 1995: 231): a tool for the efficient delivery of shelter and humanitarian aid to displaced people, on the one hand, and a means of immobilizing and isolating them, on the other. Recognizing the tension between these imperatives, in 2014 the United Nations Refugee Agency (UNHCR) adopted a policy of seeking alternatives to camps that stresses the 'significant negative impacts' they can have (UNHCR 2014: 4). But the emphasis on control that makes camps uncomfortable for UNHCR, not to mention their residents, is the thing that often makes them appealing to states. The sites chosen for refugee camps often indicate the host state's commitment to holding refugees at a distance, from the military transit camps where France accommodated Spanish Republican exiles in 1939 to the remote Azraq or Dadaab camp complexes in contemporary Jordan and Kenya. The prior and later functions of such sites often also show how refugees are grouped with other 'controlled' populations: in the French example, a camp like Rivesaltes, created to keep colonial troops away from the metropolitan population, was adapted first into a refugee camp, then into an internment camp for 'undesirables' and prisoners of war (POWs), and later still into accommodation for migrant workers, and then an immigration detention centre (Mémorial du camp de Rivesaltes n.d.).

What holds for camps also holds for individual structures and complexes of buildings. In 1914–19, for example, the theatre and other buildings at Earls Court showground were adapted to house thousands of refugees, mostly Belgians (British Government War Refugees' Camp 1920). The central location and minimal restrictions on residents' movements indicated the British government's commitment to caring for, rather than controlling, the citizens of its war allies. But in other cases, the location and biography of buildings used to shelter refugees can indicate a desire to contain and isolate them that may be at odds with the rhetoric of protection. In this chapter I explore that tension between care and control, protection and isolation, using site biographies of two distinctively Australian cases: the old quarantine stations at North Head, Sydney, and Point Nepean, near Melbourne. Both of these sites have also been used to house humanitarian evacuees – groups of refugees who were ostensibly benefiting from a particularly generous form of protection. In their buildings, we see a logic underlying refugee shelter that is as much carceral as humanitarian.[1]

Quarantine and Confinement in Australia

The coastline of Australia is dotted with old quarantine stations, often set near to, but apart from, major cities. For much of the country's modern history, control of disease meant control of mobility, often in locations that were also used for other kinds of confinement. On Torren's Island near Adelaide in South Australia, for example, a quarantine station was later joined by a notorious First World War internment camp for 'enemy aliens'. At Woodman Point near Perth in Western Australia, a quarantine station became a Second World War POW camp. Near Darwin in the Northern Territory, the immigration detention centres at Bladin Point and Wickham Point, recently closed, stood on what was previously known as Mud Island, where Chinese and Aboriginal men with leprosy were quarantined in the late nineteenth and early twentieth centuries; even at the time, the appalling conditions there drew considerable criticism (Find & Connect n.d.; *Northern Standard* 1928).

Australia's history of quarantine is different from that of other countries in Europe and Asia. Maritime quarantine regulations were enacted later, but lasted longer, and they had a more central place in government policy. At federation in 1901, quarantine was the only area of public health regulation to be assigned in the constitution to the new Commonwealth government, and Australia's modern Department of Health emerged from the Federal Quarantine Service (Bashford 1998: 388, 397). The notion of quarantine as part of the emerging nation's defences against invasion from abroad was central to public health policy. As such, quarantine, as Alison Bashford has argued, played an important discursive role in marking the boundaries of the Australian nation, both territorially (as an 'island-nation') and politically (with black or yellow bodies much more likely to be confined and excluded). In an article with Carolyn Strange, Bashford extended this analysis to draw connections between the history of quarantine detention going back to the nineteenth century, the twentieth-century internment of enemy aliens during wartime, and Australia's more recent policy of mandatory detention of asylum seekers and any other 'unlawful non-citizens'. All three forms of detention have served an important nation-defining role in Australia: these are indeed *national* histories (Bashford and Strange 2002: 518–19). Given these connections, it is not surprising that the same sites were often used for more than one kind of confinement.

The parallel histories of North Head and Point Nepean are apparent even from a brief visit. Each stands just inside the mouth of a natural harbour, where a port city of European settlement developed further inland. Both are today located within national parks that combine natural heritage – coastal habitats threatened by suburban sprawl – with human heritage. There are gestures to the traditional owners of the land, fairly insubstantial for the time being, but programmed to increase (Parks Victoria 2016; Peter Freeman Pty Ltd et al. 2000: 22–42). By contrast, the vestiges of coastal fortifications are extensive, as are the quarantine stations themselves: they are material evidence not of two distinct histories, but two aspects of the same history, manifested at the same locations (Bashford 1998: 394). They are beautiful but eerie places to visit.

North Head, Sydney

North Head is the older of the two stations, as Sydney is the older of the two cities. It opened in 1832 at Spring Cove, where the first European ships to enter Port Jackson had anchored sixty years earlier (Clarke and Frederick 2016: 522; Bashford and Hobbins 2015: 392). Although the central business district of modern Sydney – the site of the original settlement – is only a few miles away up the harbour, it is out of sight beyond Middle Head, which separates the main expanse of the harbour from its northern offshoots. Like its counterpart at Point Nepean, the old quarantine station at North Head feels more remote than its actual location suggests.

The buildings remaining on the site today show its development into the twentieth century. At the wharf was a luggage store, a boiler house with a tall brick chimney, and a disinfecting room where luggage was steamed in enormous cast-iron autoclaves. On the slopes above the cove, a spacious complex gradually spread out, with accommodation areas reproducing the class hierarchies and racist hierarchies that pertained aboard ship. The first-class passengers in their comfortable accommodation were protected from mingling with second-class residents by high fences and a stretch of 'neutral ground', while third-class passengers were elsewhere again and 'Asiatics' were housed in crowded dormitories with an external communal kitchen. Obliged to stay at the station in 1930, the golfer J.H. Kirkwood found the segregation insufficient (*The Argus* 1930):

> I am an Australian, and I always thought that this was a white man's country, but when I have seen Chinese, Indians, and Fijians with the same bathing and toilet facilities as white men in this quarantine station I have not been able to help feeling disgust. However, we are resigned to our fate.

For residents suspected of carrying disease or showing symptoms, there was an isolation zone at one end of the site; for those who became ill, there was a hospital and in the final necessity a burial ground.

In recent years, the site has been developed as a cultural heritage destination (Peter Freeman Pty Ltd et al. 2000) and simultaneously, thanks to a 'linkage' grant from the Australian Research Council, has been intensively studied by a large historical archaeology project based at the University of Sydney. The inscriptions that mark the site, from highly visible carvings in the sandstone by the road leading down to the wharf to faded scribbles of ink on the internal paintwork of buildings, were a key focus for this project. Some of these inscriptions are formal, clearly executed by skilled craftsmen, while others are more amateurish and/or incomplete, but they commemorate the stay at North Head of the passengers and crew of numerous ships. The oldest was made by sixteen-year-old John Dawson in 1835, but they continue late into the twentieth century, carved, painted or scratched onto external and internal surfaces (Hobbins, Frederick and Clarke 2016). Among the most interesting are those made by Chinese, Arab or Indonesian sailors, whose voices are hard to recover from other historical sources for Australia's racist nineteenth and twentieth centuries (Hobbins, Frederick and Clarke 2016: Chapter 6).

Maritime quarantine restrictions outlasted coastal naval defences, though only by a decade or two. Long-range bomber aircraft – and, later, intercontinental ballistic missiles – made coastal artillery batteries irrelevant by the middle of the twentieth century. Mass civilian air travel took a little longer to do the same for quarantine stations. In 1963, when the North Head fortifications fell permanently out of use, European immigrants were still arriving in Australia by ship, as part of the country's enormous postwar programme of state-supported immigration. But by then, one building on the site, identified by the number A20, had already been adapted to a different kind of confinement: immigration detention (Clarke, Frederick and Hobbins 2017: 405; Clarke and Frederick 2016: 531–33).

Although quarantine restrictions were winding down, Australian migration policy became steadily more restrictive in the 1960s and 1970s. From 1959 to 1976, building A20 accommodated 'non-criminal deportees': foreign citizens who had not committed any crime, but were in Australia without a valid visa. A total of 327 separate inscriptions scratched or scrawled onto the paintwork by detainees at North Head remain, despite decades of repainting and what archaeologists term 'adaptive reuse' (the building is now a wedding venue). They offer 'a counter-narrative to the rosy image and official record of late-twentieth-century immigration to Australia' (Clarke, Frederick and Hobbins 2017: 405). Indeed: one of them simply reads 'Fuck Australia' (Clarke, Frederick and Hobbins 2017: 416).

Most of the surviving graffiti in building A20 that can be dated (only about 20 per cent of the total) were inscribed in one year: 1975. In that year, another mobile foreign population was housed at North Head, this time on their way into rather than out of Australia: Vietnamese children, controversially brought into the country as part of the U.S. military's 'Operation Babylift'. This was an evacuation of children, some of them the offspring of American servicemen, from Saigon prior to its fall. About 300 were brought to Australia, mostly to Sydney, in the midst of bitter recriminations over the country's participation in the war and responsibility for Vietnamese refugees (Forkert 2012). A total of 115 of them were brought to North Head, where the now little-used quarantine station was able to accommodate them (Peter Freeman Pty Ltd et al. 2000: 68): Prime Minister Gough Whitlam visited them there (*Sydney Morning Herald* 1975). This was not the first time that the station had been used to house evacuees. As well as briefly accommodating British evacuee children in 1940 and Portuguese refugees from Timor in 1942, it had more recently housed Australians evacuated from Darwin after Cyclone Tracy struck in 1974. (It would take more Vietnamese refugees in 1977: Peter Freeman Pty Ltd et al. 2000: 87–88.)

Point Nepean, Melbourne

The quarantine station at Point Nepean was founded later than the one at North Head, in 1852, as the population boom sparked by the Victoria gold rush was just beginning. Melbourne's colonial population in 1851 was between 20,000 and 30,000, but in 1852, 619 incoming ships brought over 55,000 passengers to and through the city over just four months. The following year, over four times as many ships arrived, and the boom continued until the 1890s, by which time the city had nearly half a million people (*eMelbourne* 2008). Among the 1852 arrivals were the passengers of the clipper *Ticonderoga*, which departed Liverpool in August and arrived in Port Phillip, the large and almost completely enclosed bay on whose northern shore Melbourne stands, in November (Kruithof 2002). But by the time the clipper reached the Rip – the narrow, treacherous seaway at the bay's entrance – nearly 100 of its passengers had died, mainly of typhus, and almost 400 more were ill with fever, dysentery and diarrhoea. As a result, it was anchored at Point Nepean, where the passengers could be quarantined to protect the city. Another seventy died there. Interpretation boards at the site detail this history, and a modern memorial stone commemorates the dead.

Point Nepean is further away from Melbourne than North Head is from Sydney. It is on the long, thin extremity of the Mornington Peninsula, one of the two peninsulas that encircle Port Phillip. Like North Head, Point Nepean was heavily fortified from the late nineteenth century into the mid twentieth century, and the fortifications seem to attract more visitors than the quarantine station. The quarantine station resembles Sydney's in many ways: the boiler house, the autoclaves for disinfecting luggage, the isolation hospital and morgue standing at a slight remove from the rest of the complex. By the shore, the memorial to the passengers of the *Ticonderoga*, erected in 2002, marks the site of the station's original cemetery; in 1952, the remains were moved to protect them from coastal erosion, which also affects one of the burial grounds at North Head.

From 1952, the Point Nepean quarantine station shared its site with the military, which ran an Officer Cadet School there. It was finally closed in 1978–80. From 1985 to 1998, the site was used by the School of Army Health, and, in the early 2000s, the site was passed over to a local community trust for heritage management. In 2009, it was incorporated into the national park that occupies the rest of the point and includes other old military buildings. Whereas the North Head quarantine station was redeveloped as a heritage attraction by a private company, the Point Nepean station is directly run by the state parks and wildlife service of Victoria (Parks Victoria n.d.).

In 1999, when the site still belonged to the military, it briefly found another use that creates a further parallel with North Head. In the northern hemisphere spring of that year, during the NATO bombing campaign against Serbia, tens of thousands of Kosova Albanian refugees fled into Macedonia, a small new state with little capacity to assist them. Recognizing that its own aerial campaign had contributed to their displacement and that international public opinion might hold the alliance responsible for their suffering, NATO organized a large-scale humanitarian evacuation (Huysmans 2002). This was the first time that the term 'humanitarian evacuation' was used to describe such an international action: Sadako Ogata, the then UN High Commissioner for Refugees, described the operation as having 'no precedent' in her agency's history (White 2019: 1). Although it was not a member of the alliance, Australia participated by hosting evacuees (Carr 2011).

Of the nearly 4,000 Kosovan refugees who were brought to Australia under Operation Safe Haven, around 400 were accommodated in the old quarantine station at Point Nepean (the State Library of Victoria commissioned the photographer Emmanuel Santos to document their stay). The others were scattered around nine other military sites. The government considered but rejected the idea of housing the evacuees in very remote locations, such as the Woomera base in the South Australian desert, where an immigration detention centre would open later that year to confine 'unauthorized arrivals' under Australia's mandatory detention policy. But several sites, like the Singleton barracks in New South Wales, nonetheless held them at a remove from the general population (Carr 2011: 158–59). Point Nepean is as far away from Melbourne as it is possible to be while still remaining 'close to Melbourne': this narrow spit of land is literally at the end of the road.

Australia's response to humanitarian evacuees shifted between the earlier evacuation of children from Vietnam and the Kosovan case in the late 1990s. Operation Babylift was controversial, like the country's participation in the Vietnam War. In opposition, Gough Whitlam and the Australian Labor Party had been critical of the war; in power, their reluctance to assist refugees from South Vietnam led to 'humanitarian' criticism from the right that they were abandoning Australia's former allies to communist tyranny (Forkert 2012). Operation Babylift offered a way to offset that criticism, at a time when Australia was progressively abandoning the 'white Australia policy' that had restricted non-European immigration since federation. Whitlam's government removed the final restrictions in 1973, reversing the Labor Party's earlier adherence to 'white Australia'; his Liberal opponent and replacement as Prime Minister, Malcolm Fraser, was committed both to a liberal immigration policy and to assisting Vietnamese refugees. But by the 1990s, Australian public debate on immigration had soured, especially where asylum seekers and refugees were concerned. Both main parties were increasingly committed to restriction.

Operation Safe Haven in the late 1990s was therefore a tricky political issue for John Howard's Liberal government. Howard had diplomatic reasons for assisting NATO by participating in the evacuation, but political reasons for ensuring that the evacuees left quickly. The grudging nature of Australia's humanitarian response can be seen across several areas, from legislation to location. A new class of temporary visa was created for the evacuees, but most of the text of the legislation was given over to establishing the immigration minister's rights to shorten, revoke or withhold such visas (Parliament of Australia 1999). Evacuees received a weekly cash allowance, but it was so miserly – at first only $20, a quarter of what Kosovo evacuees in Germany received – that they were virtually confined to their 'Safe Havens' (Carr 2011: 160). Notwithstanding the claim by the then Department of

Immigration and Multicultural Affairs that 'every effort was made to enable the Kosovars to participate in the local community', everything indicates that the evacuees were to be held at a distance (Department of Immigration and Multicultural Affairs 1999). They arrived in May and June, but half were gone by September. By April 2000, only 100 or so remained, mostly for medical reasons.

Conclusion

Kate Coddington, writing of the parallels between federal policies towards Aboriginal communities in the Northern Territory and asylum seekers arriving on Australia's northern shores, has found 'a common logic toward policymaking in Australia that relies on *containment* to engage with populations perceived as threatening to perceptions of Australian nationality' (Coddington 2014: 2–3). The housing of Vietnamese child evacuees at North Head might simply be explained as a pragmatic choice determined by the availability of more or less suitable accommodation. The 'quarantining' of the Kosovo Albanians at Point Nepean more clearly indicates that these humanitarian evacuees too were caught up in the logic of containment, isolated as well as protected. Despite the Australian government's own decision to bring them to the far side of the world in recognition of their humanitarian need, the Kosovan evacuees remained within the increasingly carceral framework of Australia's asylum and refugee policy.

When we research histories of confinement, including quarantine and immigration detention, we often start with states' policies, laws and practices, and only then note specific sites where they took effect. Similarly, when we study humanitarian operations on behalf of displaced people, it is easiest to start by investigating the policies and practices of states, international organizations and humanitarian agencies – for example, the UNHCR's policy on avoiding alternatives to camps, or the actual practices of building them. To move beyond these institutional perspectives and explore the experience of people living in confinement or in camps, social scientists use ethnographic research. Historians, for their part, can use personal testimonies: oral history (Green et al. 2017), diaries or – in the example of quarantine – the 'ship's newspapers' created by passengers and crew (Foxhall 2017; Hobbins, Frederick and Clarke 2016; Maglen 2005). We also need such sources to deepen our understanding of humanitarian evacuations from the perspective of the evacuees (Carr 2011: 336; White 2019).

Another approach is to start with a specific site and move outwards to consider the *different* policies, laws and practices that have been manifested there. The inscriptions that historical archaeologists have studied at sites like North Head or Kilmainham Gaol (Clarke, Frederick and Hobbins

2017; McAtackney 2016) could be taken as a specific form of personal (or in some cases collective) testimony. But their layering over time, and across different forms of confinement, also illustrates the value of a site biography. A historian of quarantine might never learn, from legislative texts or the diaries of confined passengers, that the buildings of a quarantine station also served to house immigration detainees or shelter humanitarian evacuees; a historian of refuge might not realize that a camp where refugees were accommodated also held POWs, 'undesirable aliens' or migrant workers. Site biographies give us a richer spatial awareness of what confined populations experience. But more than that, they also allow us to understand the underlying logic of containment that is applied to very different kinds of mobile populations when, even if they are being protected, they are viewed as a threat. Researching the past and present of specific sites gives us a more textured understanding of the tension between care and control in refugee shelter.

Benjamin Thomas White teaches history at the University of Glasgow, where he is also a member of the Glasgow Refugee, Asylum and Migration Network. A Middle East historian by background, he now teaches refugee history more broadly and is researching the global history of the refugee camp.

Note

1. Descriptions of North Head and Point Nepean here are drawn from site visits in August 2017, made during a visiting fellowship at the EU Centre for Shared Complex Challenges, University of Melbourne. I would like to thank Professor Joy Damousi for suggesting that I apply for this fellowship, and Peter Freeman for making a copy of the 2000 *North Head Quarantine Station Conservation Management Plan* available to me.

References

The Argus (Melbourne). 1930. 'Aorangi Passengers: Conditions in Quarantine. Kirkwood Dissatisfied', 6 March. Retrieved 18 October 2019 from http://trove.nla.gov.au/newspaper/article/4073060.
Bashford, Alison. 1998. 'Quarantine and the Imagining of the Australian Nation'. *Health* 2(4): 387–402.
Bashford, Alison, and Peter Hobbins. 2015. 'Rewriting Quarantine: Pacific History at Australia's Edge'. *Australian Historical Studies* 46(3): 392–409.

Bashford, Alison, and Carolyn Strange. 2002. 'Asylum-Seekers and National Histories of Detention'. *Australian Journal of Politics and History* 48(4): 509–27.

British Government War Refugees' Camp, Earls Court (London). 1920. *Four Years in a Refugee Camp: Being an Account of the British Government War Refugees' Camp, Earl's Court, London, 1914–1919. Compiled under the Direction of G.A. Powell, Officer-in-Charge.* London: Baynard Press.

Carr, Robert. 2011. 'The Kosovar Refugees: The Experience of Providing Temporary Safe Haven in Australia'. Ph.D. thesis. Wollongong: University of Wollongong.

——. 2018. *Generosity and Refugees: The Kosovars in Exile.* Leiden: Brill.

Clarke, Anne, and Ursula Frederick. 2016. '"Born to Be a Stoway": Inscriptions, Graffiti, and the Rupture of Space at the North Head Quarantine Station, Sydney'. *International Journal of Historical Archaeology* 20: 521–35.

Clarke, Anne, Ursula Frederick and Peter Hobbins. 2017. '"No Complaints": Counter-narratives of Immigration and Detention in Graffiti at North Head Immigration Detention Centre, Australia 1973–76'. *World Archaeology* 49(3): 404–22.

Coddington, Kate. 2014. 'Geographies of Containment: Logics of Enclosure in Aboriginal and Asylum Seeker Policies in Australia's Northern Territory'. Ph.D. thesis. Syracuse, NY: Syracuse University.

Department of Immigration and Multicultural Affairs. 1999. 'DIMA Annual Report 1998–99'. Retrieved 18 October 2019 from http://web.archive.org/web/20060911190216/http://www.immi.gov.au/about/reports/annual/1998-99/html/safe.htm.

eMelbourne. 2008. Retrieved 18 October 2019 from http://www.emelbourne.net.au/biogs/EM00652b.htm ('Gold') and http://www.emelbourne.net.au/biogs/EM00455b.htm ('Demography').

Find & Connect. n.d. 'Mud Island Lazaret (1889–1931)'. Find & Connect: History & Information about Australian Orphanages, Children's Homes & Other Institutions. Retrieved 18 October 2019 from https://www.findandconnect.gov.au/guide/nt/YE00283.

Forkert, Joshua. 2012. 'Refugees, Orphans and a Basket of Cats: The Politics of Operation Babylift'. *Journal of Australian Studies* 36(4): 427–44.

Foxhall, Katherine. 2017. 'White Men in Quarantine: Disease, Race, Commerce and Mobility in the Pacific, 1872'. *Australian Historical Studies* 48(2): 244–63.

Green, Michael, Andre Dao, Angelica Neville, Dana Affleck and Sienna Merope (eds). 2017. *They Cannot Take the Sky: Stories from Detention.* Sydney: Allen & Unwin.

Hobbins, Peter, Ursula Frederick and Anne Clarke. 2016. *Stories from the Sandstone: Quarantine Inscriptions from Australia's Immigrant Past.* Sydney: Arbon Publishing.

Huysmans, Jef. 2002. 'Shape-Shifting NATO: Humanitarian Action and the Kosovo Refugee Crisis'. *Review of International Studies* 28: 599–618.

Kruithof, Mary. 2002. *Fever Beach: The Story of the Migrant Clipper 'Ticonderoga', Its Ill-Fated Voyage and its Historic Impact.* Mount Waverley, Victoria: QI Publishing.

McAtackney, Laura. 2016. 'Graffiti Revelations and the Changing Meanings of Kilmainham Gaol in (Post)Colonial Ireland'. *International Journal of Historical Archaeology* 20(3): 492–505.

Maglen, Krista. 2005. 'Quarantined, Exploring Personal Accounts of Incarceration in Australian and Pacific Quarantine Stations in the Nineteenth Century'. *Journal of the Royal Australian Historical Society* 91(1): 1–14.

Malkki, Liisa. 1995. *Purity and Exile: Violence, Memory, and National Cosmology among Hutu Refugees in Tanzania*. Chicago: University of Chicago Press.

Mémorial du camp de Rivesaltes. n.d. 'L'histoire du Camp de Rivesaltes'. Retrieved 18 October 2019 from http://www.memorialcamprivesaltes.eu/2-l-histoire-du-camp-de-rivesaltes.htm.

Northern Standard (Darwin). 1928. 'Mud Island', 2 October, reproducing a letter from the Sydney *Labor Daily*. Retrieved 18 October 2019 from https://trove.nla.gov.au/newspaper/article/48025023.

Parks Victoria. n.d. 'Point Nepean National Park Visitor Guide'. Retrieved 18 October 2019 from http://parkweb.vic.gov.au/__data/assets/pdf_file/0007/719701/Point-Nepean-National-Park-Visitor-Guide.pdf.

———. 2016. 'Mon Mon: Point Nepean National Park Draft Master Plan Summary Document'. Retrieved 18 October 2019 from http://parkweb.vic.gov.au/__data/assets/pdf_file/0007/689497/PNNP_Draft-MP_Summary-Brochure.pdf.

Parliament of Australia. 1999. Migration Legislation Amendment (Temporary Safe Haven Visas) Act 1999. Retrieved 18 October 2019 from https://www.legislation.gov.au/Details/C2004A00425.

Peter Freeman Pty Ltd, Donald Ellmsmore Pty Ltd, Robert Boden and Associates, Haglund and Associates, and Guppy and Associates. 2000. *Sydney Harbour National Park, North Head Quarantine Station Conservation Management Plan. Volume 1*. Prepared for New South Wales National Parks and Wildlife Service, Sydney.

Sydney Morning Herald. 1975. 'Let Adult Vietnamese Come Here, Fraser Says', 7 April.

UNHCR. 2014. 'Policy on Alternatives to Camps'. Retrieved 18 October 2019 from https://www.unhcr.org/protection/statelessness/5422b8f09/unhcr-policy-alternatives-camps.html.

White, Benjamin Thomas. 2019. 'A Grudging Rescue: France, the Armenians of Cilicia, and the History of Humanitarian Evacuations'. *Humanity* 10(1): 1–27.

Figure 15.1 *Silos* in Trieste, Italy. © Mark E. Breeze, based on an image supplied by Roberta Altin.

15
Silos in Trieste, Italy
A Historical Shelter for Displaced People

Roberta Altin

When you arrive by train in Trieste, a city in the northeast of Italy on the border with Slovenia, a huge historic building welcomes you just a few metres from the station: the so-called *Silos*. The word 'Silos' literally means a container. It was built as a granary in the commercial hub under the Austro-Hungarian Empire in the mid 1800s, during a period of rapid economic growth. The enormous warehouse covers a vast area of 45,000 sq.m, and for a long time was a tangible symbol of Trieste's wealth, which originated in its strategic position as a place for maritime transit between the Balkans and Central Europe. *Silos* was built as a huge three-storey warehouse, with a central body at the front behind which lies a long, open air space for railway tracks and freight trains. It was built using the then recently discovered technique of concrete construction and still today its location in the heart of the city is a prominent example of industrial architecture dominating the urban panorama of Trieste. It was originally constructed for purely practical purposes, as a port facility for storing grain at the edge of the quay by the sea. The trains that entered it 'loaded or unloaded goods directly from two long sheds' (Semerari and Tamaro 1998: 162).

Today, this enormous structure is private property, mostly abandoned after a fire. The one exception is a small area, occupied by a pay car park and a coach station, which is the last stop in Italian territory. After the original edifice burned down in 1994, only the facades remained, which stood as a sort of infrastructure or a mask, surviving on three sides of the building. The old walls still house beautiful floor slabs and structures that are no longer fit for use, but since 2014, many refugees and asylum seekers have been occupying this vast empty area, mostly from Afghanistan and Pakistan. They have populated the space on the ground floor with makeshift shelters, tents, cardboard boxes, blankets and rags. The average number of migrants settled in *Silos* has varied from between 50 and 150 people, but this represents only the latest layer of several streams of displaced people who have moved through the building over the past seventy years. In this chapter, I draw comparisons between the way *Silos* has been used in the past and the way it is used in the present. The aim is to illustrate how a single refugee shelter can accrue layers of meaning, becoming a regular reference point for journeys due to its important strategic position. My central argument is that the benefit of spaces like this lies in their flexibility: they are located at important crossroads, yet informal enough to develop social spaces that allow mobility and a form of partial protection on the move. In terms of structure, this chapter first looks at 'then' – the history of the shelter – before turning to 'now', discussing the same building today.

Then

The decline of Trieste as a border town began in the first half of the twentieth century, with the outbreak of the two world wars (Ara and Magris 1987). In 1938, Trieste was chosen by Mussolini as the venue to announce his new racial laws; consequently, in December 1943, *Silos* became the last gathering place for Jews and the departure point for the first train to Auschwitz. It was the first time *Silos* had been used as a container for people rather than grain. It worked as a collection point for those interned in the Risiera S. Saba, the only camp in Italy with an operating crematorium. Between December 1943 and the spring of 1945, 159 trains departed from *Silos* in Trieste, transporting them to their final destination. As a plaque on its façade reminds us, *Silos* constituted the last gathering place and departure point for many Jews, who waited and were collected there for a journey with no return.

At the end of the Second World War came the Treaty of Paris (1947) and the London Memorandum (1954). Subsequently, a large flow of Italian refugees leaving Istria and Dalmatia were hosted in *Silos*, which became the main centre of aid and first reception for people fleeing from the East. There are no official statistics even today, but historians more or less agree that an average of 280,000 Italian exiles escaped from the territory handed over to Yugoslavia under the socialist regime of Marshal Tito (Pupo 2005). Indeed, between 1943 and 1956, almost the whole of the Italian population of Istria and Dalmatia moved to Italy in several migration waves due to the effects of the war (Ballinger 2003). *Silos* became a 'CPR' or Refugee Collection Centre, which registered the new arrivals and provided an identification card for recognition and assistance. One-third of the Italian exodus from what became Yugoslavia remained at their first stop, Trieste. This use of *Silos* as a centre for first reception is well described in many archival sources and in literature. Indeed, in a novel written by Marisa Madieri, the wife of Claudio Magris, the daily life in *Silos* is depicted particularly vividly. The ground, first and second floors were almost completely dark, with no natural light, while the third floor was illuminated by large skylights in the roof that could never be opened. Thousands of Italian refugees were camped for several years here in the 1950s, and on each floor the space was divided by wooden walls into many small compartments, called 'boxes'. Each was placed right next to the other with no intervals, 'like cells of a beehive' (Madieri 1998: 68). Such sources underline that refugees felt like a series of numbers, living in modular *loculi*, in a kind of small artificial city set apart. *Silos*, in this period, was sometimes called 'the village' by refugees – a place for exiles in the heart of the real town.

The identical 'boxes' in *Silos* were all composed of two rooms. In the case of a family, there was one kitchen/dining space and a common bedroom with numerous beds separated only by a curtain. The 'boxes' were sometimes named like villas to customize them, and were also numbered and separated by thin wooden walls, connected and crossed by internal alleys named by the refugees after their place of origin. Inside the camp, there was a hierarchy based on a system of 'first come first served', sometimes disrupted by personal power. The most coveted 'boxes' were those close to the few windows or those on the third floor with sunlight, as walking through *Silos* was often like going through 'a Dantesque landscape, a nocturnal and smoky purgatory' (Madieri 1998: 68). The worst problem was the smells: a mixture of canteen, kitchen, refugee camp and sweat. Sources recount the pungent smell of the disinfectant used upon their arrival, the situation of total chaos, with temporary beds, straw mattresses and bed bugs. Sources also describe the total lack of privacy and of intimacy. Such conditions have remained etched in the memory of the displaced who transited through *Silos*, even though there are also signs of domestication of space, evident in the Christmas photos depicting decorated trees, tablecloths, furniture and posters adorning the plywood walls.

The internal pavilions in *Silos* allowed the refugees to literally share a life as a community: rather than a neighbourhood, it was more a sort of cohabitation, with both positive and negative repercussions. The doors of the boxes were always left open during the day, a common habit that helped them feel less alone in the squalor of exile, but also had more practical reasons, offering more ventilation and lighting. Within such an enormous human container, there was always a background buzz punctuated with louder pitches of the radio, coughing, screaming and children's crying. The heat in the summer was unbearable, forcing the refugees to spend as much time as possible outside. The harsh winters, with rain dripping from the skylights, obliged refugees to use emergency heaters, which constantly blew the precarious electrical system. There were communal water and sanitation facilities and an external canteen. *Silos* was supposed to be a centre for the initial period of emergency, but actually several witnesses can confirm that they lived there for many years; the youngest attended the state schools in the city, while others organized a chapel in which to pray and to celebrate the Catholic Mass.

It is interesting to observe how this community of the same national language and citizenship tried to interact and to insert itself into the local life of the new town. Often this came with an ingrained sense of shame, because the displaced people were not well accepted by the local residents and had been stigmatized due to political reasons resulting from ethnic conflict and civil war. For many decades, 'refugee' was a common insult among children in Trieste, as heavy as an insult to one's mother or family. Indeed, the meaning of the word 'refugee' is far from neutral and it is important to underline the entanglement of reactions. Like other European resettlement programmes after the war, locals were sceptical about the displaced Italians' unknown past, raising doubts about the reasons they abandoned their homes (Audenino 2016). They were often accused of political infidelity or ambiguity, considered 'not only homeless, but also without a country' and, consequently, 'with no moral and legal ties' (Vernant 1953: 4–5; Salvatici 2007: 71).

Therefore, refugees were looked upon with suspicion: as significant rivals for the few available jobs and public housing. *Silos*, meanwhile, became a place of transit and suffering, inhabited by people stuck between war and normalization. This hub became a 'temporary' centre of hospitality, with all the goods and properties of displaced people stacked and crammed into a nearby warehouse at the city's old harbour. This, famously known as Warehouse 18, is even today full of furniture, pictures, photos, piles of dishes, pots, cutlery, books, personal effects, work tools and chairs, hundreds of wooden chairs stacked one on top of each other, which remain unclaimed and have become the symbolic visual representation of this exile (Altin and Badurina 2018: 192–93). The warehouse is located in a special area of the old port in disuse, near *Silos*, where no free circulation is permitted. This has created an extraordinary zone where the objects of ordinary daily life have been interrupted, a kind of frozen frame of domesticity in other times and spaces. It is of course particularly ironic that this has taken place in a port and a train station, which also symbolize mobility and movement.

The goods and chattels are still waiting to be reclaimed by their owners, who were expected to come for them once they had settled into new homes.

But the displaced people who gradually moved out of *Silos* in the 1950s and 1960s were spread out to other structures, when the Italian government set up camps on the Karst Plateau, an area largely inhabited by the Slovenian minorities. The camps, designed with housing in wooden shacks, were built near the Yugoslavian border in order to colonize the territory linguistically through the presence of the Italian refugees. These so-called Istrian 'villages' were planned with a view to maintaining cohesion among the Italian exiles, and later still the barracks were replaced with apartment buildings as a campaign of 'public housing' for the displaced. In the meantime, many refugees moved elsewhere, throughout the Italian peninsula or abroad, leaving their possessions behind in Warehouse 18 near *Silos*.

Now

After the 'Arab Spring' and the subsequent Syrian Civil War, the Balkan route resumed its old function as an overland passage from the East to Central Europe. *Silos* therefore once again became a refugee shelter, a space of first arrivals. Part of the roof still covers the half-abandoned, semi-destroyed area of the historical building and, together with its thick walls, it provides partial protection and shelter. However, on its own, the structure is insufficient as a cover and in 2013–14, in an unobtrusive and semi-invisible way, the first of many cardboard houses were built in the internal colonnade, with wire, ropes, cardboard boxes and other materials. In 2015, which became known as 'the year of the Balkan route', over 850,000 people travelled to Central Europe over land, mostly through Greece and the Balkans. Many were passing through on their way to more northerly destinations, but at the end of 2016, around 950 asylum seekers had arrived to stay in Trieste, with approximately 50–100 of them finding no form of formal hospitality except in *Silos*. The advantage of this location was partly its accessibility: only a plastic fence divided the edifice from the railway and coach station a few metres away, so it was easy to locate and move into.

In 2016 and 2017, when the flow of people along the Balkan route slowed down, the number of asylum seekers in Trieste actually increased. A group of predominantly young males, aged twenty to thirty from Afghanistan and Pakistan, arrived overland after being smuggled over many Eastern European borders, often reporting physical violence on the way. After border closures throughout Europe, many became trapped in places like Trieste, so the numbers of asylum seekers in the city grew. A long experience with the previous inflow of refugees generated a system of integrated hospitality to deal with this inflow, which had neither a purely authoritarian nor a purely humanitarian character (Basaglia 1987; Fassin 2012; Verdirame and Harrell-Bond 2005). The system was organized through an agreement between the Prefecture, the Municipality and local nongovernmental organizations (NGOs) allocating asylum seekers to one of a network of scattered accommodation in small apartments or facilities, such as hotels or hostels in disuse. After their personal data was registered by the police and the state authorities, the migrants were entrusted by the prefecture to NGOs, which housed them in various structures with a maximum of seventy hosted per establishment. Each group of refugees was supported by a social worker, and NGOs gave them legal, medical and financial support. Nevertheless, they needed to actively throw themselves into local life in order to meet their needs.

The demographic decline and large number of elderly people in Trieste has allowed this system to fill empty houses and promote interaction between Italians and refugees. The asylum seekers tend to spend an average of two years living in small groups of the same nationality. By grouping people together in this way, refugees and other migrants are able to organize the house according to their idea of 'homing'. The difference with those living in isolated camps and barracks (cf. Altin and Minca 2017) is therefore evident: rather than waiting in a state of emergency where normal life is suspended, people in the more formal system can generate stability and a sense of community. However, the weakness of this system is its inability to provide immediate hospitality for large numbers: it cannot operate at scale. *Silos* therefore works as a buffer and decompression area in the event of mass arrivals. Everyone knows exactly what the situation in *Silos* is – and the police occasionally evict the refugees and clear out all their belongings – but after a while, everything goes back to the way it was before. Indeed, the area of *Silos* represents a black hole: a compromise that emerges from the lack of a large hub, but at the same time provides a free space for the refugees' agency. As a low threshold shelter, it is a place of rest for new arrivals in search of protection, but also a choice for people on the edge, who prefer initially to avoid the rigid apparatus of hospitality and want to resist being labelled as a bureaucratic category (Zetter 1991).

Therefore, the contemporary function of *Silos* is not only to provide a roof but also a sense of 'home' in this new unknown world, whose rules and procedures for asylum are constantly changing. In a context of increased biopolitical checks, such as fingerprints, x-rays for minors and so on, informal spaces like *Silos* offer some kind of protection or respite from surveillance. Most Afghan and Pakistani refugees arrive from the same region, the Khyber Agency in the North West Frontier, where they speak the same languages (Urdu and Pashto). As soon as they cross the Italian border, they can find in *Silos* some countrymen who provide information on their ethnic migration network. Indeed, behind *Silos* there is a large square where asylum seekers gather; even those provided with hospitality in the formal system prefer to stay here, in 'their' part of the city life, close to the centre.

They come here to talk, to play ball or cricket, and then, in the evening, they return home. It is a sort of village square and information point, a place in constant movement. Of course, it does not exist in isolation, but is part of a much wider sheltering process that includes a range of other and more formal services: the day centre for homeless people, soup kitchens, health services and NGO sites, which are all in the nearby central area.

In the huts built under the arches in *Silos*, one can find three types of migrants: irregular migrants with expulsion orders, people who have just arrived and also, paradoxically, those who have been accorded the right to international protection in too short a time. The latter have obtained a permit to stay and to travel in the European Union, but no access to the formal hospitality services of the state. If they have not had enough time to learn the Italian language, they are not able to settle or to organize their life independently, so some refugees prefer to have their first application for the status of international protection rejected in order to appeal and obtain social assistance while waiting for the procedure of recognition to be concluded. *Silos* therefore houses an 'overflow' of migrants, both in terms of numbers, when they find no hospitality, and as a form of 'surplus' humanity: displaced, rejected, undesirable (Agier 2011). However, the ambivalence of this shelter, today as in the past, is to serve as a protective and collective space, but also as a place where migrants are pushed back to the margins, to abandoned spaces, to no man's land. On the one hand, the semi-abandoned structure provides unorganized protection and semi-invisibility to the migrants. On the other hand, it allows them to get to know public spaces and practise their everyday interactions. This partial protection and invisibility escapes any controls and bureaucratic procedures, constituting a kind of social infrastructure, a buffer zone in the process of inclusion/exclusion. Migrants in transit use *Silos* as an anchorage or a temporary settlement, when they need an interim place to rest or, again, get into contact with other refugees.

Conclusion

Silos is a site with historical layers. While long being used as a refugee shelter, there have been changes in its function and use. Over the last eighty years, the same building has served as a prison, a reception camp, and finally as an informal shelter occupied by the Afghans and Pakistanis in search of international protection. While it was built to hold commodities for a rich multinational empire, it has in the twentieth century been used to shelter people on the move, and its varied functions have included reception, accommodation and detention with functional segregation. All over the world, settlements for refugees and asylum seekers have come to be known as 'camps', and the various forms of accommodation suggest a process of 'campization' (Kreichauf 2018). This is reflected architectonically and sociospatially in diverse structures, with different living conditions: the camp symbolizes a consolidated and secluded space separated from urban settlements. However, *Silos* allows asylum seekers a central dwelling with no biopolitical controls. It represents a way of resistance through urban practices and identity formation, while also offering some protection after long and dangerous journeys (Malkki 1992; Sanyal 2012).

Indeed, violence along the Balkan route emerges from many of my interviews with residents; after crossing several checkpoints, refugees trust no one and choose not to be biomonitored with fingerprints. Those who have just arrived prefer to be helped by other countrymen with the same languages and cultures, and they would rather have improvised but self-organized cooking facilities and makeshift beds than something more comfortable and formalized. Like the previous displaced Italians in the 1950s, in *Silos* 'homing' means having intimacy with their peers, achieving an almost partial form of autonomy and agency. This shelter represents the first (concrete and symbolic) step to building control over their new lives and to obtaining a settlement with a sense of protection with no external dependency. The building exists at the intersection of various infrastructures, since it is a few metres from the port, the trains and the coach station as well as close to the soup kitchen, hospital and prefecture. It allows new arrivals to start learning the everyday tactics and dwelling in a new country.

In its first era, around 1850, the sea came up as far as the ground floor of *Silos*. It was then used as a customs warehouse because at that time the whole city was a tax-free zone. Currently it is a different kind of 'free zone': used by the refugees arriving via the Balkans in Europe, finding shelter in this peripheral border area. Not accidentally, it also involves a new form of tidemark (Green 2011), a term that has been introduced into the debates to understand the processes of (re)drawing Europe's Eastern peripheries (Ballinger 2016: 44). The image of a tidemark highlights the role of a 'waiting room' for migrants, a liminal zone of transition, which describes the symbolic and tangible floating settlement of *Silos* as a hub and home. This particular environmental position makes *Silos* a perfect place of anchorage for displaced people without a definite path or final destination. The central position allows a process of learning of the local habits through daily interaction with Italian residents. As a buffer zone, it introduces a slow process of mutual knowledge for both the hosting and hosted parties, without the stress and the fear caused by the isolated organized refugee camps. In this sense, we can observe a process of a free choice of 'homing' in transit, an interstitial area where it is possible to stay without undergoing rigid controls. Whereas in large and formal reception centres the refugees become too visible, ending up trapped in the processes of racialization and territorial stigmatization, *Silos* allows mobility and a place of partial protection on the move.

Roberta Altin is Associate Professor of Cultural Anthropology at the Department of Humanities and coordinator of the Centre for Migration and International Cooperation (CIMCS) at the University of Trieste (Italy). Her research has mainly focused on migration, museum ethnography and intercultural education, and her latest projects concern the reception of asylum seekers in the border area.

References

Agier, M. 2011. *Managing the Undesirables*. Cambridge: Polity Press.
Altin, R., and N. Badurina. 2018. 'Divided Memories: Istrian Exodus in the Urban Space of Trieste', in T. Kuharenoka, I. Novikova and I. Orehovs (eds), *Memory. Identity. Culture. Collection of Essays*, vol. II. Riga: University of Latvia Press, pp. 184–200.
Altin, R., and C. Minca. 2017. 'The Ambivalent Camp: Mobility and Excess in a Quasi-carceral Italian Asylum Seekers Hospitality Centre', in J. Turner and K. Peters (eds), *Carceral Mobilities: Interrogating Movement in Incarceration*. New York: Routledge, pp. 30–43.
Ara, A., and C. Magris. 1987. *Trieste. Un'identità di frontiera*. Turin: Einaudi.
Audenino, P. 2016. 'Public Compensation and Private Permanent Loss: The Memory of Twentieth Century European Refugees'. *Yearbook of the International Society of History Didactics* 37: 81–94.
Ballinger, P. 2003. *History in Exile: Memory and Identity at the Borders of the Balkans*. Princeton: Princeton University Press.
——. 2016. 'Whatever Happened to Eastern Europe? Revisiting Europe's Peripheries'. *East European Politics and Societies and Cultures* 31(1): 44–67.
Basaglia, F. 1987. *Psychiatry Inside out: Selected Writings of Franco Basaglia*. New York: Columbia University Press.
Fassin, D. 2012. *Humanitarian Reason: A Moral History of the Present*. Berkeley: University of California Press.
Grbac, P. 2013. 'Civitas, Polis, and Urbs: Reimagining the Refugee Camp as the City'. *Refugee Studies Centre. Working Paper Series* 96. Retrieved 20 October 2019 from https://www.rsc.ox.ac.uk/files/files-1/wp96-civitas-polis-urbs-2013.pdf.
Green, S. 2011. 'What's in a Tidemark?' *Anthropology News* 52(2): 15.
Kreichauf, R. 2018. 'From Forced Migration to First Arrivals: The Campization of Refugee Accommodation in European Cities'. *Comparative Migration Studies* 6(7): 1–22.
Madieri, M. 1998. *Verde acqua: La radura e altri racconti*. Turin, Einaudi.
Malkki, L. 1992. 'National Geographic: The Rooting of Peoples and the Territorialization of National Identity among Scholars and Refugees'. *Cultural Anthropology* 7(1): 24–44.

Pupo, R. 2005. *Il lungo esodo. Istria: le persecuzioni, le foibe, l'esilio*. Milan: Rizzoli.
Salvatici, S. 2007. *Senza casa e senza paese*. Bologna: Il Mulino.
Sanyal, R. 2012. 'Refugees and the City: An Urban Discussion'. *Geography Compass* 6(11): 633–44.
Semerari, L., and G. Tamaro. 1998. *Auto Terminal in the Former Port Silo, Trieste 1986–89*. Milan: Zodiac.
Verdirame, G., and B.E. Harrell-Bond. 2005. *Rights in Exile: Janus-Faced Humanitarianism*. Oxford: Berghahn Books.
Vernant, J. 1953. *The Refugee in the Post-war World*. New Haven: Yale University Press.
Zetter, R. 1991. 'Labelling Refugees: Forming and Transforming a Bureaucratic Identity'. *Journal of Refugee Studies* 4(1): 39–62.

Figure 16.1 Modular shelter from the 'refugee villages', Denmark. © Mark E. Breeze, based on an image supplied by Zachary Whyte and Michael Ulfstjerne.

16
Flexible Shelters, Modular Meanings
The Lives and Afterlives of Danish 'Refugee Villages'

Zachary Whyte and Michael Ulfstjerne

> Little boxes made of ticky-tacky . . .
> And they all look just the same
>
> —Malvina Reynolds, 1962 (folk song)

The Danish 'refugee villages' were originally conceived and built in the early 1990s to house Bosnian refugees fleeing the Balkan War. The buildings followed a modular design that could be quickly assembled on site from prefabricated elements and, crucially, could be moved after their initial deployment. Some 20,000 Bosnian asylum seekers arrived in Denmark in 1992–94, accounting for the vast majority of the total number of asylum seekers Denmark had ever received up to that point. They were given temporary protection status by a special act of parliament in 1992 on the mistaken understanding that the Balkan War would soon be over, so they could return home. However, the sheer numbers overwhelmed institutional capacity, and a housing solution for the Bosnians was desperately needed. The Danish government initiated a quick tender process to address this issue, and a design by the architects Holm & Grut was soon chosen among the seven that made it through the prequalification stage.

This design would provide a solution by housing the Bosnians in 'flexible asylum centres', as the architects called them. The individual buildings were constructed from three modules, produced at a central facility in the town of

Esbjerg; the modules were to be assembled around a central corridor, and the house could then be finished with drop-in elements and roofing. These modules could be moved by truck to the selected site for quick assembly, requiring only the previous digging of point footings and available connections to water and utility infrastructures. The buildings were all about 8 x 30 metres with a central, communal kitchen, and plywood outer walls painted in a range of pastel colours. Corridors ran out from the kitchen along the length of the building, with rooms on either side. They had shared baths and toilets and were heated by electric radiators. About 400 units were built on a budget and put up at fifty-two sites in clusters of seven or fourteen to establish what was later known as 'refugee villages'.

Lars Coling, one of the Holm & Grut architects behind the concept, explained the thinking behind the concept as follows: 'You can think of them as a bunch of Lego bricks', he said. '[The design] had to be cheap, temporary, and it had to be quick'. Lars emphasized how the architectural value of the project was to be found in this central concept:

> We thought it was interesting to do something on a small budget [*lavpris*] – that is, modular buildings, prefabricated, yet still in a way ... that wasn't simply putting up some containers on a field. Our part [as architects] was creating these courtyards, the different building typologies, and different functions. At the same time we tried to create a design that was relatively reasonable ... each place different from each other but still using the same building blocks ... They are called asylum centres, but we thought of them as small villages ... We tried to decorate them a bit. Doing some smaller work on the façade – longitudinal and vertical panels. And then add some different colours to them ... cheap tricks to make them a bit more appealing.

Run by the Danish Red Cross, the asylum centres housed 175–350 refugees, as well as Red Cross offices and common areas. From 1991 to 1994, the number of asylum centres in Denmark more than quintupled, and this meant that a much greater number of Danish municipalities would now be hosting asylum centres. As Birte Weiss, the then Minister for the Interior, told us in an interview, the 'friendlier' design of the asylum centres was precisely meant to help get the municipalities involved in refugee reception. She told us that the original designs included a guard tower, so that centre staff could survey and control the institution, which she personally rejected. She also renamed these 'flexible asylum centres' 'refugee villages' (*flygtningelandsbyer*), a name that stuck. However, even when the buildings were first put up, the 'village feeling' was far from apparent to the people actually living in them. They called them 'camps', a name that more directly speaks to the policies of reception, which so profoundly shaped people's everyday experiences. While they waited for a decision, the Bosnians were not allowed to work or educate themselves and there was widespread frustration with the buildings, which were described as lacking privacy due to the thin walls, problematic common areas and crowded rooms (Engholm 2000; Grünenberg 2006). Similarly, their relative isolation from the surrounding community led to feelings of isolation, which was further connected to the period of extended and uncertain waiting (Whyte 2009).

Within a few years of the establishment of these 'villages', it was clear that the Bosnians would not be returning anytime soon, and in 1994, a law was passed to begin processing the Bosnian refugees' asylum claims. The majority were granted asylum and, by 1996, the asylum centres were largely empty. This created an immediate problem of surplus capacity, as the government scrambled to sell on the empty housing units. Many remained in place, but the mobility of the housing units meant that it was also possible to load the units on to trucks and move them elsewhere. In an inventory of the buildings from 1998, thirteen of the original fifty-two villages were still in use as asylum centres, with one additional village being used as a school. Fourteen had been sold on to private actors; another fourteen had been leased to municipalities at favourable rates, but with the stipulation that they could be reclaimed should the need for more asylum centres arise. Nine had been moved abroad and the last one stood empty. The buildings have since been deployed as kindergartens, schools, prisons, student housing, club houses, event centres and hostels.

Building on ethnographic fieldwork across a range of sites where the buildings currently stand, along with interviews and archival work, this chapter traces these modular shelters from their conception in the early 1990s to their current position. We focus on three concrete buildings as they stand today, each in a distinct site, describing the form and function they serve. The first shelter was a shelter repurposed as a detention and removal centre, the second repurposed as a kindergarten, and the third was shipped to Bosnia to house repatriated refugees. We analyse these buildings in light of mobility and modularity, temporality, and connectivity, arguing that despite their relatively bland appearance and relatively restricted stated purpose, the long life of these shelters demonstrates how deeply social and embedded the material forms of refugee shelter can become, even in the most constrained of circumstances.

Kærshovedgård Removal Centre, Ikast-Brande Municipality, Denmark

In 2003, a refugee village from Frederikshavn in Denmark was dismantled and moved to the site of the Kærshovedgård state prison. The buildings were used to house around fifty prisoners, which was about a third of the capacity from its time as an asylum centre. The prison was subsequently turned into a removal centre for noncitizens and, from 2016, housed rejected asylum seekers alongside criminals with deportation orders and other immigrants without accepted residence documents. It is still run by the Danish Prison Service, which uses all the old buildings and facilities. Residents of the removal centre have no income and no right to work; they can leave the fenced-in facility, but are required to check in to the centre every evening. In any case, the isolated location of the centre and the fact that the local bus stop has been closed makes it exceedingly difficult to get anywhere.

Walking to the buildings with Helle, a Prison Service guard in her fifties, we passed a group of rejected asylum seekers on hunger strike. They were huddled over a warm drink by a banner reading 'Close the camp . . . we are humans just like you, peace – love'. Apart from this small group, not many residents were around.

Kærshovedgård is composed of a variety of buildings that have been added to the site at different times; some derive from its original function as a farm. When the site was converted to a removal centre, a new set of two-storey pavilions were built to expand capacity further. The refugee village buildings themselves were retained, but were painted red and the wooden cross-panels were removed. The insides had not been restored, but the common areas had been thoroughly stripped down: the kitchens dismantled, leaving bare rooms with the odd table or stored bicycle. Helle told us that this had been done to avoid fire hazards, which also explained the many smoke alarms in the building: 'They smoke joints', she explained. At some point, it had been decided that even prefabricated shelves and drawers needed to be removed, supposedly to keep asylum seekers from defecating in them, but the removal of the kitchens was also part of making living conditions at the removal centre as 'intolerable' as possible, to use the words of the Danish Minister for Immigration and Integration. The aim, after all, was to coerce the inhabitants to leave and, in that sense, it was deliberately unhomely.

The residents were not allowed to cook at the removal centre, but were served meals in the centre cafeteria at 7 am, noon and 5 pm only. They were not allowed to bring food, plates or cutlery from the cafeteria, and food was in general a source of conflict. Residents complained about the poor quality of food and the lack of flexibility in mealtimes. The infrastructure itself, they felt, was part of the system of deterrence (Whyte et al. 2018).

Passing through a corridor, we saw a number of doors with Bible verses in English and Arabic; this was where people claiming religious conversion as an asylum motive lived. Elsewhere, there was writing on the walls showing support for football clubs, demands for freedom and humanity, and in one spot the words 'ELSKER MOR' (LOVE MOTHER) in capitals. In one corridor, the lamp had been spray-painted red, giving an eerie light to the space. All the corridors were lined with shoes and sandals. Helle had been in the job for a year and had only experienced Kærshovedgård as a removal centre. She explained to us that the experienced prison guards, who had worked there when it was still a prison, had stayed on for a little while after it was converted to a removal centre, but almost all of them had left within the first year. She spoke warmly of the former prison inmates. 'The inmates were very disciplined', she said; 'they have a hierarchy and they obey those in charge. Here, now it's simply Ragnarok [chaos]'. Unlike in normal prisons, the use of force is much more restricted in removal centres, and this, coupled with the lack of perks that could be taken away from the new inhabitants, meant that the guards felt they had few opportunities to enforce their authority.

Hestehaven Kindergarten, Odense Municipality, Denmark

In 1998, a refugee village on the outskirts of the city of Odense was partially converted in to a municipal kindergarten. When the kindergarten opened, asylum seekers were still housed in the same compound. Soon, however, this part was closed down. The buildings had been leased to Odense Municipality with a clause allowing them to be reclaimed as asylum centres, should the need arise, and so in 2001, with the number of asylum seekers on the rise, the Immigration Service attempted to activate the clause. However, parents and staff at the kindergarten raised such a commotion that it was decided instead to move additional buildings from another refugee village to allow the kindergarten to continue. In recent years, some of the extra buildings on-site were offered on a temporary basis to university students without a place to stay. In 2018, the kindergarten closed for good to make way for a massive expansion of Odense University Hospital; the original modular shelters were moved to storage until a new use can be found for them. A helicopter pad will apparently replace them.

Back at the kindergarten, four buildings are placed in the shape of a '+' and painted a crisp, dark blue. They have been significantly modified to serve the needs of a preschool. Many of the small rooms have been combined into larger rooms, sound dampeners have been added to the ceilings, and radiators have been shifted further up the walls. Near the entrance, a room had been lined with small wardrobes for the children's coats and changes of clothes. Some rooms had been dedicated to certain kinds of play: furnished with pillows, dolls and building bricks. The kitchens were in good shape, some of the appliances having been replaced, and a low table stood in the middle of them for the children to eat. These modifications in part derive from a series of possible floor plans the Immigration Service produced in the late 1990s to demonstrate the various uses for the refugee villages. The children in the kindergarten are bussed in from different parts of Odense, both from well-to-do and mostly white neighbourhoods as well as from social housing with a majority of nonwhite children. The kindergarten proudly describes its work as an 'integration success', alongside articles about its past use as an asylum centre. 'It is part of our history', said Gitte, who had worked at the kindergarten from the beginning.

Krasulje and Velagici, Kljuc Municipality, Bosnia-Hercegovina

In 1996, the Danish government decided to move two refugee villages to Bosnia to support the repatriation of refugees. This was in the immediate aftermath of the Balkan War, and policy-makers had emphasized the need for temporary shelter while returnees rebuilt their homes. Even though the costs were high, the logistics were difficult and the plan had been fiercely criticized by the Danish Refugee Council among others, it was decided to go ahead. The two refugee villages, fourteen housing modules in total, were loaded onto trucks, transported to the Danish port city of Køge, shipped to Croatia, loaded on trucks again, and taken on the difficult journey across Croatia and Bosnia to the villages of Velagici and Krasulje. These smaller villages in the municipality of Kljuc were located only a few miles from the new internal border, drawn up under the Dayton Agreement in 1995. They were chosen because many of the repatriated Bosnians, who had lived in modular buildings in Denmark, originally came from the area. Here, what came to be known locally as the 'Danish houses' (*danske kuce*) initially served as temporary accommodation for thousands of internally displaced refugees (IDPs).

These were dramatic days in Kljuc, and the movement of the refugee villages had important knock-on effects. There was little in the way of construction equipment left locally, so the Danish engineers in charge of moving the villages brought in an excavator. This excavator, in turn, was lent to local people, who used it to excavate mass graves, where hundreds of civilian Bosnian Muslims had been killed and buried by Serb forces at the beginning of the war. Therefore, when the Danish Minister for the Interior came to open the new refugee villages, she was also asked to act as a witness as local authorities brought up the dead for identification and documentation. The provision of temporary housing in exile, the reconstruction of a devastated society, and public reckoning were thereby brought together through these shelters.

When we visited Velagici in 2017, most of the buildings were still in place. While some still housed internally displaced persons, many of the modules had been reinvented as shops, offices for legal advice, interest organizations and political assembly halls. The second batch of modules, in the village of Krasulje, had been abandoned some years earlier and stood overgrown with blackberry brambles, but were otherwise in reasonably good shape. Picking around the debris, we found that they still housed a selection of abandoned items from previous occupants: homemade weights, empty plastic bottles, a broom. Two of the buildings, one from each site, had been moved again by locals within the municipality: one served as a hiking shelter in a nearby forest and one as a regatta venue by the river. The biography of these structures therefore continued to grow in surprising new directions.

In Velagici, the buildings were very worn, but still functional; they housed a handful of families, who showed us around. Amir and his family were one of these. Their kitchen was particularly run down: cupboard doors and countertops had fallen off, but one of the original stoves still worked. The electrical heating had been shut off for a number of years because neither the inhabitants nor the municipality could pay for the electricity bills, but it was back on now. Amir told us that they used the heat generated from the back of the fridge in one of the rooms for warmth. However, they did have a brand-new washing machine that was crudely patched in to the local utilities and Amir had been allowed to use some land on the other side of the road, where he planted crops and raised goats. The original signage in Danish was still up, marking emergency exits and main entrances. Plans were afoot in the municipality to move on the last inhabitants, including Amir and his family, and then to renovate these buildings and turn them into youth hostels. They wanted to keep the name of the buildings, 'Danish houses', to mark the longstanding connection with Denmark.

Conclusion: Refugees and Modular Shelter

As will be clear from the above sketches, the original plans for 'flexible asylum centres' produced housing modules that have moved in a variety of directions. Tracking the materiality and afterlives of these shelters can speak to issues of mobility, temporality and connectivity. We are inspired here by recent critical writings on infrastructure. Following Bennett (2010), one can see infrastructure as more than an aggregation of pipes, buildings, roads, etc. that make up some kind of public facility; infrastructure mediates everyday lives and translates into emerging and contesting forms of citizenship (Abourahme 2014; Anand 2017). Infrastructure also functions to maintain order – or, conversely, bring about disorder – not always in any direct or intended fashion (Harvey et al. 2017). Addressing the possible gains of thinking through infrastructure in anthropology, Larkin notes how infrastructures 'exist as forms separate from their purely technical functioning, and they need to be analyzed as concrete semiotic and aesthetic vehicles oriented to addressees' (2013: 329). Drawing on understandings of infrastructure as 'doubly relational due to their simultaneous internal multiplicity and their connective capacities *outwards*' (Harvey et al. 2017: 23, emphasis in original), we argue that the mobility and mutability of the Danish refugee villages speaks to the differential kinds of shelter offered to different kinds of people, even under literally the same roof.

A fundamental characteristic of these shelter modules, after all, is their mobility. The Danish refugee villages combined this with elements commonly associated with more fixed structures – hard walls, connection to water and electrical utilities, windows and so on. This was built into their initial design as part of their 'flexibility', and it had consequences for the afterlives of these shelters as well: the fact that they could be disassembled, moved and reassembled opened up their potential use cases tremendously. They also had an economic value and although this value was never great, it was nevertheless significant enough that they were not simply destroyed. Their continued existence invited their use for a variety of purposes, and when the Danish prison system or kindergartens needed additional capacity, they were used in part simply because they were available. In the economic calculations of the owners, reusing or selling these shelters saved money. In other words, their mobility had direct consequences for their continued usefulness and renewed meaningfulness, which in turn derived in part from the flexibility of their design and in part from their material presence as part of an available inventory available to policy-makers.

At the same time, there was a built-in temporality to these modules, which were designed and constructed to be inhabited temporarily. The Bosnian refugees for whom the structures were built to house had been granted temporary residence, as it was assumed that the Balkan War would end soon, so they could return home. This in part explained the design focus on speed, cost and flexibility. Their original design claimed no more than a 5–10-year lifespan, but the structures nevertheless lasted. Arguably, this longevity is connected to their flexibility: the sense that they always materialized a potential future usefulness was one of the reasons why they were kept around for so long.

The ideal of self-containment that also infused the 'village' model of the buildings was in part a deliberate move to isolate the refugees. The Bosnians were meant to merely make a short stop in Denmark before they returned, and the mobility and flexibility of the buildings would in principle allow for the refugees to leave little mark of their presence. In this sense, the design of the buildings as shelter also worked to hide or even erase the presence of the Bosnian refugees. However, in practice, the buildings were often fundamentally relational (Harvey et al. 2017). Our enquiries into the modules' histories and technicalities consistently opened up the opportunity for personal anecdotes, memories and accounts of social relations. Their plasticity and the derived distinct lack of historicity was thereby countered by the stories and material arrangements of the modules' current users. Old newspaper clippings, photographs and private collections were assembled, neatly kept and shown to us – in some cases mounted as a historical exposé inside the very same modules and in other cases kept privately as personal archives of sentimental value. In Bosnia, the movement of the buildings also generated a wide range of social engagements, and a number of the key actors involved in the movement of the villages maintained deep and ongoing bonds. The Danish municipality of Holmegaard, where the modules had stood before they were moved, became a sister municipality to Kljuc in Bosnia. Meanwhile, the former refugees, who had lived in the buildings in Denmark and returned to Kljuc, maintained ties and in some cases family members in Denmark. Therefore, despite being built out from a policy of isolation and temporariness, the villages involved a great deal of sociality.

Architecturally, the buildings we have described in this chapter are mostly notable for their blandness. They are nondescript, largely without identity and not the kind that would be listed or considered worth preserving. This allowed them to be continually re-placed and reinscribed in different contexts. The architects did not even put a name to the design; they were 'Lego pieces', their material attractiveness much less important than the idea of their 'flexibility'. They were, in that sense, plastic. Therefore, architectural elements were understood in relation to their placement and the ways in which they could be furnished and adapted for existing landscapes. Through a description of a few of the 400 or so of these buildings, this chapter has argued that the mobility and flexibility of this design are key characteristics that explain their rich and complex afterlives. Their continuing meaningfulness was itself modular. Despite being bland, social relations were forged through these shelters, and at the same time they invite us to rethink the process of sheltering in a wider context. In the end, tracking the trajectories of the Danish refugee villages shows how the materialization of a restrictive refugee policy is not quite the end of the story.

Zachary Whyte is an anthropologist working with asylum seekers and refugees in Denmark. He is Associate Professor at the Centre for Advanced Migration Studies (AMIS) at the University of Copenhagen. He has published on uncertainty, the asylum process, camp infrastructures, rurality, integration programmes and everyday life at asylum centres.

Michael Ulfstjerne has a background in anthropology and is Assistant Professor of Global Refugee Studies at Aalborg University. His research focuses on the emergence of new economies and its spatial effects. His publications cover diverse topics as architecture, spatial planning, humanitarian innovations, economic booms and busts, and the field of alternative currencies.

References

Abourahme, N. 2014. 'Assembling and Spilling-over: Towards an "Ethnography of Cement" in a Palestinian Refugee Camp'. *International Journal of Urban and Regional Research* 39(2): 200–17.
Anand, N. 2017. *Hydraulic City: Water and the Infrastructures of Citizenship in Mumbai*. Durham, NC: Duke University Press.
Bennett, J. 2010. *Vibrant Matter: A Political Ecology of Things*. Durham, NC: Duke University Press.
Engholm, G. 2000. 'Den lille modstand: Kontinuitet og forandring i bosniske flygtninges selvforståelse i hverdagen i Danmark 1992–97'. Ph.D. thesis. Copenhagen: Department of Anthropology, University of Copenhagen.
Grünenberg, K. 2006. 'Is Home Where the Heart Is, or Where I Hang My Hat? Constructing Senses of Belonging among Bosnian Refugees in Denmark'. Ph.D. thesis. Copenhagen: Department of Anthropology, University of Copenhagen.
Harvey, P., C. Bruun Jensen and A. Morita. 2017. *Infrastructures and Social Complexity: A Companion*. London: Routledge.
Larkin, B. 2013. 'The Politics and Poetics of Infrastructure'. *Annual Review of Anthropology* 42: 327–43.
Whyte, Z. 2009. 'In Process: An Ethnography of Asylum-Seeking in Denmark'. Ph.D. thesis. Oxford: Institute of Social and Cultural Anthropology, University of Oxford.
Whyte, Z., R. Campbell, and H. Overgaard. 2018. 'Paradoxical Infrastructures of Asylum: Notes on the Rise and Fall of Tent Camps in Denmark'. *Migration Studies* 31(8): 1–18.

Figure 17.1 Aluminium-clad improvised shelter in Goudoubo camp, Burkina Faso. © Mark E. Breeze, based on an image supplied by Craig Martin, Jamie Cross and Arno Verhoeven.

17

Shelter as Cladding

Resourcefulness, Improvisation and Refugee-Led Innovation in Goudoubo Camp

Craig Martin, Jamie Cross and Arno Verhoeven

Since 2012, growing tensions led to the fall of North Mali to Tuareg rebels, resulting in widespread mass-displacement of Malians to neighbouring states, including Burkina Faso, Mauritania and Niger. By 2017, some estimates suggested up to 33,500 Malian refugees in Burkina Faso (UNHCR 2017), based primarily in two camps: Goudoubo and Mentao. The former was a key fieldwork site for our research project, 'Energy and Forced Displacement: A Qualitative Approach to Light, Heat and Power in Refugee Camps'. This investigated the use of energy provision by refugee communities in two research settings: Goudoubo camp in Burkina Faso and Kakuma camp in Kenya. Formed of a team of researchers spanning anthropology, design and human geography, the project investigated alternative mechanisms for understanding how refugee communities engage with energy provision. Previous research provided extensive quantitative data sets (Lahn and Grafham 2015; Corbyn and Vianello 2018), but comparatively little research has engaged with the lived experiences of lighting, power and cooking in these camps. 'Energy and Forced Displacement' set out to consider how refugees actually *use* the energy products distributed by nongovernmental organizations (NGOs) such as the United Nations High Commissioner for Refugees (UNHCR). The project also sought to investigate what refugees do with such humanitarian goods (Collier et al. 2017). Are these products and services appropriate to the needs of the refugee communities? And, crucially for this chapter, how are these communities addressing their own requirements if their needs are not met by other actors?

Using these research questions as a backdrop, this chapter considers one specific energy product distributed widely in Goudoubo camp: solar cookstoves. Here we investigate what happens to energy objects when they are rejected and become redundant. Rather than seeing such lack of uptake as solely a structural failure of humanitarian provision, we argue that this rejection creates new opportunities for refugee-led innovation. We explore how redundant materials such as the sheet metals from abandoned solar cookstoves are deployed for other purposes, particularly the construction of shelters by refugees in Goudoubo camp. From this, we argue that these shelters become sites of improvised innovation, demonstrating in particular how the practice of cladding the shelters in aluminium from redundant cookstoves becomes a symbol of material resourcefulness and practical knowhow. These forms of innovation, resourcefulness and practicality – made manifest by the creation of improvised shelters in Goudoubo – highlight other important factors for ongoing debates on host–refugee relations in refugee settings, related issues of transiency and permanency (Betts and Collier 2017: 5) and, finally, the failures (and resultant potentiality) of humanitarian design and innovation.

Sheltering

Early visits by our research team to Goudoubo camp involved the typical range of practical and logistical measures: meeting translators, speaking with UNHCR representatives, agreeing dates for future visits and negotiating security protocols. However, during one of these initial trips, a significant finding emerged, one that would have a lasting impact on the research project as a whole. The configuration of the research team for 'Energy and Forced Displacement' involved in-field researchers sharing fieldnotes, photographs and videos with the entire team. Reviewing data from this preliminary camp visit, we were all struck by one photograph in particular, which had an uncanny quality to it. While it was difficult at first to fully ascertain what we were looking at, the image showed highly reflective aluminium sheeting glistening in the dry light of northern Burkina Faso. Scrutinizing the photograph in more detail and appreciating its situated context, we began to discern a structure of some sort. The fieldnotes provided further detail. More than simply a structure, it was a building, although it was difficult to fully garner its function from this one image alone. This was in part due to the way in which its depiction in the photograph was complexified by the reflective surface of the aluminium: it blended rather strangely into the background and foreground through a skewed admixture of ground and sky. Yet, a building emerged from the image – in fact, a shelter. It had a door, hinges, a roof, walls, a rudimentary lock, all elements that one associates with the classic signifiers of a building.

However, what unsettled these typical architectural forms were the aluminium sheeting and, less obviously, the scrap of blue tarpaulin above the shelter's door. Such materials marked out the building as significant to the broader findings of our research project. The aluminium sheeting, along with scrap of tarpaulin, were both remnants of UNHCR humanitarian provision: the aluminium sheeting was once part of the Blazing Tube solar cookstoves distributed to refugees in Goudoubo by the UNHCR, and the blue tarpaulin came from UNHCR tents in Goudoubo. These materials are testimony to the failed promise of humanitarian intervention in Goudoubo camp. Each has its own stories, but the assemblage of the shelter tells us so much more. It elicits a range of questions that are fundamental to the broader politics of humanitarianism and the specific contexts of energy and shelter, namely: (1) How are displaced people actually using humanitarian energy products? (2) How effectively do humanitarian goods address the everyday requirements of displaced people in camp settings? (3) What economic, material and social value do these products offer over and above their intended purpose? (4) What forms of improvisation, working knowledge and resourcefulness are required for displaced communities to address their own needs?

Reflecting on these questions and their relevance to contexts of displacement across Sub-Saharan Africa, this chapter offers a critique of humanitarian intervention, but simultaneously identifies important potentialities in refugees' utilization of redundant materials as forms of refugee-led innovation. By addressing these singular materials – the tarpaulin and particularly the sheet metal used to clad the shelter – we open up to scrutiny other discarded technologies and practices of repurposing. The chapter examines how the construction of the shelter addresses distinct forms of improvised architecture and design within refugee settings. We also explore how the reuse of aluminium sheet metal from a solar cooker and its incorporation as cladding into a shelter can demonstrate several important facets of material, social and economic culture in this particular refugee camp.

The Blacksmith's Shelter

Our team's initial visit to Goudoubo took them to the artisan centre, an important focal point for a range of social and cultural activities for the refugee community. It was here they met Yaya. He was a blacksmith in the camp, able to create a range of functional and decorative goods for both his own needs and to sell to others. His skills as a fabricator became evident when our research team visited his home, next to which stood the gleaming aluminium-clad shelter described above. Yaya's main dwelling was a standard-issue UNHCR-provided structure; like many others in the camp, this was a UNHCR Tuareg shelter constructed from eucalyptus poles forming the walls and domed roof (UNHCR 2016: 30). The roofing materials would traditionally have been tanned goat skin, although in Goudoubo this was not feasible due to limited resources, resulting in the use of the UNHCR tarpaulin. Again, where the walls might typically have been constructed out of straw matting, plastic sheeting was very often used instead. After his family's arrival in Goudoubo, Yaya kept food in the main UNHCR dwelling, but on several occasions food had gone to waste, either eaten by goats who were able to enter the Tuareg shelter or – more importantly for our discussions in this chapter – spoiled by rainwater owing to leaks in the roof of the shelter. The limitations of the design and construction of the main dwelling led Yaya to devise alternative storage arrangements: he built the aluminium-clad shelter to store food, alongside tools, gas equipment and firewood.

Yaya's shelter offers valuable insights into the logic of humanitarian intervention in refugee camps such as this one in Burkina Faso. More specifically, it highlights some of the inadequacies in design-led interventions in a range of displacement settings. Yaya's need for an additional shelter came as a result of the inefficiencies of the UNHCR shelter that leaked and spoilt his food, and this raised two essential points: first, that the UNHCR shelter was only a temporary structure and thus prone to structural limitations (although Yaya and his family have been living there for at least two years); and, second, that the promise of 'good' humanitarian design did not always materialize.

With its historical roots in appropriate technology (Hubert and Theocharopulou 2015) and the work of designers such as Victor Papanek (1973), the relationship between humanitarian intervention and design is driven by an ethics of aligning *with* local needs through a claimed sense of 'commonality' (Min Soo Chun 2015: 17). This is realized through an idea of meaningful, positive change in the lives of marginalized communities affected by conflict, forced displacement or natural disaster (Davis 1978). In recent years we have seen some strikingly effective examples of humanitarian designs, creating significant change in people's lives (Pilloton 2009; Smith 2007). PlayPump is a good example. This offered a seemingly effective solution to problems of access to clean water in Sub-Saharan Africa: the system works by using a conventional borehole, the top of which is a children's roundabout. As children play on the roundabout, water is drawn from underground reserves, stored in an overhead tank, then drawn off by the local community. However, whilst this design has had a meaningful impact, it did not provide the life-changing circumstances it claimed to promise. As some commentators have noted (Chambers 2009), the PlayPump was too complex to allow local maintenance and repair, too costly to manufacture at scale, reliant on child labour and left children vulnerable to injury. Whilst the intentions of the designers are of course admirable, the case of PlayPump indicates the overarching logic of much humanitarian design: the idea of innovation.

Innovation is often seen as the primary means to implement change, but, as a number of scholars have noted, one of its key problems is its market-driven logic (Redfield 2016; Sandvik et al. 2017; Schwittay 2014: 30; Scott-Smith 2016). As Arturo Escobar has recently argued, humanitarian design and design for displacement are increasingly fertile markets for large-scale multinational companies (Escobar 2017: 61). One of the recurring predicaments with humanitarian design is the rush to find solutions to real problems faced by displaced communities such as the Malian refugees in Goudoubo, but without adequate attempts to fulfil the key premise of humanitarian design – that of real, profound *commonality*: a meaningful understanding of what is actually needed. Rather than humanitarian design imaginaries (Redfield and Robins 2016), Yaya's shelter was, we might say, an example of humanitarian design *realities*. The lived experience of refugees like Yaya was premised on the need to adapt the standardized approaches of the UNHCR, making his own shelter to overcome the lack of appropriateness of the one provided for him. This is very often the reality of humanitarian design.

Redundancy as Resourcefulness

Yaya's storage shelter was a manifestation of the skills and practical knowledge he had initially acquired as a young apprentice in Mali. These skills were carried with him when he left his home country and – once in Goudoubo – he put them to use in order to meet his needs whilst generating a modest income. In addition, the finished shelter was also an artefact of knowledge, relationships and materials that were available in and around the camp itself. As well as being a practical structure for Yaya and his family, this shelter also offered an insight into the socioeconomic infrastructure of the camp, as well as the relationships between its inhabitants and other communities in this part of Burkina Faso. As people like Yaya seek materials to improve their lives, building structures such as this storage shelter, they simultaneously enter into diverse relationships, combining market exchanges with forms of barter, and intra-camp exchanges with external exchanges involving members of the 'host community' in the neighbouring town of Dori.

For Yaya, the artisan centre was an important resource for the construction of his shelter. He used the centre to find the materials to build and clad the shelter, but also to fabricate some of the tools to construct it. His resourcefulness was evident in his ability to procure materials through the social networks within Goudoubo and beyond in the neighbouring host community: the artisan centre did not give metal sheeting away for free, but they could be purchased with cash or bartered for other goods. Yaya's shelter required ten aluminium sheets and Yaya acquired these by paying 5,000 CFA ($9.00) and, as he put it, 'some tea and grilled meat'. The design of the shelter required other materials: he paid 2,000 CFA ($3.50) for two nail boxes at the artisan's centre, 1,500 CFA ($2.60) for iron to make the lock-holder and 12,000 CFA ($20.70) for two wooden columns at the market in Dori. The construction of the shelter demonstrates resourcefulness on a number of different levels, including the original design and planning of the structure, the fabrication of the tools to build it, the purchase of materials from within and beyond the camp, and, most crucially, the recognition of the potential of seemingly redundant scrap aluminium sheeting to clad Yaya's shelter. Like the inadequacies of the UNHCR Tuareg shelter that led him to build his own storage shelter, another failed 'humanitarian good' was fundamental to the construction of the shelter: the aluminium panels used by Yaya came from solar cookstoves distributed by the UNHCR.

On the same visit to the camp, our research team noticed a solar cookstove placed next to a tree outside the project translator's home. It was dented and battered, but still appeared to be in working order. At the artisan centre, they saw many more of these cookstoves, all abandoned; in another area of the camp, a further pile of parts from the cookstoves lay smashed and broken. This detritus seems to form a stark contrast to the typical image of humanitarian technologies as emancipatory. This particular solar cookstove came with exactly such a promise. The 'Blazing Tube Solar Appliance', as it was marketed, proved to be an important energy product for tackling issues around access to adequate cooking facilities in camps such as Goudoubo. It was developed in 2008 by John Grandinetti following prototype testing in Hawaii and went through an iterative design process through field testing. As with many humanitarian products, it adhered to the principle of simplicity and ingenuity: one of its key features is a glass tube, which sits inside a parabolic, trough-shaped reflector (or Compound Parabolic Curve) and is attached to the heat-retaining pot in the cooking box. The heat for cooking is generated by the solar heating of high-heat vegetable oil housed in the glass tube, which acts as a heat transfer fluid. The oil can reach a cooking temperature of 150°C and only needs to be changed once every eighteen months. Some reports note the positive response to 'Blazing Tube', but more recent research points to its limited long-term use on the part of displaced people in Goudoubo (Corbyn and Vianello 2018).

The reason for this is fundamentally cultural. Refugees in Goudoubo spoke of the intense heat the mineral oil reaches, which often resulted in it smoking and tainting the food (this may be the result of a design flaw, with the oil being reheated continuously over the eighteen-month period). The cooking smell was one of the primary reasons why the 'Blazing Tube' solar cooker was not widely accepted in Goudoubo, but a UNHCR representative also noted other problems. Whilst it was designed for Sub-Saharan climates, the cooler season in Burkina Faso, from November until February, and the rainy season from June to September limit cooking opportunities. Some parts of the cookstove are also quite fragile and prone to breaking, particularly the vacuum tube the researchers saw abandoned. However, even when they are broken or redundant, a 'Blazing Tube' stove can also become something else: an object of different potential and value. As we saw in the work of Yaya, it can also become the walls of a shelter.

Refugee-Led Improvised Innovation

The example of a redundant solar cookstove, repurposed as shelter cladding, offers up a more complex portrait of the relationship between humanitarian energy technologies and their contexts of use. It also raises important questions for the relationship between humanitarian provision and refugee dependency. Although it is clear that refugee communities such as those in Goudoubo require immediate humanitarian assistance through the provision of food, shelter and energy products, it is also evident that the actual usage of these goods and services does not necessarily adhere to that intended by NGOs such as the UNHCR. In other words, the construction of this shelter provides a valuable insight into the question of available resources, but critically the allied notion of *resourcefulness*. On the surface, the failure of the cookers to adequately fulfil the needs of the refugee community signalled an apparent failure and thus a waste of money. Seen in this manner, 'failure' is an entirely negative outcome: the utility of humanitarian goods severely limited and the economic outlay wasted. Yet the repurposing of the 'Blazing Tube' solar cooker and its transformation into cladding for the shelter built by Yaya signals the operation of a parallel system of value. The practice of repurposing involves a shift in value, a transformation in the meaning and utility of things. What began as an economic object to the UNHCR, a humanitarian technology designed to meet the universal basic need of cooking, was transformed into another essential human necessity – shelter. Yet this was defined by the refugee community themselves and driven by their *actual* needs as opposed to their *perceived* needs by humanitarian NGOs.

Modification is a common occurrence in the history of emergency shelter. Although set within the distinct context of postdisaster aid, Ian Davis has long noted the importance of local, ad hoc responses to housing and shelter needs (Davis 1978: 40; see also Jencks and Silver 2013). Whilst Davis identified the split between donor provision and local ad hoc responses typified by improvised shelter, the case of Yaya's shelter does not simply fall into this bifurcation between formal and informal. By modifying the redundant

'Blazing Tube' cookstove and repurposing the aluminium sheeting, Yaya was reliant on donor provision, albeit in a markedly different way from that intended by the likes of the UNHCR. Where innovation (including humanitarian innovation) has more recently been typified by the presence of market-driven ideologies, this example points to a more widespread idea of innovation as material and systemic resourcefulness. Equally, it also posits a distinct form of humanitarian 'design', where the top-down approach of NGOs such as the UNHCR is transfigured into a similar problem-solving activity, albeit informal methods of design employed by Yaya (see Manzini 2015). Building on the notion of refugee innovation, the actions of Yaya adhere to bottom-up approaches to displacement, notably the value of 'using the resources and opportunities around you in a particular context' (cited in Betts et al. 2015: 4). Like other members of the displaced Malian community in Goudoubo, Yaya took a localized or situated approach to dealing with his immediate problems and needs. His material resourcefulness emerged out of necessity. It was the result both of the failures in the humanitarian distribution of goods to adequately fulfil refugee needs and of the limitations of these goods themselves. Yaya's repurposing of available materials challenges any perception that people in his position are wholly or solely reliant on 'inbound innovation' (Mavhunga 2017: 8), via the provision of services and technologies from external agencies. Crucially, moreover, what marks out Yaya's shelter as distinct even from 'refugee innovation' is the repurposing of humanitarian goods themselves.

Indeed, the weaknesses in the design of the standard-issue UNHCR shelter (its tendency to leak) led Yaya to develop his own solution to the problem of storage. This was a solution that was dependent on his practical knowledge as a blacksmith, but also on the availability of materials such as the discarded aluminium sheeting from the broken 'Blazing Tube' solar cookstoves. Yaya's understanding of the material properties of aluminium, notably its capacity to reflect sunlight, meant that he saw it as ideal for storing food. Whereas the type of humanitarian design we see in goods such as the solar cookstove is premised on a top-down problem-solving mentality, Yaya and other refugees like him took a different approach, which was distinctly situated in the geographical context of Goudoubo rather than the abstracted assumption that inbound humanitarian technologies such as 'Blazing Tube' could universally solve problems like access to cooking facilities. Yaya's practical knowledge coupled with a resourcefulness in recognizing the potential application of discarded humanitarian materials demands to be understood as a form of design and innovation in their own right. Such examples of what are commonly called 'indigenous', 'frugal' or 'bottom-up humanitarian innovation' have not been sufficiently studied in refugee contexts, particularly the complex entanglement of inbound humanitarian provision and the lived realities of how this is actually used.

Conclusion

Taken in its situated context, the shelter built by Yaya is purely functional, offering him and his family space in which to store food and to keep tools and firewood. It also speaks to the problem of longer-term provision for refugee needs in camps such as Goudoubo, where the emergency shelter provided by the UNHCR has a finite lifespan and functionality. However, as we have suggested in this chapter, Yaya's shelter and the cladding in particular stands for so much more. First, it signals the ingenuity of displaced communities in recognizing the material and utilitarian value of broken energy products. Second, it points to the emergence of novel, localized practices around repurposed energy technologies or products. Third, it highlights the mobility of practical knowledge and skills, such as those required to design, procure parts and build a shelter. Finally, in more metaphorical terms, the use of the aluminium sheeting from 'Blazing Tube' as cladding for the shelter speaks to the multiple layers of usage that humanitarian goods potentially have.

We need to understand how the resourcefulness of refugees in camps such as Goudoubo demonstrates the *opposite* of a culture of dependency. Yet we also need to pay closer attention to contexts in which people use, adapt and repurpose material technologies. This ultimately provides insight into cultures of production and consumption, and the future provision of humanitarian goods such as energy, shelter and housing. There is a tension here between the perceived use-value of the products provided and their functional as well as cultural limitations. They do not always sufficiently meet the needs of the refugee community. Equally, the shelter constructed by Yaya also points to the need for greater provision of shelter for both the refugees themselves and their belongings: the failures in the design of the UNHCR shelter, including its propensity to leak, caused refugees to make their dwellings more efficient. This example of an improvised shelter points to a disjuncture between the intended and eventual use of energy technologies, highlighting the practice of improvised repurposing as a form of innovation distinct from that typified by humanitarian agencies. There needs to be greater recognition of the value of the informal economy of trading purportedly redundant materials, as well as the importance of the refugee's practical, design knowledge in developing their own solutions to some of the problems they encounter.

Finally, we must be mindful of the urge to scale up informal or local approaches to refugee innovation. While we need to challenge some of the assumptions around the capabilities of inbound humanitarian technologies such as 'Blazing Tube', we should also not simply drive to harness or operationalize local innovation such as Yaya's repurposing of the aluminium sheeting. Such an approach denies the situatedness of the political, geographical and social contexts of displacement. One humanitarian response to the local forms of resourcefulness and practices of innovation might be to try and 'scale them up'. Participatory or co-design – where displaced peoples are invited to develop a stake in the development of humanitarian technologies, products and services – is increasingly credited with producing a deeper understanding of the specific needs of different communities and helping to scale up. Yet, as this chapter has shown, an alternative and equally important response is to recognize and appreciate these forms of innovation in their own right, acknowledging the ways they alter the original configurations of economic and use-value in the provision of humanitarian products.

Craig Martin is Reader in Design Cultures at the University of Edinburgh. His research interests involve the social, cultural and spatial complexity of design, and how this is manifest in a range of social practices, involving three substantive themes: informal design practices; social complexity; and mobilities.

Jamie Cross is Senior Lecturer in Social Anthropology at the University of Edinburgh. His research interests are situated in the 'anthropology of development', including examination of infrastructures, low carbon energy futures, corporations and social enterprises, work, labour and global supply chains.

Arno Verhoeven is Senior Lecturer in Design, and Programme Director of M.A. Design for Change at the University of Edinburgh. His research is situated in examinations of critical design methods and practices, involving strategic decision-making to address complex issues and challenges through constructivist and interdisciplinary approaches to design.

Note

The core arguments in this chapter have been developed from earlier ideas explored in Cross et al. 2019. *Energy and Displacement in Eight Objects: Insights from Sub-Saharan Africa* (Research Paper). London: Chatham House and Moving Energy Initiative.

References

Betts, A., L. Bloom and N. Weaver. 2015. *Refugee Innovation: Humanitarian Innovation that Starts with Communities.* Oxford: Humanitarian Innovation Project, University of Oxford.

Betts, A., and P. Collier. 2017. *Refuge: Transforming a Broken Refugee System.* London: Penguin.

Bloom, L., and A. Betts. 2013. *The Two Worlds of Humanitarian Innovation.* Working Paper Series No. 94. Refugee Studies Centres, University of Oxford.

Chambers, A. 2009. 'Africa's Not-So-Magic Roundabout'. *The Guardian*, 24 November. Retrieved 22 October 2019 from https://www.theguardian.com/commentisfree/2009/nov/24/africa-charity-water-pumps-roundabouts.
Collier, S.J., C. Cross, P. Redfield and A. Street. 2017. 'Little Development Devices/Humanitarian Goods'. *Limn*, 9: 1–6.
Corbyn, D., and M. Vianello, for Practical Action. 2018. *Prices, Products and Priorities: Meeting Refugees' Energy Needs in Burkina Faso and Kenya*. London: Chatham House.
Davis, I. 1978. *Shelter after Disaster*. Oxford: Oxford Polytechnic Press.
Escobar, A. 2017. *Designs for the Pluriverse: Radical Interdependence, Autonomy and the Making of Worlds*. Durham, NC: Duke University Press.
Hubert, C., and I. Theocharopulou. 2015. 'Humanitarian Design: Notes for a Definition', in A. Min Soo Chun and I.E. Brisson (eds), *Ground Rules for Humanitarian Design*. Chichester: Wiley, pp. 20–35.
Jencks, C., and N. Silver. 2013. *Adhocism: The Case for Improvisation*. Cambridge, MA: MIT Press.
Lahn, G., and O. Grafham. 2015. *Heat, Light, and Power for Refugees: Saving Lives, Reducing Costs*. London: Chatham House.
Manzini, E. 2015. *Design, When Everybody Designs: An Introduction to Design for Social Innovation*. Cambridge, MA: MIT Press.
Mavhunga, C. 2017. 'Introduction: What Do Science, Technology, and Innovation Mean from Africa?', in C. Mavhunga (ed.), *What Do Science, Technology, and Innovation Mean from Africa?* Cambridge, MA: MIT Press, pp. 1–28.
Min Soo Chun, A. 2015. 'Introduction: Ground Rules for Humanitarian Design', in A. Min Soo Chun and I.E. Brisson (eds), *Ground Rules for Humanitarian Design*. Chichester: Wiley, pp. 9–17.
Papanek, V. 1973. *Design for the Real World: Human Ecology and Social Change*. New York: Bantam Books.
Peters, G. 2009. *The Philosophy of Improvisation*. Chicago: University of Chicago Press.
Pilloton, E. 2009. *Design Revolution*. London: Thames & Hudson.
Redfield, P. 2016. 'Fluid Technologies: The Bush Pump, the LifeStrawÒ and Microworlds of Humanitarian Design'. *Social Studies of Science* 46(2): 159–83.
Redfield, P., and S. Robins. 2016. 'An Index of Waste: Humanitarian Design, "Dignified Living" and the Politics of Infrastructure in Cape Town'. *Anthropology Southern Africa* 39(2): 145–62.
Sandvik, K.B., K.L. Jacobsen and S.M. McDonald. 2017. 'Do No Harm: A Taxonomy of the Challenges of Humanitarian Experimentation'. *International Review of the Red Cross* 99(1): 319–44.
Schwittay, A. 2014. 'Designing Development: Humanitarian Design in the Financial Inclusion Assemblage'. *PoLAR Political and Legal Anthropology Review* 37(1): 29–47.
Scott-Smith, T. 2016. 'Humanitarian Neophilia: the "Innovation Turn" and its Implications'. *Third World Quarterly* 37(12): 2229–51.
Smith, C.E. 2007. *Design for the Other 90%*. New York: Cooper-Hewitt.
UNHCR. 2016. *Shelter Design Catalogue*. Geneva: UNHCR Shelter and Settlement Section.
———. 2017. 'Mali Situation: Refugees, Internally Displaced Persons and Returnees'. Retrieved 22 October 2019 from https://data2.unhcr.org/en/documents/download/61702.

Figure 18.1 MSF IPERJUNGLE shelter in Grande-Synthe near Dunkirk. © Mark E. Breeze, based on an image supplied by Irit Katz.

18

Adhocism, Agency and Emergency Shelters
On Architectural Nuclei of Life in Displacement

Irit Katz

On the very same day that La Linière camp was opened by Médecins Sans Frontières (MSF) in Grande-Synthe near Dunkirk, its prefabricated emergency shelters had begun to change shape. Many of the standardized identical timber structures that had originally been built according to an accurate set of instructions were given, by their new residents, additional layers and extensions created ad hoc, some almost doubling their size. Insulation was added, entrances were porched, kitchens and extra rooms were constructed, and the gaps between shelters were adapted to become external storage spaces. Some of the temporary shelters were carefully decorated internally, while the external walls of others became publicly exposed canvases, manifesting the cultural and political identities of their inhabitants – mostly Iraqi Kurds. In addition, these timber prefab units, some of which were also erected in the Jungle makeshift camp in Calais, were appropriated in both camps to serve functions other than dwelling, transforming into grocery stores, barber shops and other spaces that met the economic needs of their inhabitants and the everyday needs of the camps' residents. While those who accommodated the shelters intended to live in them only temporarily during their attempts to cross the English Channel to the United Kingdom, they nevertheless invested significant time and efforts to adapt them to the needs of living in the camp.

'House' or 'home' usually refer to permanent dwellings, but 'shelter' is a notion that tends to refer to a more provisional structure, a place that provides more minimal protection. While today displaced people live in a wide range of shelters, from rented apartments to squats in abandoned buildings, emergency shelters are often created following the destruction of, or the lack of, available structures for protection. In such cases, two main types of temporary shelter can be identified: the self-built freely fabricated makeshift shelter created by local resources and skills, and the prefabricated shelter created from readymade flatpack kits and assembled on-site (see Katz 2017a). As these shelters are usually constructed on vacant and often unserviced sites, they often provide only basic protection, while the other needs of their residents – such as food and sanitary facilities – are answered in separate structures. These shelters, camps and other similar sites and spaces that are supposed to be dismantled as soon as the emergency situation ends are initially created to take care only of the essential needs of their residents, who are often conceived as anonymous people with identical features and necessities, and are seen as passive recipients of aid. However, as in the case of La Linière camp, these residents are often discovered as active and creative agents, who form very different environments from those originally planned for them.

By focusing on the 'MSF IPERJUNGLE' timber prefabricated shelters erected in Calais and Grande-Synthe during 2015–16 (see also Katz 2017b, 2019), this chapter examines the emergency shelter not as an end product, but as an ongoing spatial process. This process is divided into two main stages: the first stage is the top-down design, production and construction of the shelter as a standardized structure, while the second stage is the appropriation of the shelter by its inhabitants. These phases are explored in this chapter with a focus on the ways in which the shelter's spatial and functional roles are perceived in relation to the changing figure of 'the user'. This 'user' is differently perceived by the various actors involved in the design and inhabitation of the shelter. As the architectural historian Kenny Cupers (2013: 1–2) argues, rather than being a universal figure, the user is 'a historically constructed category of twentieth-century modernity that continues to inform architectural practice and thinking in often unacknowledged ways'. Meanwhile, the user's role as an 'agent of change' is too often marginalized and overlooked. This chapter shows that, similar to other cases of modern architecture, the actual users of the prefab MSF shelter and their specific needs were quite different from the categorical users the shelter was designed for, changing these shelters in unexpected manners.

In what ways were these 'users' so different? Prefab emergency shelters tend to be primarily designed for an *anonymous universal user* with standardized biological and human features: a 'user' that is itself a product of rationalization, industrialization and standardization. However, these shelters are inhabited and appropriated according to the particular needs, capabilities and resources of their *actual specific users*, whose potential role as agents of significant spatial change is completely absent from the design process. This chapter illustrates these differences, while arguing that displaced people need structures of protection that are always better than only a basic shelter, structures that will enable them to re-establish their lives, even temporarily, in their precarious environments and realities. The argument proceeds in two main sections: first, I examine the manual for the MSF prefabricated shelter to illustrate the designer's view of the 'user', and then I look at the way the actual users engaged with and changed the shelters in the camp.

The Shelter and the Manual

> This first version of the manual is intended to summarize and systematize the information collected from the field, for the production and assembly of a new type of transitional family shelter 'IPERJUNGLE' used for the first time in Calais and Dunkerque, France, in 2015/2016 . . . By proposing a time/resources effective solution, this manual is intended to be a practical tool to support the logistic construction activities in the field when facing emergency/post emergency shelters interventions.
> –MSF IPERJUNGLE Transitional Shelter, Operative Manual, Version 1
> Q-2016

Prefabricated emergency shelters, such as the MSF IPERJUNGLE shelter, are usually conceived from the very beginning as a manual-based product. Based on mass-produced components that should be easily and quickly transported and assembled on-site, the shelters need to be designed for two complementing situations: the situation of the flatpack, in which they are delivered, and the situation of the assembled shelter. The manual is the set of instructions needed to create the shelter and transform it from one situation to the other, and should be legible to those who will put it together wherever it will be needed. From the early twentieth-century Nissen Hut to today's IKEA shelter, the principles of the prefab shelter remain generally the same: while technologically these could be 'state of the art' structures, they are designed to meet the generic needs of no particular user or location (see Katz 2017b).

Looking at the table of contents of the IPERJUNGLE shelter manual, it is possible to identify all the measurable qualities that are considered important for such a shelter. These are all communicated through measurements, quantities and timetables, and are presented in great clarity, in opposition to the disorder and ambiguity of the emergency situation. The manual opens with two photos presented next to one another: the first is of the deplorable Basroch makeshift tent camp in Grande-Synthe in November 2015 and the second is of forced migrants – mainly women and children – entering the newly assembled and neatly organized timber shelters at the MSF La Linière camp in March 2016. The stark before-and-after difference, which connects the manual to the reality of a specific site, gives the document a clear humanitarian logic. In the pages that follow, the manual describes a step-by-step process for the construction, delivery and assembly of the shelters, which leads the refugees and humanitarians from a chaotic situation to a well-organized space.

The manual's introductory chapter presents the shelter's objectives alongside key figures, such as the size of the structure and its plywood boards, the number of workers required for fabrication, the number of shelters that could be installed per day, the number of shelters that could fit in certain sizes of container trucks and so on – all the possible information required in order to plan the successful logistics for an emergency operation. The first chapter, which describes the concept of the shelter, presents its main principles: low-tech, high value, modularity, flexibility, local production, rapid assembly and transportability. These communicate a product that answers various aims in simple methods. The second chapter, 'Ingredients', describes the materials, tools and security equipment needed for producing the shelters, while the third chapter, 'Fabrication', is accompanied by annotated illustrations with specific dimensions and details, showing how the shelter's components should be constructed in the workshop and how the transportable flatpack kit should be assembled. The fourth chapter, 'Transport', illustrates the sizes of trucks required for the transportation of different number of shelter kits, while the fifth chapter, 'On Site', is a step-by-step description of the assembly process. The sixth chapter presents the training required for those who build and assemble the shelter, while 'Flexibility', the concluding seventh chapter, describes the way in which the shelter could be adapted to different sizes and objectives. These adjustments are limited to a few options such as sanitation blocks, communal kitchens and larger shelters for an extended family. Yet, this flexibility of the shelters was later interpreted very differently by those who inhabited them.

This manual, similar to many other architectural manuals, communicates the shelter as a structure manufactured and assembled as an industrial 'type model'. This has been identified and historicized by Blau (2013: 25) as a postwar concept conceived in relation to the standardization and rationalization of the building process 'from the design of the individual spatial unit and architectural object, to the organization of its construction . . . based on rational analysis of the efficient and cost-effective organization of space and production'. As Emmons and Mihalache note on earlier industrialization processes:

> before mass production, devices may have been very well crafted individually, but the part of one product would not have worked in another of the

same sort because each was created as a singular totality . . . To standardize in the early twentieth century was a positive value associated with being efficient, hygienic, and modern. (2013: 37–38)

Just as architectural handbooks 'mark a radical separation in architecture between functional fact and aesthetic expression' (Emons and Mihalache 2013: 39), this shelter manual embraces a strictly technocratic approach that optimizes building practices while eschewing relationship to articulations developed through a more elaborate individual use. Design here is not about aesthetics but means a problem-solving practice based on a defined need calculated according to previously determined factors and measures. Importantly, the standardized buildings expressed through the manual are based on the assumed elementary needs of the standardized human body, which both assembles and inhabits them. This is clearly illustrated by the human figures drawn on both the assembly and configuration sheets of the manual, representing the number of people needed to produce and assemble one shelter and the maximum number of those who can accommodate it. Both of these building elements and sizes are predicted according to what Emons and Mihalache (2013: 39) call the 'dimensional routinization of the human activities . . . based upon the presumption of the essential dimensional similarity of humans'.

Such shelter manuals and their biologically based standards are directly linked to modern architectural studies of the human body in relation to space. Le Corbusier's Modulor (2004 [1954, 1958]) is probably the most famous example. The Modulor is an anthropometric scale of proportions used to calculate dimensions in architectural design, and it represents an ideal human 'proportioned' body according to which the generalized standardization of objects and the mathematization and geometrization of space is calculated. This, and similar abstract perceptions of the 'user', were developed as ways to regulate how people should use buildings and interact with the built environment. This modernist use-value, rather than being created by the users and occupants, is predetermined by abstract values. Such abstract space, as recognized by Lefebvre (1991), creates users who cannot recognize themselves within it. 'Authority', meanwhile, remains with the built object and its designers rather than with its occupants.

The MSF IPERJUNGLE shelters, which created La Linière camp, were enthusiastically received by the forced migrants who moved into them from the deplorable Basroch makeshift camp. However, the nickname 'chicken houses' was immediately attached to these shelters by the migrants, which aptly implies the strictly biologically animal-like environment they created (Katz 2017b: 11; Woensel Kooy 2016). This response to the institutionalized camp environment and its repetitive shelters is very similar to that of the residents of the container camp opened at the heart of the Calais Jungle in

January 2016. The migrants here complained that they lived 'like animals', warehoused in its rigid grid of identical and overcrowded shipping containers (Katz 2017b: 4), and although the heated containers provided residents with much-needed warmth in the cold European winter, they were also isolated and isolating spaces that did not allow for meaningful human interaction. While being essential for the physical protection of their residents from the elements, they did not provide sufficient privacy or an appropriate space to socialize. Externally, the containers formed an impersonal space that was easy to logistically create and manage, yet they did not provide a sense of identity and belonging. Residents in the container camp spent most days in the makeshift Jungle addressing their social, cultural and other essential everyday life needs with the camps' informal schools, churches, mosques, grocery stores, restaurants, bakeries, barber shops and community shelters. Meanwhile, the containers were used mostly for sleeping (Gueguen-Teil and Katz 2018).

Unlike the shipping containers, which could not be inhabited comfortably or spatially adjusted by the migrants, it turned out that the timber shelters in Grande-Synthe were much more flexible than they were originally intended to be.

Adhocism, Agency and the Shelter as a Nucleus of Everyday Life

> It is the first day of the move [from Basroch camp] and I am in the new [Linière] camp . . . It catches my eye how many people are already building extensions to their shelters. Despite the emergency structure of the camp, refugees seem to realize already that their stay in this camp may probably take longer than a couple of days, if not months.
> —Eelke van Woensel Kooy, a volunteer and researcher in Grande-Synthe's Basroch and La Linière camps, 7 March 2016

The broad media coverage of the opening of La Linière, 'France's first ever internationally recognized refugee camp' (Samuel 2016), was accompanied by panoramic photos of the camp's new identical timber shelters. However, this sight changed very rapidly, as most of its shelters went through an all-encompassing process of informalization. The shipping containers in Calais could not be appropriated due to their physical features, materiality and the strict form of management of the camp itself. In contrast, the MSF timber shelters could be easily adjusted and the manager in charge on building La Linière camp was satisfied with their appropriation, mentioning that beyond the provision of larger spaces for the camp's residents, the extensions also stabilized the shelters, making them more resilient to winds (interview, April 2016).

The migrants in the camp added bedrooms, kitchens and porches to their shelters, each with the help of friends and volunteers. Others took ownership over areas in-between and outside their shelters. Many shelters were also insulated with blankets and tarpaulin sheets, improving the ability of the structures to protect from the cold. The shelters were adjusted not only for specific functional needs, but also for aesthetic purposes, and many were decorated by their inhabitants to create more homely environments: the floors were covered with carpets, the walls were decorated with posters and other ornaments, and planters were fixed to the external walls and balconies, beautifying the shelters with carefully handled flowering houseplants. Many external walls were also covered by posters, murals, graffiti and flags of the migrants' home countries and desired destination. These expressed their identities, wishes and political call to treat them humanely.

The architectural term 'adhocism' coined by Charles Jencks as a response to 'pure' and blank modernist architecture and planning could accurately describe the spatial practices in La Linière. 'The phrase ad hoc, meaning "for this" specific purpose', write Jencks and Silver (2013 [1972]: 16), 'reveals the desire for immediate and purposeful action which permeates everyday life'. Adhocism denotes a principle of action 'having *speed* or economy and *purpose* or utility', which in architecture 'involves using an available system in a new way to solve a problem quickly and efficiently' (Jencks and Silver 2013 [1972]: vii). This includes the use of what are perceived as closed and completed systems, such as the MSF IPERJUNGLE timber shelter, as a starting point for spatial change. Adhocism privileges the moment, the short-term need, while the old and the new function are seen together. The prefab emergency shelter, an anonymized space used for a temporary purpose, is the natural architectural candidate for adhocist appropriations. These adjust it to the needs of its particular residents in their specific emergency situation.

Beyond its functional meaning, adhocism is also fundamentally about participatory social, cultural and political meaning. As opposed to the completed architectural building or product that carries the authorized signature of a specific author/designer, adhocism means that 'everyone can create his personal environment out of impersonal subsystems' (Jencks and Silver 2013 [1972]: 15). This turns architecture – as a practice, a product and a term – from 'the protected domain of the architect' into a radically democratic and pragmatic spatial practice (Awan et al. 2013: 28). Adhocism means that architecture does not end with a permanent and rigid outcome, but is open-ended and, as such, also more plural and inclusive, taking into account the ability of nonprofessionals to participate in its creation. Like Lefebvre's famous argument that '(social) space is a (social) product' (1991: 26), the concept of adhocism releases space and its production from the solely professional world of architects and engineers, placing it in a much broader social context that makes the idea of solely expert authorship redundant.

The fact that social space is also a dynamic space links adhocism's social meaning to its embedded temporariness and creation over time. This contrasts powerfully with single-authored architecture, which is perceived as being fixed at its moment of completion.

The point at which La Linière camp was formally completed, and its prefab shelters occupied, was also the beginning of a new phase in the camp's spatial life. This worked as an evolving sequence, an assemblage in which the residents turned from the anonymous abstract biological bodies assumed by the designers into human inhabitants who actively and creatively transformed their shelters according to their specific needs, preferences and talents. The literal meaning of the idea of inhabiting a space (in-habit) is particularly meaningful here. Adhocism is therefore also about the habits, skills and creativity of its assemblers, assuming that this creativity does not belong only to a limited number of chosen practitioners, but to all, being an embedded part of human life.

With these ad hoc spatial actions, the residents, instead of being anonymous users, became active spatial agents who negotiated with existing conditions in order to change and reform them. 'Spatial agency', argue Awan et al. (2013: 31), 'implies that action to engage transformatively with structure is possible, but will only be effective if one is alert to the constraints and opportunities that the structure presents'. Indeed, the residents of the shelters worked with the materiality of the shelter's structure, made of timber and therefore easily adjustable, and also with the management structure of the space of the camp itself and its administrators and volunteers. Agency – the capacity for action – is well explained by Anthony Giddens. 'Action', he writes (1984: 14), 'depends on the capability of the individual to "make a difference" to a pre-existing state of affairs', while 'agency' for him 'means being able to intervene in the world ... with the effect of influencing a specific process or state of affairs'. By changing their shelters, the residents in La Linière camp, who had a very limited ability to influence their difficult situation as refugees or irregular migrants who try to cross the border, have managed to influence and improve the minimal conditions of their shelters and their camp environment.

It is important to note that these changes were not merely spatial or cosmetic. While people in the camp, like many other refugee camps around the world, were mostly dependent on others for their provision, some opened small businesses, adjusting their shelters accordingly. Often these were small commercial stalls selling soft drinks, cigarettes and other everyday necessities, using shelters as storage space. Others converted their entire shelters in order to run their business; one shelter in La Linière became a barber shop, while another MSF timber shelter in the Calais Jungle has turned into a grocery store with adequate spatial adjustments. These business-oriented appropriations of the prefab shelters have continued the actions of many residents in the Jungle, who developed their makeshift shelters into more than seventy informal businesses in the camp (Chrisafis 2016; Katz 2017b).

As Betts et al. argue about refugee economies (2017: 9), 'economic outcomes are not only shaped by institutional structures but also by the agency and capacity of particular individuals – "innovators" – to transform constraints into opportunities for themselves and others'. Commercial spaces are very common in camps and they are often developed by residents (such as in Za'atari in Jordan and Kakuma in Kenya), but it is the management, context, spatiality and materiality of the camp that either allow such commercial activities to happen or prevent them from happening. Emergency shelters, as seen in the MSF IPERJUNGLE shelter, can be therefore used as nuclei for such activities that not only provide financial support for their residents and allow them to partially and temporarily reconstruct their livelihoods, but also provide relief and meaning to their life in the camp.

The conversion of the shelters into small businesses significantly changed their original use for accommodation. The users have therefore transformed not only the form of their shelters but also their function, together with the social, economic, cultural and political meaning of living in the camp. The specific 'adhocist' visual appearance of each shelter therefore also had a political meaning, presenting the residents not as anonymous bodies, but as human beings who can and want to take back control over their lives and re-establish their autonomy and freedom in any possible way.

A Conclusion with Two Warnings

The MSF's IPERJUNGLE shelters were created to provide minimal relief to the forced migrants, who lived in squalid conditions in the area. Yet by being flexible, they became nuclei for their inhabitants' everyday life. Originally, these prefabricated timber shelters were designed as manual-based minimal structures according to preconceived principles of functionalism and standardization: their scientifically based design was calculated and rationalized according to specific standards, so they could be efficiently mass-produced, easily transported and quickly assembled on-site. While the designers and manufacturers of these shelters were on the one end of the production line, acting as the qualified professional authority, the future residents of these shelters were positioned on the opposite end of the line, perceived as unknown abstract users/bodies whose only elementary needs must be taken care of. The shelters were therefore as anonymous as their imagined users, and their repetitive production and deployment on-site created an abstract camp space of multiple unified units.

However, these sterile shelters continued to evolve spatially as soon as they were occupied. Although in the MSF manual, their flexibility, adaptability and various configurations were limited only to their preconceived modules, the adhocist adaptations by their inhabitants turned them into unique spaces of specific everyday needs. From anonymous biological beings, their users became human beings, each with his or her own creativity, agency and capacity to intervene and change his or her very limited conditions. 'Agency', argues Giddens, 'presumes the capability of acting otherwise' (1984: 216). These basic shelters enabled their residents to act differently from the mere abstract users that had been imagined by the designers. Instead, they became resourceful people who actively changed their immediate surroundings and reality while abandoning the cherished designer-user hierarchy. In the end, the materiality of these shelters and the support of volunteers and the camp's managers allowed the forced migrants to participate in the creation of their spaces and transform their constraints into opportunities.

'Use has been a critical motor for architectural invention', argues Cupers (2013: 1). In this example, it is clear how the alternative use of the forced migrants has invented not only the shelters but also the camp environment as a whole. Such form of use should invite professionals to rethink not only what emergency shelters are, but also what they can be. However, before jumping to the drawing board for the design and development of new shelters that could be easily appropriated by their inhabitants and be more suitable for their particular lives, it is important to reflect on two important issues highlighted with clear warning signs.

The first warning relates to the one posed by the feminist science and technology scholar Donna Haraway in her seminal piece 'Situated Knowledges', contending that there is a 'serious danger of romanticizing and/or appropriating the vision of the less powerful while claiming to see from their position' (1988: 583–84). Researchers, planners, architects, engineers, humanitarian actors and spatial thinkers must remember their positioning when studying and reinventing spaces inhabited by weak populations such as displaced people who are heavily controlled and limited in their precarious situation. This is evident in the fact that while the shelters were creatively appropriated, La Linière camp has remained an extremely unstable and harsh environment until it was destroyed by fire in April 2017.

This is related to the second warning, posed by Lefebvre when reflecting on the ambivalent meaning of the user as both an instrument of control and a potential generator of a revolutionary political form of collectivity. Users' participation in spatial creation, stated Lefebvre, should be based on self-management. If participation is abstracted from a process of community self-management, he argued, then it is not real and 'has no meaning; it becomes an ideology, and makes manipulation possible' (Lefebvre 1976: 120). Therefore, the participation of inhabitants in crafting their emergency shelters should not be divorced from processes of self-management, empowerment and agency with real social and political meaning, otherwise it could risk becoming an empty tool of spatial playfulness or, worse, an instrument for their manipulation on behalf of some kind of an external architectural, economic, social or political ideology. While it is important to develop shelters that would be better than only minimal and inflexible shelters, it is also important to ensure that they will be used as part of an approach that will enable not only participation but real collaboration and agency in places of displacement and refuge, rather than being used as sophisticated professional experimental playgrounds imposed on vulnerable people out of a make-do ideology or other visions of sorts.

Finally, it is important to remember that agency, as 'acting otherwise', is not only about an agreeable and predictable change, but also about the capacity to act and exert power. Agency is therefore always political, and shelter as a nucleus of a real spatial change should happen in tandem with building capacities and creating opportunities for other real social, economic and political changes for supporting forced migrants in their new environments. A shelter that is 'better than a shelter', then, will never be only an architectural, engineering, planning or design question. It also needs to be a social and a political question, which must be addressed by more encompassing policies and practices to support life in displacement.

Irit Katz is Lecturer in Architecture and Urban Design at the Sheffield School of Architecture, Associate Researcher at the Urban Institute, and has practised as an architect in Tel Aviv and London. Her work focuses on built environments created and reshaped in extreme conditions, and is strongly engaged with spatial, cultural and political theories.

References

Awan, N., T. Schneider, and J. Till (eds). 2013. *Spatial Agency: Other Ways of Doing Architecture*. London: Routledge.
Betts, A., L. Bloom, J.D. Kaplan and N. Omata. 2017. *Refugee Economies: Forced Displacement and Development*. Oxford: Oxford University Press.
Blau, E. 2013. 'ISOTYPE and Modern Architecture in Red Vienna', in K. Cupers (ed.), *Use Matters: An Alternative History of Architecture*. Abingdon: Routledge, pp. 15–34.
Chrisafis, A. 2016. 'French Court Rejects Bid to Demolish Shops at Jungle Refugee Camp'. *The Guardian*. 12 August. Retrieved 22 October 2019 from https://www.theguardian.com/world/2016/aug/12/french-lille-court-calais-jungle-refugee-camp.
Cupers, K. (ed.). 2013. *Use Matters: An Alternative History of Architecture*. Abingdon: Routledge.

Emmons, P., and A. Mihalache. 2013. 'Architectural Handbooks and the User Experience', in K. Cupers (ed), *Use Matters: An Alternative History of Architecture*. Abingdon: Routledge, pp. 35–50.

Giddens, A. 1984. *The Constitution of Society: Outline of the Theory of Structuration*. Berkeley: University of California Press.

Gueguen-Teil, C., and I. Katz. 2018. 'On the Meaning of Shelter: Living in Calais' Camps de la Lande', in I. Katz, C. Minca and D. Martin (eds), *Camps Revisited: Multifaceted Spatialities of a Modern Political Technology*. London: Rowman & Littlefield, pp. 83–98.

Jencks, C., and N. Silver. 2013 [1972]. *Adhocism: The Case for Improvisation*. Cambridge, MA: MIT Press.

Haraway, D. 1988. 'Situated Knowledges: The Science Question in Feminism and the Privilege of Partial Perspective'. *Feminist Studies* 14(3): 575–99.

Katz, I. 2017a. 'Pre-fabricated or Freely Fabricated?' *Forced Migration Review* 55: 17–19.

——. 2017b. 'Between Bare Life and Everyday Life: Spatialising Europe's Migrant Camps'. *Amps: Architecture_Media_Politics_Society* 12(2): 1–21.

——. 2019. 'En Route: The Mobile Border Migrant Camps of Northern France', in A. Pieris (ed.), *Architecture on the Borderline: Boundary Politics and Built Space*. London: Routledge, pp. 119–138.

Le Corbusier. 2004 [1954]. *The Modulor: A Harmonious Measure to the Human Scale, Universally Applicable to Architecture and Mechanics*. Basel: Birkhäuser.

Lefebvre, H. 1976. *The Survival of Capitalism*. London: Allison & Busby.

——. 1991. *The Production of Space*. Oxford: Blackwell.

Médecins Sans Frontières. 2016. 'IPERJUNGLE Transitional Shelter, Operative Manual'. OCP-LOGOSTIC, Version 1. Editor: H. Bouhabib, curator: I. Primo de Rivera, project by: L. Vacca.

Samuel, H. 2016. 'France's First Ever Internationally Recognised Refugee Camp Opens Near Dunkirk'. *The Telegraph*, 7 March. Retrieved 22 October 2019 from https://www.telegraph.co.uk/news/worldnews/europe/france/12186407/Frances-first-ever-internationally-recognised-refugee-camp-opens-near-Dunkirk.html.

Woensel Kooy, E. 2016. 'Living in between: How Refugees and Volunteers in Negotiation (Re)Construct Citizenship and Humanitarian Care in the Camps of Grande-Synthe, France'. M.Sc. thesis. Utrecht: Utrecht University.

Figure 19.1 Za'atari refugee camp. © Mark E. Breeze, based on an image supplied by Diane Fellows.

19

Social Media, Shelter and Resilience

Design in Za'atari Refugee Camp

Diane Fellows

If you search 'Syrian artists Za'atari' on the internet, you will find a photograph of Al Khidaiwi Al-Nabulsi in his casual cap alongside his fellow artists from Dara'a Province, southern Syria. In Za'atari refugee camp in northern Jordan, artists like Mr Al-Nabulsi paint and sculpt replicas of now-destroyed iconic monuments in the Syrian landscape: the ancient ruins of Palmyra, the ablution fountain of the Grand Mosque in Aleppo and the Deir ez-Zor pedestrian bridge over the Euphrates River, to name but a few. These clay and wood models are a remembrance of cultural spaces the artists want to 'never forget'. Among these objects of memory are also less grand historical designs such as paintings of familial village homes and courtyards filled with vegetable and flowering gardens, where family and friends chat and relax. These paintings portray a domestic calm, but they also present a future intentionally shaped by imagination, resilience and contestation. Syrian artists in Za'atari have painted cultural motifs on paper, canvas, metal caravan façades, flat metal fencing, on any surface that stands bare in the desert landscape. They paint to affirm their community's autonomy, as they are not in a refugee camp by inheritance or by choice, but to persevere.

Among the replicas of Syrian cultural monuments and traditional village housing are the pop-up books of Al Khidaiwi Al-Nabulsi. Mr Al-Nabulsi is best known for these paper sculptures, which he gifts to those who visit the Za'atari refugee camp. Al-Nabulsi's pop-up sculptures fold neatly into a book and then unfold to reveal a United Nations-issued tent shelter, or a gable roofed house, or a sculpture reflecting war's effect on his homeland. Mr Al-Nabulsi (although everyone just calls him Nabulsi) will tell you his brother immigrated to Raleigh, North Carolina, years ago. Nabulsi, though, is unsure of the plan for himself, his wife, his daughter, his son-in-law and the growing number of grandchildren that live in a series of 11 m^2 (118 sq. ft.) temporary metal shelter caravans, in the Za'atari refugee camp. In 2019, this supposedly temporary condition is in its seventh year, and 78,000 fellow Syrians also call it their home, at that time.

How does one determine a shelter to be a home, while displaced? A basic definition of shelter could be noted as a built or found environment that protects its occupants from the outside elements. In response to the many refugees who fled the Syrian Civil War, temporary shelters were placed within newly constructed refugee camps in areas of the Levant. How could a temporary shelter, a safe haven for protection, transition to a permanent space of residence? Would one characterize a space sheltering the many events of one's life over time a home? A home infers a space that may be adapted to the changing needs of its inhabitants, where personal recollections of places and people are often marked by familial objects. These objects of memory, of desire or of need project our personal identity and our sense of belonging to a community of shared values, as certain objects within our home may represent those values.

Could a home also be defined within a geopolitical framework, through property ownership that depends on regional laws, or cultural laws established through lineage, or from the perspective of gender? Laws related to the permanence of property ownership also project identity, as they belong to societal processes or particular cultural practices. However, what if a home could be defined without any physical references at all, where objects are presented or creatively invented through media, through which one's personal identity is projected? A borderless condition, such as a virtual space, where individuals share their story, connect socially and support each other's psychological wellbeing instils a sense of belonging. Can a community engaged virtually by connecting across physical barriers feel more sheltered, protected and emboldened than if it maintained a built environment in a specific geographical place, especially under dire conditions? Does physical shelter in a particular place, inclusive of the right to land for sustenance, become irrelevant as one's contemporary life on the internet allows for mobility and exchange of goods? Or is the development and connection of these two distinct conditions of sheltering – physical space and virtual space – essential for displaced communities to construct their future agency?

These are the contemporaneous concerns relevant to the Za'atari refugee camp, as the Syrian community adapts temporary shelters meant for safety to the more familiar experience of a home, while engaging the boundless space of the invisible walls of the internet.

Space-Making

Since 2011, the beginning of the Syrian Civil War, 630,000 Syrians have fled into Jordan, and since it opened in 2012, the Za'atari refugee camp has seen 450,000 people pass through its security gate. Those who fled the war and did not wish to live in a refugee camp surrounded by barbed wire made their way into neighbouring towns such as Al-Mafraq or moved towards Jordan's capital, Amman. By not staying in Za'atari, they gained a modicum of freedom, but with limited access to healthcare, education and employment. For those who stayed in Za'atari, the United Nations High Commissioner for Refugees (UNHCR) and over 300 nongovernmental organizations (NGOs) have supported rudimentary daily needs, educational activities for children and adults, and basic healthcare. In 2018, the ever-growing Za'atari population averaged eighty newborns per week (UNHCR 2018). The refugee camp is a 5.2 km^2 (2 sq. miles) sandy and rocky extent of desert ground with an infrastructure of streets and paths supported by four main north/south roads, an east/west axis at the centre of the site, and a paved perimeter ring road.

In 2012, when Za'atari opened, emergency tents were placed in the northwest quadrant. The tents were soon replaced by 11 m^2 (120 sq. ft.) prefabricated metal caravans intended to house a family of six. These caravans, organized in a linear pattern, resembled a mid twentieth-century suburban tract rather than the Syrian traditional pattern of familial housing around interior courtyards providing privacy and security. The caravan configurations formed blocks; sixteen blocks formed a single district, which consisted of 0.33 km^2 with approximately 6,500 residents. Managed by Jordan and the UNHCR, Za'atari was created with twelve districts, each with resident input for governance, often from the same families that oversaw governance in their home villages in Syria. The western part of Za'atari has become configured with caravans and private courtyard constructions; the further east one goes, towards the newer part of the site, the caravans lie in a linear pattern within the street grid, with noticeable open space between shelters. The orthogonal grid allows for efficiency: water is delivered to community area tanks and boreholes supply water to individual caravans. For electricity, Za'atari is connected to Jordan's national energy grid and has its own solar farm supplied by IKEA. The grid also allows for controlled security for the UNHCR and the host country, Jordan.

In 2013, along with the temporary caravans, community bathrooms and kitchens were constructed for expediency and cost-effectiveness. However, at night, community bathrooms became a safety concern for women and children. Within a few months, the refugee residents dismantled the bathrooms and kitchens, picked the caravans off the desert floor and placed them to form family groupings. With discarded corrugated metal and old emergency tent fabric, families constructed additional rooms and private outdoor spaces, taking clearer control over their environment. However, there are other forms of community space, most significantly a bustling Market situated along the east/west axis. Named the Champs-Élysées by the NGOs and residents, men, women and families shop at the 3,000 refugee-owned ventures established over the past six years. The Market exchanges about U.S.\$3 million a month in goods such as vegetables, cooked food items, baked goods, clothing, furniture, toys, cellphones and SIM cards. Much of the merchandise delivered to Za'atari comes from neighbouring towns and Amman.

Shelter and Social Media

In Za'atari, to arrive at one's caravan home is a temporary reprieve from the blowing desert sand, the relentless summer heat, the winter's snow and the impossible events one can sometimes see and hear just 13 km north in Syria. For Za'atari residents such as Nabulsi, home is a constant readaptation of space, materials and objects. In addition, home has moved beyond the boundaries of the official UNHCR shelter, the confines of a refugee camp surrounded by wire, the trenches and camp bureaucracy, and the constraints of power politics as evidenced by ever-changing territorial boundaries. In other words, social media anchors Nabulsi to a world larger than the camp and his memories of Dara'a, larger than the built treasures of Syrian culture he carves out of found material can contain. Nabulsi sends messages to his global Facebook friends. Most mornings, his voice lands on my iPhone with a photograph and greeting; I click 'translation' to decipher the Arabic. Often, the photograph explains the event and Nabulsi's mood. His voice lands in all the smartphones of all those to whom he has told his story to and gifted his sculpture books. Now, in his adapted caravan, he offers advice for how to 'live through this mess' and how 'art can keep us feeling alive, to get us through'. In this time of global political madness, I want to believe him.

While every example of displacement is unique, the twenty-first-century refugee camps such as Za'atari are globally visible. Social media enables those displaced to experience shelter at multiple scales: from temporary emergency shelters to the virtual public space of personal experiences shared in real time. In a world of increasing uncertainty, social media is a means to build a personal presence out of a feeling of overwhelming anonymity: to share one's story and one's frustrations, and to network one's ambitions and hopes within a global community. Social media, a borderless space, offers emotional refuge and a personal address. Unprecedented in modern and contemporary refugee crises, conditions of displacement and refuge are observable in the moment.

Za'atari's internet presence can be experienced in a number of ways: UNHCR monthly reports that are posted online; visitors walking away with photographic and video recordings; bloggers keeping virtual diaries of their experience when working with the NGOs and residents; and, because many Za'atari resident adults have a smartphone, the Facebook pages of those living in the camp. In 2015, Facebook, Inc. with the UNHCR made Facebook freely available to the Za'atari residents so that families could connect from different global locations. Much of the social media activity occurs in the evening, when residents have more access to electricity and WiFi. During the day, teenage boys primarily are seen by the exterior fence of Za'atari's base camp where the onsite UNHCR and NGOs are headquartered. Crouching by their bicycles, siphoning UNHCR server signals, the boys browse for music, videos, games and retail, and check Facebook.

The Facebook platform enables Za'atari refugee residents to assert a global presence. However, social media is a complex space of engagement, incorporating the policies of governments influencing how refugees, migrants and immigrants are perceived and welcomed. A palpable tension exists between social media and the physical space of Za'atari, as the constraints of living in a refugee camp frames one's ability to act upon opportunities found on the internet.

In the Space of Engagement

Social media (primarily Skype) enabled the collaboration between my undergraduate architecture studios (MUHabitat, Miami University, Ohio) with Nabulsi and the other artists, designers and engineers residing in Za'atari during the spring of 2016 and 2017. The NGO International Relief and Development (IRD) and the UNHCR facilitated our collaboration; Laurie Balbo, a Miami University alumna working in Amman, introduced us to the multiple conditions of Za'atari in a November 2015 email. In January 2016, sixteen architecture undergraduates became Studio MUHabitat, and our conversation with the resident artists in Za'atari began. Generally, an architectural studio's academic focus may concern the process of design within theoretical, aesthetic and technological frameworks inclusive of environmental, economic and sociopolitical forces that shape people and place. However, the collaboration we embarked upon included many more concerns and unknowns than we could anticipate.

During our first Skype session, through translators, we introduced ourselves and the students simply asked the artists: 'What do you need?' The artists responded with the following list: a new market area in the camp to resemble the Al-Hamidiyah Souk in Damascus, to replace the converted caravan storefronts; separate spaces in the caravans so that husband and wives could also have privacy, as the lack of privacy caused innumerable tensions within families; chairs and tables; gardens and trees; transportation for women and those disabled, and children's playgrounds with educational equipment. Through our virtual apertures, the artists showed us a tabletop model of the Umayyad Mosque, saying: 'This is important to us, especially the children. They need to know.' For the American students, the desire to effect change grew exponentially, but, within the design work requested, we really did not know what 'change' might mean or, ultimately, what impact it would have. What sort of change besides the constructed physical ones could we understand to consider? The question of what architecture can actually do to effect change, such as political change, or what could we do collectively when working 6,000 miles apart in a global and local political landscape continuously in flux did not deter the students or the artists from considering what could be proposed in the moment and actualized.

Our collaboration resulted in 138 pages of design documentation of sun shelters, transportation, furniture and beds for the disabled. All elements were detailed using recycled materials found in Za'atari, from the demolished bathrooms and kitchens using various-sized structural metal posts and kitchen-counter marble to plastic bags and old emergency tents. We tested similar materials in the MUHabitat studio as we wanted to be sure that any habitable element could be constructed with ease on site. Students learned to weld in order to understand materiality and constructability. They proposed a hybrid of aesthetics based on our collective conversations presenting contemporary modern design with traditional components responding to the Syrian culture and desert climactic conditions. We emailed the work to the IRD facilitator Mais Abu Laila, and the artists held their own workshop to critique the designs and make revisions.

From the many designs we developed, it was the need for publicly accessible sun shelters for the Za'atari perimeter ring road that was chosen as a priority concern. This ring road encircles the camp boundary and also serves as its main bus route; the sun shelters were necessary because the elderly, the disabled, women and children had no respite from the desert climate as they walked to various destinations within the refugee camp or tried to catch the bus around its edge. Using a collaborative design process, local construction materials, skilled labour provided by refugee craftsmen and a small UNHCR grant generated by our IRD facilitator, our team succeeded in having fourteen sun shelters constructed in August 2016 that are now public spaces (Kissel 2016). The design adapted was less complex than others and certainly did not need a whole design studio and our Za'atari counterparts to accomplish, but the shelters needed our collective connection, our visibility with each other, in order for the process to be realized. This may not be what one thinks about when imagining refugee shelter, but protection from the sun was clearly one of the most central priorities emerging from this particular process of design.

In Place

The virtual realm offers views into each other's worlds, although the lens is often narrowly pointed towards a specific view. Physically connecting, in the same geographical space, is therefore still key to any engagement. In November 2016, I travelled to the Za'atari refugee camp and was joined by Laurie Balbo. Facilitated by the IRD, we met Nabulsi and the other artists: Mohammad Almari, Ahmad Hariri, Mahmoud Hariri and Eyad Sabagh. Nabulsi gifted the MUHabitat studio two pop-books: a UN tent constructed from a tent that had burnt with catastrophic consequences, and a paper gable roofed house.

The IRD and the studio discussed connecting with women in our collaboration, but the men were our primary contact. It was difficult for the women to engage during our Skype conversation in the same space as the men, as they encountered cultural difficulties within their family to do so. When in Za'atari, Laurie Balbo and I conducted a design workshop with resident women engaged in the education of young girls in Za'atari. Back in Syria, the women were practicing nurses, engineers and teachers, as well as homemakers. For the workshop, the women created drawings and models recalling traditional and more contemporary homes in Dara'a and Damascus, and imagined ones shaped like moons and round sculptural forms. Noticeably, each drawing had a garden. We talked about life before the war and now in Za'atari. Yes, gardens were desired for practical reasons such as growing vegetables, but also for cultural reasons, to bring beauty to a life under pressure – to ease the heaviness of living in a refugee camp, in a relentless open desert.

Green spaces became an ongoing discussion with the IRD and the UNHCR throughout our collaboration. The increased population in Za'atari, and major cities such as Amman, has put an increasingly difficult load on most resources in Jordan, especially water. Za'atari refugee camp sits on one the largest aquifers in Jordan. As green spaces were highly desired, they were discussed in every community meeting. However, widespread green spaces had not been realized because the administration believed that facilitating a water reclamation system for irrigation would be too difficult.

During the 2017 spring semester of the MUHabitat design studio, the IRD changed management as well as staff. Since 2016, the IRD management had changed four times. While this did not alter our engagement, it did shift the emphasis of the exchange from the artists to the NGO. The studio missed our direct discussions with the artists and, while we chatted on Facebook, the effectiveness of our collaboration seemed in doubt. However, the IRD directed the focus of work towards playgrounds, sports facilities and themed community spaces. Based on our continued Facebook connections with the artists, and images of their shelters, the studio also decided to engage housing, as well as consider a more hypothetical urban plan. However, addressing immediate concerns, the students asked: 'What can one do now with existing caravans, what could the future of housing look like with best material practices, and how could we introduce a low-budget, low-maintenance water reclamation system?' Based on the refugee practice of relocating caravans into courtyard configurations, the students proposed the rearrangement of homes into similar safe familial communities and, in the interior, building flexible furniture doubling as storage and room dividers. The students also suggested a rainwater collection system for potable water, and grey water recycling for courtyard gardens.

In May 2017, I visit Za'atari for the second time, and this time my colleague J. Elliott and two former students, Joshua Gabbard and Madison Scheper, joined me. We left another substantive design packet with the UNHCR and the IRD, and, at the behest of the IRD, we conducted workshops with the artists and other residents to review the second design packet, as well as working with children (we brought a suitcase of LEGO that proved to be a tremendous teambuilding event among the children). We also met with the girls' soccer team to consider a proper football pitch with an addition of bathrooms and viewing stands.

When I saw Nabulsi during this visit, he greeted me with the same warmth I had come to know through our Skype sessions. This time, however, his smile noted a slight disapproval. He asked: 'What happened to your hair?' I gave him a sidelong glance, shrugged and said 'American style'; the cut was short, but too short for women according to Nabulsi. Through his half-hearted disapproval, Nabulsi insisted we come to his home for coffee and to see his newly built furniture and his new kitchen. Walking through the Za'atari Market, we glanced down side streets towards informal courtyard arrangements of one-storey caravans. Additions had been constructed from corrugated siding roughly attached with old tent material. A few caravans had more elaborate additions. One family constructed a gable wood roof placed on top of the caravan's metal flat roof. The gable roof is not an additional space; it is a distinct beacon, an address among the sea of caravan shelters.

Nabulsi at Home

In his caravan, Nabulsi, with design packet in hand, took one look, brushed the back of his hand across the pages and emphatically stated 'we have done some of this already', suggesting that he and his community are way ahead of any plans the studio had on paper. Accompanied by Loay Jalamdeh, an IRD staff member, Nabulsi then gave us a tour. He coughed a bit too much, blamed the cigarettes and told us he was still trying to quit. He proudly showed us the furniture he made from caravan floorboards; the kitchen he has culled together from recycled salvaged camp materials. In the kitchen addition to the main caravan, he pointed to the u-shaped shelving with sink and running water, and wryly said: 'You see, a modern kitchen.' The shelving was made from discarded weather resistant plywood, or marine board, and a two-burner counter-top stove was sitting on one side of the kitchen counter with dishes neatly stacked on the other. Nabulsi brought us to the main caravan space, to the large armoire and bed frame he and his son-in-law constructed from some of the original caravan floorboards with refurbished wood brought in from Al-Mafraq and the neighbouring towns. As he replaced his caravan floorboard with a concrete one, the retrofit caravan construction is not constructed as mandated by the Jordanian government. Shelter has to be temporary and not permanent, and concrete suggests permanence, but the UN and NGO administrative staffers do not interfere. After six years, repurposing materials to create a more habitable shelter occurs frequently, out of necessity.

Nabulsi came to Za'atari in 2013 and has made the UN-issued caravan a semblance of a place to settle in well, even if temporarily. When he showed us the armoire, he nodded assuredly. It is a beautiful piece of craftsmanship. With shelving, covered by decorative material, on either side, the armoire is separated from the main caravan by a makeshift wall. While Nabulsi's ability to repurpose materials to meet his family's needs is not so unique in Za'atari, many families, especially those headed by women, do not have the skillsets to create the sort of changes Nabulsi and his son-in-law can craft. Nabulsi told us he wants to return to his village and rebuild: to bring his grandson, born in the refugee camp, home to Syria. This guided our conversation over the next hour.

The IRD staffers, Zain Sultan and Mais Abdel Haleem, urged us to visit more caravans to better understand Za'atari. Nabulsi got on his motorized bicycle; we followed along through the sandy terrain of alley roads. The wind blew heat at our face; there was not a tree in sight. The four of us got into the NGO van and set out for the far eastern side of Za'atari, the newer area where rows of caravans still remain in a linear pattern. As we travelled along the perimeter ring road, we saw the fourteen bus shelters designed during our 2016 collaboration painted in different thematic motifs by the

Za'atari artists: abstract Islamic designs, landscapes and even an aquarium motif.

Shelter and Culture

In the eastern part of the Za'atari refugee camp, we visited a builder, whose enclosed plot of land, with caravan and adjoining kitchen, contained a good-size vegetable garden, a pigeon coop with a roof made of reclaimed timber and metal, and, in one corner of the garden, a chicken coop with four chickens milling about. We entered a two-room caravan, created by a divider from floorboards; two children had been born in Za'atari since the family's arrival. He offered us coffee in the front room. We sat on the UNHCR-issued mattresses that his wife covered with beautiful grey cloth and rested our legs on brown patterned rugs bought from the Market. The builder told us that he had just finished building a house for his family in Dara'a when the war began. One day, an aerial bomb blew the house apart. The next day, the family fled to the Jordanian border, crossed and found their way along with so many others of his community to Za'atari. It is difficult in the camp, he said. The UNHCR and NGOs have meetings with community members about family relationships, regarding the UNHCR and the host country's policy about domestic violence and corporeal punishment of children. These meetings, he said, embarrassed him. He felt his privacy was being attacked, and he was uncomfortable listening to personal issues from governmental social service officials. When disciplining his children, he told us: 'I don't understand, now, what I should do.' We sat quietly, drinking our coffee. The social construction of Za'atari is as profoundly complex as its infrastructure and shelter needs. Many social services assist families, women, children and men to navigate not just a new physical landscape, but also new dynamics of social and criminal laws exercised by the international governing organizations.

We next visited the caravan next door to the builder. A woman greeted us, offering each of us a coffee. Her adult son, who had a learning disability, shook our hands and nodded his welcome. She motioned to us to follow her to the kitchen area, an attached makeshift space of corrugated siding attached with old tent material and sewn paper. She showed us the water drip under her kitchen sink, and then hurriedly ushered us to the other side of the kitchen wall to the main caravan. We could smell the problem before we entered: rotting floorboards. We went back around to the kitchen area and attempted to crimp the kitchen hose to stop the water drip, while one of our team completed some paperwork to solve this plumbing problem through Za'atari administrative channels. The paper trail underscored the incredible bureaucracy that has to be involved just to fix a leaking water hose causing the woman's caravan floor to rot away and become uninhabitable. The ability of neighbours to give mutual support, the very strength at the core of the Dara'a community, seemed not to be present. The IRD staffers and the UNHCR suggested that mutual community responsibility had broken down due to the war and prolonged exile. Families turn inward. Survival becomes foremost. Administratively, specific NGO organizations facilitate specific concerns, and paperwork ensues. I could not understand why a builder, and his neighbour, a single woman with a disabled son, with rotting floorboards due to a leaking water hose that could easily be fixed, weren't supported to assist each other. Frustrated, my colleagues and I noted that we came armed with the wrong tools. We came with a paper design packet; we should have come with plumbing gaskets and pliers.

Conclusion

For those residing in Za'atari, to take rudimentary shelters and adapt them to create liveable habitat is necessary. The majority of Za'atari people – 57 per cent in fact – are under eighteen. A generation will not know the Syria of their parents or grandparents such as Nabulsi. Building shelter constructs a future. The physical materials of this shelter are only one part of the process; social connections are in many ways just as important and the space of the internet empowers those who are displaced to construct how they wish to live.

Beginning in 2015, the internet became part of daily life in Za'atari. Due to these connections, a number of cultural traditions changed for those residing in Za'atari. Some experiences were culturally experienced for the first time, such as girls' playing football and celebrating their accomplishments through sports, while some traditions, separating women's and men's activities in the cramped quarters of Za'atari, upheld traditional cultural rules of decorum. The internet connected refugees to the world beyond Za'atari's boundaries. Through social connectivity, an emotional protective envelope was constructed within the tenuous conditions of the everyday, as the refugees' frustrations, desires and hopes became visibly palpable through internet exchanges. These global exchanges presented a powerful affirmation of the refugees resolve.

For a number of refugees, the return home to Syria is physically and politically difficult. Returning to a vastly transformed Syrian landscape, Syrians may find the internet's borderless and supportive social space not as accessible as it was in Za'atari. Because the internet's efficacy is contingent upon the governing politics of place, if monitored by governing entities, the internet may become less a means for free expression, yet a means to be easily situated at any moment within any geographical location.

What does the future hold for Nabulsi and his community, and all who are born in the Za'atari refugee camp that, in terms of population, is Jordan's fourth-largest area? Does a temporary way station, with embedded infrastructure, a Market, emergency shelters becoming habitats and global communication, develop into a permanent space? Perhaps. If the region found it economically advantageous to develop such a permanent condition, undoubtedly policies would be structured to support such a development. On the internet, Za'atari is often referred to as a city because of its infrastructure and services. The studio explored the following question: is Za'atari a city? An affirmative answer, without clarifying the implications for cultural identity within the region, employment opportunities beyond Za'atari's boundary and governance structures, would be troubling. Displaced, the Syrian people are constructing their lives. However, the Za'atari refugee camp is not the new norm for social engagement, habitation or community permanence; no refugee camp is.

Diane Fellows is Associate Professor in the Department of Architecture and Interior Design at Miami University (Ohio). She teaches architecture studios, and seminars exploring cinema and architectural design processes. Her creative work in video and photography concerns displacement through generations and how, in unfamiliar landscapes, places of personal and cultural meaning are created.

References

Kissel, M. 2016. 'Miami Students Bring Shade to Syrian Refugee Camp'. Retrieved 22 October 2019 from http://miamioh.edu/news/top-stories/2016/07/nuhabitat-studio-design-with-syrian-refugees.html.

UNHCR. 2018. 'Za'atari Refugee Camp – Factsheet'. Retrieved 22 October 2019 from https://reliefweb.int/report/jordan/zaatari-refugee-camp-factsheet-february-2018.

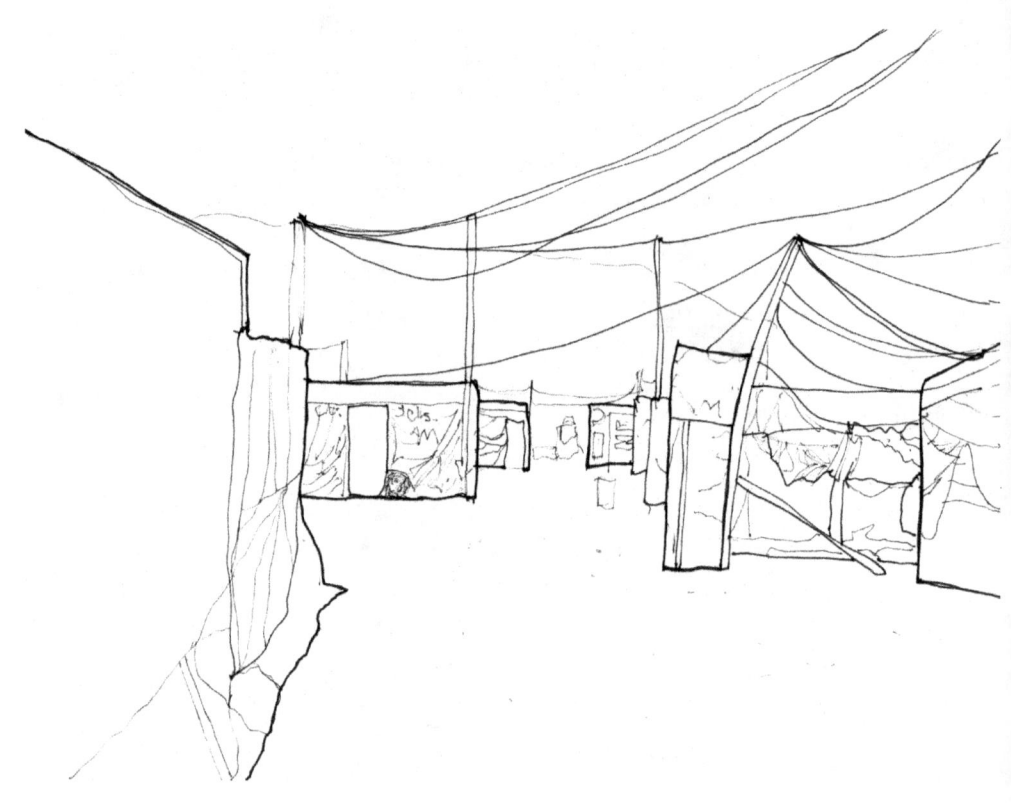

Figure 20.1 Informal settlement in Kab Elias, Bekaa, Lebanon. © Mark E. Breeze, based on an image supplied by Faten Kikano.

20

Confinement, Power and Permanence in Informal Refugee Spaces

Syrian Refugees in Lebanon

Faten Kikano

Media narratives and discourse emanating from the far right have engendered a politics of fear that feeds on negative representations of migrants and refugees. Through a strategy of delegitimization (Agamben 1998), refugees have become the 'others' that cause chaos and endanger the order of organized societies (Ahmed 1999; Arcimaviciene and Baglama 2018). This stigmatization creates a binary opposition between them and us, and initiates the separation of the world in two distinct parts: one for fortunate, regular citizens, and another, where undesirable populations, including refugees and asylum seekers, representing a threat to political, social, and environmental safety and balance, are excluded (Bauman 2007).

This exclusion is expressed through the will of most countries in the world to protect their territories from refugee influx. Countries of the Global North, due to their geographical distance from war-prone zones and the control they are able to enforce on their national borders, host a relatively limited number of refugees (Malkki 1995), whereas developing countries host almost 85 per cent of the world's refugees (UNHCR 2018). Most of these countries suffer from economic and political fragility. They perceive refugees as a security threat and an economic burden, and seek to implement policies aiming to prevent refugees' integration into the socioeconomic and the urban structure of the country (Agier 2010; Black 1998). Regarding refugee settlements, they are faced with two main solutions: settling refugees in organized camps or allowing them to self-settle.

Organized camps are often built in an emergency situation to shelter refugees temporarily and to provide them with protection and welfare. They are often built on a land provided by the host government. They are controlled by the country's authorities and managed by the UNHCR, the UN Refugee Agency. Camps are usually located in remote areas leading to the isolation of refugees (Bernardot 2008). Some scholars theorize them as apolitical spaces that control, confine, and segregate refugees (Bauman 2007; Verdirame and Harrell-Bond 2005). In their view, encampment is a dehumanizing process wherein welfare is exchanged for mobility and in which refugees become passive recipients of aid deprived of their basic civil rights. But for host countries with fragile governance structures, organized camps are constantly at risk of devolving into self-governed spaces beyond state control and endowed with emerging implicit power structures. Such countries fear that the confinement of refugees might lead to the ghettoization and the permanence of their spaces (Doraï 2006; Sanyal 2011). To avoid this risk, they often allow refugees to self-settle.

Self-settlement solutions are often based on informal agreements between owners and refugees. They include rooms and apartments, nonresidential structures, tented settlements, unfinished buildings, etc. In such spaces, refugees lack humanitarian aid and protection (Bakewell 2014), which puts them at risk of evictions, exploitation and abuse (Jacobsen 2006; Landau 2014). But self-settlement also allows refugees to enjoy a certain degree of freedom and autonomy in housing and livelihood, and a chance to integrate into host communities (Agier and Lecadet 2014). Host countries balance this 'freedom' with institutional exclusion in order to keep the pressure on refugees and entice them to leave (Long 2013).

Based on the longitudinal case study of an informal settlement for Syrian refugees in Lebanon, this chapter challenges the paradigm that associates settlement policies with the evolution of refugee spaces. It helps to understand how refuges spaces, whether camps or noncamp solutions, are produced and transformed, and the limited impact of settlement policies on the complex process of their transformation and on their duration. It challenges the dichotomy between encampment and self-settlement by setting out the common patterns of both. It extends the analysis of refugee spaces beyond the spatial characteristics of each type of settlement solution. It shows that while encampment is based on spatial exclusion, self-settled refugees often face institutional and socioeconomic exclusion that limits their freedom of movement and the legality of their situation, and leads paradoxically to their spatial exclusion. It demonstrates that formal and informal refugee spaces evolve similarly along a continuum of vulnerability and power. Their evolution is the result of: (1) intertwined politics adopted by different sets of actors – donor countries, host governments, local authorities, humanitarian actors, formal and informal settlement managers, host communities, property owners and the refugees themselves; (2) the power structures that emerge in and around these spaces; and (3) the spatial, institutional and socioeconomic conditions of refugees that are often impacted by the dynamics of their inclusion/exclusion in the host state.

Syrian Refugees in Lebanon

The Lebanese government did not initially engage in the management of the Syrian refugee crisis. Lebanon's initial response was to keep the border with Syria open and – with a few rare exceptions – to prohibit organized camps. As a result, seven years after the onset of the Syrian conflict, Lebanon is now host to almost 1.5 million Syrian refugees, a number close to 30 per cent of the country's population.

At first, the Lebanese response was praised by the international community. Today, many describe it as a groundless policy that is not aligned with the country's governance and economic capacities (AUB/UNHABITAT 2015; El Mufti 2014). However, a thorough analysis of the political and economic context in Lebanon reveals that there are several reasons for the policy (Turner 2015). One of the main reasons is the fear that the experience of Palestinian camps, which evolved into self-governed, armed ghettos and became autonomous states within the state (Hudson 1978), will be repeated. In fact, several political parties, especially those representing religious minorities, feared that organized camps for Syrians would become permanent, adding a large Sunni population to the 500,000 Palestinians who have resided in Lebanon since 1948, thus constituting a threat to the fragile sectarian balance that characterizes the country. They also worried that the camps would become a haven for extremist groups and a site for the potential radicalization of refugees (Onishi 2013).

Moreover, Syrians have not been classified by the Government of Lebanon as refugees, a category that does not exist in Lebanese law, but as displaced persons (*Nazihoun*). As for the spaces they occupy, they were referred to as gatherings in official documents and reports (*Tajamouat*). The word 'camp' was completely banned from the government's lexis (Fawaz et al. 2014; Loveless 2013; Naufal 2012).

The disengagement of the government has resulted in municipalities becoming the principal authorities in the management of the Syrian refugee crisis. Municipalities adopted hosting policies ranging from complete exclusion to hospitality and the socioeconomic inclusion of refugees. Those policies were compatible with the sociocultural, economic and religious contexts of the regions that municipalities administered. The municipalities' varied hosting and settlement policies translated into significant differences in the numbers of refugees hosted, in the types and forms of sheltering and housing solutions adopted by Syrians, and in disparities in their evolution in terms of size, structure and durability (Sanyal 2017).

Without camps, Syrian refugees settled informally in more than 2,000 locations all over the country in several types of sheltering arrangements, ranging from apartments and rooms to informal settlements (Kikano et al. 2015). They concentrated in areas where the local authorities were lenient, straining service systems and infrastructure that had not been upgraded since before the Civil War. These areas are often the poorest and refugees compete with Lebanese for affordable housing and low-skilled jobs, a situation that generates significant tensions (Loveless 2013).

In 2014, with the crisis protracting, the Lebanese government adopted a drastic reversal in dealing with Syrian refugees. It issued a number of rules prohibiting Syrians from entering the country and exerted institutional exclusion on those who were already present. Expensive fees that refugees could seldom afford were required for the renewal of residency and work permits. For the latter, Syrians needed a Lebanese sponsor. The latest United Nations High Commissioner for Refugees (UNHCR) census shows that, as a result of these measures, more than 70 per cent of Syrians have become illegal settlers in Lebanon (Janmyr 2016).

An Informal Settlement in Kab Elias, Bekaa

Between 2014 and 2018, I studied an informal settlement in Kab Elias, a city located in eastern Lebanon, in the district of Zahleh in the Bekaa valley. I chose to study a settlement in the Bekaa because it is one of the Lebanese regions with the largest number of refugees. Syrians settled in this area for several reasons. First, the Bekaa is located near the Syrian border. Second, it is a region with vast agriculture land and, prior to the Syrian war, it hosted a large community of Syrian temporary workers. To avoid commuting, workers lived in tents raised on the agriculture land itself. When the Syrian conflict erupted, they hosted family and friends fleeing the war in Syria. More tents were erected to shelter newcomers and most settlements developed rapidly. Third, the decrease in humanitarian aid forced most Syrians to work and, in the Bekaa, it was easier for them to find jobs, especially in agriculture.

Kab Elias is a town of 32 km^2 with a population of 50,000. It is the third-largest city in the Bekaa. Inhabitants belong to various religious groups, but an important Christian community resides in the city, imbuing it with Western culture and influence. It presently hosts 60,000 Syrian refugees (around 30,000 are registered with the UNHCR), some of whom rent apartments in the town centre, while others live in tented settlements on the outskirts of the town.

My fieldwork involved direct observation of refugee spaces, including pictures, plans, and drawings of the settlement and semi-structured interviews with ten stakeholders, including three ministers, the head of municipal councils, the informal camp manager or *shaweesh* and three humanitarian aid workers. The most important part of this information came from group discussions with refugees and host communities. Information was completed with a review of documents and reports produced by the UNHCR, non-governmental organizations (NGOs) (the Norwegian Refugee Council, the World Bank, UN-HABITAT, UNICEF, the World Food Program, UNRWA and the Lebanon Inter-Agency) and the Lebanese government. These documents examined the legal, economic and social situation of Syrian refugees and the living conditions in various types of shelters.

The settlement I studied is built on 14,000 m^2 of agriculture land. It hosts seventy families (almost 350 people) who live in forty tented shelters. It is constituted of a series of heterogeneous, temporary self-built shelters, created from heaps of panels, tarpaulins and other recovered materials that cover precarious wood or metal structures. The dimensions of most shelters are 7 m x 6 m. The monthly rent for each tent is around U.S.$200, excluding the price of illegal electrical connections (almost U.S.$25 per month). Irregular passages between shelters form a labyrinth where, every now and then, lean plants grow sporadically in plastic containers and pots. White latrines marked with the UNHCR logo are located near each shelter. Electrical cables hang between makeshift wood posts, creating a scattered canopy covering the settlement.

Throughout my field visits that spanned over four years, I was able to observe the 'visible' and 'invisible' transformations of the settlement. The overall external appearance reflected extreme precariousness. Shelters deteriorated with the passage of time due to the harsh climatic factors that characterize the area. This significant deterioration is also due to the initial use of materials with a short lifespan. But it is also caused by the restrictions imposed by the Ministry of Social Affairs (the ministry assigned by the government to manage refugee spaces) on both NGOs' and refugees' improvements and modifications of shelters. Restrictions sought to prevent upgrading and the construction of permanent fixtures. Ministry representatives were tasked with periodically controlling shelter modification. They allowed only minimal maintenance such as waterproofing.

On the local level, the head of the municipal council, known for his support for the Syrian regime, expressed very little empathy towards refugees during our interview. Other sources of information such as group discussions with refugees and interviews with humanitarian aid workers show that he did not cooperate with international nongovernmental organizations (INGOs) and refugees claimed that municipal representatives slowed down and sometimes prevented them from receiving aid. Local authorities imposed additional restrictions. First, they prohibited refugees from building new shelters, with the result that the existing shelters became overcrowded since their inhabitants were forced to accommodate new dwellers who had either fled the war and had just arrived in the country or had been displaced from other areas in Lebanon. Second, for security reasons and for better control over refugees' movement, refugees had no right to change their location. Despite exploitative rents, they were obliged to remain on the land they had initially rented (Kikano 2017).

This led to the creation of a new category of actors exerting their control over refugees: private landowners. Every year, they raised the (informal) rent price of the land occupied by refugees, benefiting from the new regulation that forbade refugees from moving the settlement to a different location. Other implicit power structures developed in the settlement: the *shaweesh* protects but simultaneously exploits and controls refugees. He is usually Syrian himself with legal documentation. His legal standing gives him control and authority over the rest of the residents who are mostly illegal settlers. It is he who authorizes refugees to reside in the settlement. He often chooses large families with members who are young and willing to work in agriculture. This selection favours the employment deals he arranges with land managers and allows him to withhold around 60 per cent of workers' wages. He also negotiates the informal agreements concerning land rental with the Lebanese landowner and subleases parcels of the land to each household, extracting income from each of them.

Inequality in institutional, social and economic conditions between refugees translated into disparities in the interior settings of the shelters they occupied. While the external appearance of the settlement expresses generalized scarcity and poverty, the internal space of individual shelters expresses the social hierarchy that exists between residents. In fact, the *shaweesh* along with his family and relatives live in rather opulent conditions contrasting with the rest of the shelters. The floor is a concrete slab covered with carpets. The walls are covered with colourful sheets, decorated with drapes, thin cords and tassels. Cushions are placed on the floor as armchairs. Moreover, the flexibility of structures allows the creation of multiple and interconnecting rooms with wood separations and doors or with curtains and sheets, organized according to needs and the number of family members (Kikano 2018; Kikano et al. 2018). The result is a space furnished like any modest rural house. The largest and most luxurious tent is a U-shaped *majlis* where honourable guests are hosted in special occasions, with a stove for ceremonial coffee in the centre of the space, a testimonial to Syrian hospitality (Kikano 2018). However, most other shelters, especially those occupied by the elderly or by female heads of households, are in extremely poor condition. The single-spaced dwellings consist of a structure and a tarpaulin covering an uneven mud floor with none of the amenities described above (Kikano 2018).

The authority exerted by the *shaweesh* over refugees derives mainly from the illegality of the refugees' institutional status. Their movements were restricted and they feared arrest by the army. With little freedom of movement, the only jobs they could find had to be in close proximity to the settlement. Their large numbers increased the availability of cheap labour. Work conditions were exploitative and wages were very low. As in most Lebanese areas hosting large numbers of refugees, tensions between communities quickly spread. Refugees were often subject to violence and abuse, in which case they had little legal recourse. They were seldom accepted by the local community and their presence was usually unappreciated in town. This was rather surprising considering that the Sunni Lebanese shared the same religion as refugees. Refugees represented not only competition for housing and low-skilled jobs, but, as most of them came from the southern reef of Aleppo, a poor, isolated rural area, they were perceived as a threat to local social practices, culture and way of life. In sum, despite not living in an organized camp, refugees were confined to their own settlement.

Refugees' confinement generated in them a sense of fear, distrust and insecurity. Over the years, their good nature and their initial hospitality disappeared. Entering the settlement became difficult and strangers were not allowed in without being approved and accompanied by the *shaweesh*. Refugees were uncomfortable communicating with visitors and letting them enter their living spaces, especially the most opulent ones. It was only after many visits, for example, that I was allowed to visit the *majlis* and the shelters belonging to the *shaweesh* and his relatives. With difficulties for outsiders in entering and leaving the settlement, and with the emergence of power structures inside and outside the settlement controlling refugees, the Kab Elias settlement was imperceptibly and irrevocably being ghettoized.

Conclusion: Self-Settlement as an Implicit Form of Spatial Exclusion

The divisions between populations with different social and cultural categories have deepened in the past few decades, resulting in negative representations of the Other, whether this is a migrant, a refugee, a female, a Muslim or any other minority (Arcimaviciene and Baglama 2018). But if we distance ourselves from these representations, we realize that what really characterizes these populations is their status as noncitizens. In fact, their institutional status often deprives them of their basic rights, which are apportioned on the basis on citizenship, including the right to space (Kibreab 1999).

When faced with a refugee influx, countries usually perceive encampment as a strategy that instigates refugees' spatial exclusion and weakens them. Yet, countries with fragile political systems perceive organized camps as a security threat, spaces of confinement at risk of becoming self-governed ghettos controlled by empowered refugee populations. This is the case for the Lebanese government, which, in response to the Syrian refugee influx, adopted a nonencampment policy, causing the emergence of several types of informal spaces.

Informality can be a kind of confinement: due to the refugees' institutional and socioeconomic exclusion by the Lebanese government and the control exerted by authorities on their freedom of movement, their informal settlements became spaces of confinement and segregation. While organized camps are usually controlled by government authorities and managed by humanitarian actors, with self-settled refugees, new categories of actors who control refugees and regulate their spaces are created: on the one hand, private landowners exploit them and extort excessive rents for the land where their settlement is built; on the other hand, the *shaweesh* or settlement manager empowered by his legal status and his socioeconomic wellbeing protects refugees, but also abuses and exploits them.

In conclusion, our study demonstrates the nondeterministic nature of settlement policies on the nature, evolution and duration of refugee spaces and on the living conditions of refugees. It extends the analysis of refugee spaces beyond the spatial characteristics generated by the contrast between encampment and self-settlement. From this perspective, this research argues that camps and noncamps evolve similarly along a continuum between vulnerability and power, depending on refugees' institutional and socioeconomic situation, on implicit and explicit power relations that develop in and around refugee spaces, and on the tangle of conflicting interests between different government and nongovernment actors. Kibreab (1999: 389) summarizes these recommendations, asserting that the refugee 'problem' cannot be solved unless host governments, host societies and refugees themselves cooperate to integrate refugees as members in their new environment and give them equal opportunities, allowing them to develop a 'feeling of belonging and identity that would benefit both refugee and host populations'.

Faten Kikano is a Ph.D. candidate in environmental studies at University of Montreal. Her research explores the implications of hosting policies on refugees' living conditions and on space appropriation in refugee spaces. Her findings enable her to set frameworks aiming at the implementation of appropriate living environments for refugees and sustainable solutions for host countries. Her thesis focuses on the case of Syrian refugees in Lebanon.

References

Agamben, G. 1998. *Homo Sacer: Sovereign Power and Bare Life*. Stanford: Stanford University Press.

Agier, M. 2010. 'Forced Migration and Asylum: Stateless Citizens Today', in C. Audebert and M.K. Doraï (eds), *Migration in a Globalised World: New Research Issues and Prospects*. Amsterdam: Amsterdam University Press, pp. 183–90.

Agier, M., and C. Lecadet. 2014. *Un monde de camps*. Paris: La Découverte.

Ahmed, S. 1999. 'Home and Away: Narratives of Migration and Estrangement'. *International Journal of Cultural Studies* 2(3): 329–47.

AUB/UNHABITAT. 2015. *No Place to Stay? Reflections on the Syrian Refugee Shelter Policy in Lebanon*. Beirut: American University of Beirut.

Arcimaviciene, L., and S. Baglama. 2018. 'Migration, Metaphor and Myth in Media Representations: The Ideological Dichotomy of "Them" and "Us"'. *SAGE Open* 8(2): 1–13.

Bakewell, O. 2014. 'Encampment and Self-Settlement', in E. Fiddian-Qasmiyeh, G. Loescher, K. Long and N. Sigona (eds), *The Oxford Handbook of Refugee and Forced Migration Studies*. Oxford: Oxford University Press, pp. 127–38.

Bauman, Z. 2007. *Le présent liquide: peurs sociales et obsession sécuritaire*. Paris: Seuil.

Bernardot, M. 2008. *Camps d'étrangers*. Paris: Éditions du Croquant.

Black, R. 1998. 'Putting Refugees in Camps'. *Forced Migration Review* 2: 4–7.

Doraï, M.K. (2006). *Les réfugiés palestiniens du Liban: Une géographie de l'exil*. Paris: CNRS Éditions.

El Mufti, K. 2014. 'Official Response to the Syrian Refugee Crisis in Lebanon, the Disastrous Policy of No-Policy'. Beirut: Civil Society Knowledge Centre. Retrieved 22 October 2019 from https://civilsociety-centre.org/pdf-generate/17211.

Fawaz, M., N. Saghiyeh and K. Nammour. 2014. *Housing, Land and Property Issues in Lebanon, Implications of the Syrian Refugee Crisis*. Beirut: UNHCR.

Hudson, M.C. 1978. 'The Palestinian Factor in the Lebanese Civil War'. *Middle East Journal* 32(3): 261–78.

Jacobsen, K. 2006. 'Refugees and Asylum Seekers in Urban Areas: A Livelihoods Perspective'. *Journal of Refugee Studies* 19(3): 273–86.

Janmyr, M. 2016. 'Precarity in Exile: The Legal Status of Syrian Refugees in Lebanon'. *Refugee Survey Quarterly* 35(4): 58–78.

Kibreab, G. 1999. 'Revisiting the Debate on People, Place, Identity and Displacement'. *Journal for Refugee Studies* 12(4): 384–410.

Kikano, F. 2017. *Collecte de données (3)*. Unité de Recherche AME 7109. Montreal: Faculty of Planning, University of Montreal.

———. 'Informal Settlements as Social Places of Life', in M. Fawaz, A. Gharbieh, M. Harb and D. Salamé (eds), *Informal Settlements as Social Places of Life*. Beirut: Issam Fares Institute for Public Policies and International Affairs, American University of Beirut, pp. 144–150.

Kikano, F., M. Fayazi and G. Lizarralde. 2015. 'Understanding Forms of Sheltering by (and for) Syrian Refugees in Lebanon'. Paper presented at the 7th iRec Conference 2015: Reconstruction and Recovery in Urban Contexts, London.

Kikano, F., D. Labbé and G. Lizarralde. 2018. 'Physical Variables Affecting Space Appropriation in Places of Refuge', in R. Bologna (ed.), *New Cities and Migrations*. Florence: Dida, pp. 55–68.

Landau, L. 2014. 'Urban Refugees and IDPs', in E. Fiddian-Qasmiyeh, G. Loescher, K. Long and N. Sigona (eds), *The Oxford Handbook of Refugee and Forced Migration Studies*. Oxford: Oxford University Press, pp. 139–50.

Long, K. 2013. 'When Refugees Stopped Being Migrants: Movement, Labour and Humanitarian Protection'. *Migration Studies* 1(1): 4–26.

Loveless, J. 2013. 'Crisis in Lebanon: Camps for Syrian Refugees?' *Forced Migration Review* 43: 66–68.

Malkki, L. 1995. 'Refugees and Exile: From "Refugee Studies" to the National Order of Things'. *Annual Review of Anthropology* 24(1): 495-523.

Naufal, H. 2012. *Syrian Refugees in Lebanon, the Humanitarian Approach under Political Divisions*. Migration Policy Centre Research Report, Robert Schuman Centre for Advanced Studies. Florence: European University Institute.

Onishi, N. 2013. 'Lebanon Worries That Housing Will Make Syrian Refugees Stay'. *New York Times*, 11 December. Retrieved 22 October 2019 from https://www.nytimes.com/2013/12/11/world/middleeast/lebanon-worries-that-housing-will-make-syrian-refugees-stay.html.

Sanyal, R. 2011. 'Squatting in Camps: Building and Insurgency in Spaces of Refuge'. *Urban Studies* 48(5): 877–90.

———. 2017. 'A No-Camp Policy: Interrogating Informal Settlements in Lebanon'. *Geoforum* 84: 117–25.

Turner, L. 2015. 'Explaining the (Non-)Encampment of Syrian Refugees: Security, Class and the Labour Market in Lebanon and Jordan'. *Mediterranean Politics* 20(3): 386-404.

UNHCR. 2018. *Global Trends: Forced Displacement in 2017*. Geneva: United Nations High Commissioner for Refugees.

Verdirame, G., and B.E. Harrell-Bond. 2005. *Rights in Exile: Janus-Faced Humanitarianism*. Oxford: Berghahn Books.

Figure 21.1 Tempelhof Airport in Berlin, Germany. © Mark E. Breeze, based on an image supplied by Toby Parsloe.

21

From Emergency Shelter to Community Shelter
Berlin's Tempelhof Refugee Camp

Toby Parsloe

Buildings often come to symbolize particular geopolitical moments. German Chancellor Angela Merkel's open-door policy famously allowed over one million refugees to enter Germany during the so-called 'refugee crisis' of 2015, and the emergency refugee shelters that proliferated throughout the country at that time became tangible structures that appeared to incarnate national ethical reactions in space. School gyms, military barracks, office blocks, town halls and many other structures were famously co-opted by state authorities to act as *Notunterkünfte* (emergency shelters). For some people, these shelters came to symbolize a profound moment of openness that gave hope to thousands of desperate people. For others, they were sites of squalor, neglect and mismanagement that could become breeding grounds for dissatisfaction and violence, or gateways into the country for the threatening foreign invader. Almost all of the emergency shelters erected since 2015 had closed by 2018 and were replaced by a new type of long-term shelter called *Gemeinschaftsunterkünfte* (community shelters). These have attracted significantly less attention than the initial shelters. However, they are equally as important symbolic structures, whose implications are arguably more profound and revealing as Germany addresses the complex long-term questions of hosting refugees.

Years after Merkel's historic decision, the supposed state of emergency is ostensibly over. The once prominent debates around refugee arrivals have receded and there is a sense that, for better or worse, the country has 'dealt with' the crisis. Public discussions now address broader questions and abstract concepts of migration, as tensions mount over refugee distributions and the responsibility taken by different European nations. Yet Germany stands at a critical moment where the sobering long-term realities of hosting already arrived refugees have become part of the country's everyday existence. The hospitable façade of the famous *Willkommenskultur* (welcome culture) quickly dissolved, as the major gains of the far right in mainstream politics suggest an increasingly polarized society (Lees 2018). Outbreaks of violence, such as those in Chemnitz in the summer of 2018, demonstrated that tensions rooted in asylum debates remain high (Knight 2018). Within this context, it is increasingly important to consider how cities provide long-term accommodation for the thousands who need significant support to establish their new lives in an unfamiliar country and culture.

Throughout Germany, finding available permanent housing proved difficult, but it is within major cities such as Berlin, on which this chapter focuses, where affordable housing pressures made the issue particularly acute (Katz et al. 2016). In 2017, Berlin experienced the greatest global increase in property prices and in 2018 it was ranked as the number one city for European real estate investment and development for the fourth year in a row (PricewaterhouseCoopers 2018). Refugees in 2018 had to contend with this often overpowering search for profit in the contemporary neo-liberal city, and some 27,000 refugees still lived in institutionalized shelter provided by the Berlin Landesamt für Flüchtlingsangelegenheiten (LAF – the state office for refugee affairs) in August 2018. While the emergency shelters catered to the most basic needs in their provision of accommodation, meals and hygiene facilities to refugees as they applied for asylum, the new community shelters are instead intended to provide long-term shelter as refugees attempt (and mostly fail) to find their own accommodation. These new structures are neither refugee camps as commonly understood, nor can they be considered proper urban dwellings. Instead, they are a type of imitation home: an ambiguous space wherein refugees supposedly choose to live, but in reality have little choice as they attempt to establish themselves in the city.

This chapter seeks to provide insight into the development of refugee shelter in German cities by interrogating the spatial distinctions between emergency and community shelters. It focuses on one of the most problematic cities, Berlin, to explore the transition from one type of shelter to another, which has largely been internationally ignored. It examines the development of arguably the most iconic shelter in Germany, the former Berlin-Tempelhof Airport, which transformed from an emergency shelter to a community shelter, a *Notunterkunft* to a *Gemeinschaftsunterkunft*. In this chapter I explore the various architectural characteristics and fundamental logics that define these shelter typologies, examining their sociopolitical implications. In essence, I ask what do an emergency shelter and a community shelter look like and what do they mean? By examining the evolution of a single site, this chapter contributes towards a growing understanding of a broader urban process of shelter situated in space and developing over time, revealing the extent to which specific contexts create distinct spatialities, but also the challenges and meanings that are general to all the city's shelters. Approaching the refugee situation shelter by shelter, city by city and country by country will help to begin to disentangle and elucidate the complex web of camp-like structures that has proliferated throughout Europe since 2015.

Tempelhof: An Urban Spectacle of Asylum

Of all Germany's emergency shelters, none arguably captured the same level of imagination and international attention as the Berlin-Tempelhof camp. This was at one point the largest in Germany, but it was the context for which it became famous. The camp was situated in the hangars of the former Berlin-Tempelhof Airport: a building originally constructed by the Nazis, which went on to play a key role in providing supplies to the city during the Berlin Blockade in 1948–49 and acted as the iconic gateway for arrivals to West Berlin during the Cold War (Copley 2017). Because of its history, the entire site stands under *Denkmalschutz* (historic monument protection), meaning that nothing can be added that will permanently affect the structure. Refugees came to dwell behind the building's imposing neo-classical façades, which were made from scintillating Muschelkalk stone.

The building's monolithic architecture has long attracted film-makers; indeed, its aesthetics also became the dramatic backdrop to cinematic explorations of the German refugee situation in Karim Aïnouz's 2018 film *THF Central* and Ai Weiwei's 2017 film *Human Flow*. In 2008, the wider airfield became Berlin's largest public park after the airport closed, and it made headlines in 2014 due to a public referendum that legally protected this exceptionally popular place from future urban development (Fahey 2015). However, the camp forced the protective legislation to be overturned, causing significant upset for some locals as they feared this would open up the park to real estate developers. The building was chosen to host a camp because it was state-owned and offered a large area in which to temporarily house refugees; however, it came with historical, architectural and political baggage that produced multiple tensions (Parsloe 2017). The site may be vast and open with sparse material features, but it is strikingly dense in its associations. Through its context, the camp became an urban spectacle of Merkel's open-door policy, attracting international politicians, academics and journalists (Katz et al. 2018).

Notunterkunft: A Shelter of Emergency

The municipal government had already discussed the possibility of using the former airport to accommodate refugees in the spring of 2015, months before Merkel's open-door policy. Yet it was not until late October that year that the plans came to fruition. Like many other emergency shelters, the timescale between confirmation and opening date was exceptionally rapid. Tamaja, the social service company that ran the emergency shelter, were given a single weekend to prepare one of the hangars for its first residents. Arrival numbers into Germany had reached their peak by the autumn, resulting in a lack of resources and a situation of uncertainty that effectively shut down the city's administrative structures for refugees.

The emergency shelter established in Tempelhof's hangars had two primary functions: to sort refugees and to offer temporary shelter. It was a centralized site to concentrate a particular population, which could be registered and categorized under complex migration legislation and consideration of legal statuses. It was, in effect, a concentration of state power that sought to determine 'worthy' and 'unworthy' asylum seekers; it also became a space to house migrants who had been accepted for asylum, but were yet to be transferred to more permanent governmental accommodation or find their own accommodation in the city. Throughout its existence, the emergency camp was not a pleasant environment, and the earliest iteration was the most structurally basic and problematic. Tents, each of which housed six bunk beds, were hastily erected inside one of the hangars. Portaloos were placed outside on the airport apron due to the building's unsuitable ancient plumbing. Residents had to be taken by bus to nearby swimming pools to shower at designated times. The airport's similarly ancient heating system proved to be inadequate, as Berlin's infamous winter began to bite. Keeping the hangars at a habitable temperature was an impressive feat, though operating the new heating system would cost the Berlin government €20,000 per day (Smale 2016). In such difficult conditions, tensions ran high and culminated in a physical scuffle in a food queue in December 2015. The event was sensationalized by the international media, which took the opportunity to criticize the living conditions and highlight internal camp divisions (Hall 2015).

However, the quality of accommodation and facilities did improve as the geopolitical situation became more stable. Shelter structures became more formalized both in their administration and architecture: open-top living cubicles made of prefabricated boards quickly replaced the tents, while on-site shower facilities were constructed and the original toilets were refurbished in each hangar. Security checkpoints to the hangars were implemented with swipe-card access for the residents, as well as airport-style security scanning facilities. There was a noticeable dissipation of tension as the declining numbers of new arrivals and administrative changes improved the situation considerably.

The camp authorities were subsequently able to pursue more innovative pursuits that went beyond providing the absolute minimum of basic needs. During Ramadan, one hangar was transformed into a large dining hall where Muslim residents from each hangar could break their daily fast together. The same hangar went on to become a sports centre called Tentaja: a space where residents and the general public could interact through sport activities. A newly formed local citizen initiative called 'THF Welcome' set up a clothes donation bank for camp residents and, more ambitiously, a café in a large side room in Hangar 1. Residents operated the café's daily functions, which also hosted various events and a mobile library several times a week. Although it had limited success and footfall, the café was open to the public to encourage interaction between Berliners and camp residents. Another initiative entitled 'Portals' placed a live video link between the camp and various other locations around the world, such as the U.S. Holocaust Museum in Washington DC. The intention was to allow others around the world to hear the stories of refugees. Although these initiatives had various levels of success, they nevertheless demonstrated creative experiments to engage with, and support, the incoming population through camp spaces. Such developments reflect the broader praise Berlin has received for pursuing more creative approaches in response to refugee arrivals (Katz et al. 2016). Although limited, they showed hints of looking beyond the immediate emergency situation of providing the most basic necessities, and moving towards the longer-term goal of incorporating a new population into the existing city.

These apparent improvements were still a far cry from creating a permanent and sustainable form of dwelling; indeed, the *Notunterkunft* remained a mostly prescriptive, stifling and disempowering space. Residents complained about the stark industrial lighting that glared down upon them and the noise that echoed around the vast hangars and over which they had little power to change. Food also became a major grievance. Cooking or bringing fresh food into the living areas was forbidden, and this forced residents to eat the poor-quality and unfamiliar offerings in the camp canteens; the only way to gain some influence over their subsistence was to (as many did) go into the city to eat. Increased security measures impinged on everyday actions, and any move into or out of the camp was controlled and monitored. Graffiti and colourful murals, which were common occurrences on the early wall panels, were banned due to the appearance of highly offensive markings, and the resultant gleaming white wall panels reinforced the institutionalized environment. Stencils of Berlin landmarks, which were added by camp authorities, remained an imposed and somewhat kitsch attempt to replace the original creativity of the residents. The camp gained such a negative reputation amongst the network of refugees in Berlin that when another emergency shelter nearby was closed and its residents were supposed to be moved to Tempelhof, they staged a protest by camping in tents outside their former shelter, stating that 'we would rather sleep on the street than go to Tempelhof' (Wimalasena 2016).

Problems with the early mass-shelters are more understandable if we consider the logistical challenges that inevitably arose from trying to accommodate such a large population at such short notice in such a politically charged context. The criticisms of Tempelhof's conditions were justifiable, though it would be conspiratorial to pin an obvious insidious motive by either the municipal government or the camp authorities. Tempelhof, after all, was never meant to act as a permanent dwelling. It would also be unjust to over-emphasize comparisons with other refugee shelters such as those in Palestine or in other countries, which struggle to provide basic necessities such as food and water, or which intentionally seek to permanently exclude the entire camp population. Unlike Tempelhof's emergency shelter, some of these have suspended a refugee population for decades. Rather than the conditions themselves, the emergency shelter's most traumatic injustice on residents was the normalcy of uncertainty that came to define their everyday lives. Many stayed far beyond the initial timeframe given to process an application: for months and even years. They did not know when they would be informed of the status of their asylum application or when they would be moved elsewhere. As Maria Kipp, spokeswoman of Tamaja, suggested when I interviewed her on this topic, people are able to adapt to and endure difficult situations if they know when they will end. But at Tempelhof they didn't know; instead, they were stuck for months in a space intended to house someone for days, and could not orient their lives towards a predictable reality.

In December 2017 the *Notunterkunft* eventually closed and the residents moved to supposedly better long-term accommodation. By then, however, many were demotivated, demoralized and had suffered psychological issues from the months and years spent living in the hangars.

Gemeinschaftsunterkunft: A Shelter of Community

When the *Notunterkunft* closed, the new *Gemeinschaftsunterkunft* opened a few metres away outside on the airport's former apron. Many residents moved from one to the other, experiencing two very different forms of shelter. In many ways, the challenges of creating long-term shelter is more complex than providing the most basic of necessities: the *Gemeinschaftsunterkunft* is part of the process to house, employ and absorb a large population into existing urban structures in more permanent ways, which inevitably takes more time and resources to achieve.

The terminology used by the authorities is indicative of their intentions and hopes: an 'emergency shelter' in contrast to a 'community shelter'. The former denotes a temporary solution to address an immediate problem, while the latter suggests the creation of enduring social connections between individuals. German theorists Ferdinand Tönnies and Max Weber famously distinguished the term *Gemeinschaft* (community) from *Gesellschaft* (society) and explored them as a dichotomy (Tönnies 1988; Weber 2013). *Gemeinschaft* embodies more personal interactions concerning subjective feelings, in contrast to *Gesellschaft*'s more rational and impersonal relations. Based on these ideals, a very different philosophy underpins the spatial characteristics of the *Gemeinschaftsunterkunft* that replaced the *Notunterkunft* at Tempelhof: Berlin's provision of long-term shelter demonstrates a diverse approach, which deploys multiple types of structure in attempts to achieve the vision of a community shelter. This is an experiment that adopts a range of potential solutions to housing a population that cannot find their own accommodation in the neoliberal economic climate.

The community shelter at Tempelhof constituted one of seventeen so-called Tempohome developments in the city, which utilize adapted shipping containers to create multiple small units, each with its own kitchen and bathroom and housing up to four adults (Tempohomes FAQ 2019). Tempelhof's 1,000-person capacity, in comparison to a standard of 256 elsewhere, made it the city's largest Tempohome development. Other shelter typologies include stacked shipping containers called 'container villages', new-build dormitories termed *Modulare Unterkünfte für Flüchtlinge* (MUF-modular accommodation for refugees), as well as adapted buildings such as old people's homes and medical clinics. It is important to consider all these shelters as a single spatial phenomenon that manifested simultaneously. Nevertheless, everyday life in one structure can greatly differ from another, and even within these categories experiences can be diverse, depending on local geographical, social and political contexts. Consequently, the specificities of these sites must accompany the identification of general trends.

Tempelhof's community shelter was plagued by problems apparent in all Tempohomes. The arguably rushed decision to use particular sites was made during the height of uncertainty in 2016 and, rather than renting the containers, the municipal government opted to purchase them, which fully committed it to the plans rather than giving flexibility to reconsider and adapt to changing circumstances. The quality of construction and materials was incredibly low in order to save costs, yet the need for constant repairs and replacements negated any savings. Like other shelters, Tempelhof opened six months late in order to rectify these issues, wasting more time and money. Once opened, the low quality of ventilation and insulation was particularly problematic, and in winter the containers were exceptionally cold. To compensate, residents turned the radiators to their maximum setting, which subsequently broke as they were the cheapest models. Moreover, in the summer of 2018, the extreme European heatwave created unbearable conditions of over 40°C in the very same shelters, forcing residents to leave them during the day (Fritzsche 2018).

Aside from these technical issues, the most problematic characteristic Tempelhof shared with other community shelters around the city was the façade of better living conditions that failed to overcome the exceptional and exclusory realities of life in a camp. As one resident who had lived in the hangars for two years before being moved to the Tempohomes explained to me: 'It doesn't matter that this [the *Gemeinschaftsunterkunft*] is better than the other one [the *Notunterkunft*]. It is a camp, not a home. You have security and you cannot have guests after 10 pm. A camp is a camp'. Supposed improvements became somewhat cosmetic, as many residents were acutely aware that their living situation continued to exist outside the paradigm of conventional urban dwelling. Institutionalized shelters tend towards an ideal, but can never reach it, as the shadow of the camp continues to loom over them. The exclusion they create only becomes increasingly obscured rather than eradicated.

Outside of these factors, many of Tempelhof's pertinent issues were specific to its unique context. The containers were exceptionally exposed to both rain and wind in the open space of the airfield. Seemingly neverending vistas into the park, formed through the orthogonal grid layout, created the impression of a stranded and regimented space. The boulevards between containers were unconventionally wide and the paving was undifferentiated, in contrast to other Tempohomes in the city, which had newly paved and more intimate passageways to create a more domestic streetscape. Despite their broadness, the passages at Tempelhof were nevertheless too narrow for dustbin lorries to proceed down in order to collect refuse from the vast site: the large collection bins therefore had to be loudly trundled to the main gateway on a regular basis. The street's design satisfied neither the residents nor practical considerations; instead, weeds grew through the cracks of the original 1940s paving. In winter or when wet, the stones became dangerously icy and slippery, while in summer they became unbearably hot. Unlike the hangars, which had a buffer zone between themselves and the park space, the containers sat pushed up against the edge of the park behind a large fence. While proximity and visibility can be positive forces, in this context they hinted at a certain voyeurism, as the public could peer into the caged village of containers for refugees.

Tempelhof's protection as a historic monument defined the architecture of this community shelter as it did the emergency shelter before it. Crucially, the paving stones could not be dug up, so all infrastructure had to be placed above ground, rendering it more clearly visible. This made the *Gemeinschaftsunterkunft* a form of floating shelter, where the physical architecture was literally uprooted and suspended in space, reflecting the legal condition of the population who lived there. Subsequently, the infrastructure came to define the site's aesthetics: water piping traced and emphasized the street's vistas into the horizon. It aptly framed the shelter's entrance, acting as an industrial gateway. In addition, sewage and electric lines ran along ground level, covered by wooden boards and steps, around which people of reduced mobility found it difficult and inconvenient to circulate. The usually concealed mechanics of buildings were always plainly clear both above head height and on the ground, reminding any resident that they lived in an exceptionally unconventional dwelling.

In many ways, the *Gemeinschaftsunterkunft* at Tempelhof was a unique shelter, which faced unconventional issues. Certain spatial characteristics were not evident in most Tempohomes, yet the fame of Tempelhof continued to attract the majority of international attention. Overall, the community shelters did not have anywhere near the same public interest as the emergency shelters that preceded them. Nevertheless, Tempelhof still acted as an urban spectacle for the city in the emerging era of providing long-term shelter. Its prominent location in the park made it the most visible and present in the everyday lives of Berliners – far more than the emergency shelter that had stood at the same site. The authorities have increasingly realized the importance of the public image of these spaces, and learned many lessons after the initial media reaction to emergency shelters, where sensationalist media explorations created impressions that came to define the camp long after the emphasized issues were rectified. A media ban by the Berlin government allowed the problems of Tempelhof's community shelter to be addressed before the first public representations of the site could be formed. On the one hand, there was always a problematic desire to control the public image of these shelters, but on the other hand, it arguably cleared space for more considered representations and dialogues to emerge.

The most problematic aspect of Tempelhof's fame was not in creating misrepresentative impressions of the community shelters during its presence, but the more profound misrepresentations that will occur in its absence. Tempelhof was unique in that it was the only community shelter that had a definitive closure date. All structures had to be removed by December 2019. This was to abide by the historic monument protection legislation. By July 2019, all residents had been moved out, leaving an eerily empty ghost shelter. In comparison, all others opened for indefinite periods of time. Tempelhof's abandonment and subsequent deconstruction, like its construction, was a very public and visible disappearance, yet this may make it a false symbol to the city, and even the world, that the refugee accommodation situation in Berlin has been 'solved'. In reality, the housing issues refugees face will just become concealed as they are located elsewhere in less visible and more banal sites. Long-term shelters are in danger of concentrating those who are not deemed to have the social capital, such as the personality or employable skills, to fit into the contemporary neoliberal European city.

Conclusion

From the naissance of German flight and the Nazis to the Cold War and now reunified Berlin, the story of Tempelhof encapsulates over a century of urban and global history in a single site. The emergency and community shelters demonstrated Tempelhof's continued importance as a poignant and relevant urban space that is deeply entwined with geopolitical developments. To examine this development is to reveal the evolution of refugee accommodation from which a spectrum of camp-like structures emerged throughout Europe since 2015 (Kreichauf 2018). The switch to longer-term shelter was always a critical stage of a transition that is equally as important, if not more so, than the emergence of the initial emergency shelters. It is arguably the enduring actions of a society and government that best reflect their politics and ethics, and the structures and conditions in which refugees are expected to live in the long term are important indicators of these qualities. However, there has been a worrying lack of continued engagement with these shelters: the so-called 'crisis' is deemed to be over, yet the impacts of arrivals continue in protracted forms and take a spatial arrangement in long-term shelters. While the *Gemeinschaftsunterkünfte* may offer better conditions, the injustices they inflict only become increasingly concealed. Improvements will inevitably reach an impasse, as refugees still cannot reach the next step of proper urban dwelling in the sense of non-institutional accommodation. Instead, a significant population may remain stuck within ambiguous spaces that are neither fully a camp nor fully part of the city.

Exploring the evolution and meanings of Berlin's shelters helps us to understand the continued processes of accommodation in an emergency and its afterlives. As Matthias Nowak of Tamaja in Tempelhof suggested to me: 'The process of integration is a marathon not a sprint. The first year was only the first 50 metres, and now we are perhaps a few hundred metres in; there are still many kilometres to go, and this is where the real work needs to be done.' During this process, analyses must cut across all forms of accommodation and, in many ways, Tempelhof's shelters are misleading representations of other shelters around the city. However, they might be reframed to enable their absurd existences to attract attention to the injustices of the broader situation that all the city's new shelters embody. If Tempelhof's shelters are to act as symbols, they should be ones that reflect the reality: icons for the inflexibility, unpreparedness and exclusory housing systems of the contemporary European neoliberal city, whose urban structures are incapable, and perhaps even unwilling, to practically enact the ideals of European liberal democracy.

Toby Parsloe is a Ph.D. candidate in Architecture at the University of Cambridge, based in the Centre for Urban Conflicts Research and Pembroke College. His research investigates the long-term institutionalized shelter for refugees in Berlin that has developed since the so-called 2015 'European refugee crisis'.

References

Copley, C. 2017. 'Curating Tempelhof: Negotiating the Multiple Histories of Berlin's "Symbol of Freedom"'. *Urban History* 44: 698–717.

Fahey, C., 2015. 'How Berliners Refused to Give Tempelhof Airport over to Developers'. *The Guardian*, 5 March. Retrieved 23 October 2019 from http://www.theguardian.com/cities/2015/mar/05/how-berliners-refused-to-give-temp elhof-airport-over-to-developers.

Fritzsche, M., 2018. 'Geflüchtete in Berlin: Tempohomes heizen sich in der Sonne extrem auf'. *Der Tagesspiegel Online*, 13 August. Retrieved 23 October 2019 from https://www.tagesspiegel.de/berlin/gefluechtete-in-berlin-tempohomes-heizen-sich-in-der-sonne-extrem-auf/22899384.html.

Hall, M., 2015. 'Brawls in Food Queues and Migrants' Pleas to Be Segregated by Nationality: Inside Berlin's Tempelhof Airport Where Refugees Say Arabic Speaking Guards Stir Racial Tension and Start Fights'. *Mail Online*, 7 December. Retrieved 23 October 2019 from http://www.dailymail.co.uk/news/article-3346277/Brawls-food-queues-migrants-pleas-segregated-nationality-Inside-Berl in-s-Tempelhof-Airport-refugees-say-Arabic-speaking-guards-stir-racial-tension -start-fights.html.

Katz, B., L. Noring and N. Garrelts. 2016. *Cities and Refugees: The German Experience*. Washington DC: Brookings.

Katz, I., T. Parsloe, Z. Poll and A. Scafe-Smith. 2018. 'The Bubble, the Airport, and the Jungle: Europe's Urban Migrant Camps', in I. Katz, D. Martin and C. Minca (eds), *Camps Revisited: Multifaceted Spatialities of a Modern Political Technology*. London: Rowman & Littlefeld, pp. 61–82.

Knight, B. 2018. 'Violence in Chemnitz as Leftist and Far-Right Protesters Clash'. *Deutsche Welle*, 27 August. Retrieved 23 October 2019 from https://www.dw.com/en/violence-in-chemnitz-as-leftist-and-far-right-protesters-clash/a-45250620.

Kreichauf, R. 2018. 'From Forced Migration to Forced Arrival: The Campization of Refugee Accommodation in European Cities'. *Comparative Migration Studies* 6(7): 1–22.

Lees, C. 2018. 'The "Alternative for Germany": The Rise of Right-Wing Populism at the Heart of Europe'. *Politics* 38: 295–310.

Parsloe, T. 2017. 'Appropriating Buildings to House Refugees: Berlin Tempelhof'. *Forced Migration Review* 55: 35–36.

PricewaterhouseCoopers. 2018. *Emerging Trends in Real Estate®: Europe 2018.* London: PwC.
Smale, A. 2016. 'Tempelhof Airport, Once a Lifeline for Berliners, Reprises Role for Refugees'. *New York Times*, 10 February. Retrieved 23 October 2019 from http://www.nytimes.com/2016/02/11/world/europe/tempelhof-airport-once-a-lifeline-for-berliners-reprises-role-for-refugees.html.
Tempohomes FAQ. 2019. 'LAF'. Retrieved 23 October 2019 from https://www.berlin.de/laf/wohnen/allgemeine-informationen/tempohomes-faq.
Tönnies, F. 1988. *Community and Society.* New Brunswick, NJ: Transaction.
Weber, M., 2013. *Economy and Society.* Berkeley: University of California Press.
Wimalasena, J. 2016. 'Neukölln: Flüchtlinge protestieren gegen Verlegung nach Tempelhof'. *Berliner Zeitung*, 11 July. Retrieved 23 October 2019 from http://www.berliner-zeitung.de/berlin/neukoelln-fluechtlinge-protestieren-gegen-verlegung-nach-tempelhof-24379114.

Conclusion

Towards Better Shelter: Rethinking Humanitarian Sheltering

Mark E. Breeze

The diverse range of structures elucidated in this collection illustrate the complexities of humanitarian shelter and its symbiotic relationship with nonphysical structures of protection. Regardless of the broad variety of contexts, it is striking how consistently inadequate these physical structures are in terms of even providing basic shelter from the elements, let alone enabling life to thrive. One can be forgiven for thinking that there is no specialist profession with experience and expertise in the design, construction and effective implementation of shelter, and no professional individuals who undergo lengthy practical, theoretical and in-the-field experience to be licensed to practice in such an area. As an architect, I will analyse the institutional humanitarian approach to shelter and in so doing will offer a different strategy that rethinks the humanitarian shelter process. I will analyse key humanitarian documents and representative shelter approaches. I will argue that the institutional humanitarian approach is characterized by a reductive, rationalist, spreadsheet-mentality and that there needs to be more architectural engagement in the shelter sector.

Humanitarian Shelter Guidance

The recent Humanitarian Emergency Response Review conducted by the U.K. government acknowledged that 'providing shelter is one of the most intractable problems in international humanitarian response' (Ashdown 2011: 25). Huge resources and expertise are channelled into the provision and maintenance of humanitarian shelter, from the various United Nations (UN) agencies to numerous nongovernmental organizations (NGOs) across the world; indeed, the range of shelter solutions is remarkable – from the emergency, the transitional and the permanent – as the numerous Global Shelter Cluster reports make clear.[1] Given the importance of shelter as part of the humanitarian response, it does not seem entirely unreasonable that humanitarian shelter guidance would extensively engage with architectural approaches and architects. However, there is a striking absence of explicit architectural engagement in the key humanitarian shelter guidelines, even if measured by the almost facile metric of the use of the words 'architecture', 'architectural' and 'architect' in the institutional reference publications.

In the 403 pages of the current edition of the *Sphere Handbook* (2018), for example, the word 'architecture' is only ever used to refer to the nonbuilding systems of health and legal protection. The word 'architect' appears only once and then it is to advocate for specialist professionals being hired for specific tasks. The word 'architectural' is never used. Meanwhile, in the 351 pages of the current version of the globally used field manual *Shelter after Disaster* (2010),[2] the word 'architecture' is used twice: once to recommend studying vernacular architecture to minimize environmental impact and once generically as part of evaluating 'housing standard' qualities. The word 'architect' is also used twice: once in the context of being one of many experts who could help with building damage assessment and once in passing as being involved in the response to the Nicaraguan earthquake. The word 'architectural' is used only once, to mention that 'overall architectural quality' is affected by a house's form, size, materials, and nearby historical and vernacular elements, without further elaboration. Nevertheless, this is one more mention of the word 'architectural' than in the current edition of the consensus publication *Transitional Shelter Guidelines* (2012), where there is no single use of the word; these *Guidelines* make one mention of the word 'architect' – as a professional stakeholder to be considered when ensuring the private sector understands the process of transitional shelter. And there is only a single mention of 'architecture' in the whole text: 'designs should be made involving the community but must be approved by either a local or external professional qualified in architecture, structural, or civil engineering' (Kelly 2012: 180). Assuming the punctuation is deliberate, the clear implication is that the professional required for shelter is a *type* of engineer, at best an engineer of architecture (not an architect), and even then it is in the role of verifying and applying standards (rather than as an engaged creative professional developing and realizing an agreed appropriate solution). The terms 'architecture', 'architect' and 'architectural' do not make a single appearance in any one of the indexes of these key reference texts for humanitarian shelter.

Therefore, these guidelines offer little guidance to the humanitarian sector regarding what 'architecture' is, how it can be understood or how it might be at all relevant, other than making it clear that studying vernacular architecture might help minimize environmental impacts (there are apparently no other possible benefits). They are also of little help in defining what 'architectural' means or how that might be relevant. There is no real role defined for 'architects' either, other than stating that they are professionals (seemingly only of the private sector) suited to specific tasks, who can be used to verify and apply standards if an engineer is not more readily available. As *The Sphere Handbook* makes clear through its silence, quality is improved and accountability is enhanced without architecture or architects. The multiple years of training and field experience at all stages of design and construction that the licensed architect undergoes is seemingly not relevant to providing humanitarian shelter.

Architectural Involvement

However, architecturally trained individuals have not been totally absent in the institutional humanitarian approach to shelter, despite this seeming lack of explicit discussion of 'architects', 'architecture' and anything 'architectural'. Indeed, they have been remarkably influential in some respects, as shown by the work of Professor Ian Davis. His fundamental approach to the relationship between architecture and shelter builds on his doctoral work on emergency shelter and postdisaster reconstruction, the related and influential 1978 book *Shelter after Disaster*, and then years of experience as a one-time architectural designer, author, academic, NGO director and international development consultant.[3] Through his collaborations with the consultant Fred Cuny, Davis honed his approach into five key principles, which he summarized as follows: (1) use local material and labour whenever possible; (2) avoid duplication of survivors' efforts; (3) look at the wider issues of recovery (e.g. social, psychological and economic); (4) focus on small-scale projects (to reduce corruption); and (5) support demand-driven (not supply-driven) products and services (Davis 2011). Many of his ideas are evident in various UN and NGO shelter policy/guidelines such as those discussed above, as the acknowledgements in such publications make explicit; indeed, it is no coincidence that the seminal United Nations

Disaster Relief Organization (UNDRO) publication *Shelter after Disaster: Guidelines for Assistance* (1982) uses the title of Davis's 1978 book.

Importantly, neither Davis, nor the UNDRO guidelines, nor even the concurrent United Nations High Commissioner for Refugees (UNHCR) *Handbook for Emergencies* (1982) argue for a distinct or explicit role for architects in the shelter process;[4] their skills as a creative professional working collaboratively within limits to develop and realize an effective and meaningful shelter seemingly has no role in this system. Rather, humanitarians of specifically unspecified background (although the inference is that an engineering background is best) are often tasked as an observer and facilitator for responses that are as locally driven as possible, in terms of materials, labour and vernacular design. The role of the humanitarian in the provision of shelter – even one who is trained architecturally – is essentially laid out as an engaged observer and development facilitator, who becomes the arbiter of *technical* standards at best.

Engineering Management

This institutional technomanagerial development drive can perhaps be better understood through the ethnographic case-study approach and engaged field experience of Davis's long-time colleague and collaborator at UNDRO and the UNHCR, the American management consultant and engineer Fred Cuny (see Cuny 1977; Cuny and Adams 1983). After two years of international relief work (notably in the Biafra Civil War), he founded his consulting company 'Intertect Relief and Reconstruction Corporation' (often just referred to as 'Intertect') in 1971. This reduction of the word 'architect' through amalgamation with 'international' to create 'Intertect' was more than symbolic: there is little mention of an 'architect' in his work, but rather an international professional engaged especially with disaster response, who brings economically engaged *technical* solutions and training, and empowers the survivors (Cuny and Adams 1983).

Cuny's engineering mentality is further evident not only in his support for camps and his technically efficacious planning of them, but also in his strong advocacy for adaptable technical standards as enabling effective local responses (Cuny 1977; Cuny and Adams 1983). Revealingly, Cuny had trained as a civil engineer, specializing in urban planning. The formative role of Davis and Cuny in UNDRO and the UNHCR enabled Intertect's technical settlement guidelines to become standardized through the institutional guidance that was only ever really updated rather than comprehensively revised: a technomanagerial development approach to shelter as settlements (primarily at the scale of planning) thus became institutionally embedded.

Technical Performance

The institutional nature and mandate of the UNHCR shifted in the 1990s from one primarily of legal protection to one focused as much on physical forms of protection and the delivery of humanitarian assistance. As a large administrative institution operating globally, there is clearly a considerable tension involved in providing effective shelter that is quickly deployed as well as locally driven, locally relevant and yet meets-agreed minimum standards.

The UNHCR acknowledged the failings and immense challenges of their work as they searched urgently for improvements in response to refugee shelter needs in their 'First International Workshop on Improved Shelter Response and Environment for Refugees' in the summer of 1993 (see UNHCR 1993: 14–17). Strikingly, Douglas Stafford, the Deputy High Commissioner for Refugees at the UNHCR, described it as a unique event that had brought together the UNHCR, NGOs, donors, manufacturers and researchers to discuss ways of improving refugee shelter (UNHCR 1993: 9). Note the absence of any mention of architects in any form. Wolfgang Neumann, the Senior Physical Planner and Architect in the UNHCR Programme and Technical Support Section, and also the initiator of the Workshop, opened the proceedings by emphasizing the importance of *technical performance* considerations for shelter (UNHCR, 1993: 9); it is revealing that technical performance was the primary concern of the first professional architect employed by the UNHCR at the institution's first workshop focused on shelter.

Neumann proposed two eminently sensible workshop objectives: an improved shelter strategy for the preparedness and delivery of shelter, and the formation of a network of collaborators including the UNHCR, NGOs, academic institutions and manufacturers (UNHCR 1993: 9). The workshop made eighteen recommendations – a swathe of further actions, forms of coordination and capacity-building activities – most of which were to be enabled and led by two newly created entities: a Shelter Task Force and an International Shelter Network. Together, these would enable a 'comprehensive shelter strategy with appropriately developed standards, supply methods, specifications and production capabilities related to local needs and circumstances' (UNHCR 1993: 2). There is no specific mention of architects or any unique contribution they can make, only vague references to general 'professional' capacities and expertise. The solution to better shelter provision seemingly lay in better administration and management structures rather than better design or deeper engagement with design professionals. The workshop was initiated by an architect. There was no 'second' workshop.

Better Shelter

In 2015, following over five years of development, and with the collaboration and funding of the UNHCR and the IKEA Foundation, the branded 'Better Shelter' Refugee Housing Unit (BSRHU) went into mass production. This flatpack, 17.5 square metre, 144 kg, postemergency modular shelter was developed according to Sphere standards. Designed to accommodate up to five people within its steel-framed structure, the shelter includes four 'windows', a lockable door, ventilation openings and a small solar panel to power the included built-in lamp and mobile phone charger. It is delivered flatpacked in two 80 kg boxes, which include all the necessary tools for assembly, and in optimal conditions it can be assembled manually by four people in under six hours. The BSRHU is marketed as a solution to large-scale displacement in situations where only temporary structures are permitted and locally sourced solutions are not available (see Better Shelter RHU AB, 2018). It currently costs U.S.$1,250 and has been designed to last for three years. As a shelter developed with, endorsed by, partially funded by and used by the UNHCR, it does not seem wholly unreasonable to understand the BSRHU as a model example of the institutional humanitarian approach to the architecture of shelter.

The BSRHU certainly has many benefits and as a logistical and technical product, it fulfils a wide range of criteria: it meets the Sphere minimum standards; it is easily shippable anywhere given the international pallet-sized dimensions of its two boxes; it is notionally transportable by hand to remote sites, given the weight and size of each of the two boxes; it does not require technical skills to assemble; it has translucent panels and a lockable door, thereby giving some privacy and security; although costing twice as much as an emergency family tent, the amortized cost should be less given its at least three year lifespan; and it has thoughtful extra benefits like the solar-powered lamp and phone charger. Indeed, its 'house-like' shape makes it feel like a simple housing structure. It was collectively designed by engineers and industrial designers, without any competitive process, so there has seemingly been no role for a specialist in housing and building design – no role for an architect. Even if its plastic composite panels are not recyclable, it is almost the model fulfilment of the technical criteria and the broader institutional technomanagerial performance approach elucidated above.

An Implicitly Imperfect Shelter

No shelter will be perfect for every geography, climate and sheltering situation, so the idea of a universal shelter is implicitly compromised. Similarly, the requirement to make a shelter that will sell at around U.S.$1,000 imposes tight constraints on what it can be and do. The manufacturers of the BSRHU are quite clear on the limits of the shelter, including how and when it is to be used (Terne 2017). And yet, despite these limits, the BSRHU had the luxury of multiyear funding and an extended period for development, with significant, relevant institutional backing (through the Ikea Foundation and the UNHCR), which was all provided in a noncompetitive environment (Karlsson 2017). Surprisingly for such a significant international and public commission, there was not even an open competition for the initial commission. These optimal institutional development circumstances make the BSRHU the epitome of the institutional approach to shelter. As such, it is a case study for understanding the implications for the current nonarchitectural method.

The technologistical performance approach of the BSRHU has created a product with many architectural oversights that negatively affect its ability to provide effective shelter: the 'floor' provided is a tarpaulin sheet, which provides no insulation (a great deal of heat is lost through the ground), minimal protection from the ground surface (and creatures that burrow through the ground), and as a large sheet of plastic it has a considerable resale value (so is often sold). The 'wall' and 'roof' panels do not tightly join at the corners and ground, creating gaps for insects and small creatures, as well as allowing dust and hot/cold air penetration. Furthermore, the thin panels are so minimally insulating in themselves that the shelter can become incredibly hot in warmer climates and extremely cold in cooler climates; heavy rain becomes deafening inside. The structure of galvanized steel tubes has considerable financial value (especially in emergency situations) and these also make sturdy weapons. The 'windows' are small, loosely fitting, opaque, sliding plastic panels behind a mosquito mesh, so to let light in also lets in outside air and sounds. It has a lockable door, but it is only lockable from the outside (so you can be locked in), and its position on the short side means that when it is opened it reveals the whole living space (thereby eviscerating any privacy, as well as letting in the outside air). There are over 100 parts, so even though a few spares are provided, assembly is impossible if there are too many losses/breakages (thereby doubling the cost of the unit in effect) and replacements are not easy to come by. This is to say nothing of the problematic environmental impact of 160 kg of plastic and metal being transported around the world.[5] It is ultimately a lightweight structure, so despite the basic anchoring provided (which in itself assumes suitable ground conditions), it cannot withstand winds over 60 mph assuming all else is optimal (Better Shelter RHU AB 2018). Furthermore, it is not disabled-accessible. And all of this is to say nothing of the fact that it is essentially an empty room, providing no other services (cooking or sanitation) or adaptability to such, over its intended three-year lifespan.

The above problems are significant issues that consequentially compromise daily human liveability, protection from the elements, and ultimately the ability to survive and start rebuilding a life, in a shelter that is supposed to be used for up to three years. The BSRHU reveals the problems of envisaging shelter as a product. It is yet another standardized package on which the humanitarian relief system has become dependent.[6] Moreover, the underlying technical engineering approach reveals a belief in a singular solution, a commitment to the idea that there can be an *optimal* (or at least 'better') solution that is an *object*.

The Problems with Architects

It is a meaningless and naïve counterfactual to claim that the involvement of architects would have necessarily solved the enumerated problems of the BSRHU; the problem and object-based approach is more complex than that. But it does raise the question why more architects – those trained specifically over a long period as licensed specialists in shelter – are not involved in specific humanitarian shelter solutions more generally. It is not for any lack of interest on the part of architects, as the architect and humanitarian Ian Davis noted several decades ago (Davis 1977: 24).

There are many reasons for not using an architect for humanitarian shelter, especially in urgent situations (Breeze 2017). There are, for example, complexities of defining the 'client': the key figure or entity that defines the aims and limits of the project. There are issues about who is demarcated as an 'architect' in a transnational situation, given nation states variously define the qualifying criteria for themselves. It is difficult to ensure that the social, economic, political, historical, geographical, environmental, legal, planning and built context is sufficiently understood to make any engagement appropriate and effective, as well as how experienced design, construction/manufacturing and related services can be quickly, reliably and fairly procured, especially in a range of locations where professional structures and standards are not so clearly defined. Moreover, it is very important that local social, political and cultural sensitivities are addressed or taken account of to ensure that the shelter solution does not alienate and disrupt existing communities. Architects also face challenges relating to the logistics of using appropriate materials that can be easily, quickly and sustainably sourced and delivered on time to often hard-to-access locations, as well as to the extremely tight constraints of time and money in its execution. All these issues severely limit the ability of an architect to integrate a diverse range of inputs, working collaboratively and iteratively to develop a meaningful, engaged and relevant shelter, especially in an urgent situation. Therefore, it is easy to understand why the institutional humanitarian shelter approach is one of top-down technical criteria with the abstract encouragement of 'local' solutions.

Architects (or at least architecturally trained people) have been involved in humanitarian shelter as institutional administrators (e.g. Wolfgang Neumann at the UNHCR) and development practitioners (e.g. Ian Davis), as I have elucidated above. Even within this position of relative influence and control, they were not explicitly advocating for a bigger role for architects per se, or indeed a more iterative building design-centric approach to shelter, perhaps realizing the limits of using professional architects in their traditional capacities. As discussed above, they have helped make humanitarian shelter policy increasingly focused on disaster response and locally driven solutions, within a framework of agreed international minimum standards. Given the complexities of coordinating and executing these standards on a global scale within tight timelines and budgets, the technomanagerial approach has understandably predominated. The question of why anything more might be needed goes to the heart of thinking architecture and the very nature of shelter itself.

Defining Success Successfully

The predominating technologistical performance approach to shelter relies on measurable metrics (e.g. space standards and logistical criteria); 'success' in this system is something that can be rationally measured, so it can be directly compared and subsequently optimized, as part of a global 'just-in-time' capitalist system of production. Such a system requires repeatable methods with repeatable solutions to be efficiently scalable. The result is shelters engineered to meet technical performance criteria, executed within a managerial administrative framework. Risk is thereby reduced and accountability to donors is made simple. The notion of shelter is reduced to a two-dimensional series of managerial spreadsheets and technical data points. Significantly, this metric of success is a self-created one for measuring a current approach; as Maynard (2017) makes clear, there still remains a lack of evidence for effective shelter interventions.

The practice of architecture implicitly involves engaging with this technologistical approach, but within locally specific temporal and geographical terms: architects develop effective design solutions by working to tightly defined constraints and budgets within administrative and managerial frameworks to meet agreed technical performance criteria. However, architecture uniquely involves working within these criteria three-dimensionally to take account of, engage with, and create the much more subjective and less directly measurable social, political, environmental and cultural contexts over time. These geographically local criteria affect the expected temporality of any shelter. More significantly, such local criteria involve creative development, which requires time to develop and realize. Nevertheless, the result should very likely be more contextually relevant and effective shelter that works for the specific people in need, in those specific climactic and geographical conditions, to help them rebuild *their* political, cultural, social and economic lives in an environmentally aware way, and that is relevant for *them* and the timescales of that *particular* humanitarian situation.

Institutionally embedded humanitarian architects (such as Ian Davis and Wolfgang Neumann) sought to reconcile these challenges by prioritizing locally driven solutions within an institutional humanitarian system of technical performance metrics (see Davis 1978; UNCHR 1993). This approach avoided having to meaningfully engage with these local complexities or indeed measure these less tangible criteria. This deference to locally driven solutions assumes that such local parties exist and are sufficiently organized, vocal and representative to speak with a clear and coherent voice about such specific spatial, cultural, economic, social and political needs with critical awareness and insight for the situation at hand, and promptly.

Both Davis and Neumann propose that local lessons can be learned and such experience accumulated over time within these institutional frameworks to help with such interventions. It is striking that over forty years after his early engagement with humanitarian shelter, Davis still pushes for more evidence and more information as the solution (Global Shelter Cluster 2018: 9–14). Davis and Neumann want it both ways: locally driven solutions informed by nonlocal lessons. The nuances and varieties of shelter challenges are so multifarious that the meaningful applicability of such lessons and experience is problematic, not to mention the challenges of how or through whom they would be realistically implemented.

The variety and unique situations of the few shelters discussed in this volume hint at the complexity of such a challenge: given the immense complexities of 'life' that shelter is tasked to protect and enable, the possibility of defining 'success' meaningfully in any singular way is highly questionable.

Informed and evidence-based decision-making is no doubt important in the institutional humanitarian approach to shelter, but relying on it alone is simplistic, given the constantly shifting social, cultural, political, resource, environmental, temporal and economical complexities. As a result, shelter can never be a repeatable rational solution. If a definition of 'success' is appropriate or even possible in this context, it must be less prescriptive, one that is open to failing universal criteria on a spreadsheet in order to prioritize what is needed most in that specific context at that specific time in order to enable life to survive and thrive.

Sheltering without Shelter Solutions

Making shelter that is more temporally and geographically relevant, and hence more socially, culturally, politically, environmentally and economically engaged, requires hybridizing current approaches to humanitarian shelter. I am in no way arguing for traditional modes of architectural practice to be copy-pasted into the humanitarian shelter sector; nor am I arguing for humanitarian shelter to necessarily become more permanent in any way. Indeed, architecture does not just involve buildings, or even building new objects; it is a *process* of transforming spaces and environments to work more effectively for its users and contexts. A more architectural approach to shelter*ing* needs to be layered into humanitarian responses to ensure that humanitarian shelter better protects life and enables livelihoods to be rebuilt on relevant timescales in a contextually productive way.

To become a licensed architect usually requires around seven years of education and practice-based experience in most jurisdictions (see Association of Collegiate Schools of Architecture 2013).[7] This professional training and licensure verifies that that individual knows how to execute a project ethically and effectively, and that they can collaboratively realize solutions involving all the relevant stakeholders and affected participants from the beginning of the project to its final completion. As an intellectual and physical undertaking, based on a combination of theory and practice, the architectural act engages with the structures of social, economic, legal and political protection. The architectural approach is one of integrated thinking, working within the limits of site, context, budget, resources and much more to realize a comprehensive structure of protection from more than just the elements, that engages with its context beyond its physical boundaries. These are not skills or approaches that can be substituted by data points on a spreadsheet.

In 1977, Ian Davis tentatively proposed six key criteria[8] for a valid approach to humanitarian shelter, with eight related policy recommendations,[9] all of which are eminently sensible and as appropriate now as they were then (Davis 1977: 36–37). However, his conclusion was for an international strategy, with (yet again) a total belief in more knowledge (see Davis 1977, 1978): if only there was more data, a solution could be found.

Sheltering is a creative act, an approach for protecting and enabling irrational humans in highly specific ways, in unique geographies, with very individual needs. Humanitarian sheltering is only different in that it operates on different temporalities for people in much more precarious circumstances and that requires more creativity and professional knowledge, not less.

A different approach is needed. This approach is not about wholesale disregard for the existing humanitarian system. Nor is it about imposing traditional modes of architectural practice; the challenges are too great for that, as elucidated above. And this is not about imposing any form or system, as is often currently the case, with often severely damaging effects, as this volume has shown; it is about *strategically* engaging the skills and experiences of architects to create a more specific and nuanced approached. In this way, architecture can become a meaningful part of the aid and development process, empowering people locally to make and remake spaces into their own sustainable places.

Engaging architects tactically will no doubt add costs at certain stages of the sheltering process. However, by taking a more macro-approach to the aim and funding of shelter, there is no reason why this different approach should cost more in the bigger picture. Sheltering is a process that needs to be conceived in the whole – from beginning to end: the emergence of the initial sheltering needs, to their resolution in sustainable longer-term solutions where life can thrive and be protected by locally specific structures. By conceiving of sheltering conceptually and financially in this bigger picture, there is no reason why engaging with architects should add any costs; if anything, the social, cultural, political and economic benefits of the integrated, sustainable, architectural solutions should reduce longer-term costs.

Ultimately, this is about making the architecture of humanitarian sheltering more inclusive and effective for those who need structures of protection. By reducing the obsession with measuring and imposing technologistical performance-based criteria, trust and belief in those needing sheltering can be restored. To do this effectively and meaningfully, local and non-local experienced shelter specialists – architects – need to be embedded and empowered to operate collaboratively, freely and adaptively to local situations, to enable those needing sheltering to build their own futures, and to enable life and livelihoods to survive and thrive. In this way, the sheltering process can go beyond tokenistic participatory structures of protection and it can help us to rethink the nature of architecture and the very act of architecting itself.

Mark E. Breeze is a Harvard-trained architect and the Director of Studies in Architecture at St John's College, University of Cambridge. He recently completed his postdoctorate at the University of Oxford Refugee Studies Centre. His work explores the theories and forms of human shelter.

Notes

1. The Global Shelter Cluster annual reports are available at https://www.shelter cluster.org/working-group/shelter-projects-working-group/documents (retrieved 24 October 2019).

2. These guidelines are the revision of the key publication *Shelter after Disaster: Guidelines for Assistance*, published in 1982 by the office of the United Nations Disaster Relief Coordinators (now United Nations/Office for the Coordination of Humanitarian Affairs)
3. His Ph.D. was supervised by Otto Koenigsberger – a trained architect, one-time UN Technical Program Advisor, and the first Director of Housing in India – who started the Architectural Association's Department of Tropical Studies, which later became the Development Planning Unit at UCL. Before becoming a professor at the UCL Institute for Risk and Disaster Reduction, Davis practised as an architect in the office of Minuro Yamasaki (leaving on the day that the office won the competition for the World Trade Center in New York), worked peripatetically at the small 'Tearfund' charity, consulted widely as a development practitioner and for many years lectured in the Department of Architecture at Oxford Polytechnic (later renamed Oxford Brookes University), where he established the Disasters and Settlement Unit, which developed into the Centre for Development and Emergency Practice (CENDEP).
4. Note that Davis ran the UNHCR Emergency Management Training Program in 1982
5. The net weight of the BSRHU is 144 kg (as noted above) and the gross weight with all packaging is 160 kg.
6. See Scott-Smith (2013) on the broader fetishism of humanitarian objects.
7. Many jurisdictions have limited or no architectural education infrastructure or professional accreditation system. My point here is to elucidate what a formal and rigorous architectural training and licensing process aims to do, and the vital relevance of these skills and experiences to the humanitarian sheltering process. Unfortunately, it is beyond the scope of this chapter to discuss how jurisdictions could effectively build and strengthen more local, accessible, professional architectural capacity through education infrastructures and accreditation systems.
8. These were: (1) utilize local resources; (2) avoid the implementation of novel solutions; (3) encourage labour-intensive solutions; (4) recognize the need for shelter provision in different areas to vary according to local cultural patterns, local materials and the local climate; (5) recognize that it is better to sell or rent than to give; and (6) recognize that emergency shelter must be rapidly available.
9. These were: (1) an awareness of the range of factors; (2) the need for reliable objective data; (3) education of the public; (4) donor or indigenous shelters?; (5) application of Western skills; (6) identifying roles; (7) land tenure; and (8) strategies with clear delineation of responsibilities.

References

Association of Collegiate Schools of Architecture. 2013. 'How Long Does it Take?' Retrieved 24 October 2019 from https://www.acsa-arch.org/resources/data-resources/how-long.

Ashdown, P. (ed.). 2011. *Humanitarian Emergency Response Review*. London: DfID. Retrieved 24 October 2019 from https://webarchive.nationalarchives.gov.uk/+tf_/http://www.dfid.gov.uk/emergency-response-review.

Better Shelter RHU AB. 2018. *Better Shelter 1.2: Product Information.* Hägerstern: Better Shelter.org. Retrieved 24 October 2019 from https://bettershelter.org/wp-content/uploads/2018/09/Better-Shelter-Product-Information-1.2-ENG.pdf.
Breeze, M. 2017. 'Building for a New Life'. *Four Thought.* BBC Radio 4. 1 February.
Cuny, F.C. 1977. 'Refugee Camps and Camp Planning: The State of the Art'. *Disasters* 1(2): 125–43.
Cuny, F.C., and S. Adams (eds). 1983. *Disasters and Development.* New York: Oxford University Press.
Davis, I.R. 1977. 'Emergency Shelter'. *Disasters* 1(1): 23–39.
——. 1978. *Shelter after Disaster.* Oxford: Oxford Polytechnic Press.
——. 2011. 'Disasters and the Role of the Built Environment Professional'. Lecture, Eden Project, Cornwall, 2 September. Retrieved 24 October 2019 from http://vimeo.com/23018842.
De Muyser-Boucher, I. (ed.). 2010. *Shelter after Disaster: Strategies for Transitional Settlement and Reconstruction.* Geneva: Shelter Centre.
Global Shelter Cluster. 2018. *The State of Humanitarian Shelter and Settlements 2018.* Geneva: United Nations High Commissioner for Refugees.
Hollein, H. 1968. 'Alles ist Architektur'. *Bau: Schrift für Architektur und Städtebau* 1(2): 7–16.
Karlsson, J. 2017. Interview with Tom Scott-Smith, 18 May. Stockholm.
Kelly, B. (ed.) 2012. *Transitional Shelter Guidelines.* Geneva: Shelter Centre.
Maynard, V. 2017. *The Effectiveness and Efficiency of Interventions Supporting Shelter Self-Recovery Following Humanitarian Crises: An Evidence Synthesis.* Oxford: Oxfam.
Scott-Smith, T. 2013. 'The Fetishism of Humanitarian Objects and the Management of Malnutrition in Emergencies'. *Third World Quarterly* 34(5): 913–28.
Terne, M. 2017. Interview with Tom Scott-Smith, 18 May. Stockholm.
Sphere Association. 2018. *The Sphere Handbook: Humanitarian Charter and Minimum Standards in Humanitarian Response,* 4th edn. London: Shortrun Press.
UNHCR. 1993. *Summary of Proceedings: First International Workshop on Improved Shelter Response and Environment for Refugees.* Retrieved 24 October 2019 from http://repository.forcedmigration.org/pdf/?pid=fmo:5319.

Index

accommodation, 128–29, 150–52
action and agency, 242
adhocism, 10, 229–30
  architecture and design and, 240–42
  of MSF IPERJUNGLE, 235, 240–43
administrative incarceration, 85–92
Agamben, Giorgio, 115, 128, 137
agency, 242–44
agriculture, 100–102, 266–67
Ahmed, Aslya Aden, 36
AHRC. *See* Arts and Humanities Research Council
Alef model, 139–40
Anti-Infiltration Law, 98
appropriation, 118, 242–43, 244
architecture and design, 9–10
  adhocism and, 240–42
  of Danish refugee villages, 212, 219
  of detention centres, 57–58
  engineering management, 288–89, 290
  of Goudoubo Camp, 224–25
  of Hal Far military barracks, 48–49
  of ICC, 164–65
  of Melissa Day Centre, 138–39
  of Moria, 57–58
  of MSF IPERJUNGLE, 236–44
  of North Head station, 189–90
  problem with architects, 294–95
  of Rathaus Friedenau, 178–79
  shelter betterment with, 288–97, 299n7
  of *Silos*, 199, 201
  social media and, 253–55
  of Tempelhof camp, 277–78, 281–83
  Tempohome site design, 18–20
  of Za'atari, 253–55
  See also shelter betterment
Architectures of Displacement project, 2, 3
Arendt, Hannah, 130, 137
Arts and Humanities Research Council (AHRC), 2
asylum seekers, 3, 21, 88–89, 175–76
  in Canada, 83–84, 93n8
  in Denmark, 211–13, 216–17
  in Europe, 33–35, 39n5, 40n9, 57–60
  in France, 112, 114–20
  in Germany, 276–77
  in Greece, 125–26, 128–29
  in Israel, 97–100, 104–5
  in Italy, 203–4
  in Jordan, 250–60
  See also specific shelters
Athens
  border control in, 125–26, 128–29
  citizen-run shelters in, 136–45
  City Plaza hotel in, 8, 141–45, 146nn7–8
  democratization in, 136, 141–44
  Melissa Day Centre in, 8, 134–40, 143–45, 145nn4–5
  music in, 123–24, 126–30
  police in, 126, 128
  redignification in, 8, 136–38, 143–45
  social community in, 123–25
  social integration in, 136, 138–40

Athens (*cont.*)
  sound and voice in, 122, 123–31
  voicing the squat, 129–31
Australia
  North Head station in, 9, 189–91
  Operation Babylift in, 193
  Operation Safe Haven in, 193–94
  Point Nepean Quarantine Station in, 9, 186, 188, 189, 191–94
  quarantine in, 188–94

Balkan route, 199, 203–4
Balkan War, 10, 211–12, 216
Bashford, Alison, 188–89
bed bugs, 163, 168, 169
Bedouins, 98, 102–3
belonging, 1
Berlin, Germany
  ICC in, 9, 162, 164–73
  Rathaus Friedenau in, 174, 175–83
  Tempelhof camp in, 274, 275–85
  Tempohomes in, 6, 11, 14, 15–16, 17–25
Better Shelter Refugee Housing Unit (BSRHU), 292–94
blacksmith's shelter, 225–27
Blazing Tube stove, 228–30
boat crossings, 23, 31–35, 40n9, 49–51, 119–20, 169
border control
  in Athens, 125–26, 128–29
  in Canada, 83–85
  incarceration and, 2, 84–85
  in Israel, 104–5
  in Italy, 200–201
  in Lebanon, 265–66
  Moria and, 73–79
  sovereignty and, 105
  at US-Mexico border, 84
  walls and, 105
Bosnians, 10, 211–13, 216–19
Brussels, Belgium, 8–9, 148
  Citizen Platform in, 149–59
BSRHU. *See* Better Shelter Refugee Housing Unit
Burkina Faso. *See* Goudoubo Camp

Calais, 10
  contingent camps in, 111–20
  humanitarianism in, 117
  invisibility in, 110, 111–12, 117–19
  Invisible Church near, 110, 111–12, 118–19
  living conditions in, 115–20
  police in, 112, 114–16, 118–19
  protective containment in, 113–16
  resistance in, 116–17
  social community in, 118–19
  zero-camp tolerance in, 111, 114, 117–18
Canada
  asylum seekers in, 83–84, 93n8
  border control in, 83–85
  Central East Correctional Centre in, 82
  detention centres in, 7, 82–92
  IHCs in, 84, 85
  incarceration in, 85–92
  IRPA in, 85
  IRPR in, 85
Canada's Criminal Code, 85
Canadian Border Services Agency (CBSA), 83, 87, 89
caravans, 251–52, 257–59
CBSA. *See* Canadian Border Services Agency
Central East Correctional Centre, 82
child separations, 83, 84, 88, 90–91
Citizen Platform
  accommodation by, 150–52
  history of, 150–52
  host-guest relations in, 153–54
  humanitarianism by, 150–51, 154–58
  politics and, 155–58
  social community and, 150, 152–56
  social media and, 149–50, 155, 157
  virtual social spaces and, 155–56
citizen-run shelters, 136–45
citizenship, 32, 39n2, 102, 130
City Plaza hotel, Athens, 8, 141–45, 146nn7–8
Cold War, 277
commonality in displacement, 226–27
commoning, 127

community shelter, Germany, 275–76, 280–84
conflict-resolution and voice, 142
consensus-based models, 141–42
containment, 6, 100
  disperse-contain process and, 113–14
  in Europe, 31–34, 38–39
  in Malta, 31–39
  protective, 113–16
  quarantine and, 188–89, 194–95
  shipping containers for, 19–23
contingent camps, 8
  in Calais, 111–20
cooking, 180, 214, 257, 279
  with solar cookstoves, 224, 227–31
criminalization of migration, 88–92
cultural expression, 127–28, 130–31
culture and shelter, 8, 258–59
Cuny, Fred, 289, 290

daily tasks, 176–80
Danish refugee villages
  architecture and design of, 212, 219
  Bosnians in, 10, 211–13, 216–19
  Hestehaven kindergarten and, 215–16
  Kærshovedgård prison and, 213–15
  mobility of, 212, 218
  modular shelters in, 210–19
  repurposing shelters from, 213, 215–16
Davis, Ian, 229, 288, 289–90, 296, 297, 299n3, 299nn8–9
deaths
  in detention centres, 84, 88
  in refugee shelters, 36, 38, 40n8, 60–61, 77, 200
  at *Silos*, 200
decision-making and voice, 141–42
dehumanization, 116
delegitimization, 263–64
democratization, 136, 141–44
Denmark
  asylum seekers in, 211–13, 216–17
  Danish refugee villages in, 10, 210–19
  Kærshovedgård prison in, 213–15
design workshops, 255–56

detention centres, 5
  architecture and design of, 57–58
  in Canada, 7, 82–92
  child and family separations in, 83, 84, 88, 90–91
  cost to operate, 90
  deaths in, 84, 88
  human rights and, 35–36, 86–87
  infrastructure of, 37–38
  isolation of, 37–38, 49–51, 85–87
  in Israel, 7, 96–106
  living conditions in, 32–33
  in Malta, 32–38, 39n3, 45–55
  mental health and, 84–88
  open centres, 45–55
  Pagani, 62–63
  shackling in, 87, 89, 93n9
  trauma and, 83–84, 87–92
  violence and, 36–38, 84, 88, 90–92
detention periods, 39n5
dignity, 202
  attacks on, 116
  defining, 138
  redignification, 8, 136–38, 143–45
  refugee shelter and, 8, 136
discrimination, 51–52, 53
disperse-contain process, 113–14
displacement
  commonality in, 226–27
  'Energy and Forced Displacement' project and, 223–25
  human experience of, 9–10, 124
  humanitarianism and, 225–27
  mobility and, 10, 23, 115–16, 127–28
  shipping containers and, 15, 19–23
  social community and, 158–59
  voice and, 130–31
distribution and shipping, 19–25
Dublin Regulation, 59
Dunkirk, 10
  MSF IPERJUNGLE in, 234, 235–45

EASO. *See* European Asylum Support Office
Economic and Social Research Council (ESRC), 2

Egypt, 104–5
emergency shelter, Germany, 275–76, 278–80
emergent shelters, 48–49, 52–54
energy access, 223–25, 251
'Energy and Forced Displacement' project, 223–25
engineering management, 288–89, 290
English Channel, 119–20, 149, 235
Escobar, Arturo, 227
ESRC. *See* Economic and Social Research Council
Europe
  asylum seekers in, 33–35, 39n5, 40n9, 57–60
  containment in, 31–34, 38–39
  See also specific countries
European Asylum Support Office (EASO), 57–59
exile, 7, 97–98, 104–6, 187

family separations, 83, 84, 88, 90–91
Fassin, Didier, 128
flexibility, 6, 200, 218–19
food, 167–68, 180, 214, 257, 279
forced migration, 2, 3
  'Energy and Forced Displacement' project and, 223–25
  refugee shelter and, 4–5
forced shelter, 5, 7, 84–85, 91
  See also detention centres
Foucault, Michel, 137
France, 187
  asylum seekers in, 112, 114–20
  Calais contingent camps in, 111–20
  Dunkirk, 10, 234, 235–45
  processing centers in, 111–16
fulfillment, 155–56

gardening, 255, 258
Gemeinschaftsunterkunft (German community shelter), 275–76, 280–84
Germany
  asylum seekers in, 276–77
  emergency shelter in, 275–76, 278–80
  Merkel and, 165, 275–78
  permanent housing in, 276
  See also Berlin, Germany
Giddens, Anthony, 242, 244
globalization, 16, 23–25
global mobility, 23–25
global trade, 16–17, 21
Goudoubo Camp, 10, 222
  architecture and design of, 224–25
  blacksmith's shelter, 225–27
  innovation and resourcefulness at, 224–32
  solar cookstoves at, 224
  UNHCR and, 223, 225–31
Grandinetti, John, 228
Greece
  asylum seekers in, 125–26, 128–29
  Moria, 7, 56, 57–66, 70
  politics in, 135–37, 142–43
  See also Athens

Hal Far military barracks, 34–35, 44, 45–46
  architecture and design of, 48–49
  living conditions at, 46, 48–51
  privacy at, 48, 53
  social community at, 49–51
Handbook for Emergencies (UNHCR), 290
Haraway, Donna, 244
hébergement system, 151–52. *See also* Citizen Platform
Hestehaven kindergarten, 215–16
Holot, Israel
  detention centres, 7, 96–106
  Holot Residence Centre, 96, 97–100
  isolation of, 99–100
  living conditions in, 99
  Negev Desert and, 100–106
  noncivilian settlement in, 103–4
  spatiality of, 99–100
home
  belonging and, 1
  mental health and, 176–77
  property ownership and, 250
  shelter compared to, 235–36, 250
homines sacri, 115

host community, 227–28
host-guest relations, 153–54
hosting refugees, 152–54. *See also* Citizen Platform
hotspot approach, 59–60, 66, 74. *See also* Moria
humanitarian evacuation, 192–95
humanitarianism
 in Calais, 117
 by Citizen Platform, 150–51, 154–58
 displacement and, 225–27
 fulfillment and, 155–56
 innovation and, 225, 226–27
 in Kab Elias, 266–69
 in Lebanon, 266–69
 mental health and, 177
 in Moria, 58–60
 shelter betterment and, 287–98, 299n2
 shipping containers, war, and, 17
human rights, 98
 detention centres and, 35–36, 86–87

ICC. *See* International Congress Centre
identity, 11, 124, 155, 179–80
IHCs. *See* Immigration Holding Centres
IKEA
 BSRHU and, 292–94
 kit 'houses', 75–76, 79
immigration, 7
 incarceration and, 87–92
 Italy and, 200–201
 in Malta, 31–32, 34–36, 39n1, 45–55
 politics and, 36–37
 quarantine, 190–94
 See also detention centres
Immigration and Refugee Protection Act (IRPA), 85
Immigration Holding Centres (IHCs), 84, 85
Immigrations and Refugee Protections Regulations (IRPR), 85
immobility. *See* mobility
incarceration
 administrative, 85–92
 border control and, 2, 84–85
 in Canada, 85–92
 immigration and, 87–92
 in Kærshovedgård prison, 213–15
inclusivity, 2–3
Individual Investor Programme, 39n2
industrialization, 237, 238–40
infiltrators, 98–99
informal settlement, 264–70
information, 157
infrastructure
 of detention centres, 37–38
 shipping container and, 16–17
innovation
 agency and, 242–43
 at Goudoubo Camp, 224–32
 humanitarianism and, 225, 226–27
 technology and, 224–32
International Congress Centre (ICC), 9, 162
 architecture and design of, 164–65
 bed bugs in, 163, 168, 169
 care and control in, 167–68
 door from, 172–73
 food in, 167–68
 isolation and, 170–71
 legal status of, 170
 living conditions at, 163, 164–71
 mental health and, 168–69, 171–72
 privacy at, 168–69
 remains from, 171–73
 safety at, 168–69
 time and light in, 166
international law, 89
International Organization for Standardization (ISO), 16, 24
International Relief and Development (IRD), 253–59
International Shelter Network, 291
Intertect Relief and Reconstruction Corporation, 290
invisibility, 110, 111–12, 117–19
Invisible Church, 110, 111–12, 118–19
IRD. *See* International Relief and Development
IRPA. *See* Immigration and Refugee Protection Act

306 | Index

IRPR. *See* Immigrations and Refugee Protections Regulations
ISO. *See* International Organization for Standardization
isolation
   of detention centres, 37–38, 49–51, 85–87
   of Holot, 99–100
   ICC and, 170–71
   of open centres, 49–51
   protection and, 9–10, 20, 22, 187–94
   quarantine and, 187–94
   social community and, 49–51
   spatial exclusion and, 263–70
   of Tempohomes, 20, 23
Israel
   Anti-Infiltration Law in, 98
   asylum seekers in, 97–100, 104–5
   border control in, 104–5
   detention centres in, 7, 96–106
   Egypt and, 104–5
   infiltrators in, 98–99
   Negev Desert in, 7, 97–98, 100–106
   sovereignty of, 105
Italy
   asylum seekers in, 203–4
   border control in, 200–201
   immigration and, 200–201
   Silos in, 198, 199–207

Japan, 17
Jencks, Charles, 241
Jesuit Refugee Service (JRS), 35, 40n9
Jews, 97, 100–103, 105, 200
Jordan, 250–60
JRS. *See* Jesuit Refugee Service

Kab Elias, Bekka, 10–11, 262
   deterioration in, 267
   humanitarianism in, 266–69
   informal settlement in, 264–70
   property ownership in, 268
   spatial exclusion in, 263–70
Kærshovedgård prison, 213–15
Kamara, Mamadou, 36, 38, 40n8
Kara Tepe, 65

kindergarten, 215–16
Kosovan refugees, 192–94

language, 139, 140, 205
leadership, 141–42, 144
Lebanon
   border control in, 265–66
   humanitarianism in, 266–69
   Kab Elias in, 10–11, 262, 263–70
   Syrian refugees in, 263–70
Lefebvre, H., 239, 241, 244–45
Lesvos, 64–65, 74. *See also* Moria
lighting, 166, 201
La Linière, 235–45
living conditions
   in Calais, 115–20
   daily tasks and mental health, 176–80
   in detention centres, 32–33
   at Hal Far, 46, 48–51
   in Holot, 99
   at ICC, 163, 164–71
   in Moria, 61–65, 71–72
   of MSF IPERJUNGLE, 240–43
   at *Silos*, 201–2
   in Tempelhof camp, 278–79, 281–82
locks, 180
London shipping containers, 22–23

Mali. *See* Goudoubo Camp
Malkki, Liisa, 154
Malta
   containment in, 31–39
   detention centres in, 32–38, 39n3, 45–55
   emergent shelters in, 48–49
   Hal Far military barracks, 34–35, 44, 45–51, 53
   immigration detention history in, 34–36
   immigration in, 31–32, 34–36, 39n1, 45–55
   Individual Investor Programme, 39n2
   open centres in, 45–55
   refugee shelter in, 6–7, 31–39, 45–55
   Safi military barracks in, 30, 32–33
   beyond shelters, 51–52

maritime quarantine, 188–89, 190
materiality, 77–79
material structure, 9–10. *See also*
  architecture and design
Médecins Sans Frontières (MSF), 10, 72,
  176–77
Médecins Sans Frontières (MSF)
  IPERJUNGLE
  adhocism of, 235, 240–43
  agency and, 242–44
  architecture and design of, 236–44
  industrialization of, 237, 238–40
  La Linière and, 235–45
  living conditions, 240–43
  shelter and manual of, 237–40,
    243–44
  spatiality of, 242–45
  users, 236–45
media, 61–64, 157–58, 165, 240, 263,
  283. *See also* social media
Melissa Day Centre, 8, 134–40, 143–45,
  145nn4–5
mental health, 9, 58, 62
  daily tasks and, 176–80
  detention centres and, 84–88
  home and, 176–77
  humanitarianism and, 177
  ICC and, 168–69, 171–72
  Rathaus Friedenau and, 175–83
  sheltering mind, 183
  spatiality and, 178–79
Merkel, Angela, 165, 275–78
Mexico-US border, 84
migrant activism, 129–30
migration, 1–2
  criminalization of, 88–92
  discrimination of migrants, 51–52,
    53
  forced, 2–5, 223–25
  hotspot approach to, 59–60, 66, 74
  international law and, 89
  politics and, 53–54, 112, 130, 135–37,
    263–65
  in United States, 89
  violence and, 59–60
mobile commons, 127

mobility
  of Danish refugee villages, 212, 218
  displacement and, 10, 23, 115–16,
    127–28
  global, 23–25
  movement and, 129–30
  shipping containers and global
    mobility, 23–25
  social community and, 52–54
modular shelters
  at Danish refugee villages, 210–19
  IKEA kit 'houses', 75–76, 79
  at Tempelhof camp, 281–82
Modulor, 239
Moria
  architecture and design of, 57–58
  border control and, 73–79
  genealogy of, 73–74
  history of site, 62–63
  humanitarianism in, 58–60
  as institutional grey zone, 60–63
  living conditions in, 61–65, 71–72
  local perspectives on, 63–65
  materiality in, 77–79
  neglect in, 72–73, 77–78
  order from chaos in, 74–77
  overcrowding in, 77–78
  political tensions in, 58–60, 74
  refugee shelter in, 7, 56, 57–66, 70–79
  sewage system in, 64, 78
  spatiality of, 72–74, 77–78
  violence in, 62, 64, 66
MSF. *See* Médecins Sans Frontières
music, 123–24, 126–30

The Need to Help (Malkki), 154
Negev Desert, 7
  Holot and, 100–106
  Jews, Zionism, and, 100–103
  militarization of, 103–4
  noncivilian settlement in, 103–4
  from redemption to exile, 97–98,
    104–6
neglect, 72–73, 77–78
Neumann, Wolfgang, 291, 296
noise complaints, 130

noncivilian settlement, 103–4
North Head station, 9
  architecture and design of, 189–90
  quarantine at, 189–91
Notunterkunft (German emergency
  shelter), 275–76, 278–80

Ober, Josiah, 138
open centres, 97
  background on, 46–48
  detention centres, 45–55
  emergent shelters and, 48–49, 52–54
  isolation of, 49–51
  in Malta, 45–55
  Melissa Day Centre, 8, 134–40,
    143–45, 145nn4–5
Operation Babylift, 193
Operation Safe Haven, 193–94
overcrowding, 33
  in Holot, 99
  in Moria, 77–78

Pagani detention centre, 62–63
perles d'accueil (pearls of welcoming)
  website, 155
permanency, 4, 77, 78
permanent housing, Germany, 276
Pikpa, 64–65
Platoon Kunsthalle Development
  Center, 22
PlayPump, 226–27
Point Nepean Quarantine Station, 9,
  186, 188, 189
  quarantine at, 191–94
police
  in Athens, 126, 128
  brutality, 59–60, 88, 112, 126,
    156–57
  in Calais, 112, 114–16, 118–19
politics, 11
  Citizen Platform and, 155–58
  of dehumanization, 116
  in Greece, 135–37, 142–43
  immigration and, 36–37
  migration and, 53–54, 112, 130,
    135–37, 263–65

political tensions in Moria, 58–60, 74
  voice and, 124, 130, 142–43
pollution, 64
Porte d'Ulysse, 152
prisoners of war (POWs), 187–88
privacy
  at Hal Far, 48, 53
  at ICC, 168–69
  at Rathaus Friedenau, 179
  in Tempohomes, 19
  at Za'atari, 258
processing centers, France, 111–16
property ownership
  home and, 250
  in Kab Elias, 268
protection
  isolation and, 9–10, 20, 22, 187–94
  shelter and, 5
protective containment, Calais, 113–16

quarantine
  in Australia, 188–94
  containment and, 188–89, 194–95
  immigration, 190–94
  isolation and, 187–94
  maritime, 188–89, 190
  at North Head station, 189–91
  at Point Nepean Quarantine Station,
    191–94

Rathaus Friedenau, 174
  architecture and design of, 178–79
  daily tasks and identity at, 179–80
  mental health and, 175–83
  privacy at, 179
  relationships at, 181–82
  repurposing of, 175–76
  safety at, 180, 183
redignification, 8, 136–38, 143–45
redistribution and shipping, 19–25
redundancy, 224, 227–28
refugee, defining, 3
Refugee Convention, 3
refugee distribution, 21–25
refugee economies, 127–28, 227–28,
  252

refugee shelters
  citizen-run shelters, 136–45
  deaths in, 36, 38, 40n8, 60–61, 77, 200
  defining, 2–4
  dignity and, 8, 136
  forced migration and, 4–5
  forced shelters, 5, 7, 84–85, 91
  humanitarianism and shelter betterment, 287–98, 299n2
  in Malta, 6–7, 31–39, 45–55
  modular, 75–76, 79, 210–19, 281–82
  in Moria, 7, 56, 57–66, 70–79
  shipping containers as, 6, 15–25
  social community of, 49–54
  sound and, 125–29, 131
  summarizing, 6–11
  theorizing, 4–6
  'unconditional,' 113–16
  voice and, 124–31
  warehousing effects of, 137–38
  See also specific shelters; specific topics
Refugee Studies, 1–2, 11
Refugee Support Aegean (RSA), 61
relationships, 181–82. *See also* social community
resistance
  in Calais, 116–17
  voice and, 124
resourcefulness
  at Goudoubo Camp, 224–32
  redundancy as, 224, 227–28
RSA. *See* Refugee Support Aegean

safety, 36, 61–62, 77, 91–92
  at ICC, 168–69
  at Rathaus Friedenau, 180, 183
Safi military barracks, 30, 32–33
segregation, 190
self-settlement, 264–70
settlement
  in Kab Elias, 264–70
  in Negev Desert, 103–4
sewage system, 64, 78
shackling, 87, 89, 93n9
shelter, 1–2
  conceptualizing, 4–6
  culture and, 258–59
  defining, 4
  home compared to, 235–36, 250
  protection and, 5
  social media and, 252–53
  spatiality of, 4
  'unconditional,' 113–16
  See also refugee shelter
Shelter after Disaster (Davis), 288, 289–90
shelter betterment
  with architecture and design, 288–97, 299n7
  BSRHU and, 292–94
  engineering management and, 288–89, 290
  humanitarianism and, 287–98, 299n2
  humanitarian shelter guidance, 288–89, 299n2
  imperfection and problems in, 292–94
  problem with architects and, 294–95
  sheltering without shelter solutions, 297–98
  success measurement, 295–96
  technical performance and, 291, 295–96
  UNHCR and, 290–92
sheltering mind, 183
sheltering social process, 50–51, 54, 129
Shelter Task Force, 291
shipping containers
  for containment, 19–23
  displacement and, 15, 19–23
  in distribution and redistribution, 19–25
  global mobility and, 23–25
  global trade and, 16–17, 21
  infrastructure and, 16–17
  ISO on, 16, 24
  in London, 22–23
  as refugee shelter, 6, 15–25
  size and dimensions of, 16, 25n1
  Tempohomes, 6, 11, 14, 15–16, 17–25
  war, humanitarianism, and, 17
Silos, 198
  architecture and design of, 199, 201

Silos (cont.)
    deaths at, 200
    history behind, 199–200
    in Italy, 198, 199–207
    living conditions at, 201–2
    migrant types at, 205
    now, 203–5
    then, 200–203
Smith, Merril, 137
social community
    in Athens, 123–25
    in Calais, 118–19
    Citizen Platform and, 150, 152–56
    displacement and, 158–59
    at Hal Far, 49–51
    host community and, 227–28
    host-guest relations and, 153–54
    isolation and, 49–51
    mobility and, 52–54
    of refugee shelters, 49–54
    relationships and social interactions, 181–82
    sheltering social process and, 50–51, 54, 129
    in Tempelhof camp, 280–84
    in Za'atari, 252–55
social integration, Athens, 136, 138–40
social media, 10
    architecture and design and, 253–55
    Citizen Platform and, 149–50, 155, 157
    engagement, 253–55
    shelter and, 252–53
    Za'atari and, 249–60
solar cookstoves, 224, 227–31
solar energy, 251
solidarity, 157
sound, 8, 201–2
    in Athens, 122, 123–31
    cultural expression and, 127–28, 130–31
    from Invisible Church, 111–12
    noise complaints and, 130
    refugee shelters and, 125–29, 131
sovereignty, 105

spatial exclusion, 263–70. *See also* isolation
spatiality, 1, 3
    of Holot, 99–100
    of Melissa Day Centre, 138–39
    mental health and, 178–79
    of Moria, 72–74, 77–78
    of MSF IPERJUNGLE, 242–45
    of shelter, 4
    space-making and, 251–52
    user and, 244–45
    virtual social spaces and, 155–56
Sphere Handbook manual, 288, 289
Stafford, Douglas, 291
stigmatization, 263–64
Strange, Carolyn, 189
success measurement, 295–96
Sudanese migrants, 157–58
Swarming Solidarity, 143
Syrian Civil War, 251, 258, 265–66
Syrian refugees, 10–11
    in Lebanon, 263–70
    spatial exclusion of, 263–70
    at Za'atari, 249–60

technical performance, in shelter betterment, 291, 295–96
technology
    innovation and, 224–32
    virtual social spaces, 155–56, 249–60
Tempelhof camp, 274
    abandonment of, 283–84
    architecture and design of, 277–78, 281–83
    Gemeinschaftsunterkunft in, 275–76, 280–84
    living conditions in, 278–79, 281–82
    modular shelters at, 281–82
    Notunterkunft in, 275–76, 278–80
    social community in, 280–84
Tempohomes
    in Berlin, Germany, 6, 11, 14, 15–16, 17–25
    containment in, 19–23
    isolation of, 20, 23
    locations of, 20

overview of, 17–19
  privacy in, 19
  site design, 18–20
Tempohousing, 20–21
temporality, 4, 212, 218
tidemark, 206
time and lighting, 166
Tönnies, Ferdinand, 281
trade, global, 16–17, 21
Transitional Shelter Guidelines manual, 288
trauma, from detention, 83–84, 87–92
Trieste, Italy, 199–207

'unconditional' shelter, 113–16
UNHCR. *See* United Nations High Commissioner for Refugees
United Kingdom, 22–23, 119–20, 288
United Nations High Commissioner for Refugees (UNHCR), 24, 71–72, 125, 137, 145n2, 264
  Goudoubo and, 223, 225–31
  Handbook for Emergencies by, 290
  shelter betterment and, 290–92
  on Syrian refugees in Lebanon, 266–67
  Za'atari and, 251, 253, 258
United States
  Mexico border with, 84
  migration in, 89
University of Oxford discussions, 2

Vietnamese refugees, 191, 193
Vietnam War, 17, 193
violence, 258
  detention centres and, 36–38, 84, 88, 90–92
  migration and, 59–60
  in Moria, 62, 64, 66
  police brutality, 59–60, 88, 112, 126, 156–57
virtual social spaces
  Citizen Platform and, 155–56

  design workshops in, 255–56
  spatiality and, 155–56
  technology, 155–56, 249–60
  Za'atari as, 249–60
voice, 8
  in Athens, 122, 123–31
  citizenship and, 130
  conflict-resolution and, 142
  decision-making and, 141–42
  displacement and, 130–31
  politics and, 124, 130, 142–43
  refugee shelters and, 124–31
  resistance and, 124

walls, 105
war
  Balkan War, 10, 211–12, 216
  Cold War, 277
  POWs, 187–88
  shipping containers, humanitarianism, and, 17
  Syrian Civil War, 251, 258, 265–66
  Vietnam War, 17, 193
  World War II, 200–201
warehousing effects, 137–38
Weber, Max, 281
Weidman, Amanda, 130
World War II, 200–201

Za'atari, 248
  architecture and design of, 253–55
  caravans in, 251–52, 257–59
  culture and shelter, 258–59
  design workshops in, 255–56
  energy access in, 251
  engagement spaces, 253–55
  IRD and, 253–59
  privacy at, 258
  social community in, 252–55
  social media and, 249–60
  space-making at, 251–52
  UNHCR and, 251, 253, 258
zero-camp tolerance, 111, 114, 117–18
Zionism, 97, 100–103

www.ingramcontent.com/pod-product-compliance
Lightning Source LLC
Chambersburg PA
CBHW070909030426
42336CB00014BA/2348